# THE FUTURE OF UNIONS AND WORKER REPRESENTATION

This book charts the path to revitalisation for trade unions in Australia, the USA, the UK and Italy. It examines the examples of innovation and digital campaigning that are enabling unions to build new forms of worker power – and overcome decades of declining membership wrought by neoliberalism, globalisation, and hostility from employers and the state.

The study evaluates the responses of unions in each country to falling membership levels since the 1980s. It considers the US 'organising model' and its adoption in Australia and the UK, comparing this with the strategies of Italian unions which have been more deliberately focused on precarious and migrant workers. The increasing reliance of US unions on community alliances, as seen in the 'Fight for $15' and similar campaigns, is scrutinised along with new union prototypes like Hospo Voice in Australia, the Independent Workers' Union of Great Britain and SI Cobas in Italy. The book includes an in-depth analysis of union responses to the gig economy in the four countries, and the emergence of self-organised worker collectives to combat this exploitative business model. The vital role played by unions in defending the interests of workers during the COVID-19 pandemic is also examined.

As well as highlighting the most successful union initiatives to meet the challenges of the past 30 years, the book assesses the strengths and deficiencies of the legal framework for union representation in the four nations. It identifies the labour law reforms needed to rebuild collectivism, but argues that more is needed than favourable laws. This cross-national study provides a rich basis for identifying the combination of reforms, strategies and linkages required to ensure that unions can remain relevant for a new generation of digitally-active workers.

# The Future of Unions and Worker Representation

*The Digital Picket Line*

Anthony Forsyth

•HART•
OXFORD • LONDON • NEW YORK • NEW DELHI • SYDNEY

HART PUBLISHING

Bloomsbury Publishing Plc

Kemp House, Chawley Park, Cumnor Hill, Oxford, OX2 9PH, UK

1385 Broadway, New York, NY 10018, USA

29 Earlsfort Terrace, Dublin 2, Ireland

HART PUBLISHING, the Hart/Stag logo, BLOOMSBURY and the Diana logo are trademarks of Bloomsbury Publishing Plc

First published in Great Britain 2022



A catalogue record for this book is available from the British Library.

Library of Congress Cataloging-in-Publication data

Names: Forsyth, Anthony, author.

Title: The future of unions and worker representation : the digital picket line / Anthony Forsyth.

Description: Oxford ; New York : Hart, 2022. | Includes bibliographical references and index.

Identifiers: LCCN 2021044674 (print) | LCCN 2021044675 (ebook) | ISBN 9781509924974 (hardback) | ISBN 9781509956432 (paperback) | ISBN 9781509924998 (pdf) | ISBN 9781509924981 (Epub)

Subjects: LCSH: Labor unions—Law and legislation. | Labor unions—Organizing. | Employees—Effect of technological innovations on. | Labor unions—Law and legislation—Australia. | Labor unions—Law and legislation—United States. | Labor unions—Law and legislation—Italy. | Labor unions—Law and legislation—Great Britain.

Classification: LCC K1721 .F67 2022 (print) | LCC K1721 (ebook) | DDC 344.01/88—dc23/eng/20211105

LC record available at https://lccn.loc.gov/2021044674

LC ebook record available at https://lccn.loc.gov/2021044675

ISBN: HB: 978-1-50992-497-4
ePDF: 978-1-50992-499-8
ePub: 978-1-50992-498-1

Typeset by Compuscript Ltd, Shannon

To find out more about our authors and books visit www.hartpublishing.co.uk. Here you will find extracts, author information, details of forthcoming events and the option to sign up for our newsletters.

*For Ron, Doss and Susan Forsyth – who knew much about hard work*

# FOREWORD

This is a fabulous book. The breadth and depth of its review of labour relations over the last 40-plus years in four countries, Australia, Italy, the United Kingdom and the USA is really impressive. All these countries have faced the onslaught of neoliberalism expressed through legislation, government policy, employer (and public) attitudes and changes to the legal nature of individual work relations. As the author points out, the central tenet of neoliberalism so far as labour relations are concerned is the elimination, or at least the weakening, of trade unions which, it holds, distort what should be a free labour market. He explains, in just the right amount of detail, how this ideology has manifested itself in each of the four jurisdictions he surveys and what the response of the labour movement has been in each. From the failures and successes of these responses he draws conclusions as to general strategies and specific objectives for the future. He warns that the future is not assured and that unless unions 'revitalise' successfully, the labour movement is, effectively, doomed (my words, not his).

Unsurprisingly, as a labour lawyer, he points both to the use of the law in effecting neoliberal ideology in these countries and to reforms of the law necessary to reverse the damage. He is right to do so. The fact is that (without discounting the role of government and media in seeking to embed neoliberalism in thought, attitudes and culture) so much of the adversity faced by the labour movement over the last four decades has been the product of legislation, changes to individual contractual arrangements, and legislative refusal to protect against those contractual changes.

But this is far from a book for lawyers. The examination of legal developments is only part of the story and the author gives most of the text to the unions' endeavours in each country and at all levels (from shop floor to government) to develop ways of preserving the interests of workers from what has been an unstoppable rising tide over the last 40 years.

The author is well aware of the dangers of advocating the transplanting of laws and legal institutions between jurisdictions. Nonetheless, his book proves 'the utility of cross-national comparative analysis as a basis for identifying the strategies, reforms, linkages and coalitions required to turn the fortunes of unions around'.

His comparative study shows one essential feature which distinguishes Italian (and continental European) labour relations from that of Australia, the UK and the US. As he points out,

> … the labour laws of the US, UK and Australia generally only allow collective bargaining at the level of the enterprise. In each country, the law has not kept pace with fissured work arrangements through which businesses interpose other entities, to distance

> themselves from the responsibilities of direct employment. Unions are unable to organise around and bargain with the host business in an agency/labour hire arrangement, multiple employers across industries, or lead businesses at the summit of supply chains. These limitations have contributed to falling levels of collective bargaining coverage in each of these countries. In contrast, in Italy, collective bargaining has long been conducted at the national level for agreements covering each industry (with only a minimal role in recent years for firm-level negotiations). Bargaining coverage remains very high.

Accordingly, 'the labour laws of these three countries must be altered to permit unions to bargain beyond the direct employer, with business entities who exercise significant economic power over workers' wages and conditions.' In short: sectoral collective bargaining, which, as he notes, is being reintroduced by legislation in New Zealand.

Sectoral bargaining is but one of his eight recommendations for essential changes to the law (especially in the three anglophone countries).

These are his conclusions. The bulk of the book is taken up with a comprehensive examination of the decline in union membership, collective bargaining coverage (so much more significant than membership numbers) and power in each of the four countries, noting that so much is attributable to changes in the respective labour law regimes and the 'new' forms of worker 'employment'. Of course, globalisation and outsourcing to cheap labour countries have also contributed greatly to the weakening of unions, which is one reason why apparently novel forms of employment (which are often no more than a reversion to 19th-century casualisation) are found so frequently in service industries (like food delivery) which cannot be outsourced overseas.

Of yet greater interest is the analysis, country by country, of the response of the unions. The author lays out in detail the innovative campaigns, moves to involve communities, forging links to broader campaigns which are not confined to the workplace, lobbying legislators (nothing new in that), super-union mergers (and de-mergers), the failures of the Organising Model in Australia, the UK and the USA, emphasis on grassroots organising, new forms of industrial action, the interesting parallel strategies of seeking to unionise the whole food supply chain by the UWU in Australia and the USB in Italy (developed, apparently, entirely independently), the use of new forms of membership going beyond the workplace, and the development of social and other media tools.

These chapters bring together in an invaluable way all the developments of which the scholar of labour relations may have been vaguely aware from articles in academic and union journals and from the newspapers – and many initiatives of which, for myself, I was not aware.

The book also usefully chronicles the rise, in each country, of the gig economy and the union campaigns, legislation and litigation in response to it. The final chapter 'examines the critical role of unions in each of the four countries during the COVID-19 pandemic, safeguarding workers' lives and livelihoods'. It points out the opportunity the crisis presents both for an alternative narrative about trade unions (and the economic system) to that of neoliberalism and, more importantly, the fact that the case 'for unionising has never been so compelling'.

The book concludes with a plea 'to rebuild collectivism'. The author believes 'that union revitalisation can be achieved.' What is needed (whether or not the legislation he advocates is achieved) is to continue to organise, recruit and retain members, developing more opportunities to participate and be part of the union – 'especially to attract the all-important younger generation of workers'. Unions must 'have a broader purpose than just increasing membership numbers', and they must 'respond to the demands of many marginalised workers for a more confrontational posture'. It is a truism that the more active unions are, the more they increase members – and power.

I congratulate Anthony on a unique and invaluable contribution to labour relations literature – and to the future of the labour movement.

Lord John Hendy QC[1]
*24 October 2021*

[1] Honorary Professor in the Faculty of Law, University College, London.

# PREFACE

I have wanted to write a book about trade unions for my whole academic career. Twenty-two years later, here it is.

I originally pitched to Hart Publishing a proposal for a book comparing the problems facing unions in Australia and the UK and their future prospects. Hart's generous anonymous reviewers encouraged me to broaden that horizon with one or two other country studies and a close examination of the implications for unions of the gig economy. These suggestions tied in well with my long-standing interest in the US labour movement, a fascination with Italian employment and labour law, and an unfolding research focus on the regulation of gig work.

I completed most of the writing in the period since the onset of the COVID-19 pandemic in early 2020, through various stages of lockdown and reopening in Melbourne. Although a strange and unsettling time, it has been quite conducive to productivity. The pandemic has reinforced my already firm views about the importance of unions in the lives of workers. I hope this is conveyed persuasively in the pages of this book.

There are many people whose assistance I would like to acknowledge.

I am especially indebted to: Paolo Tomassetti, who provided extensive feedback on draft sections of the book dealing with Italian labour law and trade unions (he greatly enriched my understanding, especially when it came to the baffling question of the respective roles of RSAs and RSUs in the Italian industrial relations system!); and Mark Perica, who reviewed and commented on several sections of the book, and gave me constant encouragement (especially in the difficult final stages).

Leaders and staff of a number of Australian unions helped in various ways, for which I am very grateful. They include Tim Kennedy, Paul Richardson, Godfrey Moase and George Robertson from the United Workers Union; Tim Petterson from Hospo Voice; Hyeseon Jeong from the Migrant Workers Centre; Felicity Sowerbutts from the Young Workers Centre; Tim Colwill from Game Workers Unite Australia; and Jack Boutros from the Transport Workers Union.

Thank you to Antonio Aloisi and Valerio De Stefano; Alan Bogg and Tonia Novitz; Veena Dubal and Wilma Liebman, who kindly responded to queries and requests for information about the Italian, UK and US union and labour law scenes. *Grazie mille* to my friend, Luca Esposito, who constantly sent me news items about food delivery rider strikes and other developments in Italy. Lily Raynes provided fabulous research assistance as the project neared completion.

In addition to those already mentioned, I have benefited greatly from collaboration and discussion of work, unions and labour law (over many years) with

# TABLE OF ABBREVIATIONS

| | |
|---|---|
| AB5 | Assembly Bill 5 (California) |
| ABS | Australian Bureau of Statistics |
| ACCC | Australian Competition and Consumer Commission |
| ACTU | Australian Council of Trade Unions |
| ADCU | App Drivers and Couriers Union |
| AFL-CIO | American Federation of Labor and Congress of Industrial Organisations |
| AMWU | Australian Manufacturing Workers' Union |
| ANMF | Australian Nursing and Midwifery Foundation |
| ASU | Australian Services Union |
| ATUI | Australian Trade Union Institute |
| AWU | Australian Workers' Union |
| BFAWU | Bakers Food and Allied Workers Union |
| CAC | Central Arbitration Committee |
| CFMEU | Construction, Forestry, Mining and Energy Union |
| CFMMEU | Construction, Forestry, Maritime, Mining and Energy Union |
| CGIL | Confederazione Generale Italiana del Lavoro |
| CISL | Confederazione Italiana Sindacati Lavoratori |
| CJRS | Coronavirus Job Retention Scheme |
| CPSU | Community and Public Sector Union |
| CTU | Chicago Teachers Union |
| CWA | Communications Workers of America |
| EAT | Employment Appeal Tribunal |
| ECHR | European Convention on Human Rights |

| | |
|---|---|
| EFCA | Employee Free Choice Act |
| EDR | Exclusive driver representative |
| EU | European Union |
| FELSA | Federazione Lavoratori Somministrati Autonomi ed Atipici |
| FILCAMS-CGIL | Federazione Italiana dei Lavoratori del Commercio, Alberghi, Mense e Servizi-CGIL |
| FILT-CGIL | Federazione Italiana Lavoratori Trasporti-CGIL |
| FISASCAT-CISL | Federazione Italiana Sindacati Addetti Servizi Commerciali, Affini e del Turismo-CISL |
| FLAI-CGIL | Federazione Lavoratori dell'Agroindustria-CGIL |
| FLSA | Fair Labor Standards Act, 1938 |
| FW Act | Fair Work Act 2009 (Cth) |
| FWC | Fair Work Commission |
| FWO | Fair Work Ombudsman |
| FWRO Act | Fair Work (Registered Organisations) Act 2009 (Cth) |
| GMB | GMB Union |
| GWUA | Game Workers Unite Australia |
| HERE | Hotel Employees and Restaurant Employees Union |
| HSR | Health and safety representative |
| IBEW | International Brotherhood of Electrical Workers |
| IDG | Independent Drivers Guild |
| IER | Institute of Employment Rights |
| ILO | International Labour Organization |
| IWGB | Independent Workers Union of Great Britain |
| LHMU | Liquor, Hospitality and Miscellaneous Workers' Union |
| LIUNA | Laborers' International Union of North America |
| MEAA | Media, Entertainment and Arts Alliance |
| MUA | Maritime Union of Australia |
| MWC | Migrant Workers Centre |
| NHS | National Health Service |

| | |
|---|---|
| NIDiL | Nuova Identitá di Lavoro |
| NLRA | National Labor Relations Act, 1935 |
| NLRB | National Labor Relations Board |
| NTEU | National Tertiary Education Union |
| NUW | National Union of Workers |
| NYTWA | New York Taxi Workers Alliance |
| OECD | Organisation for Economic Co-operation and Development |
| OUR Walmart | Organization United for Respect at Walmart |
| Prop 22 | Proposition 22 (California) |
| PPE | Personal protective equipment |
| PRO Act | Protecting the Right to Organize Act |
| RAFFWU | Retail and Fast Food Workers Union |
| RDU | Rideshare Drivers United (USA) |
| RSA | Rappresentanze sindacali aziendale |
| RSDAA | Ride Share Drivers Association of Australia |
| RSDU | RideShare Drivers United (Australia) |
| RSU | Rappresentanze sindacali unitarie |
| RWDSU | Retail, Wholesale and Department Store Union |
| SDAEA | Shop, Distributive and Allied Employees Association |
| SEISS | Self-Employment Income Support Scheme |
| SEIU | Service Employees International Union |
| TCFUA | Textile, Clothing and Footwear Union of Australia |
| TDL | The Doctors Laboratory |
| Teamsters | International Brotherhood of Teamsters |
| TGWU | Transport and General Workers Union |
| TLC | Taxi and Limousine Commission |
| TUC | Trades Union Congress |
| TULRCA | Trade Unions and Labour Relations (Consolidation) Act 1992 |
| TWU | Transport Workers' Union |

| | |
|---|---|
| UAW | United Automobile, Aerospace and Agricultural Implement Workers of America |
| UCU | University and College Union |
| UFCW | United Food and Commercial Workers International Union |
| UFW | United Farm Workers |
| UGL | Unione Generale del Lavoro |
| UIL | Unione Italiana del Lavoro |
| UILTUCS | Unione Italiana Lavoratori Turismo Commercio Servizi |
| Unison | The Public Service Union |
| UNITE | Union of Needletrades, Industrial and Textile Employees (USA) |
| Unite | Unite the Union (UK) |
| UPHD | United Private Hire Drivers (Branch of IWGB) |
| USB | Unione Sindacale di Base |
| USDAW | Union of Shop, Distributive and Allied Workers |
| UV | United Voice |
| UVW | United Voices of the World |
| UWU | United Workers Union |
| VTHC | Victorian Trades Hall Council |
| WHS | Work health and safety |
| WHS Act | Work Health and Safety Act 2011 (NSW) |
| YWC | Young Workers Centre |

# TABLE OF CASES

**Australia**

**Italy**



**United Kingdom**

**United States of America**

# TABLE OF LEGISLATION

**Australia**

**European Union**



**Italy**

**New Zealand**



**United Kingdom**

**United States of America**

# 1

# Introduction

## I. Unionising Big Tech

Amazon, the multinational e-commerce behemoth, is renowned for its anti-unionism. The company has pioneered a model of work in its 'fulfilment centres' based on surveillance, oppressive performance targets and precarious labour with a heavy reliance on third-party agencies.[1] Trade unions are not welcome, because Amazon does not want any interference with its ability to retain maximum managerial control.[2] This is a familiar refrain, sung by corporations all over the world from the 1980s on. However, it is one thing to *resist* union involvement in the business. The last couple of years have shown more clearly *the lengths Amazon will go to*, in countering efforts to unionise its workforce. In 2020, the company posted advertisements in the United States for two intelligence analysts whose role would include monitoring 'labor organizing threats' (Amazon subsequently deleted the job postings, claiming they were erroneous).[3] Leaked internal documents showed the extent of Amazon's surveillance of labour, environmental and social justice groups in Europe, including the use of operatives from the notorious Pinkertons spy agency.[4] The intelligence provided to the company's Global Security Operations Centre covers intricate details of labour-organising activities at Amazon distribution centres, including the numbers of workers involved, types of campaigning or protests undertaken and their 'risk level' to the business.[5]

[1] See, eg, B Cattero and M D'Onofrio, 'Organizing and Collective Bargaining in the Digitized "Tertiary Factories" of Amazon: A Comparison Between Germany and Italy', in E Ales, Y Curzi, T Fabbri, O Rymkevich, I Senatori and G Solinas (eds), *Working in Digital and Smart Organizations: Legal, Economic and Organizational Perspectives on the Digitalization of Labour Relations* (Cham, Palgrave Macmillan, 2018) 141, 143–49; J Bloodworth, *Hired: Six Months Undercover in Low-Wage Britain* (London, Atlantic Books, 2018), chs 1–5; P Hatch, 'In Amazon's "hellscape" workers face insecurity and crushing targets', *The Age* (7 September 2018); Open Markets Institute, *Eyes Everywhere: Amazon's Surveillance Infrastructure and Revitalizing Worker Power* (August 2020).

[2] Cattero and D'Onofrio (n 1) 151, 154, 156–57.

[3] L Franceschi-Bicchierai, 'Amazon is hiring an intelligence analyst to track "labor organizing threats"', *Vice* (2 September 2020). This led to concerns that Amazon workers in other countries would be subjected to data mining with the same objective: see J Taylor, 'Amazon denies it planned to spy on workers in Sydney to stop them unionising', *The Guardian* (4 September 2020).

[4] L Gurley, 'Secret Amazon reports expose the company's surveillance of labor and environmental groups', *Vice* (24 November 2020). See also E Loomis, *A History of America in Ten Strikes* (New York, The New Press, 2018) 53, explaining that: 'The Pinkerton National Detective Agency was one of several private strikebreaking and security firms that served employers in the Gilded Age. To this day, the term *Pinkerton* is synonymous with violent strikebreaking' (reference omitted).

[5] Gurley, ibid

In the early stages of the COVID-19 pandemic, Amazon fired at least six workers (and disciplined others) who had taken a stand on inadequate safety precautions at its US warehouses.[6] Chris Smalls, who led a walkout at the Staten Island, New York facility, was the subject of personal denigration by Amazon management following adverse media publicity of his termination.[7] Then, in late 2020, Amazon workers in Bessemer, Alabama instigated the National Labor Relations Board process for a vote on recognition of their chosen representative, the Retail, Wholesale and Department Store Union (RWDSU).[8] In what became an epic contest over the right to unionise in America's deep south, the world saw the full panoply of the company's obstructive tactics on display. As the vote on union recognition at the Bessemer warehouse loomed in the early months of 2021, Amazon urged staff to vote down the union drive through text messages and a specially created website (#DoItWithoutDues), telling them: 'We've got you covered with high wages, health care, vision, and dental benefits, as well as a safety committee and an appeals process.'[9] These messages were reinforced on posters installed in bathrooms at the warehouse[10] and at mandatory employee meetings (known in the US as 'captive audience' meetings).[11] Newly elected US President, Joe Biden, spoke publicly in support of the rights of American workers to a 'free and fair choice' about whether to unionise (although without naming Amazon).[12] Despite this and a number of celebrities getting behind the union cause, the workers voted *against* recognition of the RWDSU for collective bargaining: 1,798 to 738, out of 5,876 eligible voters.[13] Amazon's no-holds-barred effort to thwart the union organising drive won out.

Although the company's actions are just another chapter in the long history of union-busting by US employers,[14] the Amazon example illustrates the depth of the challenges faced by unions in the modern world of globalised capital. Indeed, it has been argued that with five of the leading US technology companies union-free (Amazon, Apple, Microsoft, Facebook and Alphabet, Google's parent entity): 'The tech

[6] G Bellafante, '"We didn't sign up for this": Amazon workers on the front lines', *New York Times* (3 April 2020); M Sainato, 'Amazon is cracking down on protestors and organising, workers say', *The Guardian* (6 May 2020).

[7] J Wong, 'Amazon execs labeled fired worker "not smart or articulate" in leaked PR notes', *The Guardian* (3 April 2020); see also C Smalls, 'Dear Jeff Bezos, instead of firing me, protect your workers from coronavirus', *The Guardian* (2 April 2020).

[8] A Press, 'Amazon is facing an unprecedented union vote in the right-to-work south', *Jacobin* (30 November 2020).

[9] L Gurley, 'Amazon launches anti-union website to derail Alabama union drive', *Vice* (16 January 2021).

[10] J Greene, 'Amazon's anti-union blitz stalks Alabama warehouse workers everywhere, even the bathroom', *Washington Post* (2 February 2021).

[11] K Candaele, 'Alabama Amazon workers say they're fed up and not taking it any more', *Salon* (6 April 2021).

[12] L Aratani, 'Biden gives tentative support to Amazon workers in union push', *The Guardian* (1 March 2021).

[13] 'Amazon defeats historic Alabama union effort', *BBC News* (9 April 2021); A MacGillis, 'The union battle at Amazon is far from over', *The New Yorker* (13 April 2021).

[14] See, eg, R Feurer and C Pearson (eds), *Against Labor: How U.S. Employers Organized to Defeat Union Activism* (Urbana, University of Illinois Press, 2017); J McAlevey, *A Collective Bargain: Unions, Organizing, and the Fight for Democracy* (New York, Harper Collins, 2020) 61–82.

industry is the biggest failure of the union movement in the 21st century.'[15] However, this does not tell us the full story. Even at Amazon, workers and their unions are fighting back. As will be recounted in Chapter 8, Italian unions utilised strike activity during the 'Black Friday' sales in late 2017 to extract a world-first collective agreement at Amazon's warehouse in Piacenza. Unions in many countries (including Germany, Bangladesh and Australia) have since organised collective actions impacting Amazon at peak sales periods.[16] Britain's GMB Union is organising around a campaign called 'Amazon workers are not robots'.[17] In the US, Chris Smalls has drawn on the profile generated by his dismissal to kick-start a protest movement demanding higher pay and improved safety protections for the company's warehouse workers.[18]

Other parts of the tech industry have seen significant worker mobilisation in recent years,[19] such as the walkouts in late 2018 of thousands of Google employees concerned about sexual harassment and racial inequality.[20] That was a largely spontaneous action, without union involvement.[21] But in early 2021, around 400 Google workers voted to form the Alphabet Workers Union (an affiliate of the Communication Workers of America), providing stronger support to worker activism at Google – albeit without engaging in collective bargaining.[22] In the wake of this, the Professionals Australia union declared it was ramping up its organising of tech-workers at Google and Apple (based on concerns over unpaid overtime and discrimination) and forming an alliance with the new micro-union for video game developers.[23] Union organising drives in the digital media sector in the US since 2015 have resulted in collective bargaining contracts at news outlets including *BuzzFeed*, *Vice*, *Slate*, *Vox* and the *Huffington Post*.[24] As shown in Chapters 9

[15] H Nolan, 'The failure to unionize the tech industry will eat the labor movement alive', *In These Times* (26 August 2020).

[16] See, eg, A Thomson and M Day, 'Thousands of Amazon workers will walk off the job today to fight for fair pay and COVID protections', *Fortune* (27 November 2020).

[17] GMB, 'Amazon workers are not robots'. Available at: www.gmb.org.uk/campaign/amazon-workers-are-not-robots.

[18] A Wood, 'Chris Smalls: "Now is the time" to confront corporate oligarchy', *Diem 25* (5 October 2020).

[19] N Nedzhvetskaya and JS Tan, 'What we learned from over a decade of tech activism', *The Guardian* (23 December 2019); G De Vynck, N Tiku and J Greene, 'Six things to know about the latest efforts to bring unions to big tech', *Washington Post* (26 January 2021).

[20] E Sullivan and L Wamsley, 'Google workers walk out to protest company's treatment of women', *NPR* (1 November 2018); N Scheiber, 'Google workers reject Silicon Valley individualism in walkout', *New York Times* (6 November 2018).

[21] Nolan (n 15); D Peetz, *The Realities and Futures of Work* (Acton, Australian National University Press, 2019) 179.

[22] K Conger, 'Hundreds of Google employees organize, culminating years of activism', *New York Times* (4 January 2021).

[23] D Marin-Guzman, 'Union push to organise Google workers', *Australian Financial Review* (27 January 2021). See the examination of Game Workers Unite Australia in ch 6.

[24] M Walker, 'Tech innovators start to see old-fashioned benefits of collective bargaining', *The Conversation* (19 July 2018); N Cohen and G de Peuter, 'What's behind the new push for unionization by journalists?', *The Conversation* (1 September 2020). See further N Cohen and G de Peuter, *New Media Unions: Organizing Digital Journalists* (Abingdon, Routledge, 2020); and Part V below.

and 10 of this book, unions are making headway in organising and representing workers in the uniquely hostile terrain of the gig economy.

## II. Aims and Scope

Trade unions have acted as the main form of representation for workers and the primary vehicle for countering managerial power for more than 200 years. Spurred on by the industrial revolution in Britain, unions came to occupy a highly influential position in the economies of many countries in the post-war period of the twentieth century. However, the power of the unions has taken a markedly downward turn since the 1980s. Neoliberal economic and political thought has laid down fundamental challenges to the legitimate role (and sometimes, the very existence) of trade unions. The intense competitive pressures brought to bear by globalisation have unleashed successive waves of economic restructuring, eroding traditional mainstays of union strength such as manufacturing industries. Businesses have engaged in various strategies of re-invention through new business models, to avoid traditional forms of protective employment regulation and the representative role of unions. At the same time, unions have had to contend with deregulatory labour law reforms, prioritising individualised employment relationships and removing long-standing support for collective organisation. This shifting role of the state has been accompanied by and has enabled growing employer hostility to unions. As if all that were not enough, the COVID-19 pandemic has presented major new tests for unions: pushing them into the primary role of defender of workers' basic rights to income security and a safe workplace and requiring nimble adaptation to digital organising on a massive scale.

This book explores the recent experience and future prospects of unions and newer forms of worker representation in four countries: the United States of America, Australia, the United Kingdom and Italy. It considers the extent of union membership decline in each nation and its causes. The book illustrates the differing strengths and deficiencies in the legal frameworks for union representation in the four countries. It also explores employer opposition to unions and the impact of business models, including agency/labour hire arrangements, independent contractor relationships (whether genuine or 'sham' in nature), supply chains and the gig economy. The book examines how unions in the four nations have sought to meet these various tests through a range of strategies. These include the 'organising model', which originated in the US and its adoption in Australia and the UK; union mergers and new approaches to union structures and membership models; lobbying for more favourable legislation; running litigation in the courts to contest various business models and expand recognition and bargaining rights; concerted efforts to engage with the hardest-to-recruit groups (precarious, migrant and younger workers); and innovative forms of campaigning, both in the workplace and in the broader communities, that unions inhabit.[25] The book also considers other manifestations of collectivism which are filling the gap left by the retreat or absence of unions. Among these are self-organised worker coalitions (some of which exist only online), worker centres and 'alt-labour' groups.[26] These phenomena are now widespread in the US, with green shoots starting to appear in the other three nations considered in this study (eg, the spontaneous collectives of food delivery riders and new independent unions which have emerged in Italy and the UK).

Drawing on this account and assessment of developments in the four countries – and an in-depth examination of the role of unions in the gig economy – a central purpose of the book is to identify how the revitalisation of unions can be achieved and what collectivism must look like to ensure the effective representation of workers' interests into the future. In an important contribution to the scholarly debate on these issues in 2019, Visser outlined 'four possible futures' for trade unions globally.[27] First, marginalisation: 'the continuation of present trends with decreasing rates of unionization and trade unions becoming less relevant or powerless in shaping the newly emerging labour markets.'[28] Secondly, dualisation: 'unions will defend their positions and resist where they are currently strong', but this will lead to 'a sharper distinction between unionized and non-unionized firms and a smaller share for the former'.[29] Thirdly, replacement: 'Unions will gradually give way to other forms of social action and representation', including those based on legislation (eg, works councils); employer-driven substitutes (eg, employee voice and participation schemes); and 'more or less spontaneous, intermittent forms of social and community action'.[30] Fourthly, revitalisation: 'Unions will find ways to strengthen existing practices of trade union renewal, reverse the current trend, rejuvenate, expand beyond their current membership base and succeed in organizing parts of the "new unstable workforce" in the digital economy.'[31] Visser concludes that 'the four futures for trade unions are [already] happening' to a

[25] These and other approaches adopted by unions around the world have been explored in the extensive academic literature on union renewal: see, eg, P Fairbrother and C Yates (eds), *Trade Unions in Renewal: A Comparative Study* (London, Routledge, 2003); C Frege and J Kelly (eds), *Varieties of Unionism: Revitalization in a Globalizing Economy* (Oxford, Oxford University Press, 2004); J Kelly, 'Trade Union Membership and Power in Comparative Perspective' (2015) 26:4 *Economic and Labour Relations Review* 526; C Ibsen and M Tapia, 'Trade Union Revitalisation: Where Are We Now? Where To Next?' (2017) 59:2 *Journal of Industrial Relations* 170, 178–84; G Murray, 'Union Renewal: What Can We Learn from Three Decades of Research?' (2017) 23:1 *Transfer* 9. See also A Tattersall, *Power in Coalition: Strategies for Strong Unions and Social Change* (Ithaca, ILR Press/Cornell University Press, 2010).

[26] See, eg, Murray (n 25) 15; S Ashby, '"Traditional" and "Alt" Labor: Comparisons, Critiques and Perspectives' (2018) 43 *Labor Studies Journal* 101.

[27] J Visser, *Trade Unions in the Balance* (ILO/ACTRAV Working Paper, International Labour Organization, 2019) 10.

[28] Ibid, 10; see also 59–62.

[29] Ibid; see also 62–66.

[30] Ibid; see also 66–68.

[31] Ibid; see also 68–70.

varying extent around the world, but the 'bottom line' for unions is that: 'adding new members or creating some other form of engagement involves doing things differently, albeit for the same old purpose: organizing and expressing solidarity among workers'.[32] This book is premised on the view that Visser's revitalisation option for unions is viable, as long as they commit to its underlying pre-conditions: it is not a promise of a return to the past, rather it requires experimentation with new ideas and technologies, a fundamentally different approach to the concept of membership, openness to less-rigid forms of engagement with the union (especially for young workers) and forming alliances with other social movements.[33]

My subscription to the revitalisation pathway is a product of the specific contours of the debate about union decline – and how to reverse it – which has been taking place for some time in Australia. There has been a strong emphasis placed by some union leaders on the hostile legal and institutional framework for unions – leading to the conclusion that more favourable labour laws will save the day. For example, National Tertiary Education Union officials Ken McAlpine and Sarah Roberts contended (in a 2017 paper) that the 'systemic hurdles' in Australia's labour legislation 'operate as the central and critical factor' which prevents organising and recruitment strategies from succeeding.[34] Their proposal to change the law to allow collective bargaining in 'bargaining electorates' made up of employees across enterprises, industries, occupations or supply chains would (they suggested) 'rapidly bring union density to well above fifty percent of the workforce'.[35] In short, McAlpine and Roberts argued, unions will not recover 'until the basic rules of the game are changed'.[36] In the lead-up to the 2019 federal election, the Australian Council of Trade Unions (ACTU) marshalled a major campaign to fix the nation's broken laws governing employment relations under the banner 'Change the Rules'.[37] The campaign focused public attention on important issues including wage theft, income inequality and insecure work. However, it did not succeed in its main objective of unseating the (conservative) Coalition government and having a Labor government implement wide-ranging labour law reforms. In my view, the legislative changes sought by the ACTU in its 'Change the Rules' campaign are absolutely necessary to give workers and unions a fair chance of building power. But they are *not enough, on their own*, to bring about the revival of Australian unions[38] (nor would similar improvements in the law solve

[32] Ibid, 71.

[33] Ibid, 70.

[34] K McAlpine and S Roberts, *The Future of Trade Unions in Australia* (Paper for the Association of Industrial Relations Academics of Australia and New Zealand Conference, Canberra, 9 February 2017) 1.

[35] Ibid, 9.

[36] Ibid, 5. See also J Bornstein, 'Employees Are Losing: Have Workplace Laws Gone Too Far?' (2019) 61:3 *Journal of Industrial Relations* 438.

[37] See ch 5.

[38] It should be noted that ACTU Secretary, Sally McManus, has said that changing legal rules is a big piece in the 'jigsaw' of turning around union membership decline – along with innovation in union membership offerings: 'Life membership might help unions turn corner: McManus', *Workplace Express* (26 June 2017).

the problems encountered by unions elsewhere). The focus of those efforts must also be on *what unions need to do themselves.*

This perspective is reflected in other contributions to this exchange, which recognise the imperative of unions adapting to the contemporary and future world of work. Tim Lyons, a former Assistant Secretary of the ACTU, put this position forcefully in a 2016 article in which he argued that Australian unions had put too much faith in 'electoral politics', whereas: '... for a social movement such as unionism the real game is elsewhere – it's in what you do to build permanent organised power in workplaces and communities'.[39] He went on to state the essential problem for unions, and the solution to it, as follows:

> The workplaces and communities in which we organised politically and industrially have disappeared underneath us. ...
>
> ... The world has changed much more than the labour movement has changed. ...
>
> Unions have to transform to catch up with the world as it is. ...
>
> ... [U]nions can transform by returning to a focus on work and organising, but in transformative ways. Our workplace laws, and most union tactics, were designed for places such as car factories – large workplaces where people worked for decades. ... But ... in the world of casual work and the contracting chain, *new models of what it means to be union and to bargain collectively must be worked out.*[40]

Leading US worker advocates, Sarita Gupta, Stephen Lerner and Joseph McCartin, expressed a similar view in 2019, contending that: 'Laws will not save us. Workers' struggles and organizations must play a central role in shaping the twenty-first century if we are to win the changes we need.'[41] Importantly, they added this caveat:

> But that does not mean that legal reform isn't important or that it doesn't have a crucial, indeed indispensable role to play. We don't see legal reform and movement-building as an either/or. We simply meant to address the vital question "Which comes first?".[42]

In the wake of the Australian union movement's disappointment about the 2019 election outcome, Centre for Future Work director and economist Jim Stanford maintained that legislative fixes to overcome Australia's 'unusual and intrusive' barriers to union organising 'must remain a central priority, complementing the ongoing effort to organise workers and rebuild the union movement'.[43] This indicates, again, that the future path for unions is not a binary choice between pushing for legal change or innovating. It is a matter of striking the right balance between

[39] T Lyons, 'The Labour Movement: My Part in its Downfall', *Meanjin* (Spring 2016) 87, 91.
[40] Ibid, 94 (emphasis added). See also G Moase, 'A New Species of Shark: Towards Direct Unionism' (2012) 4:2 *Interface: A Journal for and about Social Movements* 280; and ch 11.
[41] S Gupta, S Lerner and J McCartin, 'Why the Labor Movement Has Failed – And How to Fix It', *Boston Review* (1 May 2019).
[42] Ibid.
[43] J Stanford, *Union Organising and Labour Market Rules: Two Sides of the Same Coin* (Briefing Note, Centre for Future Work, The Australia Institute, 13 June 2019) 9, 11.

these and the other strategies open to unions, and (consequently) where they should focus their energy and resources.

Stanford also utilised data from the World Economic Forum and the Organisation for Economic Co-operation and Development (OECD), to make the case that: 'there are *no countries* where union membership is strong (above 20% of employment) without the presence of strong protections for workers' rights and labour freedoms'.[44] The connection between unions' (lack of) power and the regulatory environment and the broader relationship between unions and the state have been extensively scrutinised in international literature.[45] Another main purpose of this book is to examine how unions and other worker representatives have tried to utilise the labour laws of Australia, the UK, USA and Italy. It will show how the legal rules in the first three countries have inhibited effective representation (compared with Italian law). Based on this analysis, the book argues for reforms to ensure that workers have a genuine opportunity to exercise collective power.

## III. Why Compare the USA, the UK, Australia and Italy?

These four nations have been chosen because (in the case of the first three) there are significant commonalities in their industrial relations and labour law systems and in their stories of the 'rise and fall' of trade unions. The USA, the UK and Australia are all usually categorised as falling within the Anglophone industrial relations tradition:[46] countries typified by firm-level systems of collective bargaining[47] and which adopt a 'single channel' approach to worker representation dominated by trade unions (rather than the 'dual channel' of unions alongside works councils or other firm-level structures).[48] Historically, unions in these three countries developed along craft, occupational and industry lines[49] and remain structured mostly

[44] Ibid, 1.

[45] See, eg, Ibsen and Tapia (n 25) 184; R Adams and R Markey, 'How the State Influences Trade Union Growth: A Comparative Analysis of Developments in Europe, North America and Australasia' (1997) 13:4 *International Journal of Comparative Labour Law and Industrial Relations* 285; C Howell, *Trade Unions and the State: The Construction of Industrial Relations Institutions in Britain, 1890–2000* (Princeton, Princeton University Press, 2000).

[46] R Gumbrell-McCormick and R Hyman, *Trade Unions in Western Europe: Hard Times, Hard Choices* (Oxford, Oxford University Press, 2013) 24–27.

[47] OECD, *OECD Employment Outlook 2017* (Paris, OECD Publishing, 2017) 134.

[48] P Davies, 'A Challenge to Single Channel' (1994) 23 *Industrial Law Journal* 272.

[49] See, eg, N Lichtenstein, *State of the Union: A Century of American Labor* (Princeton, Princeton University Press, revised and expanded edition, 2013) ch 2; B Ebbinghaus and J Visser, *Trade Unions in Western Europe since 1945* (Basingstoke, Palgrave Macmillan, 2000) 715–16; A Stewart, A Forsyth, M Irving, R Johnstone and S McCrystal, *Creighton and Stewart's Labour Law*, 6th edn (Sydney, Federation Press, 2016) 835–36.

on the basis of industry formations. As will be shown further in Chapter 2, similarities can also be seen among the US, the UK and Australia in the extent and causes of union decline; in the nature of employer opposition to unions; in the adoption of various business models or 'fissuring'[50] through which businesses have sought to keep unions at a distance; and (the subject of later chapters) in union responses to these and other challenges, including heavy reliance on organising as a path to revitalisation.[51] In most of these areas, trends in the USA have been followed by similar developments in the UK and Australia.

In several respects, Italy provides an interesting counterpoint to the other three countries examined in this study. Italy belongs to the southern European model of trade unionism and labour relations,[52] characterised historically by 'relatively late industrialisation, a large agricultural sector, and a high proportion of self-employment'.[53] Again, as Chapter 2 will make clear, the nature of worker representation in Italy has always differed from the Anglophone systems (including union structures, with three ideologically-orientated national union confederations, and a more pronounced role for workplace-level representative bodies); unions have a higher degree of legitimacy in Italian society and closer integration within the state; and union decline has not been as pronounced in Italy as in the US, the UK and Australia. In addition, the organising approach 'has not been central to the revitalization project of Italian unions'.[54] In other ways, similar trends can be observed in Italy to those evident in the other three countries: for example, the proliferation of agency work, engagement of workers through platforms and other disruptions to conventional employment arrangements.[55] Like their counterparts in Australia, the US and the UK, Italian unions have sought to contest precarious work and income inequality, while pushing back on the exploitative business model of the gig economy has seen a greater role for newer collectivist groups in Italy. Finally, parallels can be seen in the vital role played by unions in response to the COVID-19 pandemic in all four countries.

These various points of similarity and contrast between the USA, the UK, Australia and Italy make for a rich comparative focus in this book. This kind of comparison is useful in that it can enable a 'better perception of one's own national system' and contribute to the process of law reform.[56] It also allows the researcher 'to

[50] D Weil, *The Fissured Workplace: Why Work Became So Bad for So Many and What Can Be Done to Improve It* (Cambridge MA, Harvard University Press, 2014).

[51] E Heery and L Adler, 'Organizing the Unorganized', in Frege and Kelly (n 25) 45.

[52] OECD (n 47) 134; I Regalia and M Regini, 'Trade Unions and Employment Relations in Italy during the Economic Crisis' (2018) 23:1 *South European Society and Politics* 63, 68–69.

[53] Gumbrell-McCormick and Hyman (n 46) 20.

[54] Heery and Adler (n 51) 55.

[55] See ch 2.

[56] R Blanpain, 'Comparativism in Labour Law and Industrial Relations', in R Blanpain (ed), *Comparative Labour Law and Industrial Relations in Industrialized Market Economies* (Alphen aan den Rijn, Kluwer Law International, 2010) 3, 4–5.

set aside the discourse, value assumptions and intellectual repertoire that constrict the imagination and confine the actions of participants within a closed system'.[57] There is also a bolder objective, articulated by Stone, which informs this study: the use of 'comparative analysis to identify possibilities for action and forge alliances that can bring about a renewed progressive social agenda'.[58] She has suggested the necessity of a comparative approach in response to the forces of globalisation, in particular: 'to understand how flexible work practices are undermining established collective labor relations and to explore efforts in different places to adapt organizational forms to the new work practices'.[59] Previous studies, such as Frege and Kelly's edited collection examining labour movement revitalisation in the US, the UK, Germany, Italy and Spain, have demonstrated the utility of cross-national comparative analysis as a basis for identifying the strategies, reforms, linkages and coalitions required to turn the fortunes of unions around.[60]

To the extent that this study involves *legal* comparison, it is noted that comparative analysis is fraught with potential difficulties. A considerable body of comparative law and comparative labour law literature counsels on the need, when undertaking comparison of the laws and legal institutions of different countries, for consideration of *context*: the economic, social, political, historical, cultural and other contexts in which laws and institutions have developed. Scholars have long disagreed on which of those contexts matters most.[61] Their warnings have been sounded in relation to the specific question of the transplantability of labour laws and legal institutions between jurisdictions.[62] This study does not engage in transplant analysis, but it does undertake a comparative assessment of the legal

[57] H Arthurs, 'Cross-National Legal Learning: The Uses of Comparative Labor Knowledge, Law, and Policy' in K Stone and H Arthurs (eds), *Rethinking Workplace Regulation* (Russell Sage Foundation, 2013) 353, 356.

[58] K Stone, 'A New Labor Law for a New World of Work: The Case for a Comparative-Transnational Approach', in B Aaron and K Stone (eds), *Rethinking Comparative Labor Law: Bridging the Past and the Future* (Lake Mary, Vandeplas Publishing, 2007) 193, 209.

[59] Ibid, 203, 204–7. See also R Locke and K Thelen, 'Apples and Oranges Revisited: Contextualized Comparisons and the Study of Comparative Labor Politics' (1995) 23:3 *Politics and Society* 337.

[60] L Turner, 'Why Revitalize? Labour's Urgent Mission in a Contested Global Economy', in Frege and Kelly (n 25) 1, 4–6. See also G Mundlak, *Organizing Matters: Two Logics of Trade Union Representation* (Cheltenham, Edward Elgar Publishing, 2020).

[61] See, eg, O Kahn-Freund, 'On Uses and Misuse of Comparative Law' (1974) 37 *Modern Law Review* 1; A Watson, 'Legal Transplants and Law Reform' (1976) 92 *Law Quarterly Review* 79; P Legrand, 'The Impossibility of "Legal Transplants"' (1997) 4 *Maastricht Journal of European and Comparative Law* 111; G Teubner, 'Legal Irritants: Good Faith in British Law or How Unifying Law Ends Up in New Divergences' (1998) 61 *Modern Law Review* 11. See also D Schiek, 'Enforcing (EU) Non-discrimination Law: Mutual Learning between British and Italian Labour Law' (2012) 28:4 *International Journal of Comparative Labour Law and Industrial Relations* 489, 506–9; P Almond and H Connolly, 'A Manifesto for "Slow" Comparative Research on Work and Employment' (2019) 26:1 *European Journal of Industrial Relations* 59.

[62] See, eg, Kahn-Freund (n 61); B Hepple, 'Can Collective Labour Law Transplants Work? The South African Example' (1999) 20 *Industrial Law Journal (South Africa)* 1; R McCallum, 'Plunder Downunder: Transplanting the Anglo-American Labour Law Model to Australia' (2005) 26 *Comparative Labor Law and Policy Journal* 381; M Rawling and J Howe, 'The Regulation of Supply Chains: An Australian Contribution to Cross-National Legal Learning', in Stone and Arthurs (n 57) 233, 245–47.

frameworks of the USA, the UK, Australia and Italy, to obtain deeper insights into their strengths and limitations as bases for effective worker representation. The suggestions for law reform that are made in Chapter 11 include some ideas about each nation looking to the others' labour laws (or proposed laws) for inspiration. In putting these views forward, I am cognisant of the lessons of comparative labour law scholarship: that there are important differences in the broader landscapes in which each country's labour laws have evolved and operate (including their economic and industrial relations systems, union traditions and strategic choices, and business cultures) and that legal rules cannot simply be ripped out of one national system and dropped into another.

## IV. Chapter Overview

Chapter 2 provides a snapshot of the extent and causes of union membership loss in the US, the UK, Australia and Italy. In doing so, it further highlights the areas of congruence and contrast which justify the choice of these four nations for this study. This is followed, in Chapter 3, by an overview of the legal framework for trade unions and worker representation in each country. It highlights, in particular, the inadequacies of the laws regulating union recognition, collective bargaining and industrial action in the US, the UK and Australia, in contrast to the more favourable legal and institutional setting for Italian unions. The book then moves onto the four country studies, examining the range of strategies adopted by unions in each nation to counter membership decline, beginning in Chapter 4 with the USA. This traces the implementation of the organising model by US unions, its limited success in terms of increasing overall levels of union membership and other approaches including voluntary union recognition agreements with employers and the pursuit of pro-union labour law reforms. The increasing engagement of US unions with other social movements and the emergence of alt-labour groups and campaigns (eg, the Fight for $15) are also explored.

Chapters 5 and 6 focus in some depth on the position of Australian unions: their adoption of US-style organising as their political power waned at the end of the Accord era; their switch, as the limits of organising became apparent, to heavy reliance on electoral politics as a basis for obtaining more supportive labour laws (on two separate occasions in the last 15 years, with different outcomes); and their growing recognition that recovery lies in innovating and experimenting with new membership models. Six examples of these novel forms of unionism or digital prototypes (eg, Hospo Voice) are considered. along with the recent wave of union mergers and the campaign by one Australian union to organise beyond the workplace in the fresh-food supply chain.

In Chapter 7, the UK variant of organising is examined, along with the simultaneous pursuit of workplace partnerships by British unions in the New Labour years; their responses to austerity and Brexit and positioning for labour law reform as the prospect of Labour returning to government glimmered (then faded); and the more recent emergence of combative, grass-roots unions mobilising low-paid workers (eg, the Independent Workers Union of Great Britain). Chapter 8 explores the somewhat different path of Italian unions: in place of the US organising model, they have focused their activism and recruitment efforts on marginalised worker groups (including migrants and those engaged in precarious work). The growing influence of independent unions, such as SI Cobas in the logistics sector, is also highlighted.

Chapters 9 and 10 shift the focus of the study to union efforts to organise and represent workers in the gig economy. The core business model of platforms like Uber, Lyft, Deliveroo and Foodora – the assumption that workers are self-employed contractors, until they prove otherwise – has meant the denial of basic employment rights for millions of workers *and* limitations on their ability to engage in collective action. The intervention of unions is critical to combating the exploitative effects of this newest iteration of fissured work. These two chapters chronicle how unions – and self-organised worker collectives – in all four countries have risen to this challenge, by revealing the reality of gig work as a basis for advocacy, campaigning and mobilising; using litigation to contest the platforms' sham contracting model; and engaging in collective bargaining and other efforts to reach collectively negotiated improvements in the situation of these workers.

Chapter 11 sets out the book's analysis in response to its two central objectives, as stated above. First, drawing on the accounts of union revival strategies in the country studies and the roles being played by unions in the gig economy, the chapter identifies the steps unions should take and issues they need to consider to rebuild collectivism. Among the conclusions are that union revitalisation can be achieved by supplementing organising and other recruitment efforts with innovation in membership offerings and opportunities to participate – especially to attract the all-important younger generation of workers. The need for unions to have a broader purpose than just increasing membership numbers; to incubate digital and campaign-based forms of unionism (and see where these lead); to respond to the demands of many marginalised workers for a more confrontational posture; and to move workers from online to offline forms of collectivism, is also articulated.

Secondly, Chapter 11 outlines eight priority areas for labour law reform that will also help unions and workers to rebuild – including multi-employer bargaining, realistic thresholds for establishing the right to bargain through non-ballot methods, union rights of access to and communication with workers, removing limits on strike action, and bringing gig workers within the protection of employment and labour laws. Finally, Chapter 12 examines the critical role of unions in each of the four countries during the COVID-19 pandemic, safeguarding workers' lives and livelihoods. It also considers the implications of the health and economic crisis for unions and the opportunity it presents: the case for unionising has never been so compelling.

## V. The Digital Picket Line

The book's sub-title – 'the digital picket line' – encapsulates the melding of the rich tradition of unions at the peak of their strength (symbolised by the exercise of collective power through strikes and picketing) and the use of innovative technological tactics to win gains for a new generation of workers. As early as the eighteenth century, striking workers in Britain engaged in '"picketing": either touring the district to persuade others to come out and join them, or standing in front of a workplace to scare substitute labour away'.[63] By the time of the 1972 miners' strike, British unionists had perfected the art of the picket (combined with secondary action) as an industrial tactic, as Lyddon tells of the conflagration at Saltley, east Birmingham:

> … Engineering and car workers struck in support [of the miners], with sufficient thousands of them marching to the coke depot to seal if off, forcing the police to shut it …. As [National Union of Mineworkers General Secretary Lawrence] Daly acknowledged a few days afterwards, "the industrial workers of Birmingham marched in their thousands to join our picket line".[64]

The idea of employees being able 'to mirror real-life collective action in online transactions' was articulated in the January 2020 final report of the Harvard Labor and Worklife Program's 'Clean Slate for Worker Power' project – an ambitious redesign of US labour law to enable working people to create economic and political power.[65] As part of Clean Slate's recommendations for a new suite of collective action rights, the report argued that workers should be able to appeal for support from the public and consumers as follows:

> … the digital picket line would require employers to allow workers to inform online customers about strikes occurring at the employer's physical site. For example, when a customer goes to book a hotel room on the Marriott website (or a third-party site, such as Expedia or Booking.com), the company would be required to accede to the union's request to show the customer a pop-up window stating, "There is a strike occurring at this location; do you still want to proceed?" Then, the customer could click yes (an online analog to crossing a picketing line) or no.[66]

After *The New Yorker* magazine shifted its annual festival in 2020 online due to the pandemic, The New Yorker Union organised a digital picket line of the opening night event featuring Senator Elizabeth Warren and Representative Alexandria Ocasio-Cortez. The union was in dispute with the magazine's owner, Condé

[63] A Reid, *United We Stand: A History of Britain's Trade Unions* (London, Penguin Books, 2005) 21.

[64] D Lyddon, '"Glorious Summer", 1972: The High Tide of Rank-and-File Militancy', in J McIlroy, N Fishman and A Campbell (eds), *The High Tide of British Trade Unionism: Trade Unions and Industrial Politics, 1964–79* (Monmouth, Merlin Press, 2007) 326, 331 (reference omitted).

[65] S Block and B Sachs, *Clean Slate for Worker Power: Building a Just Economy and Democracy* (Harvard Law School, 2020) 1; see ch 11.

[66] Ibid, 64.

Nast, over negotiations for a new contract. Both congresswomen pulled out of the event in solidarity with the magazine's staff,[67] 'AOC' tweeting to her 9 million followers: 'Love the @NewYorker, but @ewarren and I don't cross picket lines'.[68] Of course, one of the main purposes of a picket line is to ensure that employees of the target business do not cross it. The New Yorker Union's digital picket line was accompanied by a virtual walkout (employees closed their computers and set up out-of-office messages).[69] These tactics triggered 30 hours of Zoom talks on the weekend before the festival, resulting in the resolution of the dispute (including management's agreement to a key union claim: ending at-will employment by including a 'just cause' termination provision in the contract).[70]

Unions representing rideshare drivers in the gig economy have used local and global online pickets to encourage sympathy action from third parties such as customers and supporters.[71] A digital picket line can also be used to bolster a traditional physical picket. In the context of industrial action in UK universities in late 2019, University and College Union (UCU) members were urged to 'respect the digital and non-campus picket line':

> Remember that striking includes not working from home, not dealing with your emails …, no work-related social media, and generally not doing anything that counts as work, wherever it might be done.[72]

Another form of the digital picket line is simply an online protest, such as that organised by the Victorian Trades Hall Council (VTHC) to mobilise support for the broader Australian union movement campaign for wage subsidies following the first COVID-19 lockdown. This was a nine-hour, live-streamed event held on 31 March 2020, featuring interviews with migrant workers, retail and hospitality staff, health and safety experts, journalists and politicians.[73] While the Australian government had (reluctantly) announced an income protection scheme (JobKeeper) on 30 March, it left out many groups of workers.[74] VTHC's

[67] K Robertson, 'Ocasio-Cortez and Warren pull out of New Yorker festival', *New York Times* (30 September 2020).

[68] H Aizenman, S Frey and M Schotz, 'We finally won just cause protection at The New Yorker after AOC and Warren refused to cross our picket line', *Labor Notes* (23 October 2020).

[69] Ibid.

[70] Ibid; K Flynn, 'New Yorker Union wins fight for just cause in contract', *CNN* (6 October 2020); The New Yorker Union, 'The era of at-will employment at *The New Yorker* is over'. Available at: www.newyorkerunion.com/.

[71] See ch 9.

[72] University of Leeds UCU, 'News on negotiations, the digital picket line, hot breakfasts and more' (27 November 2019). Available at: www.leedsucu.org.uk/news-on-negotiations-the-digital-picket-line-hot-breakfasts-and-more/. See also L Spurgin, 'Never cross a digital picket line', *Medium* (30 November 2019); C Bertram, 'University strikes: can workers fully withdraw labour in the digital age?', *The Conversation* (23 March 2018).

[73] N Montague, 'Online Picket Line Guide', *The Commons Social Change Library*. Available at: https://commonslibrary.org/online-picket-line-guide/.

[74] 'Pay $1500 wage subsidy to all casuals, visa workers: Unions', *Workplace Express* (31 March 2020). See ch 12.

online picket, and a virtual picket organised by the United Workers Union (UWU), highlighted these gaps and kept up pressure on the federal government to address them (using the campaign slogan #WageSubsidyForAll).[75] VTHC repeated the tactic, holding an online picket on 1 March 2021 to protest against the government's legislative proposals to weaken employment protections (ostensibly intended to help businesses recover from the pandemic).[76]

In its various manifestations, the digital picket line is emblematic of the transformation in union forms and tactics that, this book argues, is needed to ensure that unions continue to play an effective role as the representative voice of workers into the future.

[75] Ibid; UWU, 'Nationwide virtual picket line calls for no worker to be left behind', *Media Release* (3 April 2020).

[76] VTHC, 'Online picket-line to stop Scott Morrison's job-destroying laws' (27 February 2021). Available at: www.weareunion.org.au/online_picket_line_20210301?utm_campaign=omnibus_picket_line&utm_medium=email&utm_source=victorianunions. See ch 12.

# 2

# A Snapshot of Union Decline in the Four Countries

## I. Introduction

So much has been written about falling trade union membership levels in many industrialised countries since the 1980s. It is not the purpose of this book to replicate earlier accounts of the extent and causes of union decline during this period.[1] Rather, the study identifies similar and contrasting trends which help us to understand what has happened to the union movement in each of the four nations under consideration. This begins with the following comparative snapshot, which also draws out further the common features of the situation facing unions in the USA, the UK and Australia, compared with the position of the Italian unions.

## II. Challenging Times for Trade Unions in the USA, the UK and Australia

### A. Extent of Falling Union Membership

Fostered by the National Labor Relations Act, 1935 (NLRA), union membership in the United States peaked at around 35 per cent of total employment in 1954.[2] However, membership numbers fell by almost 9 million in the private sector between 1970 and 2005: 'in the heart of the economy where society's wealth is extracted, the unions lost over half their members'.[3] By 2019, just 10.3 per cent of the US workforce were union members.[4] In 2020, there was a slight increase

[1] See, eg, S Fernie and D Metcalf (eds), *Trade Unions: Resurgence or Demise?* (London, Routledge, 2005); T Bramble, *Trade Unionism in Australia: A History from Flood to Ebb Tide* (Port Melbourne, Cambridge University Press, 2008); S Greenhouse, *Beaten Down, Worked Up: The Past, Present, and Future of American Labor* (New York, Alfred A Knopf, 2019); R Gumbrell-McCormick and R Hyman, *Trade Unions in Western Europe: Hard Times, Hard Choices* (Oxford, Oxford University Press, 2013).

[2] D Weil, *The Fissured Workplace: Why Work Became So Bad for So Many and What Can Be Done to Improve It* (Cambridge MA, Harvard University Press, 2014) 41.

[3] K Moody, *US Labor in Trouble and Transition: The Failure of Reform from Above, the Promise of Revival from Below* (New York, Verso, 2007) 98.

[4] US Bureau of Labor Statistics, *Union Members Summary* (22 January 2020).

to 10.8 per cent,[5] although only 6.3 per cent of workers in the private sector were in unions (compared with 34.8 per cent in the public sector).[6] Rosenfeld, pointing to the fact that public sector union density has held reasonably steady since the 1970s, suggests that: 'Union decline in the United States is entirely a private-sector phenomenon.'[7]

In the UK, union membership increased by 4 million from 1950 to 1979, when density reached its highest point of 55.4 per cent.[8] This was followed by the precipitous decline from the Thatcher era on, which saw the loss of 5.5 million members between 1979 and 1999.[9] Since the mid-1990s, the proportion of UK employees in unions has generally continued to decline (although at a slower rate), falling to a low of 23.3 per cent in 2017.[10] However, this has been followed by three successive years of gradual increases in membership density: to 23.4 per cent in 2018 and 23.5 per cent in 2019 (13.3% in the private sector; 52.3% among public sector employees),[11] then to 23.7 per cent in 2020.[12] Worryingly, though, private sector density continues to fall (to 12.9% in 2020).[13]

Union membership density in Australia climbed to a height of 63 per cent of the workforce in 1953, dipped to 49 per cent in 1969, rebounded to 56 per cent by 1975 and remained fairly stable until the mid-1980s.[14] From that point on, the shift 'from flood to ebb tide' in unionisation became unmistakable.[15] Overall, union membership numbers dropped from around 2.5 million in 1976 to 1.5 million in 2016 and union density fell from 51 to 15.6 per cent.[16] In 2018, only 14.6 per cent of Australian workers were union members;[17] by 2020, the proportion had fallen

[5] US Bureau of Labor Statistics, *Union Members Summary* (22 January 2021), noting that due to the impact of the COVID-19 pandemic, specifically 'the disproportionately large decline in total wage and salary employment (mostly among non-union members) compared with the decline in the number of union members', the 2020 figures should be treated with caution. See also ch 12.

[6] Ibid.

[7] J Rosenfeld, *What Unions No Longer Do* (Cambridge MA, Harvard University Press, 2014) 2–4.

[8] S Fernie, 'The Future of British Unions: Introductions and Conclusions', in Fernie and Metcalf (n 1 above) 1; J McIlroy and A Campbell, 'The High Tide of Trade Unionism: Mapping Industrial Politics, 1964–79', in J McIlroy, N Fishman and A Campbell (eds), *The High Tide of British Trade Unionism: Trade Unions and Industrial Politics, 1964–79* (Monmouth, Merlin Press, 2007) 93, 120.

[9] Fernie ibid, 1.

[10] Department for Business, Energy and Industrial Strategy, *Trade Union Membership, UK 1995–2019: Statistical Bulletin* (27 May 2020) 1, 5.

[11] Ibid.

[12] Department for Business, Energy and Industrial Strategy, *Trade Union Membership, UK 1995–2020: Statistical Bulletin* (27 May 2021) 1, noting that the 2020 statistics should be viewed with caution 'due to the Labour Force Survey … being weighted to pre-[pandemic] population projections'. See also ch 12.

[13] Ibid, 1, 5.

[14] D Peetz, *Unions in a Contrary World: The Future of the Australian Trade Union Movement* (Cambridge, Cambridge University Press, 1998) 24–30.

[15] Bramble (n 1) 154–55.

[16] Parliament of Australia, Department of Parliamentary Services, *Trends in Union Membership in Australia* (Research Paper Series, 2018–19, 15 October 2018) 1–2; Australian Bureau of Statistics (ABS), *Characteristics of Employment, Australia* (Cat 6333.0, August 2016).

[17] ABS, *Characteristics of Employment, Australia* (Cat 6333.0, August 2018).

further, to 14.3 per cent.[18] The most recent available figures providing a breakdown, from 2016, showed union membership at 38 per cent in the public sector and only 9 per cent in the private sector.[19]

## B. The Rise of Neoliberalism and State Hostility to Unions

The neoliberal agenda which has held sway for decades in the USA had the objective of weakening or eliminating unions, which its proponents considered to be 'the source of unacceptable interference in the labour market'.[20] The ideological godparent of this view, Milton Friedman, portrayed unions as monopolistic organisations possessing special immunities and causing the public harm by 'distorting the use of labor'.[21] Similarly, Friedrich Hayek asserted that unions were 'uniquely privileged institutions to which the general rules of law do not apply', fixated on the objectives of 'monopoly' and 'the coercion of fellow workers'.[22] These views formed part of a broader set of assumptions about the limited role that law should play in economic activity generally[23] and in employment relations specifically which should mostly be left to the free market and the common law of contract and tort.[24]

The work of Friedman, Hayek and 'New Right' scholars like Epstein[25] provided the intellectual fodder for the shift to a more hostile state stance towards unions from the 1980s in the USA and the UK, and later, Australia. In the US, the foundations for employer anti-unionism were laid down in the 1947 Taft-Hartley amendments of the NLRA.[26] Under President Reagan, an overt form of state antipathy towards labour unions emerged, exemplified by the US government's confrontation with air-traffic controllers in 1981.[27] Reagan fired over 11,000 striking members of the Professional Air Traffic Controllers Organisation, brought in replacement workers and had the union decertified.[28] This revealed (according to

[18] ABS, *Trade Union Membership* (Cat 6335.0, August 2020). See also ch 12.

[19] ABS, *Characteristics of Employment, Australia* (Cat 6333.0, August 2016).

[20] R Milkman, 'Back to the Future? US Labour in the New Gilded Age' (2013) 51:4 *British Journal of Industrial Relations* 645, 652.

[21] M Friedman, *Capitalism and Freedom*, 40th anniversary edn (Chicago, University of Chicago Press, 2002) 123–24, 131.

[22] FA Hayek, *The Constitution of Liberty* (London, Routledge and Kegan Paul, 1959) 267–69; see also FA Hayek, *Law, Legislation and Liberty: A New Statement of the Liberal Principles of Justice and Political Economy* (London, Routledge and Kegan Paul, 1979), vol 3, 89–97.

[23] M Friedman, *Capitalism and Freedom* (Chicago, University of Chicago Press, 1962) 14–15.

[24] R Epstein, 'A Common Law for Labor Relations: A Critique of the New Deal Labor Legislation' (1983) 92 *Yale Law Journal* 1357, 1359, 1366.

[25] Ibid.

[26] See ch 3.

[27] Greenhouse (n 1) 127–36; E Loomis, *A History of America in Ten Strikes* (New York, The New Press, 2018) 179–99.

[28] See J McCartin, *Collision Course: Ronald Reagan, the Air Traffic Controllers, and the Strike that Changed America* (New York, Oxford University Press, 2011).

Fantasia and Voss) the US state's propensity to inflict 'economic violence' on workers, while also encouraging employers to engage in 'an assault on unions in the private sector'.[29] From 2011, several US states significantly limited the collective bargaining and organisational rights of public sector unions,[30] adding to the 'right to work' laws already applying in many parts of the country.[31]

In the UK, state confrontation with unions took shape in the Thatcher and Major governments' step-by-step legislative programme of dismantling union rights (including the right to take industrial action and the 'closed shop') over the course of the 1980s and into the 1990s.[32] Here we see the most explicit connection with the Hayekian blueprint:[33] these statutes were cast as diluting trade union power by taking away unions' legal immunities and privileges and protecting the rights of the individual (ie, non-unionists).[34] Legislative reform with similar ideological foundations did not come to Australia until the election of the Liberal/National Coalition government in 1996[35] (although conservative governments in several Australian states had implemented free market-orientated labour laws in the early 1990s).[36] The Howard administration's 2005 'Work Choices' legislation demonstrated both an extreme anti-union animus and a retreat from the traditionally strong role of the state in regulating labour relations in the 'public sphere'.[37] In both the UK and Australia, labour laws implemented by Labour/Labor governments (in the years 1997–2010 and 2007–2013, respectively) did not restore meaningful support for union organisation. The subsequent return of conservative governments has led to new manifestations of state control over British and Australian unions.[38]

[29] R Fantasia and K Voss, *Hard Work: Remaking the American Labor Movement* (Berkeley, University of California Press, 2004) 67–68.

[30] See, eg, Rosenfeld (n 7) 37–39; A Walker, *Divided Unions: The Wagner Act, Federalism, and Organized Labour* (Philadelphia, University of Pennsylvania Press, 2020) ch 7.

[31] Enabled by section 14(b) of the NLRA, these state laws prohibit union-shop provisions and other forms of union security aimed at countering non-member 'free-riders': R Gorman, M Finkin and T Glynn, *Cox and Bok's Labor Law: Cases and Materials*, 16th edn (St Paul MN, Foundation Press, 2016) 375, 1150–53. See ch 11.

[32] S Auerbach, *Legislating for Conflict* (Oxford, Clarendon Press, 1990).

[33] J McIlroy, 'A Brief History of British Trade Unions and Neoliberalism: From the Earliest Days to the Birth of New Labour' in G Daniels and J McIlroy (eds), *Trade Unions in a Neoliberal World: British Trade Unions under New Labour* (London, Routledge, 2009) 21, 30–31.

[34] S Fredman, 'The New Rights: Labour Law and Ideology in the Thatcher Years' (1992) 12:1 *Oxford Journal of Legal Studies* 24; P Fosh, H Morris, R Martin, P Smith and R Undy, 'Politics, Pragmatism and Ideology: The "Wellsprings" of Conservative Union Legislation (1979–1992)' (1993) 22:1 *Industrial Law Journal* 14.

[35] R Cooper and B Ellem, 'The Neoliberal State, Trade Unions and Collective Bargaining in Australia' (2008) 46:3 *British Journal of Industrial Relations* 532.

[36] Largely inspired by the enactment of the Employment Contracts Act 1991 in New Zealand; for its primary intellectual underpinning see P Brook, *Freedom at Work: The Case for Reforming Labour Law in New Zealand* (Auckland, Oxford University Press, 1990).

[37] J Murray, 'Work Choices and the Radical Revision of the Public Realm of Australian Statutory Labour Law' (2006) 35:4 *Industrial Law Journal* 343.

[38] See ch 3.

## C. Hardened Employer Opposition

Emboldened by state antipathy, employer opposition to union organisation firmed up considerably from the 1980s onwards. As noted in Chapter 1, union-busting has a long pedigree in the USA. It took on greater vehemency as major corporations sought to emulate the President's aggressive stance in the air-traffic controllers' dispute, using permanent replacement workers to defeat strikes and 'break the unions'.[39] Employer opposition to union recognition campaigns became more widespread; tactics like firing union activists and deploying 'union avoidance' consultants were used to hammer home the purported harmful effects of voting for union representation.[40] This aggression escalated into the 2000s.[41] Elements of it were exported to the UK,[42] where the Thatcher-era laws had provided the basis for 'a very real institutional shift of power toward employers … that helped to deligitimize unions in the wider socio-political context'.[43] Many British employers have continued to stave off union recognition for collective bargaining, through tactics which the Blair 'New Labour' government's statutory recognition procedure has not sufficiently countered.[44] In Australia, the Coalition government's legislative reforms sponsored vigorous employer de-unionisation strategies on the waterfront and in the mining, telecommunications and finance industries in the 1990s and 2000s.[45] Since 2009, this kind of aggressive employer opposition to collective bargaining has been replaced by a range of new avoidance strategies, exploiting weaknesses in the Fair Work legislation introduced by the former Labor government.[46]

## D. Economic Restructuring and the Changing Nature of Work and the Workforce

Neoliberalism also brought with it globalisation and rapid technological change, which have eroded the traditional strongholds of US unions.[47] After the loss of

[39] Greenhouse (n 1) 137–39.

[40] J Logan, 'The Union Avoidance Industry in the United States' (2006) 44:4 *British Journal of Industrial Relations* 651.

[41] K Bronfenbrenner, *No Holds Barred: The Intensification of Employer Opposition to Organizing* (EPI Briefing Paper #235, Economic Policy Institute, 20 May 2009).

[42] J Logan, *US Anti-Union Consultants: A Threat to the Rights of British Workers* (London, Trades Union Congress, 2008).

[43] M Simms, J Holgate and E Heery, *Union Voices: Tactics and Tensions in UK Organizing* (Ithaca, Cornell University Press, 2013) 23.

[44] A Bogg, *The Democratic Aspects of Trade Union Recognition* (Oxford, Hart Publishing, 2009), chs 5 and 6. See ch 3.

[45] R Cooper, B Ellem, C Briggs and D van den Broek, 'Anti-unionism, Employer Strategy, and the Australian State, 1996–2005' (2009) 34:3 *Labor Studies Journal* 339.

[46] See ch 3.

[47] Milkman (n 20) 647, 652.

2.7 million American manufacturing jobs in just four years (1979–1983) came the increasing spectre – and reality – of further layoffs as companies relocated production overseas to reduce labour costs.[48] The UK and Australia have also witnessed the loss of large numbers of traditionally unionised jobs in sectors like manufacturing, mining and transport.[49] Visser notes that in all three countries (along with Canada and New Zealand): 'the average union density rate in manufacturing dropped from 47 per cent around 1980 to 17 per cent in 2017'.[50] Employment growth has occurred instead in service sectors such as (in Australia) finance, insurance, business services, wholesale and retail trade, restaurants and hospitality.[51] Unions have found organising and recruiting members in the service industries very difficult.[52] As at 2017, union density in some of the fastest-growing UK industries was lower than the private sector average of 13.4 per cent (12.1% in construction; 11.4% in retail; 10.1% in information and communication; 8.3% in professional, scientific and technical activities; and just 2.5% in food and accommodation services).[53]

Growing levels of casual employment, contracting and other types of insecure work or temporary jobs have also inhibited union membership growth.[54] In addition to the generally lower unionisation rates among migrants,[55] attracting younger workers has been another major problem.[56] Only 5 per cent of Australian workers aged 15 to 19 were union members in 2020[57] and just 4.4 per cent of those aged 16 to 24 in the UK in 2019.[58] Referring to the experience of several countries, including the USA, the UK and Australia, McIlroy and Daniels observe that:

> The general picture since the emergence of neoliberalism is one of union decline, significantly greater in the private sector and among the young, with increases in female density counteracted by falls in male density.[59]

[48] Greenhouse (n 1) 142–46.

[49] C Howell, *Trade Unions and the State: The Construction of Industrial Relations Institutions in Britain, 1890–2000* (Princeton, Princeton University Press, 2000) 154, 160–61; M Crosby, *Power at Work: Rebuilding the Australian Union Movement* (Sydney, Federation Press, 2005) 25.

[50] J Visser, *Trade Unions in the Balance* (ILO/ACTRAV Working Paper, International Labour Organization, 2019) 21.

[51] Crosby (n 49) 25; Parliament of Australia, Department of Parliamentary Services (n 16) 3.

[52] See, eg, Visser (n 50) 27–29.

[53] C Tait, *Future Unions: Towards a Membership Renaissance in the Private Sector* (The Changing Work Centre, 2017) 17.

[54] See, eg, R Bales, 'Union Trends' in R Bales and C Garden (eds), *The Cambridge Handbook of U.S. Labor Law for the Twenty-First Century* (Cambridge, Cambridge University Press, 2020) 3, 9–10; M Bernaciak, R Gumbrell-McCormick and R Hyman, *European Trade Unionism: From Crisis to Renewal?* (Report 133, European Trade Union Institute, 2014) 20–21; D Peetz, *The Realities and Futures of Work* (Acton, Australian National University Press, 2019) 201–02.

[55] See, eg, Visser (n 50) 33–34.

[56] Ibid, 24–26; Peetz (n 54) 191.

[57] ABS (n 18).

[58] Department for Business, Energy and Industrial Strategy (n 10) 16.

[59] J McIlroy and G Daniels, 'Introduction: Trade Unions in a Neoliberal World' in Daniels and McIlroy (n 33) 1, 6.

The higher level of female membership is, in fact, one of the few bright spots for unions:[60] in Australia, women accounted for 55 per cent of total union membership in 2020,[61] while in the UK, the female union density rate in that year was 27.2 per cent (compared with 20.2% for men).[62] This reflects the concentration of women workers in sectors that are now more likely to be unionised, such as education, health and social care, in both countries.[63]

## E. New Business Models

Putting organised labour even further on the defensive, in the last 30 years, employers have adopted a range of business models to distance themselves from responsibility for minimum employment standards – and keep unions at bay. Weil has persuasively shown that this formed part of a deliberate strategy on the part of many US companies to 'shed activities deemed peripheral to their core business models' (such as cleaning, security, payroll and information technology) and have these functions performed instead by a range of external providers.[64] The benefits for 'lead' businesses have included 'substantially reducing costs and dispatching the many responsibilities connected to being the employer of record'.[65] The business forms through which this 'fissuring' of work has occurred include, in the USA, franchising, third-party management, subcontracting and supply chain systems.[66] In Australia, independent contractor and labour hire arrangements have been widely utilised, along with franchising and complex supply chains.[67] Similarly, in the UK, various 'multilateral work arrangements' have been implemented including outsourcing, the parcelling of employer functions among several entities and the supply of workers through temporary agencies.[68]

According to Weil, the deployment of these business models has produced effects including 'downward pressure on wages and benefits, murkiness about who bears responsibility for work conditions, and increased likelihood that basic labor standards will be violated'.[69] Further, by 'shedding employment' through fissuring,

[60] Although not in the USA, where 11% of men in the workforce are union members, compared with 10.5% of women: US Bureau of Labor Statistics (n 5).

[61] ABS (n 18).

[62] Department for Business, Energy and Industrial Strategy (n 12) 7.

[63] Ibid, 8; Parliament of Australia, Department of Parliamentary Services (n 16) 4.

[64] Weil (n 2) 3–4.

[65] Ibid, 3; see further 49–58.

[66] Ibid, 8–9, 14–15, 24–26.

[67] T Hardy, 'Reconsidering the Notion of the "Employer" in the Era of the Fissured Workplace: Traversing the Legislative Landscape in Australia' in H Nakakubo and T Araki (eds), *The Notion of the Employer in the Era of the Fissured Workplace: Should Labour Law Responsibilities Exceed the Boundary of the Legal Entity?* (Alphen aan den Rijn, Kluwer Law International, 2017) 53.

[68] J Prassl, *The Concept of the Employer* (Oxford, Oxford University Press, 2015) 1–6.

[69] Weil (n 2) 8; see also 17.

lead businesses have been able to 'shift away from a highly unionized workforce or move work to forms of employment that are both legally and strategically difficult for unions to organize'.[70] This is because workers in these various contexts are less likely to join unions, and it is often unclear who is the direct employer (if there is one at all) to base a union campaign around. These difficulties are magnified in the context of the newest form of fissured work, the gig economy, which is examined in detail in Chapters 9 and 10 of this book.

# III. The Differing Trajectory of Union Membership and Worker Representation in Italy

## A. Less Pronounced Union Decline

Union membership density in Italy reached a peak of between 50 and 55 per cent of the workforce in 1977–1978.[71] From there, it fell to 48 per cent in 1980, and 33 per cent in 2010,[72] but had rebounded to 37.3 per cent by 2013.[73] These figures somewhat mask peaks and troughs which occurred within these periods. For example, Locke and Baccaro wrote of the 'resurgence of Italian unions' from the early 1990s, after 'more than a decade of declining political power [and] membership loss'.[74] By 2018, according to Organisation for Economic Co-Operation and Development (OECD) figures, trade union density in Italy was 34.4 per cent.[75] It must be noted, though, that Italian union membership figures are bolstered by the inclusion of retired members, who made up 38.5 per cent of overall union membership in 1990,[76] almost 50 per cent in 2007[77] and 44.1 per cent in 2016.[78] The high level of retired members is a 'distinctive feature of Italian trade unionism', reflecting an ageing population and 'a system

[70] Ibid, 77; see also 56, 254.

[71] T Treu, *Labour Law in Italy*, 3rd edn (Alphen aan den Rijn, Wolters Kluwer, 2011) 152. See also M Regini, 'Trade Unions' in E Jones and G Pasquino (eds), *The Oxford Handbook of Italian Politics* (Oxford, Oxford University Press, 2015) 528, 531.

[72] Gumbrell-McCormick and Hyman (n 1) 5.

[73] I Regalia and M Regini, 'Trade Unions and Employment Relations in Italy during the Economic Crisis' (2018) 23:1 *South European Society and Politics* 63, 68.

[74] R Locke and L Baccaro, 'The Resurgence of Italian Unions?' in A Martin and G Ross, *The Brave New World of European Labour: European Trade Unions at the Millennium* (New York, Berghahn Books, 1999) 217.

[75] OECD, OECD Data on Trade Union Density (undated). Available at: https://stats.oecd.org/Index.aspx?DataSetCode=TUD.

[76] Locke and Baccaro (n 74) 267.

[77] S Leonardi, 'Union Organisation of Employees in Atypical and Precarious Work in Italy' (2008) 4:3 *International Journal of Action Research* 203, 205.

[78] S Leonardi, 'Trade Unions and Collective Bargaining in Italy during the Crisis', in S Lehndorff, H Dribbusch and T Schulten, *Rough Waters: European Trade Unions in a Time of Crisis* (European Trade Union Institute, 2018) 87, 92–93.

of selective incentives offered by trade unions' to assist pensioners through welfare and cultural programmes.[79]

Factoring retired members into the equation, overall union membership among the active working population is likely to be lower in Italy than in the UK. Nevertheless, this does not detract from this book's premise that union decline (taking into account the overall strength and impact of a nation's union movement)[80] has not been as extensive in Italy as in the US, the UK or Australia. As Regini explains, 'the actual influence of unions in Italy has always been somewhat greater than might appear from indicators such as membership levels or the results of collective bargaining', due to the high 'institutional involvement' of unions in the public policy framework.[81] In any case, collective bargaining coverage in Italy is considerably higher than in the other three countries examined in this study.[82] Another important distinguishing feature is that the private sector union membership rate exceeds that in the other three nations, and, in fact, grew from 34.4 per cent in 2011 to nearly 40 per cent in 2016.[83] Writing in 2018, Leonardi maintained that although the qualitative power of Italian unions was weakening (as reflected in 'modest outcomes' in respect of workers' wages and conditions and welfare outcomes), their 'associative power' remained strong (as evidenced by 'membership, bargaining coverage, mobilisation capacity, [and] finances').[84] He concluded that they 'still manifest a remarkable associative vitality and presence in Italian society'.[85]

## B. Closer Integration between Unions and the Italian State

According to Regalia and Regini, unions have a 'widespread, almost ubiquitous, presence' in Italy, second only to that of the Catholic church, and operate at national, regional and workplace levels across the country.[86] This reflects a long-standing meshing of Italian unions and the state, another significant difference from the position in the other three countries examined here. While the Italian industrial relations system traditionally had low levels of formalised regulation

[79] Regini (n 71) 533. See also Leonardi (n 78) 93, 103–4; B Chiarini, 'The Composition of Union Membership: The Role of Pensioners in Italy' (1999) 37:4 *British Journal of Industrial Relations* 577.

[80] See J Kelly and C Frege, 'Conclusions: Varieties of Unionism', in C Frege and J Kelly (eds), *Varieties of Unionism: Revitalization in a Globalizing Economy* (Oxford, Oxford University Press, 2004) 181, 185, proposing that 'union revitalization could be examined along four dimensions: membership …, economic (or bargaining) power, political power, and institutional vitality'.

[81] Regini (n 71) 537.

[82] See ch 3.

[83] Leonardi (n 78) 94.

[84] Ibid, 88.

[85] Ibid, 113.

[86] Regalia and Regini (n 73) 70; see also R Hyman, *Understanding European Trade Unionism: Between Market, Class and Society* (London, Sage Publications, 2001) 154.

of employer–union relations,[87] state support for trade unions was manifested in different forms. Unions have for some time played a role in the implementation of government policies (for example, social security and welfare programmes) and engaged with public authorities on labour market issues.[88] Indeed, Agnoletto describes trade unions as the 'main actors' in the development of the post-war welfare state in Italy.[89]

In contrast to the USA, UK and Australia (which have no constitutional protections of workers' rights), the 1947 *Costituzione della Repubblica Italiana* contains guarantees of freedom of association, trade union activity, collective bargaining and the right to strike.[90] Direct institutional support for Italian unions as industrial relations actors came in the wake of the 'Hot Autumn' strikes and protests in 1969, through legislation 'guaranteeing the freedom of workers as citizens' and allowing workplace-based union structures (the *Statuto dei Diritti dei Lavoratori 1970* or Statute of Workers' Rights).[91] Collective bargaining in Italy, traditionally conducted through the negotiation of national-level agreements for each major industry, has become the subject of increasing levels of state facilitation. A significant point in this transition was the July 1993 government-initiated accord between the main employer and union confederations, which permitted a managed form of company-level bargaining within the framework of industry agreements.[92] Firm-level derogation from national collective labour agreements was more clearly encouraged through legislation passed in 2011, although with limited practical effect.[93]

The adoption of this measure reflected the external competitive pressures for some time facing the Italian industrial relations system.[94] These led inevitably to various forms of labour market deregulation under the centre-right Berlusconi governments from 2001 and again from 2008,[95] and through the Renzi

[87] M Regini and I Regalia, 'Employers, Unions and the State: The Resurgence of Concertation in Italy?' (2007) 20:1 *West European Politics* 210, 227.

[88] Regalia and Regini (n 73) 65. See also Chiarini (n 79) 586–91; D Comande and S Giubboni, 'The Social Partners in the Welfare System in Italy: From Coordination to Fragmentation' (2020) 26:3 *International Journal of Comparative Labour Law and Industrial Relations* 315, 318–21.

[89] S Agnoletto, 'Trade Unions and the Origins of the Union-Based Welfare State in Italy (1950s–1970s)' (2012) 3:2 *California Italian Studies* 1.

[90] See ch 3.

[91] R Locke, *Remaking the Italian Economy* (Ithaca, Cornell University Press, 1995) 71–72, 76–77. See also F Carinci, 'Fifty Years of the Workers' Statute (1970–2020)' (2020) 13:2 *Italian Labour Law E-Journal* 1.

[92] Locke and Baccaro (n 74) 246–48.

[93] See ch 3.

[94] M Pallini, 'Italian Industrial Relations: Toward a Strongly Decentralized Collective Bargaining?' (2016) 38:1 *Comparative Labor Law and Policy Journal* 1, 1–4. See also M Tiraboschi, *Labour Law and Industrial Relations in Recessionary Times* (Newcastle-upon-Tyne, Cambridge Scholars Publishing, 2014).

[95] L Baccaro and C Howell, *Trajectories of Neoliberal Transformation: European Industrial Relations Since the 1970s* (Cambridge, Cambridge University Press, 2017) 121, 128, 136–41; P Vesan, 'Labor Market Policy and Politics' in Jones and Pasquino (n 71) 491, 494–95.

government's 2015 Jobs Act.[96] A more general erosion of the traditional closeness of unions and the state was occurring – particularly under the strain of the 'acute economic and social crisis' triggered by the financial meltdown of 2008 and its austerity aftermath.[97] Prime Minister Monti's government (2011–2013) distanced itself from the national social partnership model, while that of Renzi (2014–2016) chose to 'pursue reforms without seeking union consent'.[98] The separation was hastened during the period of the *Lega/Movimento Cinque Stelle* government from 2018.[99] The main union confederations have resumed their conventional role as social partners in deliberations with Italian governments since the onset of the COVID-19 crisis.[100]

## C. Italian Union Structures and Workplace-Level Representation

While unions in the other three countries developed predominantly on craft, occupational and industry bases,[101] since 1948 Italian unionism has been mainly organised around three major (rival) union confederations: the communist/socialist-orientated *Confederazione Generale Italiana del Lavoro* (CGIL), the Christian Democrat-led *Confederazione Italiana Sindacati Lavoratori* (CISL), and the smaller *Unione Italiana del Lavoro* (UIL) made up of dissident socialists and republicans.[102] Various new union groups, independent of the main confederations, emerged from the 1980s (particularly in the public sector).[103] More recently, independent or 'base' unions have come to play a more prominent role.[104] National-level collective bargaining has remained predominantly the preserve of CGIL, CISL and UIL (on the unions' side) and employer associations

[96] See ch 3.

[97] Leonardi (n 78) 88.

[98] N Durazzi, T Fleckenstein and S Lee, 'Social Solidarity for All? Trade Union Strategies, Labour Market Dualization, and the Welfare State in Italy and South Korea' (2018) 46:2 *Politics and Society* 205, 216–17. See also S Negrelli and A Signoretti, 'Between Berlusconi and Monti: Trade Unions and Economic Crisis in Italy' (2014) 59:4 *The Singapore Economic Review* 1.

[99] See, eg, E Schumacher, 'Italy: Hundreds of thousands protest populist government', *DW.com* (9 February 2019). Available at: www.dw.com/en/italy-hundreds-of-thousands-protest-populist-government/a-47443707. However, note that this government legislated the 2018 Dignity Decree, restoring some worker protections which had been removed by the Jobs Act: S Merler, 'Italy's "Dignity Decree"', *Bruegel* (23 July 2018).

[100] See ch 12.

[101] See ch 1.

[102] Gumbrell-McCormick and Hyman (n 1) 23; see further R Locke, 'The Demise of the National Union in Italy: Lessons for Comparative Industrial Relations Theory' (1992) 45:2 *Industrial and Labour Relations Review* 229, 231–32. On the earlier emergence of national unions in Italy 'mainly on the basis of occupational identity', see B Ebbinghaus and J Visser, *Trade Unions in Western Europe since 1945* (Basingstoke, Palgrave Macmillan, 2000) 381–82.

[103] Treu (n 71) 153–54; Locke (n 91) 99–100.

[104] See ch 8.

(such as *Confindustria* in the manufacturing sector).[105] National unions covering specific industries generally affiliate to one of the three confederations, with each union also performing a representative role for members at regional and workplace levels.[106] The 1970 Workers' Statute provided strong institutional support for workers from 'the "most representative" unions' to form workplace or plant-based structures known as '*rappresentanze sindacali aziendale*' (RSAs) (company union representatives).[107] This basically gave CGIL, CISL and UIL 'a representational monopoly within most large and medium-sized Italian firms'.[108] This system was reformed through the tripartite agreement of July 1993, under which '*rappresentanze sindacali unitarie*' (RSUs) (unitary union representatives) can be elected on the initiative of any union able to obtain the support of at least 5 per cent of the workforce.[109] Through this second channel of worker representation, Italian unions maintain a more significant presence at the enterprise level than their counterparts in the US, the UK and Australia.

## D. Similarities in the Situation of Italian Unions

In addition to the differences identified above, some of the causes of union decline in the USA, the UK and Australia have also been evident in Italy. Commencing in the 1980s, the economy underwent significant transformation through technological innovation and restructuring in the composition of firms (including the growth of small-medium enterprises).[110] Italy also saw a major 'shift from industrial to post-industrial employment', weak unionisation in the expanding services sector (for example, among IT and knowledge workers), the growth of atypical jobs (especially self-employment) and 'subcontracting'.[111] This Italian variant of fissuring has taken the form, as well, of widespread temporary agency work and complex contracting chains through which lead companies have avoided minimum wage and workplace safety standards.[112] The 'flexibilisation' of employment relationships has created conditions 'that are totally unfavourable for the individual choice of [workers to become] union members'.[113] Misclassification of employees as independent contractors has become common in Italy,[114] as has (in recent years) the exclusion of gig economy workers from

[105] See ch 3.
[106] Treu (n 71) 156–57.
[107] Regini (n 71) 533.
[108] Locke (n 91) 77.
[109] Locke and Baccaro (n 74) 253. Both RSAs and RSUs may be formed in enterprises with more than 15 workers; see further ch 3.
[110] Ibid, 224–25.
[111] Leonardi (n 77) 206–7.
[112] E Menegatti, 'Mending the Fissured Workplace: The Solutions Provided by Italian Law' (2015) 37 *Comparative Labor Law and Policy Journal* 91, 96, 101–3, 105–10. See ch 8.
[113] Leonardi (n 77) 207.
[114] Menegatti (n 112) 112–13; Leonardi (n 78) 89.

employment protections including leave and pension entitlements, minimum pay rates and regulation of working time.[115] Italian unions have faced the challenges of organising groups with less inclination to join (including women, young, precarious and migrant workers).[116] Finally, while unions in Italy have not encountered the virulence of US-style union-busting, employers have been known to utilise 'divide-and-rule' tactics[117] and efforts to counter collective organisation have become more evident in the context of platform work.[118]

## IV. Conclusion

This chapter has identified the common features contributing to declining union membership levels in the USA, the UK and Australia: the rise of neoliberalism and state restrictions upon traditional union rights of organisation and representation; more aggressive employer anti-unionism; economic restructuring and changes in the make-up of the workforce; and the growth of new business models generating fissured forms of work. It was shown that while some of these factors have also been at play in the Italian context, unions there have not encountered the erosion of their power to the same extent as in the other three countries. This is partly attributable to the closer interaction between trade unions and the Italian state, compared with the more hostile institutional setting faced by unions in the US, the UK and Australia – a subject explored in closer detail in the next chapter, which examines the legal framework for unions and worker representation in each of the four nations.

[115] V De Stefano and A Aloisi, *Digital Age: Employment and Working Conditions of Selected Types of Platform Work – National Context Analysis, Italy* (European Foundation for the Improvement of Living and Working Conditions, 2018) 5. See chs 9–10.

[116] Leonardi (n 77) 207–8, 94–95.

[117] Gumbrell-McCormick and Hyman (n 1) 24.

[118] See A Tassinari and V Maccarrone, 'Riders on the Storm: Workplace Solidarity among Gig Economy Couriers in Italy and the UK (2020) 34:1 *Work, Employment and Society* 35, 48; and chs 9–10.

# 3

# The Legal Framework for Unions and Worker Representation in the Four Countries

## I. Introduction

It has already been observed in Chapters 1 and 2 that the neoliberal turn from the 1980s unleashed a harsher stance toward unions on the part of governments in the USA, the UK and (later) Australia. It was also seen that unions and the Italian state long had a more symbiotic relationship, which has largely been maintained although with some loosening in the period since the 2008 financial crisis. This chapter turns to consider in greater depth the legal and institutional framework for unions and worker representation in each of the four countries. It focuses on the arrangements for union recognition for collective bargaining in the US, the UK and the similar process in Australia, drawing out in each instance how the laws have not proven to be effective in extending the reach of collectively determined employment conditions. Constraints placed upon industrial action by the laws of these three countries are also briefly considered, along with the minimal role of alternative worker representative bodies. The contrasting legal position in Italy is then presented, highlighting the supportive framework for collective bargaining through framework agreements negotiated between the social partners; the relatively permissive approach to strikes; the system of firm-level worker representation; and strong statutory rights underpinning the various representative functions of unions.

## II. The USA

### A. Background

Of the four countries examined in this study, the legal framework for collective representation of workers in the USA is the most fraught. Strong support for collective bargaining was enacted through the National Labor Relations Act,

1935 (NLRA).[1] This legislation was very important both in legitimating unions[2] after many years of often brutal suppression of workers' attempts to collectivise[3] and extending democracy 'into the heart of market capitalism: the economy and the workplace'.[4] However, the NLRA was weakened through amendments passed by Congress in 1947. US unions do not face competition from alternative worker representative bodies like works councils.[5] As Lichtenstein explains: 'the framers of the [NLRA] were determined to stamp out "company unionism", that is, employee organisations that were set up or dominated by management'.[6] The internal affairs of unions are regulated by the Labor Management Reporting and Disclosure Act, 1959. This legislation includes 'crucial rights for union members and provisions for union democracy'[7] and imposes extensive financial reporting and accountability obligations upon labour organisations.[8]

## B. Legal Support for Collective Bargaining in the National Labor Relations Act, Reined in by the 1947 Amendments

The NLRA is the principal statute governing labour relations in the US private sector, covering around 43 per cent of the workforce.[9] It explicitly aims to encourage the practice of collective bargaining and to protect 'the exercise by workers of full freedom of association, self-organization, and designation of representatives of their own choosing'.[10] These rights are given effect by section 7: employees 'shall have the right to self-organization, to form, join, or assist labor organizations, to bargain collectively through representatives of their own choosing, and to engage in other concerted activities for the purposes of collective

[1] The NLRA and the National Industrial Recovery Act, 1933 which preceded it were central to President Roosevelt's 'New Deal' program of economic recovery after the Great Depression. See N Lichtenstein, *State of the Union: A Century of American Labor* (Princeton, Princeton University Press, revised and expanded edition, 2013) ch 1.

[2] J McAlevey, *A Collective Bargain: Unions, Organizing, and the Fight for Democracy* (New York, Harper Collins, 2020) 49–50.

[3] E Loomis, *A History of America in Ten Strikes* (New York, The New Press, 2018) 27, 53, 60–61, 64–66, 82.

[4] McAlevey (n 2) 48.

[5] Section 8(a)(2) of the NLRA prohibits employers from engaging in any domination or interference with the formation or administration of a labour organisation or contributing financial or other support to it.

[6] Lichtenstein (n 1) 37.

[7] C Estlund, *Regoverning the Workplace: From Self-Regulation to Co-Regulation* (New Haven, Yale University Press, 2010) 29.

[8] K Griffith and L Gates, 'Worker Centers: Labor Policy as a Carrot, not a Stick' (2019) 14 *Harvard Law and Policy Review* 601, 603.

[9] R Gorman, M Finkin and T Glynn, *Cox and Bok's Labor Law: Cases and Materials* 16th edn (St Paul, Foundation Press, 2016) 56–57; see also 58–59, noting the exclusion from the NLRA of federal, state and local government employment (just over 15% of the workforce).

[10] NLRA, s 1. Although the legislation excluded agricultural and domestic workers, a 'damning compromise … codifying the racial and sexual stratification of the working class': McAlevey (n 2) 49.

bargaining or other mutual aid or protection'. The NLRA establishes a process through which representatives 'designated or selected for the purposes of collective bargaining by the majority of employees in a [bargaining] unit appropriate for such purposes' become the exclusive representatives of those employees in negotiating 'rates of pay, wages, hours …, or other conditions of employment'.[11] A union seeking to instigate this process must be a 'labor organization' as defined in section 2(5): an 'organization of any kind … in which employees participate and which exists for the purpose, in whole or part, of dealing with employers concerning grievances, labor disputes, wages, rates of pay, hours of employment, or conditions of work'. The National Labor Relations Board (NLRB) oversees representational elections held under the NLRA and deals with complaints of unfair labour practices.[12] In respect of *employers*, the proscribed practices include interfering with, restraining or coercing employees in the exercise of their rights under section 7, discriminating against employees to encourage or discourage union membership, or refusing to engage in collective bargaining with employees' chosen representatives.[13]

The Labor Management Relations Act, 1947[14] cut across the framework of rights supporting union representation enacted in 1935.[15] As a result, section 7 of the NLRA also provides for the right of employees to refrain from being involved in unions or collective bargaining; section 8(b) proscribes certain *union* unfair labour practices (for example, coercing employees in the exercise of their section 7 rights); and section 9(c) requires that certification of a union as the exclusive representative of employees be determined through a secret ballot election. Under section 8(c), the free expression of views does not constitute an unfair labour practice provided that 'such expression contains no threat of reprisal or force or promise of benefit'. Section 8(d) provides that collective bargaining is the mutual obligation of the employer and employees' representative to meet at reasonable times and confer in good faith, but this does not compel either party to agree to a proposal or make concessions.

## C. The NLRA's Ballot-based System for Union Recognition: A Recipe for Union-Busting

The NLRA therefore establishes a system whereby, unless an employer voluntarily recognises a union,[16] representation of employees for collective bargaining

[11] NLRA, s 9(a).

[12] Gorman, Finkin and Glynn (n 9) 73–87.

[13] NLRA, s 8(a).

[14] Enacted 'at the behest of business' after the rise in union growth and economic power in the NLRA's early years of operation: K Andrias, 'The New Labor Law' (2016) 126 *Yale Law Journal* 2, 17–18.

[15] W Liebman, 'Labor Law Inside Out' (2008) 11 *Working USA: The Journal of Labor and Society* 9, 9–10.

[16] See ch 4.

is contingent on a union establishing majority support through a secret ballot election. Unions must engage in these elections at each enterprise (precluding multi-employer bargaining).[17] The process is initiated through a 'showing of interest' by at least 30 per cent of the employees in the bargaining unit, evidenced by their signing a petition or union authorisation cards.[18] However these methods are not available for the ultimate determination of employee preferences. The US system's reliance on workplace-based elections as the route to certification of a recognised union could be viewed as enshrining employees' freedom of choice if they were able to express a *genuine* choice. Putting this another way, Bodie pointed to NLRB jurisprudence establishing that employees should exercise their rights through an election conducted under 'laboratory conditions'.[19] This is far from the reality, though, as union recognition ballots in US workplaces have become fiercely fought contests.[20]

In the late 2000s, Logan highlighted the tactics businesses engage in to counter organising campaigns including anti-union videos, dismissal of union supporters and threats of business closures.[21] These and other strategies are used to intimidate employees 'against exercising their right to organize', by convincing them that unionisation would be futile (as the employer would never enter into a collective agreement).[22] Logan also traced the evolution of the industry of anti-union consultants and lawyers, developing by the 1970s into aggressive advocacy of employers' '"right" to operate union free'.[23] This approach has continued unabated in the last few decades.[24] Greenhouse, referring to campaigns against union recognition by companies like FedEx, Coca-Cola and Staples, summed up the US position thus: 'In no other industrial nation do employers fight so hard to defeat, indeed quash, labor unions.'[25]

Anti-union practices are so widespread and effective because the NLRA, as interpreted by the NLRB and the courts over more than 85 years, does not present a sufficient bulwark against employer anti-unionism. Instead, the rights of individuals to be free from union involvement have been prioritised over

[17] Andrias (n 14) 30–32.

[18] Gorman, Finkin and Glynn (n 9) 81.

[19] Emanating from *General Shoe Corp.* 77 NLRB 124 (1948): see M Bodie, *Mandatory Disclosure in the Market for Union Representation* (Saint Louis University Legal Studies Research Paper Series, No 2011-02, 2011), 1–2.

[20] C Garden, 'Tactical Mismatch in Union Organizing Drives' in R Bales and C Garden (eds), *The Cambridge Handbook of U.S. Labor Law for the Twenty-First Century* (Cambridge, Cambridge University Press, 2020) 199, 200.

[21] J Logan, *U.S. Anti-Union Consultants: A Threat to the Rights of British Workers* (London, Trades Union Congress, 2008) 5.

[22] Ibid, 6–8.

[23] Ibid, 13–15. See also McAlevey (n 1) 64–65.

[24] C McNicholas, M Podock, J Wolfe, B Zipperer, G Lafer and L Loustaunau, *Unlawful: U.S. Employers are Charged with Violating Federal Law in 41.5% of All Union Election Campaigns* (Economic Policy Institute, Report, 11 December 2019).

[25] S Greenhouse, *Beaten Down, Worked Up: The Past, Present, and Future of American Labour* (Alfred A Knopf, New York, 2019) 154–56.

the legislation's original goal of promoting collective bargaining.[26] Employers can conduct captive audience meetings in which they communicate anti-union messages to employees at the workplace, unchallenged by employees or their union representatives.[27] One NLRB ruling described this as allowing a 'free exchange of views in a "market place of ideas"'.[28] However, in the assessment of Wilma Liebman (who served as Chair of the Board under President Obama) the latitude given to employers to engage in anti-union speech suggests that 'employee free choice may not be that free'.[29] Further, campaigning in support of a union cannot take place during working time and union officials 'may almost never gain access to target employees on company premises'.[30] Bogg explained this in terms of 'the sanctity of private property', which the US Supreme Court determined in *Lechmere v NLRB* prevailed over a union's organisational rights.[31]

## D. Limits on Industrial Action

Compounding the absence of a level playing field in union recognition contests, US strike law has become increasingly restrictive. Again, the NLRA was initially fairly permissive of industrial action,[32] but limits were imposed by the 1947 amendments to curb 'perceived … excesses of industrial conflict and union power'.[33] Workers are prohibited from engaging in secondary boycotts (industrial action in support of workers engaged in a dispute with another firm) and employers may permanently replace striking workers.[34] Over time, the NLRB and the courts have added new constraints on intermittent strikes, partial strikes and slowdowns, leaving extended strikes as the main protected form of industrial action – although faced with the employer bringing in a replacement workforce, 'workers are usually the first to call it quits'.[35] Unsurprisingly, the reported incidence of strikes in the

[26] J Gross, 'Conflicting Statutory Purposes: Another Look at Fifty Years of NLRB Law Making' (1985) 39:1 *Industrial and Labor Relations Review* 7, 13–14.

[27] P Secunda, 'Toward the Viability of State-Based Legislation to Address Workplace Captive Audience Meetings in the United States' (2008) 29 *Comparative Labor Law and Policy Journal* 209, 214–15; see also Andrias (n 14) 25.

[28] *Aladdin Gaming, LLC*, 345 NLRB 585 (2005), 586: see Liebman (n 15) 18.

[29] Liebman (n 15) 18 (footnote omitted).

[30] C Craver, 'The National Labor Relations Act at 75: In Need of a Heart Transplant' (2010) 27:2 *Hofstra Labor and Employment Law Journal* 311, 326 (footnote omitted).

[31] (1992) 502 US 527: see A Bogg, *The Democratic Aspects of Trade Union Recognition* (Oxford, Hart Publishing, 2009) 186–88.

[32] Treating it as protected concerted activity of workers within s 7, along with an express provision supporting the right to strike in s 13: see A Colvin, 'Strike Ballot Law and Practice in the United States: Order without Law in Labour Relations?' (2016) 29:2 *Australian Journal of Labour Law* 243, 245.

[33] Ibid, 246 (footnote omitted). On the legality of industrial action (and its limits) in the context of collective bargaining under the NLRA, see Gorman, Finkin and Glynn (n 9) 487–96 and Part IV.

[34] Andrias (n 14) 18, 23, 26.

[35] S Block and B Sachs, *Clean Slate for Worker Power: Building a Just Economy and Democracy* (Harvard Law School, 2020) 60–61. See also D Reddy, '"There is No Such Thing as an Illegal

US has fallen dramatically since the 1980s,[36] although something of a resurgence in strike activity occurred in 2018–2019.[37]

## E. As the NLRA Withers, Collective Bargaining Coverage Falls

Even where a union finally succeeds in securing a majority vote in favour of recognition, employers engage in further efforts to thwart collective bargaining. Litigation is often pursued, challenging the validity of the ballot outcome and delaying a union's ability to commence bargaining.[38] Or an employer may sit down to engage in agreement negotiations, but drag the process out by 'talking the union to death'[39] or contracting out the work performed by employees in the bargaining unit.[40] The effect of the range of aggressive employer anti-union tactics has been to substantially reduce (over more than four decades) the proportion of US workers participating in union recognition elections, the union success rate in those elections and the total number of workers ultimately able to obtain a first collective agreement.[41] In turn, collective bargaining coverage declined from 25 per cent of the workforce in 1980 to 11.2 per cent in 2018.[42] Writing in 2007, Liebman declared that the NLRA 'by virtually all measures, is in decline if not dead': unions and workers had increasingly given up on utilising the legislation.[43] Almost a decade later, Andrias noted the continuation of this trend as the 'legal roadblocks' had 'rendered the traditional NLRA electoral mechanisms inadequate'[44] (amplified by employer fissuring strategies to take even more workers out of the statute's reach).[45] As Chapter 4 will make clear, efforts by US unions to obtain labour law reform have generally proved futile in

Strike": Reconceptualizing the Strike in Law and Political Economy' (2021) 130 *Yale Law Journal Forum* 421, 436–38.

[36] Colvin (n 32) 252; see further J Rosenfeld, *What Unions No Longer Do* (Cambridge MA, Harvard University Press, 2014) ch 4.

[37] See ch 4.

[38] Craver (n 30) 335. See also Andrias (n 14) 26, on lengthy delays in the pursuit by unions of unfair labour practice remedies against employers.

[39] A Cox, 'The Duty to Bargain in Good Faith' (1958) 71 *Harvard Law Review* 1401, 1413, 1417; see also M Mandelman and K Manara, 'Staying Above the Surface: Surface Bargaining Claims under the National Labor Relations Act' (2007) 24 *Hofstra Labor and Employment Law Journal* 261 (surface bargaining is technical compliance with good faith bargaining requirements without intending to conclude an agreement).

[40] Block and Sachs (n 35) 67.

[41] L Mishel, L Rhinehart and L Windham, *Explaining the Erosion of Private-Sector Unions* (Economic Policy Institute, Report, 18 November 2020) 8–15.

[42] C Schnabel, *Union Membership and Collective Bargaining: Trends and Determinants* (University of Erlangen-Nuremberg, Labor and Socio-Economic Research Center, LASER Discussion Papers No 121, 2020) 39.

[43] W Liebman, 'Decline and Disenchantment: Reflections on the Aging of the National Labor Relations Board' (2007) 28 *Berkeley Journal of Labor and Employment Law* 569, 571–72.

[44] Andrias (n 14) 41.

[45] Ibid, 28–32, including consideration of the NLRA's exemption of independent contractors; see also ch 10.

the face of strident business and Republican Party opposition (a dynamic which seems set to play out again under President Biden).

# III. The UK

## A. Background

Trade unions in the UK face an unwelcoming legal setting. Historically, the state played a minimal role in regulating collective labour relations.[46] It largely left the development of collective bargaining rules to employers, employees and unions, with no legal provisions for union recognition, freedom of association or the enforcement of collective agreements.[47] However, this abstentionist position began to change by the mid-1960s, as union militancy and widespread strikes came to be seen as problems that needed to be addressed through the law.[48] The Conservative government introduced a union recognition procedure in the Industrial Relations Act 1971, adopting the NLRA's ballot-based approach to establishing majority employee support for collective bargaining.[49] Because unions had to register to access this framework, it was not widely taken up.[50] Another recognition process was introduced by the Labour government's Employment Protection Act 1975,[51] enabling the use of methods such as questionnaires and surveys to assess the level of employee support for recognition.[52] Although the 1975 procedure was better utilised than its predecessor,[53] the election of Margaret Thatcher's Conservative government brought an end to state support for all forms of collectivism – beginning with the repeal in 1980 of statutory recognition.[54] This was the first in a series of enactments through which the

[46] See O Kahn-Freund, 'Legal Framework', in A Flanders and H Clegg (eds), *The System of Industrial Relations in Great Britain: Its History, Law and Institutions* (Oxford, Blackwell, 1954), discussed in P Davies and M Freedland, *Labour Legislation and Public Policy* (Oxford, Clarendon Press, 1993) ch 1. For contrasting accounts, see K Ewing, 'The State and Industrial Relations: "Collective Laissez Faire" Revisited' (1998) 5 *Historical Studies in Industrial Relations* 1; C Howell, *Trade Unions and the State: The Construction of Industrial Relations Institutions in Britain, 1890–2000* (Princeton, Princeton University Press, 2000).

[47] Davies and Freedland (n 46) 9, 16–20; see also 20–22, noting that '"negative" law' in the form of the Trade Disputes Act 1906 was put in place to remove common liability for '[p]eaceful industrial action'.

[48] Ibid, ch 6; Howell (n 46) ch 4. See also Lord Donovan (Chair), *Royal Commission on Trade Unions and Employers' Associations* (Report, Cmnd 3623, 1968).

[49] Bogg (n 31) 55–60; R Dukes, 'The Statutory Recognition Procedure 1999: No Bias in Favour of Recognition?' (2008) 37 *Industrial Law Journal* 236, 242.

[50] A Bogg and T Novitz, 'Recognition in Respect of Bargaining in the United Kingdom: Collective Autonomy and Political Neutrality in Context' in B Creighton and A Forsyth (eds), *Rediscovering Collective Bargaining: Australia's Fair Work Act in International Perspective* (New York, Routledge, 2012) 225, 227.

[51] Bogg (n 31) 65–66.

[52] Ibid, 66–67; see also Dukes (n 49) 243–44.

[53] Dukes (n 49) 244.

[54] Employment Act 1980: see Bogg and Novitz (n 50) 230.

Conservatives constrained union activity and stripped away collective regulation of employment conditions.[55]

Prime Minister Tony Blair's New Labour government, elected to office in 1997, was committed to restoring some union rights which had been dismantled in the Thatcher/Major years – but with significant limitations.[56] Blair notoriously said there would be 'no going back' to the pre-1979 order on industrial action and that even after his government's reforms the UK would retain 'the most lightly regulated labour market of any leading economy in the world'.[57] The 'limited re-regulation' he foreshadowed saw the introduction of a statutory union recognition procedure, framed to intrude as little as possible on business interests.[58] Other reforms included establishing a Low Pay Commission to set the National Minimum Wage;[59] legislative enshrinement of the freedom of association rights of individual union members;[60] support for union organisation at the workplace through provision for 'union learning representatives' to have paid time off for organising union education and training;[61] and legislation implementing the European Commission's 1994 European Works Councils Directive[62] and 2002 Information and Consultation Directive,[63] requiring experimentation with continental-style worker participation within Britain's traditional single channel of union representation.[64]

## B. The Statutory Union Recognition Procedure

Under the Trade Union and Labour Relations (Consolidation) Act 1992 (TULRCA), trade unions can become listed by a government agency (the Certification Officer).[65] Only a listed union can obtain a certificate of independence,[66]

[55] See ch 2.

[56] J McIlroy, 'A Brief History of British Trade Unions and Neoliberalism in the Age of New Labour' in G Daniels and J McIlroy (eds), *Trade Unions in a Neoliberal World: British Trade Unions under New Labour* (London, Routledge, 2009) 63, 79–80.

[57] Foreword of *Fairness at Work* (London, Department of Trade and Industry, 1998) 2. See also ch 7.

[58] McIlroy (n 56) 83.

[59] National Minimum Wage Act 1998; see P Davies and M Freedland, *Towards a Flexible Labour Market: Labour Legislation and Regulation Since the 1990s* (Oxford, Oxford University Press, 2007) 46–48.

[60] Employment Relations Act 1999 and Employment Relations Act 2004, both seeking to counter the effects of the House of Lords' decision in *Wilson and Palmer v United Kingdom* [1995] 2 AC 454; see H Collins, KD Ewing and A McColgan, *Labour Law* 2nd edn (Cambridge, Cambridge University Press, 2019) 490–98.

[61] Employment Act 2002, inserting s 168A in Trade Union and Labour Relations (Consolidation) Act 1992; see Davies and Freedland (n 59) 215.

[62] Transnational Information and Consultation of Employees Regulations 1999 (SI 1999/3323).

[63] Information and Consultation of Employees Regulations 2004 (SI 2004/3426).

[64] On the uneasy fit between these two approaches, see P Lorber, 'National Works Councils: Opening the Door on a Whole New Era in United Kingdom Employment Relations?' (2003) 19:3 *International Journal of Comparative Labour Law and Industrial Relations* 297.

[65] TULRCA, ss 2–4.

[66] TULRCA, s 5, defining an 'independent trade union' as one that is not under employer domination or control and is not liable to employer interference through financial or other means.

the gateway to accessing statutory rights including recognition for collective bargaining.[67] Unions are subject to extensive regulation of their internal affairs, including provisions governing administration and financial management, elections for office-holders and the rights of members.[68] The Schedule A1 recognition procedure was introduced by the Employment Relations Act 1999, taking effect on 6 June 2000. The UK adopts an enterprise-based focus for collective bargaining, rather than industry or sectoral bargaining. An application for recognition under Schedule A1 is limited to the employer of the workers in the relevant bargaining unit[69] and cannot be made in enterprises with 20 workers or less.[70] While opening access to union recognition for collective bargaining beyond employees to 'workers',[71] judicial interpretation has excluded certain gig economy workers from the application of Schedule A1.[72] The emphasis is on parties entering into voluntary recognition agreements, with Schedule A1 as a fall-back.[73] In the absence of such agreement, a union may apply to the Central Arbitration Committee (CAC),[74] by showing it has at least 10 per cent membership in the bargaining unit; and that a majority of workers in that unit would be likely to favour recognition.[75] The latter requirement can be met by a petition, signed employee statements or evidence of majority union membership.[76]

## C. The UK Variant of the Ballot-based Approach

In determining whether to grant recognition based on majority worker support, the CAC has two main options open to it. Recognition could be granted automatically, if the union can provide evidence that the majority of the bargaining unit are its members.[77] Alternatively, majority support might be established through a secret ballot. The CAC has the discretion to order a ballot (even where a union has provided evidence of majority membership), if any one of three conditions is met: holding a ballot is 'in the interests of good industrial relations'; there is credible evidence 'from a significant number of union members' that they do not want the union to bargain for them; or the circumstances in which relevant workers became union members leads the CAC to doubt whether a significant number of

[67] Collins, Ewing and McColgan (n 60) 525, 588.
[68] TULRCA, Pt I, Chapters III–V.
[69] See, eg, TULRCA, Sch A1, paras 2(4), 19B.
[70] Ibid, para 7, therefore excluding around 31% of the UK workforce: G Gall, 'Union Recognition in Britain: The End of Legally Induced Voluntarism?' (2012) 41:4 *Industrial Law Journal* 407, 408.
[71] TULRCA, Sch A1, para 7.
[72] See ch 10.
[73] Dukes (n 49) 251–52. On the negotiation of voluntary recognition agreements between employers and unions, see TULRCA, Sch A1, para 10 and Part II; Collins, Ewing and McColgan (n 60) 582–86.
[74] TULRCA, Sch A1, paras 11–12.
[75] Ibid, paras 14(5) and 36(1).
[76] Collins, Ewing and McColgan (n 60) 591.
[77] TULRCA, Sch A1, paras 22(1)–(2).

them want the union to bargain.[78] Collins, Ewing and McColgan explain that the ability of unions to obtain recognition without a ballot was intended to '[reward] their recruitment efforts' and bypass the problem of anti-union campaigns of the kind found in the US.[79] However, the addition of provisions for the 'forcing' of a secret ballot reflects the fact that 'employers do not like recognition without a ballot', giving them 'an important opportunity to derail a union campaign'.[80] Where a ballot is held, it must be 'conducted by a qualified independent person appointed by the CAC'.[81] To succeed, a union must meet the dual threshold of securing support from a majority of the workers who vote and 'at least 40 per cent of the workers constituting the bargaining unit'.[82] The UK procedure therefore sets up the same kind of workplace-based contest for testing worker support for union representation as the NLRA, although with important differences. In Bogg's view, Schedule A1 'avoids many of the design flaws identified in the US system' – but 'still falls short of ensuring genuine parity' in the competition over workers' preferences.[83]

## D. The 2004 Amendments: Attempting to Counter Employer Avoidance Tactics

The UK procedure was intended to allow unions to communicate freely with workers, without employer pressure, but the original provisions needed to be fortified in 2004 to address this.[84] Evidence had emerged that employers were 'using a range of techniques to undermine recognition claims through the subversion of worker free choice'.[85] These US-style tactics included surveillance of workers' interactions with union organisers, threatening closure or relocation of the business, dismissal and intimidation of union activists, and undermining attempts to collectivise through offers of improved pay and benefits during a recognition ballot.[86] Originally, Schedule A1 imposed duties on the employer to cooperate with the union seeking recognition and the person conducting the ballot;[87] give

[78] Ibid, para 22(3)–(5). See, eg, *Unite the Union v Rhys Davies Logistics* (TUR1/864/2014); *Unite the Union v Primopost* (TUR1/869/2014); *Unite the Union v Citizen Advice Merton & Lambeth* (TUR1/954/2016); see also *Independent Workers Union of Great Britain v The Doctors Laboratory Limited* (TUR1/1016/2017), discussed in ch 10.

[79] Collins, Ewing and McColgan (n 60) 595.

[80] Ibid, 595–96.

[81] TULRCA, Sch A1, para 25(2), (7).

[82] Ibid, para 29(3); for critiques, see Bogg and Novitz (n 50) 225, 230; Dukes (n 49) 250.

[83] Bogg (n 31) 160.

[84] Employment Relations Act 2004.

[85] A Bogg, 'Employment Relations Act 2004: Another False Dawn for Collectivism' (2005) 34:1 *Industrial Law Journal* 72, 75–76.

[86] Ibid, 76; see further KD Ewing, S Moore and S Wood, *Unfair Labour Practices: Trade Union Recognition and Employer Resistance* (London, Institute of Employment Rights, 2003).

[87] TULRCA, Sch A1, para 26(2).

the CAC specified information about the workers in the bargaining unit;[88] and allow the union reasonable access to those workers 'to seek their support'.[89] The 2004 amendments added further forms of employer conduct constituting breach of the duty to provide access – for example, unreasonably refusing to allow the union to meet with workers in the absence of the employer, attending such a meeting without invitation, or seeking to record or be informed of what occurs at the meeting.[90] Employers are encouraged to reach agreement with unions on access arrangements, including the posting of union communications at the workplace and making equivalent arrangements for union meetings to those which an employer itself has with the workers.[91] The CAC's interpretation of the employer's access duty, 'routinely' allowing full-time union officers onto employer premises during working time, contrasted with the US Supreme Court's defence of 'property and managerial rights'.[92]

The 2004 changes proscribed several other employer practices: making unreasonable offers to workers in the bargaining unit to induce them not to attend meetings with the union seeking recognition;[93] and taking action against a worker because they took part in a union meeting.[94] In addition, a number of 'unfair practices' aimed at influencing the result of a recognition ballot – whether engaged in by an employer or a union – were prohibited by the 2004 amendments. These include: offering to pay a worker entitled to vote in the ballot, to sway the worker's vote or have them abstain; coercing a worker into disclosing how they voted or will vote; dismissing, taking disciplinary action or subjecting a worker to other detriment; or using undue influence on a worker entitled to vote.[95] Bogg initially predicted that these provisions retained 'scope for employers to pursue the objective of subverting the union's recognition claim through ingenious means'.[96] After several years, in which very few unfair practice complaints were initiated by unions and none were upheld, he lamented that:

> … the Government [had] enacted a mouse of a statutory provision to safeguard workers' collective freedom of choice.
>
> …

[88] Ibid, para 26(4).
[89] Ibid, para 26(3).
[90] Ibid, para 26(4D).
[91] Bogg (n 31) 193–94; Collins, Ewing and McColgan (n 60) 598, discussing Department of Trade and Industry, *Code of Practice: Access and Unfair Practices during Recognition and Derecognition Ballots* (2005).
[92] Bogg (n 31) 195–96, referring to decisions under Sch A1 including *Amicus and South Marston Distribution Centre Ltd* (TUR1/361/2004) and *Transport and General Workers Union and King Asia Foods Ltd* (TUR1/111/2004).
[93] TULRCA, Sch A1, para 26(4A).
[94] Ibid, para 26(4C); Bogg (n 84) 78.
[95] Ibid, para 27A.
[96] Bogg (n 85) 79. Other concerns included that the provisions did not address 'concerted employer opposition' *prior to* a ballot (Bogg and Novitz (n 50) 232–33) and did not preclude 'passive' employer aggression such as establishing non-union staff associations (Collins, Ewing and McColgan (n 60) 599).

> … In the exceptional case where the union makes it as far as the statutory ballot procedure, the employer can expect wide latitude for its [anti-union] campaign activities given the CAC's [cautious] interpretive approach ….[97]

## E. Regulation of the Bargaining Process

Once the CAC declares that a union is recognised under Schedule A1 to collectively bargain on behalf of the workers in a bargaining unit, the employer and union try to agree on how they will negotiate. They can ask the CAC to assist if no agreement is reached within 30 days.[98] If the CAC is unable to resolve the parties' differences, it must determine a bargaining method for them.[99] The Trade Union Recognition (Method of Collective Bargaining) Order 2000 acts as a guide, limiting negotiations to the subjects of pay, hours and holidays.[100] The model bargaining process falls short of imposing good faith bargaining obligations[101] or otherwise addressing whether a party's bargaining conduct or substantive proposals are reasonable.[102] It simply establishes time-frames for meetings through a Joint Negotiating Body made up of union and employer representatives.[103] In practice, Gall's 2012 study indicated that Schedule A1 had limited 'the scope and depth of both voluntary and statutory union recognition agreements', creating 'a ceiling rather than a floor' for negotiation only over wages, working time and holidays.[104]

## F. Old and New Restrictions on Strikes

UK law takes a highly restrictive approach to industrial action.[105] The Thatcher laws of the 1980s removed legal immunities for: industrial action taken without the support of a ballot of employees; secondary action directed at a business not involved in a dispute; and certain forms of picketing.[106] New Labour retained these

[97] A Bogg, 'The Mouse That Never Roared: Unfair Practices and Union Recognition' (2009) 38:4 *Industrial Law Journal* 390, 393, 399, 402; at 394–98, see the discussion of CAC decisions including *Transport and General Workers Union and Comet Group Plc* (TUR1/501/2006), *Unite-the Union and Kettle Foods Limited* (TUR1/557/2007), *Communication Workers Union and Cable and Wireless Services UK Limited* (TUR1/570/2007).

[98] TULRCA, Sch A1, para 30.

[99] Ibid, para 31; see, eg, *Public and Commercial Services Union and Axis Security Services Limited* (TUR1/1159/2020).

[100] Trade Union Recognition (Method of Collective Bargaining) Order 2000 (SI 2000/1300), para 2.

[101] Collins, Ewing and McColgan (n 60) 608.

[102] Bogg (n 31) 281.

[103] Trade Union Recognition (Method of Collective Bargaining) Order 2000, paras 4–5, 14–15.

[104] Gall (n 70) 419.

[105] TULRCA, Pt V. See Collins, Ewing and McColgan (n 60) chs 16 and 17; note also (at 785) that employers may bring in temporary replacements for striking workers (although not through a third-party employment agency).

[106] B Simpson, 'Trade Union Immunities', in R Lewis (ed), *Labour Law in Britain* (Oxford, Basil Blackwell, 1986) 162; R Lewis, 'Picketing', in Lewis 195.

restrictions, although made the ballot requirements less complex.[107] However, the Conservative government's Trade Union Act 2016 again sharpened the ballot rules for lawful industrial action, requiring a turnout of 50 per cent or more of the eligible union members.[108] This was added to the pre-existing requirement of a majority vote in support of the action.[109] Further, where the proposed action involves workers providing 'important public services' (eg, health, fire or transport services), at least 40 per cent of the eligible membership must vote in favour it.[110] Ford and Novitz warned that these 'revised balloting thresholds … are likely to place insurmountable blocks in the way of much industrial action and … reduce the negotiating power of the threat of a strike'.[111] The 2016 legislation also imposed further restrictions on lawful picketing, requiring unions to appoint a picket supervisor who must comply with detailed rules relating to oversight of the picket.[112] The 2016 provisions, according to Bogg, formed part of a creeping authoritarianism and 'a wider political strategy [of the Conservatives] to suppress political opposition and dissent'.[113] Certainly, the measures seemed designed to weaken the overall resistance of civil society groups to austerity,[114] as well as the collective bargaining capacity of unions.

## G. Limited Effectiveness of Statutory Recognition and the Decline of Collective Bargaining

The Schedule A1 procedure has not acted as an effective stimulant to the extension of collective bargaining in the UK over its 20 years of operation. It initially produced an increase in recognition agreements, Marginson describing this early effect as: 'a once-off shock amongst a minority of non-union employers who were relatively agnostic towards unions'.[115] However, as Gall explains, within a few years the uptick in voluntary recognition was:

> … thrown into reverse, amounting to … the stark unmasking of the weakness of the statutory procedure as applications fell to a historical low. By 2010, the early promise and portent had clearly evaporated.[116]

[107] Davies and Freedland (n 59) 114.

[108] R Dukes and N Kountouris, 'Pre-strike Ballots, Picketing and Protest: Banning Industrial Action by the Back Door?' (2016) 45:3 *Industrial Law Journal* 337, 345.

[109] M Ford and T Novitz, 'Legislating for Control: The Trade Union Act 2016' (2016) 45:3 *Industrial Law Journal* 277, 284.

[110] Dukes and Kountouris (n 108) 346.

[111] M Ford and T Novitz, 'There is Power in a Union? Revisiting Trade Union Functions in 2019', in A Bogg, J Rowbottom and A Young (eds), *The Constitution of Social Democracy: Essays in Honour of Keith Ewing* (Oxford, Hart Publishing, 2020) 261, 278.

[112] Dukes and Kountouris (n 108) 355.

[113] A Bogg, 'Beyond Neo-Liberalism: The Trade Union Act 2016 and the Authoritarian State' (2016) 45:3 *Industrial Law Journal* 299, 308.

[114] R Darlington and J Dobson, *The Conservative Government's Proposed Strike Ballot Thresholds: The Challenge to Trade Unions* (London, Institute of Employment Rights, 2015) 6–7. See also ch 7.

[115] P Marginson, 'The Changing Nature of Collective Employment Relations' (2015) 37:6 *Employee Relations* 645, 647.

[116] Gall (n 70) 409.

Ten years later, he noted that out of 1,166 recognition applications to the CAC from June 2000 to March 2020, unions enjoyed 'a 50% success rate overall' (combining the numbers of cases in which automatic recognition was granted, recognition was obtained via ballots and employers granted recognition voluntarily).[117] Gall estimated that, taking into account the shadow effect of Schedule A1 (ie, the 3,765 voluntary recognition agreements obtained without using the legislation), almost 2.7 million UK workers were brought under union recognition over the 20-year period.[118] Yet he concluded that its overall influence 'has been limited, if not marginal', as reflected in the contraction of collective bargaining coverage 'from 37.0% in 1997 to 26.9% in 2019'.[119] Collective agreement coverage in private sector workplaces with 25 or more employees fell from 32 per cent in 1998 to 25 per cent in 2011.[120] The UK Institute of Employment Rights observes that the longer-term decline of collective bargaining's reach from the peak of 86 per cent in 1976 'has not reversed, halted or even slowed' after introduction of the Schedule A1 procedure.[121]

# IV. Australia

## A. Background

The Australian legal framework for unions and worker representation is moderately supportive, with qualified encouragement of collective bargaining but many restrictions on the statutory rights accorded to unions. Trade unions occupied a central place in the conciliation and arbitration system which evolved during the twentieth century.[122] They had an integral role in the making of awards establishing minimum wage levels and employment standards for employees covering entire industries.[123] This system delivered both compulsory unionism and de facto recognition, through the ability of unions to compel employers to participate in it.[124] All of this changed, however, through deregulatory reforms implemented in response to neoliberal pressures: beginning with the shift to enterprise bargaining

[117] G Gall, 'Twenty Years of the Third Statutory Union Recognition Procedure in Britain: Outcomes and Impact' (2020) 49:4 *Industrial Law Journal* 657, 659.

[118] Ibid, 660.

[119] Ibid, 660, 662.

[120] Marginson (n 115) 648.

[121] KD Ewing, J Hendy and C Jones (eds), *Rolling out the Manifesto for Labour Law* (Liverpool, Institute of Employment Rights, 2018) 16.

[122] M Rimmer, 'Unions and Arbitration', in J Isaac and S Macintyre (eds), *The New Province for Law and Order: 100 Years of Australian Industrial Conciliation and Arbitration* (Cambridge, Cambridge University Press, 2004) 275.

[123] R Naughton, *The Shaping of Labour Law Legislation: Underlying Elements of Australia's Workplace Relations System* (Chatswood, LexisNexis Butterworths, 2017) 30–31, 48–53.

[124] Rimmer (n 122) 276; P Weeks, *Trade Union Security Law: A Study of Preference and Compulsory Unionism* (Sydney, Federation Press, 1995) ch 3.

from the early 1990s, followed by the overt de-unionisation policies of the Howard Coalition government from 1996 to 2007.

Despite this retreat from state support, only partially reversed by the subsequent Labor government, Australian law still recognises the legitimate role of trade unions. The Fair Work (Registered Organisations) Act 2009 (Cth) (FWRO Act) encourages the formation of organisations through which employees may advance their economic and social interests under a registration system.[125] To obtain registration, a union must be 'free from control by, or improper influence from employers'.[126] Registered unions must meet standards relating to accountability to their members, efficient operation and democratic control,[127] 'in order to gain the rights and privileges' attached to registration.[128] These include rights (such as those of union officials to access employers' business premises) provided under the Fair Work Act 2009 (Cth) (FW Act). This legislation was enacted by the Rudd Labor government, with minimal amendments by the Coalition since its return to office in 2013. Alternative worker representation bodies such as works councils have not emerged in Australia.[129] Provisions introduced by the Howard government encouraging the formation of enterprise associations to compete with registered unions remain available but have rarely been utilised.[130]

## B. Enterprise Bargaining under the Fair Work Act

Changes to the system of formalised collective bargaining since its adoption in the early 1990s have given unions a pivotal or, at times a marginal, role.[131] The FW Act represents a half-way point between those positions, reinstating (as Creighton has put it) an 'attenuated' form of collectivism.[132] This hesitancy can be seen in the legislation's objects, which speak only of 'enabling' collective bargaining – and even then, 'for enterprise agreements that deliver productivity benefits'.[133] The bargaining provisions in Part 2-4 of the FW Act reflect the compromises struck

[125] FWRO Act, s 5(4).
[126] Ibid, s 19(1)(b).
[127] Ibid, chs 5–9.
[128] Ibid s 5(2)–(3); see A Stewart, A Forsyth, M Irving, R Johnstone and S McCrystal, *Creighton and Stewart's Labour Law* 6th edn (Sydney, Federation Press, 2016) 814–17, 833–34.
[129] P Gollan, R Markey and I Ross (eds), *Works Councils in Australia: Future Prospects and Possibilities* (Sydney, Federation Press, 2002).
[130] FWRO Act, ss 18C, 20. For an unsophisticated attempt to use these provisions, see '"Union-free" in 28 days: IR manager', *Workplace Express* (1 October 2020); 'Dual IR manager/union roles killed DREA registration bid', *Workplace Express* (19 March 2021), referring to *DREA (Della Rosa Employee Association)* [2021] FWC 1494.
[131] P Gahan and A Pekarek, 'Collective Bargaining and Agreement Making in Australia: Evolution of the Legislative Framework and Practice' in Creighton and Forsyth (n 50) 21; Stewart et al (n 128) 351–58.
[132] B Creighton, 'A Retreat from Individualism? The Fair Work Act 2009 and the Re-collectivisation of Australian Labour Law' (2011) 40 *Industrial Law Journal* 116, 142.
[133] FW Act, s 171(a).

by the then-Labor government, when it sought to wind back the Coalition's 2005 Work Choices legislation.[134] Unions are, in some respects, built into the FW Act bargaining scheme. A union is assumed to be the default bargaining representative of any members it has in the workplace (unless a union member explicitly chooses another representative).[135] In that capacity, a union may utilise one of several mechanisms to progress negotiations for an enterprise agreement. These include applying to the Fair Work Commission (FWC) for a majority support determination, compelling a reluctant employer to bargain;[136] seeking an order requiring an employer to adhere to prescribed good faith bargaining obligations;[137] requesting the FWC to conciliate or arbitrate a bargaining dispute;[138] or activating the dedicated low-paid bargaining stream.[139] Unions may also initiate the process enabling employees to take 'protected' (ie lawful) industrial action to advance their negotiating claims.[140]

In other ways, unions are sidelined in collective bargaining under the FW Act. They are not the *exclusive* bargaining representatives of employees: individual employees may represent themselves or appoint someone else as their representative (including someone from an unregistered union).[141] These other representatives may, like unions, activate the various FWC mechanisms to progress bargaining and take protected industrial action.[142] Further, unions are not parties to enterprise agreements. Instead agreements are made between employers and employees,[143] with a union able to become covered by an agreement where it has acted as a bargaining representative.[144] This creates the unusual situation whereby enterprise agreements made under the FW Act *may* but *do not have to* arise from collective bargaining, which has contributed to the growth of non-union agreement-making.[145] In non or lightly unionised settings, agreement-making often consists of no more than the employer complying with minimal information-provision obligations before asking employees to vote on an agreement.[146]

[134] See ch 5.

[135] FW Act, s 176(1)(b). See R Read, 'The Role of Trade Unions and Individual Bargaining Representatives: Who Pays for the Work of Bargaining?' in S McCrystal, B Creighton and A Forsyth (eds), *Collective Bargaining under the Fair Work Act* (Sydney, Federation Press, 2018) 69.

[136] FW Act, ss 236–37.

[137] Ibid, ss 228–33.

[138] Ibid, s 240.

[139] Ibid, Pt 2-4, Division 9.

[140] Ibid, Pt 3-3 (in particular s 437(1)).

[141] Ibid, s 176(1)(c); see Read (n 135).

[142] See ch 6.

[143] When the majority of employees who cast a valid vote on a proposed agreement, vote to approve it: FW Act, s 182(1).

[144] FW Act, ss 53(2) and 183; the union can then enforce the provisions of the agreement on behalf of its members.

[145] A Pennington, 'The Fair Work Act and the Decline of Enterprise Bargaining in Australia's Private Sector' (2020) 33:1 *Australian Journal of Labour Law* 68, 84–85.

[146] FW Act, ss 180–81. See U Chaudhuri and T Sarina, 'Employer-Controlled Agreement-Making: Thwarting Collective Bargaining Under the Fair Work Act' in McCrystal, Creighton and Forsyth (n 135) 138, 143–48.

## C. A Modified Form of Union Recognition without Reliance on Ballots

The FW Act does not include a union recognition mechanism of the kind found in US or UK law. Instead, a union is automatically entitled to act as bargaining representative in negotiations for a new enterprise agreement, where it has at least one member in the workplace.[147] A union can seek a majority support determination if an employer refuses to bargain.[148] If a determination is made, the formal bargaining process is triggered.[149] In deciding whether to make a determination, the tribunal must be satisfied – *by any method it considers appropriate* – that a majority of the employees who will be covered by the agreement want to bargain.[150] The FWC can therefore ascertain if the required majority exists by examining employee petitions, union membership records or the outcome of a ballot of employees.[151] Petitions have been considered sufficient in the vast majority of cases.[152] However, ballots have been ordered to eradicate doubts about the expression of employees' support for collective bargaining – for example, arising from concerns about the integrity of a petition[153] or where a long-running contest over the employer's refusal to bargain required decisive resolution.[154] The FWC has, in some cases, taken steps to ensure a fair contest in the ballot (such as by allowing paid meetings between employees and the union in the lead-up to the vote;[155] or the tribunal member attending the workplace to speak with employees directly and holding a 'show of hands' ballot to ascertain their preferences[156]).

## D. The Nature of Employer Opposition

The majority support determination process improves upon the US and UK union recognition laws, as the obligation to bargain in Australia is not dependent on

[147] FW Act, s 176(1)(b).
[148] Ibid, s 236(1).
[149] Ibid, s 173(2)(b).
[150] Ibid, s 237(2)–(3).
[151] Commonwealth Parliament, *Fair Work Bill 2008: Explanatory Memorandum* (2008), paras [r.166] and [979].
[152] See, eg, *National Union of Workers v Lovisa Pty Limited* [2019] FWC 2885; *Australian Workers' Union v Legeneering Australia Pty Ltd* [2020] FWC 4138; *Australian Manufacturing Workers' Union–Queensland Branch v Bustech Pty Ltd* [2021] FWC 924.
[153] See, eg, *Transport Workers' Union v MJ Rowles Pty Ltd* (2012) 219 IR 357.
[154] *Australian Manufacturing Workers' Union v Cochlear Ltd* (2009) 186 IR 120. Occasionally, the applicant union may ask the FWC to order a ballot: see, eg, *Retail and Fast Food Workers Union Incorporated* [2021] FWC 3068 and ch 6.
[155] *Independent Education Union of Australia v Academy of Interactive Entertainment* [2010] FWA 7733.
[156] *Australian Workers' Union v Alsco Pty Limited* [2021] FWC 1680.

union success in a fiercely contested workplace ballot.[157] This generally limits the opportunity for employers to engage in US-style union-busting tactics. However, other forms of anti-unionism have emerged under the FW Act, including: employers distributing pro forma letters of resignation from the union to employees in response to collective bargaining efforts;[158] spurious arguments to prevent the FWC making a majority support determination;[159] and aggressive litigation strategies to frustrate the making of a determination (even challenging the right of unions to represent employees).[160] In other cases, employers have exploited weaknesses in the good faith bargaining requirements:[161] for example, by engaging in surface bargaining;[162] or by telling employees that if a union's proposed agreement were voted up, the company would close within six months.[163] Employers have also successfully bypassed collective bargaining through the use of 'strategic voting cohorts':[164] the employer selects a limited number of employees in a part of the business not covered by an agreement, asks those employees to vote on a proposed agreement, then applies it (through a broadly expressed coverage clause) to a much broader workforce of 'potentially thousands of future employees'.[165]

## E. Constraints on Industrial Action

The ability of Australian employees to take lawful industrial action in support of enterprise bargaining claims has narrowed considerably.[166] The FW Act

[157] A Forsyth, J Howe, P Gahan and I Landau, 'Establishing the Right to Bargain Collectively in Australia and the UK: Are Majority Support Determinations under Australia's Fair Work Act a More Effective Form of Union Recognition?' (2017) 46:3 *Industrial Law Journal* 335, 337, 357–63.

[158] *Textile, Clothing and Footwear Union of Australia v Kennon Auto Pty Ltd* [2009] FWA 1377.

[159] See, eg, *Media Entertainment and Arts Alliance (re Australian Football League)* [2014] FWC 8898 (the tribunal rejected the employer's argument that collective bargaining was alien to its culture).

[160] *Australian Manufacturing Workers' Union v ResMed Ltd* [2016] FWCFB 22; see A Forsyth and B Ellem, 'Has the Australian Model Resisted US-Style Anti-Union Organising Campaigns? Case Studies of the Cochlear and ResMed Bargaining Disputes', in McCrystal, Creighton and Forsyth (n 135) 45, 60–63.

[161] FW Act, s 228(1) which requires bargaining representatives to meet and exchange information and responses to proposals; recognise other bargaining representatives; and refrain from capricious or unfair conduct that undermines freedom of association or bargaining. See A Bukarica and A Dallas, *Good Faith Bargaining under the Fair Work Act 2009: Lessons from the Collective Bargaining Experience in Canada and New Zealand* (Sydney, Federation Press, 2012).

[162] Permitted, because bargaining representatives are not required to make concessions or reach agreement (FW Act, s 228(2)): *Endeavour Coal Pty Ltd v Association of Professional Engineers, Scientists and Managers, Australia* (2012) 206 FCR 576; *Australian Manufacturing Workers' Union v Cochlear Ltd* (2012) 231 IR 1.

[163] *DPP Electrical Services Pty Ltd* [2019] FWCA 4999.

[164] The Senate, Education and Employment References Committee, *Corporate Avoidance of the* Fair Work Act 2009 (September 2017) 14.

[165] Chaudhuri and Sarina (n 146) 150–53 (footnote omitted), discussing case law including *Construction, Forestry, Mining and Energy Union v John Holland Pty Ltd* (2015) 228 FCR 297. See also *One Key Workforce Pty Ltd v Construction, Forestry, Mining and Energy Union* (2018) 262 FCR 527 (in which some limits on employer use of this strategy were imposed).

[166] See, eg, J Bornstein, 'Employees Are Losing: Have Workplace Laws Gone Too Far?' (2019) 61:3 *Journal of Industrial Relations* 438, 448–52.

maintained many of the former Coalition government's procedural hurdles for the taking of protected industrial action (including the requirements for majority employee approval in a secret ballot[167] and to give the employer three days' notice of intended strikes, work bans or other action[168]). The prohibition of industrial action in support of 'pattern bargaining' (pursuing common claims at more than one employer) is also still in place.[169] Employers are free to bring in short-term replacement workers when employees engage in protected action.[170] In sum, as McCrystal explains: 'it is technically difficult to engage in lawful strike action and easy to get it wrong, and when [such action] does occur [it] may be stopped'.[171] This refers to the ability of employers to have protected industrial action suspended or terminated due to its economic effects or impact on public health or community welfare.[172] In 2020, the Coalition government intervened to support an application by stevedoring company Patrick to use this provision to end a strike. Prime Minister Scott Morrison described the Maritime Union of Australia's (lawful) pursuit of pay increases as 'a campaign of extortion against the [community] in the middle of a Covid-19 recession'.[173] It is therefore not surprising that the longer-term decline in the incidence of industrial action has continued under the FW Act.[174] As Stanford has shown, the resultant weakening in the bargaining power of workers has contributed to persistently stagnant wages growth in Australia since 2013.[175]

## F. The Fair Work Act's Failure to Increase Collective Bargaining Coverage

Along with employer resistance and the limits placed on strikes, several other features of the FW Act have limited its effectiveness as a tonic for union-based collective bargaining. First, the focus of bargaining is mostly limited to a single enterprise or part of an enterprise.[176] This means agreements can be made only

[167] FW Act, Pt 3-3, Division 8; see B Creighton, C Denvir, R Johnstone, S McCrystal and A Orchiston, *Strike Ballots, Democracy, and Law* (Oxford, Oxford University Press, 2020) ch 4.

[168] FW Act, s 414(1)–(4), (6).

[169] Ibid, ss 409(4), 412 and 422.

[170] S McCrystal, *The Right to Strike in Australia* (Sydney, Federation Press, 2010) 258–59.

[171] S McCrystal, 'Why Is It So Hard to Take Lawful Strike Action in Australia?' (2019) 61:1 *Journal of Industrial Relations* 129, 130.

[172] FW Act, s 424. See, eg, *National Tertiary Education Union v Monash University* [2013] FWCFB 5982 (suspension of bans by academics on processing assessment results due to impact on students' welfare); *Sydney Trains; NSW Trains* [2018] FWC 519 (suspension of a proposed strike that would have caused disruption to users of the Sydney rail network).

[173] P Karp, 'Morrison not ruling out sending in military to settle Patrick Terminals wharf strike while urging lawful resolution', *The Guardian* (29 September 2020).

[174] J Stanford, *Historical Data on the Decline in Australian Industrial Disputes* (Briefing Note, Centre for Future Work, Australia Institute, 30 January 2018).

[175] Ibid, 6–7; J Stanford, 'The Fair Work Act and Wages' (2020) 33:1 *Australian Journal of Labour Law* 20, 32–33.

[176] FW Act, ss 12 (definition of 'enterprise') and 172(2)(a).

between a group of employees and their direct employer, and not (for example) between labour hire employees and the host business at which they are placed to work. As Bornstein points out, enterprise bargaining was designed for the Australian economy of the early 1990s and has not kept pace with business fissuring strategies.[177] Secondly, the one main avenue through which multi-employer bargaining is permitted[178] – low-paid bargaining[179] – is so fundamentally flawed that it has barely been used in over 12 years. Due to the complexity of its statutory design[180] and unhelpful interpretations by the FWC,[181] the low-paid bargaining scheme has not fulfilled its potential to lift employees in childcare, aged care, security, cleaning and other low-paid sectors off awards and into collective agreements.[182]

Thirdly, constraints have been imposed on the FW Act rules which are meant to provide support for the representative role of unions at the workplace level: the provisions for union 'right of entry' to workplaces;[183] and the 'general protections' provisions.[184] The latter, which protect union activists and members from adverse treatment by an employer because of their union affiliation or their engagement in industrial activity, have been narrowly interpreted by the courts.[185] In relation to the former, union officials have the right to enter business premises to hold discussions with members or prospective members.[186] However, this right is heavily circumscribed: the workers must be performing work on the premises and be willing to participate in union discussions;[187] the union official must hold an entry permit, and give 24 hours' notice of intended entry;[188] and discussions may only be held during employees' mealtimes or other breaks.[189] In practice, the ability of unions to use these provisions effectively for organising is hampered, as employers frequently contest entry rights

[177] Bornstein (n 166) 445–47.

[178] See also s 172(3) (dealing with multi-employer enterprise agreements) and s 172(5) (agreements for 'single interest employers' such as related companies and franchises).

[179] See, again, FW Act, Pt 2-4, Division 9; and ch 5.

[180] The provisions include stringent tests for unions to access the low-paid bargaining stream, requiring consideration not only of the necessity of multi-employer bargaining for employees (FW Act, ss 243(2)(a)–(d), 262(3)) but also its potential impact on businesses, productivity and service delivery (ss 243(3)(a),(e), 262(4)(b) and 275(b)).

[181] *United Voice and Australian Workers' Union, Queensland* (2011) 207 IR 251; *Australian Nursing Federation v IPN Medical Centres Pty Ltd* [2013] FWC 511; *Re United Voice* [2014] FWC 6441.

[182] F Macdonald, S Charlesworth and C Brigden, 'Access to Collective Bargaining for Low-Paid Workers' in McCrystal, Creighton and Forsyth (n 133) 206, 213–18.

[183] FW Act, Pt 3-4.

[184] Ibid, Pt 3-1.

[185] See ch 11.

[186] FW Act, s 484. Union officials also have entry rights to investigate suspected breaches of the FW Act, awards, agreements, and health and safety laws: ss 481, 494.

[187] FW Act, s 484(a), (c).

[188] Ibid, ss 487, 489.

[189] Ibid, s 490(2).

by disputing issues like the precise on-site location where union meetings are to be held.[190]

The upshot of these many statutory limitations is that overall collective bargaining coverage has *fallen* under the FW Act: 30.4 per cent of the workforce was covered by federal agreements in 2018 compared with 31.5 per cent in 2010;[191] and between 2013 and 2018, agreement coverage in the private sector was halved, from 22 to 11 per cent.[192] Concerted union campaigning for labour law reform is therefore an ongoing political project.[193]

# V. Italy

## A. Background

The Italian legal framework for unions and worker representation is the most encouraging of the four nations examined in this study. As noted in Chapter 2, the Italian Constitution sets down principles to protect collective organisation rights. Article 18 provides citizens with a general 'right to form associations freely and without authorization'.[194] This is supplemented by Article 39: 'Trade unions may be freely established.' Article 39 goes on to provide that the only legal restrictions which can be imposed upon unions are those relating to registration (eg, requiring democratic organisation); and that registered unions have legal personality and may 'enter into collective labour agreements'.[195] Article 40 states that: 'The right to strike shall be exercised in compliance with the law.'[196] No law requiring union registration was in fact enacted, leaving 'trade union organisation … assigned to private law alone'[197] (including the civil code dealing with non-recognised associations[198]). This vacuum was to some extent filled by the

[190] The FW Act was amended in 2013 to require discussions to be held in an area on the premises agreed with the occupier, or (failing agreement) in any area where employees usually take meal or other breaks (s 492). Nevertheless, disputes over entry rights have continued: N Kimberley and S McCrystal, 'Contested Spaces: Unions and Employer Controlled Access to Space for Organising under the Fair Work Act 2009 (Cth)' (2020) 33:1 *Australian Journal of Labour Law* 139.

[191] Australian Government, Attorney-General's Department, *Trends in Federal Enterprise Bargaining Report: June Quarter 2020*, 5, 13.

[192] Pennington (n 145) 74.

[193] See ch 5.

[194] Senato della Repubblica, *Constitution of the Italian Republic* (Roma, undated), art 18.

[195] Ibid, art 39.

[196] Ibid, art 40.

[197] F Carinci, 'Trade Union Freedom, Organization and Activities' in F Carinci and E Menegatti, *Labour Law and Industrial Relations in Italy: Update to the Jobs Act* (Milano, Wolters Kluwer Italia, 2015) 279, 282.

[198] Carinci (n 197) 290; see also T Treu, *Labour Law in Italy* 3rd edn (Alphen aan den Rijn, Wolters Kluwer, 2011) 167.

1970 Workers' Statute, described by Treu as 'the basic source of protection of trade union freedom in Italy'.[199]

## B. A Charter of Union and Worker Rights: The 1970 Workers' Statute

Reinforcing Article 39 of the Italian Constitution, Article 14 of the Workers' Statute affirms the right of all workers to form and belong to trade unions and to engage in union activities within the workplace.[200] Article 15 then provides various protections of workers' freedom of, and from, association: employment cannot be made subject to the condition of being or not being a union member and a worker cannot be dismissed or discriminated against based on union affiliation or involvement in strike action.[201] Under Article 17, employers are prohibited from providing any organisational or financial support to trade unions, a measure intended to prevent the emergence of cooperative or 'yellow' unions.[202] Article 18 enables workers dismissed without an economic or disciplinary basis, or for discriminatory reasons, to obtain reinstatement and compensation through court proceedings.[203] Articles 19–27 set down a suite of organisational rights for unions and their members at workplace level, including: the right to hold unlimited meetings after hours, and paid meetings during working time (up to the limits specified in the statute or a collective agreement); the ability to provide workers with access to information on union issues within the production unit; and the right to take paid and unpaid leave to participate in union meetings and negotiations.[204] These rights have operated in practice to assist union officials to extend their reach into new workplaces 'from the inside instead of from the outside'.[205]

The Workers' Statute includes a significant further protection for unionists against repressive anti-union conduct by employers. Under Article 28, a union can seek a court order requiring an employer to desist from engaging in behaviour that limits or denies the expression of trade union freedom or activity, including the right to strike.[206] According to Razzolini, Article 28 effectively

[199] Treu (n 198) 146.
[200] Carinci (n 197) 283.
[201] Treu (n 198) 146.
[202] Ibid, 148, noting that paid time for union delegates and activists to carry out their union activities is excluded from this prohibition.
[203] G Picot and A Tassinari, 'Politics in a Transformed Labor Market: Renzi's Labor Market Reform' (2015) 30:1 *Italian Politics* 121, 125–26; note also at 130–35 the Renzi Government's attempt to water down art 18, only partly achieved through the 2015 Jobs Act.
[204] Carinci (n 197) 292–94; see also Treu (n 198) 172, noting that these rights apply to the 'representative organs' of the unions at workplace level, that is RSAs and RSUs.
[205] Treu (n 198) 175.
[206] Ibid, 179.

'enables unions to bring unfair labor practice claims against employers'.[207] A union need not prove the intention of the employer to intrude upon its rights; only the effect of the employer's actions in that respect must be shown.[208] As unions have frequently relied upon Article 28 in disputes with employers, an extensive body of case law has developed. The provision has been applied, for example, to preclude (or overturn) employers replacing striking workers with others engaged on fixed-term contracts; non-recognition of unions in collective bargaining (for example, bypassing union representatives through direct negotiations with employees); dismissals, transfers, discrimination or reprisals against union activists; and failure to comply with mandatory provisions of an applicable collective agreement.[209] Leonardi views Article 28 as 'a key norm that for many years has allowed trade unions to seek enforcement of collective rights that would otherwise exist only on paper'.[210]

## C. Workplace-Level Representation through RSAs and RSUs

It was mentioned in Chapter 2 that the Workers' Statute provided for a system of company-level representation of workers through '*rappresentanze sindacali aziendale*' (RSAs), since adjusted by the role accorded to '*rappresentanze sindacali unitarie*' (RSUs) pursuant to the 1993 cross-sectoral agreement of the national social partner associations. Under Article 19 of the Workers' Statute (as amended by a referendum in 1995), RSAs may be established at the initiative of the workers in a production unit who are represented by the unions that are parties to collective agreements applying in that unit.[211] The amendment can be seen as part of a wider move to prise away the grip long exercised by the three main union confederations over company-level representation via RSAs. This shift to a more pluralistic approach to representation was also facilitated by provision for the creation of RSUs under the 1993 social pact, since refined under a further agreement between *Confindustria* and CGIL, CISL and UIL in 2014.[212] The delineation between RSAs and RSUs is not precise and the circumstances in which one or

[207] O Razzolini, *Collective Action for Self-Employed Workers: A Necessary Response to Increasing Income Inequality* (Centre for the Study of European Labour Law 'Massimo D'Antona', Working Paper 155/2021) 27.

[208] Treu (n 198) 180.

[209] Ibid, 179; Carinci (n 197) 296.

[210] S Leonardi, 'Employee Participation and Involvement: The Italian Case and Trade Union Issues' (2016) 22:1 *Transfer* 81, 90.

[211] M Pallini, 'Italian Industrial Relations: Toward a Strongly Decentralized Collective Bargaining?' (2016) 38:1 *Comparative Labor Law and Policy Journal* 1, 7–8, noting that subsequent decisions of the Italian Constitutional Court have established that art 19 thus establishes the representativeness of relevant trade unions for purposes of exercising certain rights under the Workers' Statute (replacing the requirement of 'most representative' union status under the original legislation; see ch 2).

[212] Ibid, 10.

the other may be present in an Italian firm vary according to a complex array of considerations. Tomassetti explains this as follows:

> In Italy there are two channels for workplace representation. The first is the union channel, regulated by Article 19 of [the Workers' Statute] … [under which] only organisations signatory to a sectoral and/or company collective agreement in force in the workplace are entitled to set up [RSAs]. As for works councils [RSUs], … [they] are formally independent from unions and are appointed by employees, regardless of their trade union affiliation. In enterprises joining employers' associations which signed the 1993 agreement [of the social partners], the [RSU] model applies. If a company is not affiliated to an employers' association, [RSAs] are elected according to Article 19.[213]

In Damiani, Pompei and Ricci's view, however, unions do play an influential role within RSUs 'because workers' representatives are elected from candidates of trade union lists'.[214] Among other functions, RSUs engage in firm-level negotiations over issues such as performance pay[215] and are the body through which workers' rights to information and consultation over business issues are channelled in the enterprise.[216] Likewise, RSAs have traditionally acted as the vehicle 'for information disclosure between management and unions, and as a permanent mechanism for workplace negotiation, joint consultation or decision-making'.[217] Both RSAs and RSUs play a role in localised agreement-making within Italy's coordinated system of collective bargaining.

## D. High Collective Agreement Coverage through National/ Industry-Level Bargaining

Unlike the USA, the UK and Australia, '[t]here is no systematic legal regime regulating collective bargaining and collective agreements in Italy'.[218] Instead, collective bargaining norms have been developed through a series of pacts or framework agreements reached between the social partners (the three major

[213] P Tomassetti, 'The Shift towards Single-Employer Bargaining in the Italian Car Sector: Determinants and Prospects at FIAT' (2013) 2:1 *E-Journal of International and Comparative Labour Studies* 93, 104. See also V Pulignano, D Carrieri and L Baccaro, 'Industrial Relations in Italy in the Twenty-first Century' (2017) 40:4 *Employee Relations* 654, 669.

[214] M Damiani, F Pompei and A Ricci, 'Opting Out, Collective Contracts and Labour Flexibility: Firm-Level Evidence for the Italian Case' (2020) 58:3 *British Journal of Industrial Relations* 558, 562.

[215] Ibid.

[216] Leonardi (n 209) 89–90. On the role played by an RSU in workplace-level management–union relationships in the metal industry in the Brescia region, see I Armaroli, 'Integrating Direct Employee Voice within the Framework of Employee Representation: The Role of an Italian Trade Union in *Organising Disintermediation*' (2020) *Economic and Industrial Democracy* (advance access).

[217] M Regini, 'Trade Unions' in E Jones and G Pasquino (eds), *The Oxford Handbook of Italian Politics* (Oxford, Oxford University Press, 2015) 528, 534.

[218] M Magnani, 'The Role of Collective Bargaining in Italian Labour Law' (2018) 7:2 *E-Journal of International and Comparative Labour Studies* 1, 2.

union confederations and employer associations).[219] As noted in Chapter 2, the cross-sectoral protocol negotiated between these organisations in 1993 was particularly significant, Grandi calling it: 'the "Constitution" of [Italian] labour relations, because it entailed the "rules" governing the collective bargaining system'.[220] The 1993 pact provided 'a clear and stable specification' to the 'respective competences and procedures' of Italy's traditional dual system of collective bargaining.[221] Under this 'two-tier model, coordinated centrally', national/industry-level collective agreements negotiated between the social partners establish 'basic common rules' while 'second-level bargaining' takes place at company/territorial level.[222] Typically, the industry agreement establishes 'the main items of the employment contract' including salary levels, working hours, holidays, health and safety and training; and the local-level agreement can only modify those rules where permitted by the nationally-negotiated agreement.[223] Tomassetti notes that another significant feature of the 1993 protocol was its stipulation that 'wage increases were to be set at industry level in line with the rate of inflation' while 'local increases were to be linked to productivity' and the performance of the firm.[224]

Further national-level collective bargaining accords followed, including those of 2009, 2011, 2013 and 2014. A major preoccupation of these various measures was the decentralisation of collective bargaining, achieved by extending the permissible boundaries of company-level derogation from national/industry collective agreements.[225] Pressure for reform in that direction arose from the economic conditions created by the global financial crisis in 2008; then from the major auto-manufacturer Fiat's complete withdrawal (in 2010–2011) from the metalworking sectoral agreements, triggering 'a crisis of industry-wide collective bargaining'.[226] In 2011, a rare legislative intervention (adopted at the urging of the European Central Bank) came in the form of the Berlusconi government's decree permitting binding company-level agreements with the goals of increasing

[219] Ibid, 4, 11–12; G Recchia, 'The Future of Collective Bargaining in Italy between Legislative Reforms and Social Partners' Responses' (2017) 23:4 *Transfer* 457.

[220] G Grandi, 'Collective Bargaining' in Carinci and Menegatti (n 197) 301, 304.

[221] S Colombo and I Regalia, 'Changing Joint Regulation and Labour Market Policy in Italy during the Crisis: On the Edge of a Paradigm Shift?' (2016) 22:3 *European Journal of Industrial Relations* 295, 296.

[222] S Leonardi, 'Trade Unions and Collective Bargaining in Italy during the Crisis', in S Lehndorff, H Dribbusch and T Schulten, *Rough Waters: European Trade Unions in a Time of Crisis* (European Trade Union Institute, 2018) 87, 99–100.

[223] A Terzi, *An Italian Job: The Need for Collective Wage Bargaining Reform* (Bruegel Policy Contribution, Issue 2016/11, July 2016) 3. Note also that industry and local-level agreements apply to all employees in the enterprise (in the case of local agreements, they must have been approved by the majority of RSA or RSU members): E Ales and I Senatori, 'Collective Bargaining and Workers' (Trade Union) Representation: The Company Level in Italy' (Paper for the Labour Law Research Network Conference, Amsterdam, 2015) 9–10.

[224] P Tomassetti, 'From Fixed to Flexible? Wage Coordination and the Collective Bargaining System in Italy' (2017) 33:4 *International Journal of Comparative Labour Law and Industrial Relations* 527, 528.

[225] Ibid, 528–29, 537; Grandi (n 220) 310–11; Pallini (n 210) 3, 10–11.

[226] Recchia (n 219) 459; see also Colombo and Regalia (n 221) 298–99.

competitiveness, wages and employment levels.[227] However, the social partners subsequently agreed not to utilise this avenue,[228] resisting its impetus for uncoordinated local-level bargaining. The three framework agreements adopted by the social partners between 2011 and 2014 produced new rules for collective bargaining, which remain in place today. As Leonardi explains, these mean that:

> Unions need to pass a threshold of 5 per cent representativeness to take part in national collective bargaining, whereas a final agreement is binding if signed by unions representing at least 50 + 1 per cent of the relevant workforce.[229]

Additional prompting of localised bargaining was implemented through provisions in the Renzi government's Jobs Act of 2015.[230] Magnani observes that despite these many recent initiatives to decentralise bargaining, 'the role of industry-level agreements remains central'.[231] According to Leonardi (referring to data compiled by Brindelli), 'the spread of decentralised-level bargaining is still very limited', applying (in 2016) to approximately 20 per cent of employers in unionised medium-large businesses, mostly in northern Italy.[232] The ongoing strength of industry-based bargaining is considered to be a major contributing factor to the retention of comparatively high levels of collective agreement coverage in Italy, measured at 80 per cent of the workforce in 2018.[233]

## E. A Definitive Right to Strike

The reinforcement of industry-level bargaining with a fairly permissive approach to strikes and industrial action again marks Italy out from the USA, the UK and Australia. In light of the constitutional protection of the right to strike, higher Italian courts have determined that this right 'cannot be limited internally and no criminal sanctions … can be imposed on employees' for participating in industrial action.[234] Santini elucidates further that as the right to strike

[227] Ibid, 459–60, referring to art 8, Decree-law No 138 of 13 August 2011 (converted into statute by Act No 148 of 14 September 2011). See further Damiani, Pompei and Ricci (n 214) 563.

[228] Grandi (n 220) 310–11; Recchia (n 219) 461.

[229] Leonardi (n 222) 99.

[230] Magnani (n 218) 5,12; Recchia (n 219) 462, 466.

[231] Ibid, 12.

[232] Leonardi (n 222) 101, referring to L Brindelli, 'Contrattazione integrative e retribuzioni nel settoro privato' (Roma, Fondazione Giuseppe Di Vittorio, 2016). See also S Leonardi, M Ambra and A Ciarini, 'Italian Collective Bargaining at a Turning Point' in S Leonardi and A Pedersini, *Multi-Employer Bargaining under Pressure: Decentralisation Trends in Five European Countries* (Brussels, European Trade Union Institute, 2018) 185, 200, noting that the spread of company-level bargaining has been constrained by the limited presence of RSUs in businesses with less than 50 employees.

[233] Schnabel (n 42) 23–24, 38.

[234] M Corti, M Delfino and C Spinelli, 'The Impact of the Global Economic Crisis on the Evolution of Labour Law in the National Legal Systems: Italian Report' (International Society for Labour and Social Security Law, European Regional Congress, Dublin, 2014) 19. Note that some limits are placed by Italian law on industrial action in essential public services: see Treu (n 198) 220–26; F Santini, 'Strike Action' in Carinci and Menegatti (n 197) 319, 329–34.

in Italian law is: 'an absolute right of the person, related to the existence of a contract, and not necessarily inherent to the relationship with the employer, it would allow the lawfulness of sympathy strikes …'[235] Permitted forms of action include indefinite, temporary and short strikes, taken by workers at company, industry or even national level.[236] Although the jurisprudence has generally required that strikes take the form of a 'collective abstention from work, called by a plurality of employees, to achieve a common goal',[237] there is an increasing 'recognition of lawfulness' of other types of action including work-to-rule and work bans.[238] Articles 15 and 28 of the Workers' Statute[239] reinforce the right of the individual worker to take strike action, Article 28 extending (in Treu's view) to prevent employers from bringing in temporary strikebreakers.[240] In practice, strikes tend to be of fairly short duration[241] and, while the incidence of industrial action in Italy has fallen since the 1990s, it remains higher than in the other three countries.[242]

## VI. Conclusion

This chapter has identified certain common weaknesses in the laws intended to promote union representation of workers through collective bargaining in operation in the USA, the UK and Australia. In each case it was seen that the enterprise focus of bargaining, combined with insufficient protections against anti-union conduct by employers and limitations on industrial action, have contributed to falling levels of collective bargaining coverage. In contrast, the non-recognition of unions is an option far less available to employers in the Italian context: unions are generally accepted social partners in the framework of national/industry-level collective bargaining, with extensive statutory rights of organisation and representation at the firm level. Another important point of distinction is that the right to engage in collective bargaining and strikes under Italian law extends beyond employees, to certain self-employed or non-subordinate workers (although not the collective rights provided for by the Workers' Statute).[243] This study now turns to consider the various strategies adopted by unions in the four countries to revive their fortunes, commencing in Chapter 4 with the USA.

[235] Santini, ibid 319, 320.
[236] Ibid, 323.
[237] Ibid, 324 (quoting from a 1980 decision of the Italian Supreme Court).
[238] Ibid, 328.
[239] See Pt V(B) above.
[240] Treu (n 198) 219.
[241] Ibid, 217.
[242] Organisation for Economic Co-operation and Development, *Negotiating Our Way Up: Collective Bargaining in a Changing World of Work* (Paris, OECD Publishing, 2019) 66.
[243] A Aloisi and E Gramano, 'A Solution in Search of a Problem? Collective Rights and the Antitrust Labor Exemption in Italy', in S Paul, S McCrystal and E McGaughey (eds), *Labor in Competition Law* (Cambridge, Cambridge University Press, forthcoming, 2022). See further ch 10.

# 4

# Unions in the USA: From the Organising Model to Alt-Labour

## I. Introduction

This chapter explores the various ways in which unions in the USA have sought to address membership decline. It begins with the adoption by the American Federation of Labor and Congress of Industrial Organisations (AFL-CIO) of the organising model as a basis for expanding the reach of unions into the private sector, from the mid-1990s. The chapter then turns to the Change to Win federation's split from the AFL-CIO in 2005 (in pursuit of a more concerted focus on strategic organising) and the bypassing of the fraught National Labor Relations Act (NLRA) process by many unions through voluntary recognition agreements negotiated with employers. This is followed by an exploration of the increasing tendency of US unions to look beyond the workplace and into the community, drawing on connections forged with other social movements to rebuild worker power. Three examples of this phenomenon (encompassing what have also been described as alt-labour or alt-bargaining approaches) are closely examined: the Fight for $15 movement, OUR Walmart/United for Respect and bargaining for the common good in public education (the #RedForEd teacher strikes). The chapter also considers the long-standing pursuit by US unions of labour law reform, explaining why this goal has proven so elusive.

## II. The AFL-CIO Organising Model

The AFL-CIO's new leadership team under John Sweeney, elected in October 1995, effected a fundamental shift to an 'organizing' model[1] – 'organizing non-union workers', in place of the traditional union role of servicing existing members.[2] In fact, an AFL-CIO publication from 1988 had explained the distinction between

[1] K Bronfenbrenner, S Friedman, R Hurd, R Oswald and R Seeber, 'Introduction' in K Bronfenbrenner, S Friedman, R Hurd, R Oswald and R Seeber (eds), *Organizing to Win: New Research on Union Strategies* (Ithaca, Cornell University Press, 1998) 1.

[2] K Bronfenbrenner and T Juravich, 'It Takes More Than House Calls: Organizing to Win with a Comprehensive Union-Building Strategy' in Bronfenbrenner et al (n 1) 19.

the 'servicing model' of trying to help union members by solving problems for them and the 'organizing model' of involving members in solutions.[3] New organising was largely a response to the decreasing union win rate in National Labor Relations Board (NLRB) recognition campaigns by the mid-1980s in the face of business closures, automation and aggressive employer opposition.[4] Bronfenbrenner's research had shown that 'in a climate of intense and pervasive employer opposition, union success in NLRB elections depends most on the quality and intensity of union organizing campaigns'.[5]

Sweeney had previously led the Service Employees International Union (SEIU) in pioneering an organising approach through its 'Justice for Janitors' campaign from the early 1990s, demonstrating how migrant workers 'in deunionized building service jobs could be galvanized into action to restore union recognition'.[6] For example, in Los Angeles, the campaign successfully targeted non-union cleaning firms through publicity stunts, direct lobbying of building owners and strikes, to win pay raises for janitors.[7] Extending these concepts more widely, 'organizing to win' focused on the one element of union campaigns that the labour movement controls: 'union strategies and tactics'.[8] On this view, even very strong employer opposition could be overcome by unions running 'aggressive bottom-up campaigns'.[9] Intensive union tactics designed to increase the chances of winning NLRB elections were deployed 'such as person-to-person contact, active representation committees, member volunteer organizers, solidarity days and building for the first contract before the election'.[10]

The AFL-CIO sought to drive this new approach among affiliates through its Organizing Institute (established in 1989) and the commitment of significant financial and staffing resources.[11] By the late 1990s, according to Bronfenbrenner et al, there was 'near-universal agreement among union leaders that the future of the movement depends on massive new organizing'.[12] The organising model

[3] B Fletcher and R Hurd, 'Beyond the Organizing Model: The Transformation Process in Local Unions' in Bronfenbrenner et al (n 1) 37, 38.

[4] Bronfenbrenner et al ibid, 6.

[5] Ibid, 10, referring to K Bronfenbrenner, *The Impact of Employer Opposition on Union Certification Win Rates: A Private/Public Sector Comparison* (Working Paper No 113, Economic Policy Institute, 1995).

[6] R Milkman and K Voss, 'Introduction', in R Milkman and K Voss (eds), *Rebuilding Labor: Organizing and Organizers in the New Union Movement* (Ithaca, Cornell University Press, 2004) 1, 1–2.

[7] R Waldinger, C Erickson, R Milkman, D Mitchell, A Valenzuela, K Wong and M Zeitlin, 'Helots No More: A Case Study of the Justice for Janitors Campaign in Los Angeles', in Bronfenbrenner et al (n 1) 102, 109–11.

[8] Bronfenbrenner and Juravich (n 2) 19.

[9] Ibid, 20.

[10] K Bronfenbrenner and R Hickey, 'Changing to Organize: A National Assessment of Union Strategies', in Milkman and Voss (n 6) 17, 19 (the full range of strategic union tactics is detailed at 21, 24–25).

[11] E Heery and L Adler, 'Organizing the Unorganized' in C Frege and J Kelly (eds), *Varieties of Unionism: Revitalization in a Globalizing Economy* (Oxford, Oxford University Press, 2004) 45, 48–49.

[12] Bronfenbrenner et al (n 1) 1.

was not without its critics though: for example, Fletcher and Hurd considered it 'to be an insufficient antidote to labor's ills'.[13] They examined the implementation of organizing in a number of SEIU 'locals', and found (among other problems) that servicing was still expected by members while increased resources were being devoted to organising.[14] Moody has also criticised 'the essentially top-down, bureaucratic view of change' of the AFL–CIO leadership which drove the organising programme, including its emphasis on public relations, institution building and 'training college students to become organizers'.[15]

According to Milkman and Voss, 'new organizing' involving 'imaginative, successful campaigns' did produce membership gains in certain industries and geographic areas, but these were not replicated 'on a large enough scale to impact the overall density problem' in the US.[16] Bronfenbrenner and Hickey observed that, by the early 2000s, major union victories were concentrated in industries such as healthcare, hotels and airlines 'while the majority of unions continue[d] to experience organizing losses and declining membership'.[17] Their research showed that the unions most utilising comprehensive organising tactics (SEIU, Hotel Employees and Restaurant Employees Union (HERE) and Union of Needletrades, Industrial and Textile Employees (UNITE)) obtained the highest levels of success in NLRB certification elections: 'even when we control for industry, corporate structure, bargaining unit demographics, and employer opposition'.[18] Milkman contends that the 'high-profile organizing drives among low-wage immigrant workers' by SEIU and HERE '[falsified] the once-widespread assumption that such workers were "unorganisable"'.[19] In an overall sense, though, new organising did not halt the downward slide: Moody points to the 'net loss of 888,000 members' during the period 1995–2005, and progressively fewer gains for unions in NLRB elections between 1997 and 2005.[20] He concludes that: 'the turn of the century represented not a new thrust in organizing, but a continued decline in the effort to organize in the private economy'.[21]

## III. Change to Win

In 2005, the 'Change to Win' federation of unions split from the AFL-CIO when agreement could not be reached over the rebating of dues to affiliated unions

[13] Fletcher and Hurd (n 3) 38.
[14] Ibid, 42–43.
[15] K Moody, *US Labor in Trouble and Transition: The Failure of Reform from Above, the Promise of Revival from Below* (New York, Verso, 2007) 134–36.
[16] Milkman and Voss (n 6) 1, 2.
[17] Bronfenbrenner and Hickey (n 10) 17.
[18] Ibid, 41–45, 53.
[19] R Milkman, 'Back to the Future? US Labour in the New Gilded Age' (2013) 51:4 *British Journal of Industrial Relations* 645, 654.
[20] Moody (n 15) 137–39.
[21] Ibid, 139.

wanting to engage more intensely in organizing efforts.[22] This seemingly technical dispute reflected bigger philosophical differences within the American labour movement over how to address its long-term downturn. The AFL-CIO was by then pursuing 'a more aggressive political agenda' with the goal of reforming US labour law 'as a precursor to union revitalization', whereas the Change to Win group urged an even more concerted focus on 'highly coordinated and strategic new member organizing'.[23] The breakaway group consisted of the SEIU, United Brotherhood of Carpenters (UBC), Laborers' International Union of North America (LIUNA), United Food and Commercial Workers International Union (UFCW), International Brotherhood of Teamsters (Teamsters), United Farm Workers (UFW), UNITE and HERE (which had merged to form UNITE-HERE).[24] Between them, they took away around 40 per cent of the AFL-CIO's total membership.[25] They aimed to zero-in on national corporate targets for unionisation like DHL and Walmart[26] and sign up millions of workers in service jobs considered less susceptible to offshoring or eradication through technology.[27]

In Milkman's assessment, the Change to Win unions were initially galvanised by their being 'unusually aggressive in their organizing efforts during the preceding decades, despite the long odds'.[28] In practice though:

> … this effort failed to achieve its own targets, much less to ignite the major labour upsurge that some if its founders had hoped for, and a few years after it occurred the split became yet another example of organized labour's disarray.[29]

Aleks's 2015 study showed that Change to Win unions had enjoyed greater success than AFL–CIO unions 'in winning elections and adding workers to the ranks of union members' over a ten-year period.[30] Yet, for Lichtenstein, the Change to Win group's achievements were outweighed by its 'divisive' tactics, such as reaching private recognition deals with employers and the fact that it 'generated no organizing breakthrough'.[31] According to Moody, the split precipitated 'a veritable civil war' among leading US unions,[32] largely attributable to the SEIU's aggressiveness under Andy Stern (who had taken over as President from Sweeney) including

[22] Ibid, 171.

[23] R Aleks, 'Estimating the Effects of "Change to Win" on Union Organising' (2015) 68:3 *Industrial and Labor Relations Review* 584, 585.

[24] Ibid, 586.

[25] Ibid, 587.

[26] Moody (n 15) 172.

[27] K Gross, 'Separate to Unite: Will *Change to Win* Strengthen Organized Labor in America?' (2005–2006) 25 *Buffalo Public Interest Law Journal* 75, 77, 101; see also D Moberg, 'Has the change led to wins?', *In These Times* (24 October 2007).

[28] Milkman (n 19) 654.

[29] Ibid.

[30] Aleks (n 23) 602.

[31] N Lichtenstein, *State of the Union: A Century of American Labor* (Princeton, Princeton University Press, revised and expanded edition, 2013) 274. See also K Moody, *In Solidarity: Essays on Working-Class Organization in the United States* (Chicago, Haymarket Books, 2014), 151, 303.

[32] Moody (n 31) 299; see also 302–4.

raids on the membership of healthcare unions and UNITE-HERE.[33] By 2011, Change to Win had transformed from 'a new labor federation' into a 'strategic organizing center', with a much lower profile than the fanfare that accompanied its launch.[34] Early suggested that: 'Six years after its founding, only a handful of the "5.5 million" workers who … "united to create Change to Win" even know what it is or why they are in it.'[35] Ultimately, Change to Win itself fractured, with several of its affiliates returning to the AFL–CIO fold.[36] Only three of the original splinter unions remain within Change to Win (SEIU, Teamsters and UFW) with the addition of Communications Workers of America (CWA) (also affiliated with AFL-CIO).[37]

## IV. Unions Bypass the Broken NLRA Process

Given the mounting problems besetting the NLRA route to union recognition for collective bargaining,[38] by the 2000s many US unions were bypassing it altogether. Instead, they turned to direct negotiations with employers aimed at securing the equivalent of recognition through so-called 'neutrality agreements'.[39] In this way, the usually heavily contested elements of a union organising drive could be resolved through 'private ordering'.[40] As Andrias explains, in these agreements:

> … employers typically pledge to remain neutral with respect to whether their employees organize; they also may allow unions access to employer property, recognize the union when a majority of workers sign cards requesting representation, or agree to some form of expedited election ….[41]

Some agreements also include time limits on organising campaigns, union access to employee lists and employer commitments to negotiate a first contract following recognition.[42] These arrangements have helped to reduce the intensity of anti-union campaigning by employers[43] and enabled unions to fast-track

[33] Ibid, 66–67.

[34] S Early, 'Whither Change to Win', *In These Times* (10 October 2011).

[35] Ibid.

[36] Ibid; K Moody, *On New Terrain: How Capital is Shaping the Battleground of Class War* (Chicago, Haymarket Books, 2017) 81.

[37] Change to Win Strategic Organizing Center, 'About Us'. Available at: www.changetowin.org/about-us/.

[38] See ch 3.

[39] A Eaton and J Kriesky, 'Union Organizing under Neutrality and Card Check Agreements' (2001) 55:1 *Industrial and Labor Relations Review* 42. On earlier adoption of this approach, see W Guzick, 'Employer Neutrality Agreements: Union Organizing under a Nonadversarial Model of Labor Relations' (1984) 6 *Industrial Relations Law Journal* 421.

[40] B Sachs, 'Labor Law Renewal' (2007) 1 *Harvard Law and Policy Review* 375, 378.

[41] K Andrias, 'The New Labor Law' (2016) 126 *Yale Law Journal* 2, 41.

[42] Eaton and Kriesky (n 39) 48.

[43] Ibid, 48–52; see also A Eaton and J Kriesky, 'NLRB Elections versus Card Check Campaigns: Results of a Worker Survey' (2009) 62:2 *Industrial and Labor Relations Review* 157.

organising without NLRB elections.[44] For example, SEIU signed up almost 5,000 janitors through an agreement with Houston's major cleaning contractors in 2005, resulting in a 'market-wide contract' providing low-paid workers with close to a 50 per cent wage rise and gains in health insurance and paid vacation leave.[45] The outcomes of many other contracts negotiated following voluntary recognition have come under scrutiny, Lichtenstein considering that union membership gains came at a price: 'employers wanted something in return' usually in the form of a collective agreement with minimal wage increases and commitments on productivity.[46]

As at November 2015, major US employers including UPS, AT&T, Safeway, Verizon and Kaiser Permanente had union neutrality agreements in place covering almost 1.5 million workers.[47] This reflects the continuing use of the mechanism by unions like CWA, Teamsters and SEIU, along with UNITE-HERE (at Hilton and Starwood hotels) and Retail, Wholesale and Department Store Union (at H&M and Zara).[48] In addition, United Automobile, Aerospace and Agricultural Implement Workers of America (UAW) has negotiated neutrality deals to extend union recognition from major car manufacturers to auto-parts supply firms.[49] Overall though, union organising through voluntary agreements with employers has not made a significant contribution to reversing union membership losses in the US.[50] This has not stopped employers and bodies like the National Right to Work Foundation vigorously contesting the legality of these arrangements.[51] They were supported in this endeavour by the Trump administration. In September 2020, then-NLRB General Counsel, Peter Robb, issued a memorandum indicating that neutrality deals under which employers facilitated union access on-site to employees – or the negotiation of collective agreement terms *before* a union

[44] J Moore and R Bales, 'Elections, Neutrality Agreements, and Card Checks: The Failure of the Political Model of Industrial Democracy' (2012) 87 *Indiana Law Journal* 147, 156, noting that of the almost 3 million workers organised by AFL–CIO unions between 1998 and 2003, only one-fifth came via traditional elections.

[45] Sachs (n 40) 378–80.

[46] Lichtenstein (n 31), 272, 274. See also J McAlevey, *No Shortcuts: Organizing for Power in the New Gilded Age* (New York, Oxford University Press, 2016) 81–83.

[47] R Freeman, M Barenberg and J Rogers, *The Legal, Economic and Business Case for Neutrality and Majority Verification of Worker Desire for Union Representation* (February 2016) 3.

[48] M Garneau, 'Neutrality agreements: a political primer', *Organizing Work* (18 November 2019). Available at: www.organizing.work/2019/12/neutrality-agreements-a-political-primer/; for a more recent example, see M Tracy, 'Journalists at The Daily News form a union, joining a wave', *New York Times* (5 February 2021).

[49] B Snavely, 'Neutrality agreements aid UAW in organizing', *USA Today* (22 June 2014).

[50] See, eg, Moody (n 31) 209–15.

[51] See, eg, National Right to Work Legal Defense Foundation, 'Supreme Court dismisses union-backed petition to overturn organizing case' (10 December 2013), referring to *UNITE HERE Local 355 v Mulhall*, 571 US 83 (2013). On the legality of neutrality agreements, see *Dana Corp.*, 356 NLRB No 49 (2010) in R Gorman, M Finkin and T Glynn, *Cox and Bok's Labor Law: Cases and Materials* 16th edn (St Paul, Foundation Press, 2016) 205–7; C Garden, 'Tactical Mismatch in Union Organizing Drives' in R Bales and C Garden (eds), *The Cambridge Handbook of US Labor Law for the Twenty-First Century* (Cambridge, Cambridge University Press, 2020) 199, 205–6.

demonstrated majority support among the workforce – would likely constitute unlawful employer support for the union.[52] President Biden's day-one removal of Robb[53] was quickly followed by the rescission, by Acting NLRB General Counsel Peter Ohr, of several of his predecessor's memoranda (including that on neutrality agreements) to more fully realise the NLRA's purpose of promoting collective bargaining and freedom of association.[54]

## V. Looking Further Afield: Unions in the Community, Alt-Labour and Bargaining for the Common Good

### A. Overview

The last decade or so has seen an even more profound shift on the part of many US unions, in their efforts to grow the labour movement.[55] In 2013, AFL–CIO President, Richard Trumka (recognising the major predicament faced by US unions) declared that the '[organisation's] door has to be – and will be – open to any worker or group of workers who wants to organize and build power in the workplace'.[56] Milkman posed the question whether this signalled 'a marriage of old and new labor'.[57] For so long, the central objective of American unions has been to obtain recognition from employers (by signing up as many members as possible) with a view to improving workers' wages and conditions through a collective agreement. Increasingly, though, unions are taking a much broader view of how the goal of advancing workers' interests can be achieved: for example, through negotiation of an agreement that also addresses community concerns or by concentrating their campaign efforts on state or local government legislators. Unions have become more deeply immersed in community-based organising, forging coalitions with other civil society groups including churches and advocates for action on climate change, LGBTQI rights and racial justice.[58]

[52] NLRB, Office of the General Counsel, *Guidance Memorandum on Employer Assistance in Union Organizing* (GC 20-13, 4 September 2020).

[53] N Scheiber, 'Peter Robb, Trump's labor appointee, is fired', *New York Times* (20 January 2021).

[54] NLRB, Office of the General Counsel, *Rescission of Certain General Counsel Memoranda* (GC 21-02, 1 February 2021). See further Part VI below.

[55] The developments discussed in this section are not novel: see, eg, R Fantasia and K Voss, *Hard Work: Remaking the American Labor Movement* (Berkeley, University of California Press, 2004) ch 4; R Needleman, 'Building Relationships for the Long Haul: Unions and Community-Based Groups Working Together to Organise Low-Wage Workers', in Bronfenbrenner et al (n 1) 71; and note the AFL-CIO's community affiliate 'Working America'. Available at: www.workingamerica.org/ (established in 2003).

[56] R Milkman, 'Introduction: Toward a New Labor Movement? Organising New York City's Precariat', in R Milkman and E Ott (eds), *New Labor in New York: Precarious Workers and the Future of the Labor Movement* (Ithaca, Cornell University Press, 2014) 1.

[57] Ibid, 18.

[58] A Tattersall, *Power in Coalition: Strategies for Strong Unions and Social Change* (Ithaca, Cornell University Press, 2010) 5; J Rosenblum, *Beyond $15: Immigrant Workers, Faith Activists, and the Revival*

Various terms have been used to identify these innovative approaches to fortifying worker power, including 'social movement unionism',[59] 'community unionism',[60] 'coalition unionism'[61] and, more recently, 'bargaining for the common good'[62] or even 'alt-bargaining'.[63] Consistent threads include unions and community organisations 'organiz[ing] workers on the basis of their identity or interests rather than their common workplace';[64] unions looking beyond contests over the employment relationship and members' grievances to pursue wider improvements in social and economic policies through political activity;[65] and unions utilising 'social bargaining' to transform conventional collective bargaining into a sectoral-orientated process that occurs 'in the public arena'.[66] Overwhelmingly, these various strategies aim to counter the chronic prevalence of low-paid work in the US economy,[67] thereby improving the lives of 'low wage workers, a disproportionate number of whom are women, Black, and Latino'.[68]

'Alt-labour' is another description of the phenomena discussed above, although this concept also takes in a range of non-union groups engaged in activism on behalf of workers.[69] These include the more than 220 worker centres across the US providing legal and advocacy services, predominantly for immigrant and irregular workers,[70] along with new worker collectives of the kind which have emerged to fight for better treatment of migrant agricultural workers[71] and those engaged in

*of the Labor Movement* (Boston, Beacon Press, 2018); J Broxmeyer and E Michaels, 'Faith, Community, and Labor: Challenges and Opportunities in the New York City Living Wage Campaign', in Milkman and Ott (n 56) 70.

[59] C Engeman, 'Social Movement Unionism in Practice: Organizational Dimensions of Union Mobilization in the Los Angeles Immigrant Rights Marches' (2015) 29:3 *Work, Employment and Society* 444; E Heery, 'Fusion or Replacement: Labour and the "New" Social Movements' (2018) 39:4 *Economic and Industrial Democracy* 661.

[60] Tattersall (n 58) 17–21.

[61] Ibid, 21.

[62] S Gupta, S Lerner and J McCartin, 'Why the Labor Movement Has Failed – And How to Fix It', *Boston Review* (1 May 2019). See also K Sánchez Ocasio and L Gertner, 'Fighting for the Common Good: How Low-Wage Workers' Identities Are Shaping Labor Law' (2017) 126 *Yale Law Journal Forum* 503.

[63] M Oswalt, 'Alt-Bargaining' (2019) 82:3 *Law and Contemporary Problems* 89.

[64] Tattersall (n 58) 21; see also Sánchez Ocasio and Gertner (n 62) 505, 511.

[65] Tattersall (n 58 above) 177. See also Andrias (n 41) 46; Sánchez Ocasio and Gertner (n 62) 506.

[66] Andrias (n 41) 47.

[67] M Oswalt, 'Improvisational Unionism' (2016) 104:3 *California Law Review* 597, 612.

[68] Sánchez Ocasio and Gertner (n 62) 504, 507–9.

[69] Oswalt (n 67) 609; Milkman (n 19) 656; T Juravich, 'Constituting Challenges in Differing Arenas of Power: Worker Centers, the Fight for $15, and Union Organizing' (2018) 43:2 *Labor Studies Journal* 104.

[70] K Griffith and L Gates, 'Worker Centers: Labor Policy as a Carrot, not a Stick' (2019) 14 *Harvard Law and Policy Review* 601; Juravich (n 69) 109–10; J Garrick, 'How Worker Centers Organize Low-Wage Workers: An Exploration of Targets and Strategies' 46:2 (2021) *Labor Studies Journal* 134. Note, also, the emergence of not-for-profit policy and campaign organisations devoted to combating income inequality and strengthening workers' rights, like the National Employment Law Project (www.nelp.org/) and Jobs with Justice (www.jwj.org/); E Larson (ed), *Jobs with Justice: 25 Years, 25 Voices* (Oakland, PM Press, 2013).

[71] M Dias-Abey, 'Justice in Our Fields: Can "Alt-Labor" Organizations Improve Migrant Farm Workers' Conditions?' (2018) 53 *Harvard Civil Rights-Civil Liberties Law Review* 167.

the gig economy.[72] For Oswalt, alt-labour is conceptualised as 'worker organizing' where 'unions are not behind the wheel' and the goal is not necessarily a collective agreement[73] – although tight definitions are elusive, as unions frequently fund and support alt-labour groups and campaigns.[74] Juravich, too, highlights the areas of overlap between traditional and alt-labour and suggests it is mistaken to view 'alt-labor as a residual category for everything that is not a traditional union'.[75]

## B. The Fight for $15

The 'Fight for $15' campaign, now a nationwide movement, had its origins in a 2011 effort by the SEIU – 'Fight for a Fair Economy' – to improve working conditions on a wider scale than could be achieved through site-by-site organising.[76] The fast-food industry became the first major target. Workers at McDonald's, Burger King, KFC and other major chains were stuck on the federal minimum wage of US$7.25 per hour, and exposed to safety risks and 'unfair firings'.[77] The SEIU began to organise these workers in partnership with community groups, such as New York Communities for Change, through a series of 'city wide stoppages that last a single day, repeat, and gradually expand to more and more cities'.[78] From the earliest strikes of hundreds of fast-food workers in New York (November 2012) and Chicago (April 2013),[79] Fight for $15 has spread across the US including nationwide strikes in 2013 and 2015 and in many midwestern cities in late 2018.[80]

Organisers use the internet and social media to attract widespread media coverage.[81] Over time, the campaign has drawn in other low-paid workers including those employed in home health care, childcare, airports and retail and it has forged links with Black Lives Matter and other social movements.[82] This has fostered the use of 'powerful' tactics like 'the "walk back"', where community leaders accompany workers on their return to the business after a strike 'in a public

[72] See chs 9 and 10.
[73] Oswalt (n 67) 609.
[74] Oswalt (n 63) 96.
[75] Juravich (n 69) 105.
[76] S Greenhouse, *Beaten Down, Worked Up: The Past, Present, and Future of American Labour* (New York, Alfred A Knopf, 2019) 232–33.
[77] Ibid, 234.
[78] Oswalt (n 67) 622–23 (footnote omitted).
[79] Ibid, 623–624.
[80] Greenhouse (n 76) 241; Andrias (n 41) 50; K Thomhave, 'Fighting for $15 – and a Union', *The American Prospect* (16 October 2018).
[81] See the Fight for $15 website (www.fightfor15.org/); L Franghi, T Zhang and R Hebdon, 'Tweeting and Retweeting for Fight for $15: Unions as Dinosaur Opinion Leaders?' (2020) 58:2 *British Journal of Industrial Relations* 301.
[82] Andrias (n 41) 49.

show of solidarity'.[83] As activist Jonathan Rosenblum puts it in the context of the successful Fight for $15 struggle at Seattle's SeaTac Airport:

> The community was not an ally of the union; it was part of the union. Community activists did the organizing work .... But they also were strategic partners in the campaign, engaged in decision-making, developing actions, and playing leadership roles in public demonstrations.[84]

Fight for $15 has achieved some significant wins by exerting pressure on employers to increase pay rates and lobbying local municipalities and state governments to raise the minimum wage above the federal level. McDonald's increased its minimum pay rate to US$8.25 an hour in 2015,[85] rising to US$10.00 per hour by 2016.[86] Target, Costco, Starbucks, Wells Fargo and even Amazon have upped pay rates[87] in response to the momentum generated by Fight for $15. Some of the more notable regulatory victories have included the increase of minimum wage rates to US$15.00 per hour in states including New York, California and Massachusetts, and at the municipal level in Washington DC, Seattle and San Francisco (among other cities).[88] By 2021, it was estimated that Fight for $15 had delivered pay rises for around 27 million American workers.[89]

According to Andrias, the pay increases generated by the movement 'would have been unthinkable' in their 'magnitude and scope' prior to 2012.[90] Using 'symbolic power to reframe low-wage work', Fight for $15 has also altered how Americans think about income inequality and the low-paid workforce.[91] However, much less has been achieved in respect of Fight for $15's other main goal: *unionising* low-wage workers (ie, the demand for '$15.00 and a union'[92]). While some companies have given in to the first demand, they have firmly denied the second.[93] SEIU's President, Mary Kay Henry, claimed in 2018 that: 'We believe union wins

[83] Sánchez Ocasio and Gertner (n 62) 514.

[84] K Brice-Lall, 'Beyond $15 (Interview with Jonathan Rosenblum)', *Jacobin* (September 2017); see further Rosenblum (n 58) chs 3–9.

[85] Andrias (n 41) 52.

[86] Greenhouse (n 79) 244, noting that the increases would only apply at company-owned stores; see also Oswalt (n 67) 622, estimating that more than 80% of McDonald's US stores are owned and run by franchisees.

[87] Economic Policy Institute and National Employment Law Project, *Why the U.S. Needs a $15 Minimum Wage* (Fact Sheet, 26 January 2021) 5.

[88] Andrias (n 41) 51–53; Greenhouse (n 79) 244–46. See further Congressional Research Service, *State Minimum Wages: An Overview* (CRS Report, R43792, 25 January 2019).

[89] Fight for $15, 'New report shows massive impact of $15/hr in communities nationwide'. Available at: fightfor15.org/new-report-shows-massive-impact-of-15-hr-in-communities-nationwide/.

[90] Andrias (n 41) 53.

[91] Juravich (n 69) 111; see also K vanden Heuvel, 'The Fight for $15 has created a road map for change', *The Nation* (23 July 2019).

[92] Thomhave (n 80).

[93] Greenhouse (n 79) 248; A Press, '$15 isn't enough to empower Amazon's workers', *Medium* (5 October 2018).

can escalate just like [they did] for $15.'[94] Yet some observers have been quite critical not only of Fight for $15's failure to develop into a durable workers' movement, but also the reluctance of those behind it to admit that shortcoming.[95] Union organiser and writer, Jane McAlevey, suggests that it has become a 'mostly publicity, social media campaign' creating 'the illusion of a huge movement' – mobilising workers behind the cause, but not organising them into unions.[96]

Following the election of President Biden, the new front in the Fight for $15 is the *federal* minimum wage. The campaign's prior efforts directed at state and local law-makers reflected the need to find 'a way around the gridlock in Washington',[97] with no increase in the federal rate of US$7.25 per hour since 2009. An increase to US$15.00 per hour was proposed in the Raise the Wage Act, introduced into Congress by House Democrats in January 2019, but defeated in the Senate due to Republican opposition.[98] Biden pledged to lift the federal standard to $15.00 and index it to median hourly wages ('so that low-wage workers' wages keep up with those of middle income workers').[99] Since taking office, he has increased the minimum wage for federal contractors to $15.00 per hour from 2022 (having unsuccessfully tried to include an overall federal minimum wage increase in a COVID-19 relief-funding measure).[100] However, the prospects of a refreshed Raise the Wage Act being passed by Congress are probably as limited as those of labour law reform more broadly.[101]

## C. OUR Walmart/United for Respect

Organization United for Respect at Walmart (OUR Walmart) was originally a UFCW-backed venture directed at breaking through the virulent anti-unionism of the largest private sector employer in the US. It has since evolved into a broader worker campaign organisation called United for Respect. OUR Walmart was established in 2010, following years of unsuccessful UFCW organising drives using the traditional NLRA process.[102] OUR Walmart aimed to improve working

[94] Thomhave (n 80).

[95] See, eg, J Rosenblum, 'Fight for $15: Good Wins, but Where did the Focus on Organizing Go?' (2017) 42:4 *Labor Studies Journal* 387, 389.

[96] M Rozworski, 'Having the hard conversations (Interview with Jane McAlevey), *Jacobin* (4 October 2015). See Part VII below; and ch 11.

[97] Juravich (n 69) 111.

[98] A Campbell, 'The $15 minimum wage bill has all but died in the Senate', *Vox* (16 August 2019).

[99] J Biden, 'The Biden Plan for Strengthening Worker Organizing, Collective Bargaining, and Unions'. Available at: www.joebiden.com/empowerworkers/.

[100] N Scheiber, 'Biden orders $15 minimum wage for federal contractors', *New York Times* (27 April 2021).

[101] See Part VI below.

[102] N Lichtenstein, 'Wal-Mart, John Tate, and Their Anti-Union America' in N Lichtenstein and E Shermer (eds), *The Right and Labor in America: Politics, Ideology and Imagination* (Philadelphia, University of Pennsylvania Press, 2012) 252, 264–75. See also Greenhouse (n 79) 157–58, indicating that the company preferred to close stores (or departments within stores) rather than recognise any union.

conditions for the company's more than 1.4 million US employees by building a support network based on the worker centre model.[103] OUR Walmart activists sought to build solidarity around key concerns of the workforce: low pay rates, intrusive surveillance, unpredictable shift schedules and health and safety for pregnant store-workers (through demands that management 'respect the bump').[104] OUR Walmart also contested 'Walmart's dominant framing of the employment relationship as one in which workers were part of a well-treated "family"', highlighting instead the company's retribution against workers who dared to collectivise and the disparity between the wealth of its owners and the poverty wages of 'associates'.[105]

Much like the Fight for $15, OUR Walmart organised coordinated, sudden work stoppages at stores in many US cities, starting with the 2012 '"Black Friday" day of action'.[106] This was repeated in 2013 and 2014, these protests leading to the arrests of some employees while (between the various strikes) 'aggressive demonstrations on Walmart property … made creative use of the element of surprise'.[107] The establishment of an 'internet facilitated network' to bolster on-the-ground activism was a significant feature of OUR Walmart.[108] This included dedicated social media channels to provide 'accessible space[s] beyond the workplace', connecting Walmart's disparate workforce and forging 'a collective identity of exploited workers'.[109] Facebook and Twitter were used to 'amplify offline collective actions by increasing their visibility',[110] in turn generating media coverage.[111] Wood explains that a central purpose of all this activity was to harm the company's brand: OUR Walmart deployed 'symbolic power' to improve employment standards 'through reputational damage'.[112] In this, it could claim some modest success: the company increased hourly pay rates for store-workers to $US9.00 in 2015 and $US10.00 in 2016, and introduced fixed schedules for some staff.[113]

[103] V Pasquier and A Wood, *The Power of Social Media as a Labour Campaigning Tool: Lessons from OUR Walmart and the Fight for 15* (Brussels, European Trade Union Institute, Policy Brief No 10/2018) 2; A Wood, 'Networks of Injustice and Worker Mobilisation at Walmart' (2015) 46:4 *Industrial Relations Journal* 259, 260, 262.

[104] Oswalt (n 67) 615, 617–18; Pasquier and Wood, ibid, 2.

[105] Pasquier and Wood ibid; see also A Kroll, 'Walmart workers get organized – just don't say the U-word', *Mother Jones* (March/April 2013), noting that the average Walmart associate's pay was US$8.31 per hour 'and many rely on food stamps and Medicaid'.

[106] Pasquier and Wood (n 103) 3.

[107] Oswalt (n 67) 616–17.

[108] Wood (n 103) 260.

[109] Ibid, 264–65; see further B Caraway, 'OUR Walmart: A Case Study of Connective Action' (2016) 19:7 *Information, Communication and Society* 907.

[110] Pasquier and Wood (n 103) 3.

[111] Wood (n 103) 267–68.

[112] Ibid, 270–71.

[113] Ibid, 271; J Kasperkevic, 'Walmart to boost pay for half a million workers', *The Guardian* (20 February 2015). In 2020, Walmart further increased pay for around 11% of its workforce to US$15.00 per hour: M Corkery, 'Walmart to raise wages for some workers', *New York Times* (17 September 2020).

Yet, according to Reich and Pearman, as only a miniscule proportion of the Walmart workforce had engaged in OUR Walmart's activism, it could not:

> ... impact the company's production process .... OUR Walmart had symbolic leverage but not yet structural leverage. It succeeded in creating a public relations problem for Walmart that the company answered with policy changes that were just big enough to change the narrative.[114]

By 2015, it was apparent that OUR Walmart was faltering. A change in UFCW leadership led to questioning of the estimated US$7–$8 million the union had spent on the campaign annually, without any increase in membership.[115] Later that year, it was significantly defunded by UFCW and relaunched as a broader organising initiative.[116] Confusingly, OUR Walmart was also relaunched by a splinter group of organisers and workers who had been involved in the original outfit.[117] Led by Dan Schlademan, the new grouping attracted support from over 20 not-for-profit worker organisation partners.[118] One of its early ventures under Schlademan's direction was the 'WorkIt' app, enabling Walmart employees to obtain speedy responses to questions about their treatment at work.[119]

It is not precisely clear when the remnants of OUR Walmart morphed into United for Respect, but the new organisation has taken on a wider remit. It continues to strive for better treatment of workers at Walmart,[120] but United for Respect also campaigns to counter the influence of private equity firms and hedge funds which has seen the loss of thousands of jobs at Toys "R" Us, Sears and Kmart.[121] Through the Fair Workweek Initiative, United for Respect works with the Center for Popular Democracy to tackle the problem of unfair employer scheduling practices that eat into workers' family time across the

[114] A Reich and B Pearman, *Working for Respect: Community and Conflict at Walmart* (New York, Columbia University Press, 2018) 212–13.

[115] D Moberg, 'The union behind the biggest campaign against Walmart in history may be throwing in the towel. Why?', *In These Times* (11 August 2015); see also Reich and Pearman, (n 114), 211–12. OUR Walmart itself obtained somewhere in the vicinity of 'thousands [of members] nationally': Wood (n 103) 261.

[116] P Olney, 'Where did the OUR Walmart campaign go wrong?', *In These Times* (14 December 2015). UFCW still runs a Walmart-focused campaign, 'Making Change at Walmart'. Available at: http://changewalmart.org/.

[117] N Lane and L Baertlein, 'Wal-Mart worker group splits in two; both sides vow to continue wage fight', *Reuters* (17 September 2015).

[118] Ibid.

[119] M Snider, 'Walmart, labor group clash over app that connects employees', *USA Today* (15 November 2016). See also S Berfield, 'Labor group gets IBM's Watson to help Walmart workers', *Bloomberg* (14 November 2016), describing the app as 'a mobile employee handbook'; and (on similar approaches in Australia and the UK) chs 6 and 7.

[120] United for Respect, 'United for Respect at Walmart'. Available at: www.united4respect.org/campaigns/walmart/.

[121] United for Respect, 'The Jobs Crisis in Retail'. Available at: www.united4respect.org/campaigns/wall-street/.

service industries.[122] United for Respect claims to represent 'over 16 million men and women of different ages, sexual orientations and ethnicities' and to 'build power' by bringing workers 'together – in our stores, in our communities and online'.[123] Schlademan suggests that this model of unionism is representative of the: '[e]merging worker movements … winning hard fought victories with the painful recognition that the same [old] methods for organizing don't work inside America's broken system of laws and traditions'.[124] Yet United for Respect and its predecessor have attracted criticism (similar to that of the Fight for $15) that it has generated a lot of publicity, but 'Facebook hits and likes do not make a real organizing program'.[125] There is also the view of an anonymous United for Respect organiser who feels it simply 'uses workers as media props' and is 'more about pleasing funders' than building a strong workplace-based organisation that retail store-workers can count on.[126]

## D. #RedForEd: Bargaining for the Common Good and Striking 'For the Future of Public Education'

'Bargaining for the common good', as explained by Gupta, Lerner and McCartin, involves: 'efforts by unions and their allies to remake collective bargaining and organizing campaigns … a conscious rethinking and broadening of the *participants, processes* and *purposes* of organizing and collective bargaining'.[127] Participation is broadened beyond the traditional focus on bargaining between employers and unions to include community and other stakeholders; the nature of bargaining is altered from closed door negotiations between professionals to incorporate increased militancy, transparency and political action; and the former singular goal of 'winning a serviceable contract' is replaced by 'contract campaigns as steps in a long-term strategy of worker empowerment'.[128] For Sánchez Ocasio and Gertner, 'common-good unionism' sees unions aligning their claims with those of their communities, to 'address structural inequality' for union members and

[122] United for Respect, 'Fair Workweek Initiative'. Available at: www.united4respect.org/campaigns/fair-workweek/.

[123] United for Respect, 'About'. Available at: www.united4respect.org/about-us/.

[124] D Schlademan, 'A reborn American labor movement is coming – if unions are bold enough to change', *Quartz* (6 April 2017).

[125] Olney (n 116). See Part VII below and ch 11.

[126] 'Leo', 'Burnout culture, workers as props: organizers at United for Respect speak out', *Organizing Work* (16 May 2020). Available at: www.organizing.work/2020/05/burnout-culture-workers-as-props-organizers-at-united-for-respect-speak-out/.

[127] Gupta, Lerner and McCartin (n 62); emphasis in original.

[128] Ibid. See further J McCartin and M Sneiderman, 'Collective Action and the Common Good: Teachers' Struggles and the Revival of the Strike', in R Givan and A Lang (eds), *Strike for the Common Good: Fighting for the Future of Public Education* (Ann Arbor, University of Michigan Press, 2020) 15, 16, 23–24.

'all similarly situated workers across various geographies and demographics'.[129] Oswalt illustrates bargaining for the common good (or 'alt-bargaining') with reference to the Chicago Teachers Union (CTU)'s:

> … approach to [contract] negotiations, which prioritizes community-centric demands. [This] model is central to how the [union] conceives of its membership – *each and every city resident* – and accordingly, how it develops proposals to cover that membership.[130]

In the CTU's landmark dispute with the Chicago public school district in 2012, teachers worked with parents and other community representatives to progress demands on class sizes, facilities and better financial management of the school system.[131] Their successful strike-based bargaining campaign blazed a trail for teachers nationally.[132]

In 2018, a wave of militancy by teachers combined elements of bargaining for the common good with spontaneous strikes (often in defiance of legal restrictions).[133] In five conservative 'red' states (Arizona, Oklahoma, West Virginia, North Carolina and Kentucky), teachers borrowed from the playbook of earlier campaigns in more unionised cities like Chicago and St Paul to push back against austerity measures which had seen greatly reduced funding of public education.[134] They walked out in support of the need for improvements not only in their own desperately low pay and conditions, but also the under-resourcing of school libraries, family support services and even basics like classroom equipment and textbooks.[135] Teacher chat groups on Facebook and Twitter swiftly blew up into protest movements (using the #RedForEd hashtag) that marched on state legislatures demanding change.[136] At large rallies, the ranks of teachers and unionists were swelled by parents, students and other supporters.[137]

Essentially, these were 'organizing, bargaining and political campaigns all at once'.[138] An important ingredient in the mass mobilisation of education workers (generally fearful of striking in 'right to work' states) was the level of fury felt by this predominantly female workforce.[139] Their rage was amplified by the belittling

[129] Sánchez Ocasio and Gertner (n 62) 519.

[130] Oswalt (n 63) 90; emphasis added.

[131] Gupta, Lerner and McCartin (n 62). See further S Ashby and R Bruno, *A Fight for the Soul of Public Education: The Story of the Chicago Teachers Strike* (Ithaca, Cornell University Press, 2016).

[132] R Givan, 'Introduction: On Strike for Our Students and the Common Good' in Givan and Lang (n 128) 1, 2–4.

[133] J McCartin, M Sneiderman and M BP-Weeks, 'Combustible Convergence: Bargaining for the Common Good and the #RedForEd Uprisings of 2018' (2020) 45:1 *Labor Studies Journal* 97, 98–99; Oswalt (n 63) 112.

[134] McCartin, Sneiderman and Weeks (n 133) 98–99.

[135] Ibid, 106.

[136] Oswalt (n 63) 112–13; McCartin, Sneiderman and Weeks (n 133) 105–6, 109.

[137] Greenhouse (n 79) 319.

[138] Gupta, Lerner and McCartin (n 79).

[139] Greenhouse (n 79) 308–9, 316, 318. See further G Russom, 'The Teachers' Strikes of 2018: A Gendered Rebellion', in Givan and Lang (n 128) 173.

responses of state governors and school administrators, especially where states preached belt-tightening for schools but had given tax cuts to corporations.[140] Insurgent teachers' groups were often far ahead of their unions, mapping out strike action and other tactics via social media.[141] In West Virginia, teachers who had walked out for nine school days (despite threats of fines from the state administration) sent union leaders back to the negotiating table when presented with a settlement that failed to address their concerns.[142]

Significant gains were ultimately achieved in most states, including pay rises and a commitment to invest more in public education – although Oswalt notes that, because these outcomes were not formalised in collective agreements, they were susceptible to reversal by some state law-makers.[143] In contrast, a six-day strike led by the United Teachers of Los Angeles in 2019 (taking 600,000 students out of school) produced pay increases – and common good objectives like increased 'green spaces' for children in schools – through a new collective bargaining contract.[144] Overall, the wave of teachers' strikes is credited with shifting the national discourse on public education away from the austerity agenda of deprivation and privatisation over more than a decade.[145] In addition, as Givan concludes:

> … common-good demands by striking educators are well on their way to becoming standard elements of bargaining and advocacy campaigns. … Educators are now demanding and winning the creation of antiracism programs; protection from overpolicing in public schools …; appropriate funding of support services …; and more. Class size is a central issue in almost every campaign. To focus solely on pay and benefits would feel positively quaint in this era in which collective bargaining in education has centered the deeper and more inclusive fight for social justice.[146]

## VI. A (Seemingly) Lost Cause: Unions and Labour Law Reform

The pursuit of union revival through law reform has been of greater longevity than any of the other approaches considered in this chapter, but also the most elusive. Pressure from the labour movement to rectify the many shortcomings

[140] Greenhouse, (n 79), 308, 313.

[141] Oswalt (n 63) 113–15. See further E Blanc, 'Rank-and-File Organizing and Digital Mobilizing in the Red State Revolt', in Givan and Lang (n 128) 91; R Garelli, 'Educators United Online', in Givan and Lang (n 128) 102.

[142] Greenhouse (n 79) 309–11.

[143] Oswalt (n 63) 117.

[144] J McAlevey, *A Collective Bargain: Unions, Organizing, and the Fight for Democracy* (New York, Harper Collins, 2020) ch 6.

[145] S Karp and A Sanchez, 'The 2018 Wave of Teachers Strikes: A Turning Point for Our Schools?', in Givan and Lang (n 128) 191.

[146] R Givan, 'The Strike Continues …', in Givan and Lang (n 128) 253, 254.

of the NLRA has come in waves over more than 40 years, mostly linked to the promise (then disappointment) following the election of Democratic presidents. Each time, reform ambitions have foundered on the rocks of vehement business opposition, backed by free enterprise lobby groups and Republicans in Congress. The proposed Labor Law Reform Act of 1977 would have 'mitigate[d] some of the overwhelming advantages that employers enjoy in union campaigns' and strengthened 'remedies against employer misconduct' but did not survive a filibuster in the Senate.[147] Lukewarm support from President Carter, concerned to assuage business interests, was a factor in the bill's demise.[148] President Clinton set up the Commission on the Future of Worker-Management Relations. Its moderate recommendations, along with Republican victories in the 1994 mid-term elections, paved the way for the Clinton administration to run dead on amending the NLRA.[149]

The brightest hopes for change coalesced around the proposed Employee Free Choice Act (EFCA) in President Obama's first term in office. EFCA included three main proposals: certification of a union based on a card-check procedure (rather than secret ballot elections); mandatory arbitration of disputes over negotiations for a first contract (after 120 days); and significantly enhanced penalties for unfair labour practices.[150] The campaign against EFCA was vitriolic: card-check was portrayed as 'a politically motivated subversion of American democratic values',[151] while business groups argued that 'mandatory arbitration would be intrusive, heavy-handed government at its worst'.[152] Yet again, labour law reform crumbled – this time, without a vote in Congress following 'aggressive and cohesive opposition from virtually every major employer group in the country' and their Republican allies.[153]

The result is what Estlund has described as the 'ossification' of US labour law.[154] Not only does the NLRA no longer provide a basis for union growth, it is also stuck in the New Deal economy of the 1930s. The legislation was designed for workplaces based around continuing employment at a fixed location.[155] This model,

[147] C Estlund, *Regoverning the Workplace: From Self-Regulation to Co-Regulation* (New Haven, Yale University Press, 2010) 33–34 (footnote omitted).

[148] R Perlstein, *Reaganland: America's Right Turn 1976–1980* (New York, Simon and Schuster, 2020) 313–15.

[149] J Logan, '"All Deals Are Off": The Dunlop Commission and Employer Opposition to Labor Law Reform', in Lichtenstein and Shermer (n 102) 276.

[150] S Orr, 'Is Democracy in the Cards? A Democratic Defense of the Employee Free Choice Act', in Lichtenstein and Shermer (n 102) 296, 297; Estlund (n 147) 166–67.

[151] Orr (n 150) 300; see also J Getman, *Restoring the Power of Unions: It Takes a Movement* (New Haven, Yale University Press, 2010) 258–59.

[152] Greenhouse (n 79) 202; see also C Fisk and A Pulver, 'First Contract Arbitration and the Employee Free Choice Act' (2009) 70:1 *Louisiana Law Review* 47, 94.

[153] J Logan, 'After EFCA, What Next for Unions? The Future of Labour Law Reform and of Collective Bargaining in the United States', in B Creighton and A Forsyth (eds), *Rediscovering Collective Bargaining: Australia's Fair Work Act in International Perspective* (New York, Routledge, 2012) 270, 270–71.

[154] Estlund (n 147) ch 2.

[155] W Liebman, 'Decline and Disenchantment: Reflections on the Aging of the National Labor Relations Board' (2007) 28 *Berkeley Journal of Labor and Employment Law* 569, 574; see also D Weil,

according to Liebman, is 'increasingly anachronistic' in the globalised economy where 'unionized bargaining units and bargaining unit work regularly disappear'.[156] Lobbying by US unions to remedy the legislation's deficiencies therefore makes sense, although views are divided over whether law reform should be the main priority. Some activists point out that unions have obtained no return from many years of investment in political campaigning.[157] For a number of academics, the reforms consistently sought by organised labour are reactive and mistake the need to redesign the NLRA for the modern economy.[158]

The election of President Biden has again raised hopes that improvements in US labour law might finally be attainable, this time through the proposed Protecting the Right to Organize Act (PRO Act). Among the PRO Act's main amendments of the NLRA are those that would: prevent employers from requiring employees to attend captive audience meetings during a union recognition campaign, or from permanently replacing striking workers; allow workers to engage in secondary boycotts; set time periods for negotiation, mediation and ultimately arbitration of first contract negotiations; and empower the NLRB and courts to impose stronger penalties on employers that engage in unlawful anti-union conduct.[159] The PRO Act would also allow card-check certification of a union, where employer unfair labour practices have interfered with a free vote by employees on union recognition.[160]

The AFL–CIO has lobbied consistently for passage of the PRO Act in recent years.[161] In early 2021, the proposed legislation was at the centre of the 'Workers First Agenda' it was urging upon the new Biden administration and Congress.[162] Biden had committed in his campaign to '[strengthen] public and private sector unions and [help] all workers bargain successfully for what they deserve' and, in some areas, his policy promises went beyond the PRO Act (eg, allowing card-check from the initial stages of union-organising drives).[163] In his first address to Congress, President Biden called for law-makers to pass the PRO Act 'and send it to my desk so we can support the right to unionize'.[164] The legislation was passed by

*The Fissured Workplace: Why Work Became So Bad for So Many and What Can Be Done to Improve It* (Cambridge MA, Harvard University Press, 2014), 41, 184–85.

[156] Liebman (n 155) 574–75 (footnote omitted).

[157] See, eg, McAlevey (n 144) 237.

[158] See, eg, Milkman (n 19) 648; Andrias (n 41) 27–28.

[159] B Magner, 'Breaking down the PRO Act', *Labor Law Lite* (19 January 2021). Available at: www.brandonmagner.substack.com/p/breaking-down-the-pro-act. See also C McNicholas, M Podock, J Wolfe, B Zipperer, G Lafer and L Loustaunau, *Unlawful: U.S. Employers are Charged with Violating Federal Law in 41.5% of All Union Election Campaigns* (Economic Policy Institute, Report, 11 December 2019) 23–25; and ch 11.

[160] Magner (n 159).

[161] L Gerard, 'The PRO Act: Pathway to power for workers', *AFL-CIO* (17 May 2019). Available at: www.aflcio.org/2019/5/17/pro-act-pathway-power-workers.

[162] AFL-CIO, 'The Workers First Agenda' (January 2021). Available at: www.aflcio.org/workers-first-agenda; R Trumka, 'What Biden and Congress can do to support unions', *CNN Business* (26 January 2021).

[163] Biden (n 99).

[164] The White House, *Remarks by President Biden in Address to a Joint Session of Congress* (US Capitol, 28 April 2021).

the House of Representatives in March 2021, but the Senate remains a formidable obstacle to its becoming law.[165] Perhaps recognising this reality, Biden established a White House taskforce to examine how the *executive* branch could advance worker organising and collective bargaining (eg, among government employees or through procurement requirements in federal contracts).[166]

## VII. Conclusion

This chapter has shown that the various efforts of US unions to counter many years of continuing membership decline – including the pioneering of the organising model and attempts to gain recognition from employers outside the NLRA – have not proved successful in overall terms. Community-based campaigns, alt-labour groups and bargaining for the common good have all made an impact. However, there is considerable debate as to whether these various approaches provide a viable basis for the rebuilding of organised labour and worker power, which will be explored more fully in Chapter 11. Despite the clear downward trend in membership numbers, the last few years have revealed some bright spots for the US labour movement. These include signs that young people working in traditionally less-unionised settings – art museums, digital and social media outlets, cafes, game developing and the gig economy – are taking steps to join or form unions.[167]

Another promising indication of renewed labour strength is the upsurge in strike activity across the country in 2018 and 2019. In addition to the #RedForEd teachers' strikes, large numbers of workers went out on strike at Marriott hotels, General Motors plants, Californian healthcare providers,[168] McDonald's and Google.[169] Kamper noted, in 2020, that there were: 'compared to two years ago, 500,000 more workers who have firsthand experience with a strike, and who

[165] E Mueller and H Otterbein, 'Unions warn Senate Democrats: Pass the PRO Act, or else', *Politico* (22 April 2021), noting that while business and Republican opposition remains resolute, unions cannot even count on the support of all Democrats in the Senate.

[166] N Scheiber, 'Biden forms task force to explore ways to help labor', *New York Times* (26 April 2021); S Greenhouse, 'Biden stakes claim to being America's most pro-union president ever', *The Guardian* (2 May 2021).

[167] See, eg, T Lorenz, 'Instagram memers are unionizing', *The Atlantic* (17 April 2019); S Greenhouse, 'The faces of a new union movement', *The New Yorker* (28 February 2020); D Murrell, 'Philly's new generation of unions is young, progressive, and coming to a coffee shop near you', *Philadelphia – City Life* (17 October 2020). Available at: www.phillymag.com/news/2020/10/17/philadelphia-unions/; C D'Anastasio, 'A big union wants to make videogame workers' lives more sane', *Wired* (7 January 2020). See also chs 9 and 10.

[168] S Greenhouse, 'The return of the strike', *The American Prospect* (3 January 2019); S Greenhouse, 'The Autoworkers' strike is bigger than G.M.', *New York Times* (18 September 2019); D Kamper, 'Strike wave: A preliminary assessment of US labour militancy in 2018 and 2019', *Rupture Magazine* (17 February 2020).

[169] M Oswalt, 'Short Strikes' (2020) 95:1 *Chicago-Kent Law Review* 67, 71–77; on the 2018 Google walkouts see, also, ch 1.

might therefore find it easier to strike again ….'[170] Sara Nelson, President of the Association of Flight Attendants-CWA, argues the strike wave reflects the growing demand of US workers 'to be heard' in the face of income inequality and the injustices of the Trump era.[171] Yet she cautions that: '… one strike does not a labor movement make. Nor does five or ten strikes'.[172] This view is validated by changes in the official data measuring strikes involving 1,000 or more workers, showing that 2019 saw 'the largest number of major work stoppages since 2001'.[173] However, the data for 2020 indicated only eight major stoppages had occurred: 'the third lowest number … since the series began in 1947'.[174] The COVID-19 pandemic was no doubt a factor, with unions generally forced into a more defensive posture in the face of the health and economic crisis (as we shall see in Chapter 12). Nevertheless, the rise of coalition-building, alt-labour and (to some extent) use of the strike weapon has generated a sense of dynamism in the American labour movement that belies the gloomier picture conveyed by union density statistics.

[170] Kamper (n 168).

[171] S Nelson, 'Sara Nelson: "People are ready to fight"', *Jacobin* (May 2019). See further J Kerrissey, E Weinbaum, C Hammonds, T Juravich and D Clawson (eds), *Labor in the Time of Trump* (Ithaca, Cornell University Press, 2020).

[172] Ibid.

[173] US Bureau of Labor Statistics, '25 major work stoppages in 2019 involving 425,500 workers' (14 February 2020). Available at: www.bls.gov/opub/ted/2020/25-major-work-stoppages-in-2019-involving-425500-workers.htm.

[174] US Bureau of Labor Statistics, 'Work Stoppages Summary' (19 February 2021). Available at: www.bls.gov/news.release/wkstp.nr0.htm.

# 5

# Australian Unions: From the Accord to 'Change the Rules'

## I. Introduction

The next two chapters examine in some depth how the Australian union movement has responded to falling membership levels since the early 1990s. This chapter traverses the enthusiastic adoption of the US organising model by Australian union leaders, as their influence and power in the Accord era were brought to a halt by the election of the Howard Coalition government in 1996. The effects of the implementation of organising by Australian unions are considered and assessed. This is followed by an exploration of the pivot by the union leadership to a political/legislative strategy in the lead-up to the 2007 election through the 'Your Rights at Work' campaign. Although successful in helping to remove the Howard government from office, the heavy union investment in obtaining favourable labour laws yielded a fairly disappointing outcome under the Rudd/Gillard Labor governments. The chapter recounts the reassessment by unions of their strategies for growth following the Coalition's return to office in 2013, as membership levels fell to new lows. These included innovative membership models and fee structures to provide workers with new opportunities to engage with the union movement. The chapter concludes with the renewed focus of unions on labour law reform – the 'Change the Rules' campaign – and the aftermath of its failure to unseat the Coalition at the 2019 election.

## II. Early 1990s: The Legacy of the Accord

The Australian union movement's approach to tackling membership decline from the early 1990s was shaped by the legacy of its participation in the series of Accord agreements with the Hawke and Keating Labor governments from 1983.[1] Under the Accord, the Australian Council of Trade Unions (ACTU) had partnered with Labor in an economic reform programme to combat high levels of unemployment

[1] S Carney, *Australia in Accord: Politics and Industrial Relations under the Hawke Government* (South Melbourne, Sun Books, 1988).

and inflation. This required unions to exercise restraint in wage demands in return for improvements in the 'social wage'.[2] Tangible benefits for Australian workers followed, including reduced taxes, increases in social welfare payments, universal health care (Medicare) and mandatory employer contributions to retirement funds (superannuation).[3] Union leaders such as ACTU Secretary, Bill Kelty, were closely integrated within the Labor government's processes of economic and social policy formulation throughout the 1980s and into the 1990s.[4] According to Cooper, Ellem and Wright, the ACTU adopted the posture of 'a quintessential core insider group' under the Accord agreements.[5] Over time, this approach attracted increased criticism as it came to be seen that, under the Accord, the membership and bargaining power of unions contracted and real wage levels fell.[6] As Humphreys argues in her powerful dismantling of the Accord, its import 'was that it voluntarily drew the unions into wage suppression, enwrapping them in the state's priorities in the vanguard neoliberal era'.[7]

The union leadership and the Labor government also drove an intensive process of union amalgamations from the late 1980s, eliminating many traditional craft-based organisations with the goal of forming around 20 industry-based 'super-unions'.[8] The objective here 'was to achieve sufficient economies of scale to enable unions to free up resources to focus on their declining density'.[9] The number of federally registered unions fell from 326 in 1986 to 47 in 1995.[10] By 2007, the 20 largest unions accounted for around 80 per cent of all Australian union members.[11] The amalgamation process delivered certain benefits, such as reducing multi-unionism in some workplaces and therefore strengthening the

[2] C Wright, 'The Prices and Incomes Accord: Its Significance, Impact and Legacy' (2014) 56:2 *Journal of Industrial Relations* 264, 265–66.

[3] K Hancock, 'The Accord, the Labour Market and the Economy' (2014) 56:2 *Journal of Industrial Relations* 273, 280; R Cooper, B Ellem and C Wright, 'Policy and the Labour Movement', in B Head and K Crowley (eds), *Policy Analysis in Australia* (Bristol, Policy Press, 2015) 231, 237. Compare E Humphreys, *How Labour Built Neoliberalism: Australia's Accord, The Labour Movement and the Neoliberal Project* (Chicago, Haymarket Books, 2019) 145–53.

[4] On one view, the ACTU Secretary became 'a de facto member of the Cabinet' during this period: M Crosby, *Power at Work: Rebuilding the Australian Union Movement* (Sydney, Federation Press, 2005) 57.

[5] Cooper, Ellem and Wright (n 3) 237.

[6] Ibid, 238; Hancock (n 3) 281–82; T Bramble, *Trade Unionism in Australia: A History from Flood to Ebb Tide* (Port Melbourne, Cambridge University Press) ch 5, especially 154–55; J Buchanan, D Oliver and C Briggs, 'Solidarity Reconstructed: The Impact of the Accord on Relations within the Australian Union Movement' (2014) 56:2 *Journal of Industrial Relations* 288, 290–92.

[7] Humphreys (n 3) 127.

[8] A Barnes and R Markey, 'Evaluating the Organising Model of Trade Unionism? An Australian Perspective' (2015) 26:4 *Economic and Labour Relations Review* 513, 517–18.

[9] Crosby (n 4) 58.

[10] D Peetz, *Unions in a Contrary World: The Future of the Australian Trade Union Movement* (Cambridge, Cambridge University Press, 1998) 133. See, further, K Hose and M Rimmer, 'The Australian Union Merger Wave Revisited' (2002) 44 *Journal of Industrial Relations* 525.

[11] D Peetz and J Bailey, 'Dancing Alone: The Australian Union Movement over Three Decades' (2012) 54:4 *Journal of Industrial Relations* 525, 532.

capacity to deal with employer resistance to unionisation.[12] However in Bramble's view, the wave of union mergers '[did] nothing to rebuild union membership'.[13] According to Barnes and Markey: 'By the early 1990s, the ACTU had come to the realisation that amalgamation *per se* was not enough to reverse union fortunes.'[14]

In parallel with the merger process, the ACTU and Labor implemented another major reform: the transition to an enterprise-based collective bargaining system. This arose partly in response to growing criticism from business leaders and conservative politicians, as the 1980s wore on, about the perceived inflexibility of Australia's centralised system of wage determination through conciliation and arbitration.[15] Union-Labor government responses to these pressures in the late 1980s, through the linking of wage increases under awards to 'structural efficiency' objectives,[16] evolved into the embracing of enterprise-level bargaining by the early 1990s.[17] This made it possible for employers and employee representatives to negotiate agreements suited to the circumstances of the workplace or enterprise, underpinned by the award safety net (through the application of a 'no disadvantage test' by the federal industrial tribunal).[18] This framework was fully implemented by the Keating government's Industrial Relations Reform Act 1993 (Cth), which controversially introduced both union and non-union agreement-making options.[19] Peetz contends that powerful unions such as those in the construction and transport sectors did well in the early years of enterprise bargaining while weaker unions, who had been more dependent on wage rises through arbitration, struggled.[20] Over time, the productivity-orientated project of enterprise bargaining – and its limited capacity as a vehicle for delivering improvements in workers' wages and conditions – came to be seen as yet more evidence of the weakening of the union movement in the Accord years and subsequently.[21] Critically, the shift to enterprise bargaining was one of several steps towards the more extreme deregulation of labour relations which came under the Coalition governments from 1996.[22]

[12] Peetz (n 10) 140, 143.

[13] Bramble (n 6) 176.

[14] Barnes and Markey (n 8) 518. See also ch 6.

[15] See, eg, HR Nicholls Society, *Arbitration in Contempt* (Melbourne, HR Nicholls Society, 1986); Business Council of Australia (BCA), *Enterprise-Based Bargaining Units: A Better Way of Working* (Melbourne, BCA, 1989).

[16] Facilitated by the federal industrial tribunal in successive National Wage Case decisions: R McCallum and P Ronfeldt, 'Our Changing Labour Law' in P Ronfeldt and R McCallum (eds), *Enterprise Bargaining, Trade Unions and the Law* (Sydney, Federation Press, 1995) 1, 8–11.

[17] Ibid, 11–12.

[18] I Ross, 'Bargaining in the Federal System' in Ronfeldt and McCallum (n 16) 30, 30–31.

[19] L Bennett, 'Bargaining Away the Rights of the Weak: Non-Union Agreements in the Federal Jurisdiction' in Ronfeldt and McCallum (n 16) 129.

[20] D Peetz, 'The Impacts and Non-Impacts of Enterprise Bargaining on Unions' (2012) 22:3 *Labour and Industry* 237, 245–46, 248.

[21] C Briggs, 'The End of a Cycle? The Australian Council of Trade Unions in Historical Perspective' in B Ellem, R Markey and J Shields, *Peak Unions in Australia: Origins, Purpose, Power, Agency* (Sydney, Federation Press, 2004) 236, 247–53; Bramble (n 6) ch 6; Humphreys (n 3) 195–99.

[22] See Part IV below.

# III. Adopting the Organising Model

## A. Australian Unions Look to the United States

By 1992, overall union membership in Australia had fallen below 40 per cent of the workforce.[23] Bramble observes that Australian union leaders knew that 'their relatively privileged position' in the Accord years 'was built on sand'.[24] The unexpected re-election of the Keating Labor government in 1993, a rejection of the Coalition's radical economic and industrial relations reform agenda,[25] was only a reprieve. The union movement realised a change of government at the federal level was coming – and this meant membership decline had to be addressed – but union leaders were constrained by 'the agenda of workplace reform to which they remained committed'[26] (including enterprise bargaining). Nevertheless, the lurch to the right in the Coalition's policy direction emboldened the ACTU to explore the potential of the US organising model to restore union power.[27] The report of the peak body's delegation to the USA in 1993 led to the establishment, the following year, of the ACTU Organising Works programme.[28] Under the leadership of Chris Walton, Organising Works sought to counter membership loss by: '[training] a new generation of union organisers capable of talking to non-members and working with them to extend the frontiers of unionism'.[29]

The development of 'flying squads of highly motivated young recruiters who [would] go out and sell our message'[30] drew on the experience of the AFL-CIO's Organising Institute and the Justice for Janitors campaign.[31] Not all unions were on board, though: some were concerned that Organising Works' graduates would lack real, shop-floor experience and about the 'American antecedents' of the programme.[32] Michael Crosby was centrally involved in the early implementation of the organising model in Australia. He explained that – although there were

[23] To 39.6%: Australian Bureau of Statistics (ABS), *Trade Union Members, Australia, August 1992* (Cat No 6325.0).

[24] Bramble (n 6) 176.

[25] See, eg, J Hewson and T Fischer, *Jobsback! The Federal Coalition's Industrial Relations Policy* (Canberra, Liberal Party of Australia, October 1992). This proposal, essentially to leave regulation of employment relations to the free market, was modelled on New Zealand's Employment Contracts Act 1991 and similar laws introduced in two Australian states (Victoria and Western Australia): see D Nolan (ed), *The Australasian Labour Law Reforms: Australia and New Zealand at the End of the Twentieth Century* (Sydney, Federation Press, 1998).

[26] Bramble (n 6) 176.

[27] Barnes and Markey (n 8) 518. See also B Bowden, 'The Organising Model in Australia: A Reassessment' (2009) 20:2 *Labour and Industry* 138, 145–46; and ch 4.

[28] Barnes and Markey (n 8) 518–19; D Peetz and B Pocock, 'An Analysis of Workplace Representatives, Union Power and Democracy in Australia' (2009) 47:4 *British Journal of Industrial Relations* 623, 629.

[29] Crosby (n 4) 5.

[30] Bramble (n 6) 176, quoting then-ACTU President Martin Ferguson.

[31] Ibid. See also R Cooper, 'Peak Council Organising at Work: ACTU Strategy 1994–2000' (2003) 14:1 *Labour and Industry* 1, 3.

[32] Barnes and Markey (n 8) 519.

risks in looking to the US labour movement for solutions – this was necessary because Australian employers were adopting American union-busting tactics. Further, there were clear examples of US unions 'against all the odds … growing and surviving in an environment designed to wipe them out'.[33] For Crosby, it was necessary for union leaders to shift away from their long-standing reliance on the arbitration system and industry-wide wage outcomes through awards as the basis for simply servicing existing members.[34] Most union leaders, he suggested, 'concentrated little or no time on expanding the reach of the union to non-union areas'.[35] Crosby utilised what became known as his '"scary graph" of projected doom for [union] membership and finances'.[36] It foreshadowed that 'if we changed nothing and density continued to deteriorate' at the rate it had reached by the late 1990s, the union movement 'would cease to exist in 2012'.[37]

## B. Australian Organising Campaigns

The implementation of US-style organising in Australia saw a similar concentration on '"strategic targeting", with unions identifying key industries and employers for organising activity and investing substantial resources in breakthrough campaigns'.[38] This involved concentrated efforts to increase union membership in growing private sector industries such as call centres, hotels and casinos,[39] and a 'focus on organising low-wage, minority and migrant workers'.[40] Crosby's formula urged unions to begin a workplace-based organising campaign with detailed knowledge of the business, its workforce and likely employer responses to unionisation; building face-to-face contact with potential members and activists *outside* the workplace (even in workers' homes); and then moving to gradual escalation of pressure tactics on the employer.[41] Some unions adopted the new approach with fervour. In 1999, the NSW Branch of the Transport Workers' Union (TWU) 'rebadged itself as the "TWU, Organising Union"' and 'implemented a strategy of organising around key issues and inspiring rank-and-file activists to pursue those issues'.[42] The Community and Public Sector Union (CPSU) (NSW Branch) utilised a range of 'mobilizing tactics', including

[33] Crosby (n 4) 6.

[34] Ibid, 52. See also D Peetz, *Brave New Workplace: How Individual Contracts are Changing Our Jobs* (Crows Nest, Allen and Unwin, 2006) 160–62.

[35] Crosby (n 4) 52.

[36] Peetz and Pocock (n 28) 629.

[37] Crosby (n 4) 16–17.

[38] E Heery, 'Unions and the Organising Turn: Reflections after 20 Years of Organising Works' (2015) 26:4 *Economic and Labour Relations Review* 545, 547–48.

[39] Bramble (n 6) 204, 207; Cooper (n 31) 7; R Cooper, 'Getting Organised: A White-collar Union Responds to Membership Crisis' (2001) 43:4 *Journal of Industrial Relations* 422.

[40] Heery (n 38) 553.

[41] Crosby (n 4) ch 14; see also ACTU, *Future Strategies: Unions Working for a Fairer Australia* (2003) 38–39, 42.

[42] M Hearn, *Organising Union: Transport Workers Face the Challenge of Change, 1989–2013* (Carlton, Melbourne University Publishing, 2017) 94.

workplace organising committees, demonstrations and holding 'study groups' and meetings of activists in local workers' clubs.[43]

## C. Some Early Wins through Organising in an Increasingly Unfavourable Environment

The shift to organising was reliant on unions having strong, workplace-based, delegate structures, with union representatives actively engaged in recruiting new members and (to some extent) freeing up organisers to concentrate on non-union sites.[44] However, as only 19 per cent of Australian workplaces had an active union presence in 1995, a considerable reallocation of union resources was required to develop the workplace-level infrastructure required to make organising successful.[45] Many unions made this shift, prioritising 'the training or education of workplace delegates, and diverting resources away from tribunal advocacy and "servicing" of members'.[46] For example, the TWU 'developed a network of 540 delegates and 120 activists' through a two-day training programme ('Winning in the Workplace').[47] The ACTU pointed to the US Service Employees International Union's significant membership growth and commitment of 50 per cent of its budget to new member organising activities, urging Australian unions to consider dedicated organising funds or levies.[48] The peak body had, itself, recommitted to the organising agenda in the late 1990s, seconding some Organising Works trainees to affiliated unions to work on workplace membership drives; and establishing the Organising Centre to drive future campaigns[49] (one example centred on residential hotels in Sydney and Melbourne with the Liquor, Hospitality and Miscellaneous Workers' Union (LHMU)).[50]

The new emphasis on workplace-based strategies to grow the union movement was made even more challenging by the harsher legal and institutional environment under the Coalition government from 1996. In addition to the

[43] B Carter and R Cooper, 'The Organising Model and the Management of Change: A Comparative Study of Unions in Australia and Britain' (2002) 57:4 *Relations Industrielles/Industrial Relations* 712, 731–32.

[44] Peetz and Pocock (n 28) 624, 629–30.

[45] Ibid, 629–30.

[46] D Peetz, 'Are Australian trade unions part of the solution, or part of the problem?', *Australian Review of Public Affairs* (February 2015). In some unions, however, tensions arose between leaders and officials in the balancing of traditional servicing roles with new organising responsibilities: see, eg, Carter and Cooper (n 43) 729–32, examining the CPSU NSW Branch. In other unions, Organising Works graduates reported the difficulty they encountered in their organising campaigns when these were not backed up by senior union leaders 'on the ground' in workplaces: see P Holland and G Hanley, *'Organising Works': Is It Meeting the Challenge of Declining Union Membership?* (Monash University, Faculty of Business and Economics, Working Paper 48/02, December 2002) 5.

[47] Hearn (n 42) 94.

[48] ACTU (n 41) 37.

[49] Cooper (n 31) 7–9; see also ACTU, *unions@work: The Challenge for Unions in Creating a Fair and Just Society* (1999).

[50] Crosby (n 4) 210.

loss of 'legitimacy and of political influence' that the ACTU had enjoyed in the Accord years, unions were now 'under attack' from both the government and employers.[51] At a practical level, the Coalition's 1996 reform legislation imposed new restrictions on the legal rights of union officials to access workplaces for recruitment purposes,[52] followed by even more constraints under the 2005 Work Choices legislation.[53] Nevertheless, the deployment of 'bottom-up' campaigns of the type pioneered in US organising had some success in attracting new members to Australian unions. Cooper notes that the 1994 graduates of the Organising Works programme recruited some 10,000 union members (however, from 1995, the ACTU no longer published the results of these recruitment efforts).[54] The ACTU highlighted organising campaigns in the early 2000s that bore fruit in non-union coal mines in the Hunter Valley region of NSW and in the iron ore industry in the Pilbara WA (to some extent offsetting earlier employer de-unionisation strategies).[55] The TWU NSW Branch's organising efforts 'yielded 700 new members in 2001 and 692 between January and August 2002'; by 2005, the union's Sydney sub-branch was 'signing up 111 new members per week'.[56] Overall, Peetz and Pocock ventured the view that (as at the late 2000s) there was:

> … good reason for having confidence in the "turn to organizing" that is underway in Australia, given the positive relationships we find between union power [at the local level] and an organizing approach. … There are positive signs of change – in workplace delegates' perceptions at least – about the situation of unions in some workplaces.[57]

They questioned, though, '[w]hether these signs will be enough to stem the decline in union density and power in Australia'.[58]

## D. Organising Gains were not Sustained

Indeed, the bulk of the evidence indicates that the organising model has not proved successful in its goal of boosting unionisation over the longer term. There was a levelling out in the rate of union membership decline at the turn of the century, with the move towards organising playing some part.[59] Aggregate membership

[51] Cooper (n 31) 9–10.

[52] W Ford, 'Being There: Changing Union Rights of Entry Under Federal Industrial Law' (2000) 13 *Australian Journal of Labour Law* 1.

[53] A Forsyth and C Sutherland, 'From "Uncharted Seas" to "Stormy Waters": How Will Trade Unions Fare under the Work Choices Legislation?' (2006) 16:2 *The Economic and Labour Relations Review* 215, 223–26.

[54] Cooper (n 31) 5; see also Holland and Hanley (n 46) 6–7, noting that, by 1997, Walton claimed that Organising Works had led to increased membership in the retail, horse-racing and fast-food industries.

[55] ACTU (n 41) 40, 44; see also B Ellem, '"We're Solid": Union Renewal at BHP Iron Ore, 1999–2002' (2002) 10:2 *International Journal of Employment Studies* 23.

[56] Hearn (n 42) 96 (footnote omitted).

[57] Peetz and Pocock (n 28) 648–49.

[58] Ibid, 649.

[59] Bowden (n 27) 149; Bramble (n 6) 204.

even grew in six out of the ten calendar years in the 2000s, leading to 'statements of cautious optimism from union leaders that the tide of … decline might be turning'.[60] Bowden notes, however, that the stabilisation in union membership was overtaken by the growth in overall employment levels from 1999 to 2007 and the commencement of a 'collapse' in union density in strongly organised industries including coal mining, electricity and gas and railways.[61] Bowden concluded that (as at 2009):

> … there is little evidence that the organising model has been a panacea for the Australian union movement's woes. Its most notable claim – to have halted the decline in union membership – has little credibility. The steady retreat of membership in the public sector, and in key private sector strongholds, casts doubt on the assumption that workplace organisation can protect unions from decline.[62]

Noting the support of the Australian Manufacturing Workers' Union (AMWU) for the ACTU's strategic organising approach from its inception, Ellem, Goods and Todd observed that: '[Australian] union density fell from 35 per cent in 1994 to under 16 per cent in 2016 …, although we recognize that decline might have been still greater without organizing ….'[63] By 2016, Chris Walton was recommending a new approach, acknowledging that: '… we continue to concentrate on improving our density in a dwindling pool. With a few exceptions, there is limited evidence of unions organising outside traditional areas, and certainly not to scale'.[64] All the way through, alternatives to organising were also being pursued, including a major campaign to remove the Coalition government in 2007 on the back of the deeply unpopular Work Choices legislation.

## IV. Campaigning for Legal Change: Ending Work Choices and the Return of a Labor Government

### A. Unions Look for a Political/Legislative Solution

Greg Combet, who took over from Bill Kelty as Secretary of the ACTU in 1999, had made his name in the fierce waterfront dispute of 1998. As Assistant Secretary of the ACTU and a former official of the Maritime Union of Australia (MUA), he

[60] R Cooper and B Ellem, 'Trade Unions and Collective Bargaining' in M Baird, K Hancock and J Isaac (eds), *Work and Employment Relations: An Era of Change* (Sydney, Federation Press, 2011) 34 at 37.

[61] Bowden (n 27) 149–50.

[62] Ibid, 150–51.

[63] B Ellem, C Goods and P Todd, 'Rethinking Power, Strategy and Renewal: Members and Unions in Crisis' (2019) 58:2 *British Journal of Industrial Relations* 424, 435 (references omitted).

[64] C Walton and E Locke, *The Overdue Case for Change: A Place for Unions in Modern Australia* (January 2016).

was at the forefront of resisting the Howard government's attempt to de-unionise the wharves in conjunction with Patrick Stevedores.[65] Combet was credited with successfully opposing Patrick's corporate restructure and the mass dismissal of its unionised workforce, through a strategy combining traditional industrial tactics, a broad-based community campaign and legal action that went all the way to the High Court of Australia.[66] During his eight years as ACTU Secretary, Combet supplemented the organising approach of building union strength at the workplace level and growing membership in new areas of the economy[67] with other strategies: more engagement by unions in the wider Australian society and supporting union members to engage in political activism aimed at enhancing economic and social outcomes.[68] The emphasis on political campaigning grew stronger following the Labor Party's fourth successive federal election loss in 2004. In that election, the Coalition also obtained control of the Senate, enabling it to enact Work Choices. This was the zenith of the period of state hostility to unions. In response, the ACTU pivoted to a legislative strategy premised on ensuring that Labor would win the 2007 election (then enact more advantageous laws for unions and workers).

## B. The Howard Government's Work Choices Legislation, Countered by 'Your Rights at Work'

The debate over Work Choices dominated the Coalition government's fourth term of office. The introduction of this legislation was the realisation of a long-held dream for Prime Minister John Howard, a leading advocate of radical labour-market reform since the mid-1980s.[69] His government had already implemented a first wave of deregulation in 1996, through legislation restricting the organisational and collective action rights of unions and encouraging employers to reach individual employment agreements with employees.[70] Work Choices went much further than this: it prevented most employees from having any legal recourse for unfair dismissal, handed the wage-fixing and agreement-vetting powers of the federal industrial tribunal to other statutory bodies and removed the

[65] See H Trinca and A Davies, *Waterfront: The Battle that Changed Australia* (Milsons Point, Doubleday, 2000).

[66] G Orr, 'Conspiracy on the Waterfront' (1998) 11 *Australian Journal of Labour Law* 159; *Patrick Stevedores Operations No 2 Pty Ltd v Maritime Union of Australia* (1998) 195 CLR 1.

[67] ACTU (n 49).

[68] ACTU (n 41) 4–19.

[69] P Kelly, *The End of Certainty: The Story of the 1980s* (St Leonards, Allen and Unwin, 1992) 114, 119–20.

[70] Workplace Relations and Other Legislation Amendment Act 1996 (Cth): see R Mitchell, 'Juridification and Labour Law: A Legal Response to the Flexibility Debate in Australia' (1998) 14 *International Journal of Comparative Labour Law and Industrial Relations* 113.

no disadvantage test for collective and individual agreements.[71] This last change arguably had the most profound effect. It meant that employers could offer 'take-it-or-leave it' individual agreements which stripped away employees' entitlements under awards (including penalty rates for working overtime or other irregular hours).[72]

The growing evidence about the inequality caused by these changes after their implementation in March 2006[73] formed the basis for the ACTU's 'Your Rights at Work' campaign. This path had, in fact, been decided upon at the first ACTU executive meeting held after the 2004 election.[74] It developed into a sophisticated, 'multi-platform campaign' incorporating widespread media advertising, protests and rallies involving unionists and the broader community and consistent branding of key messages and their presentation: all of this focused on winning the marginal seats necessary to change the government.[75] The central message was about Work Choices' removal of the Australian concept of the 'fair go' and the impact this had had on workers ('real people') and 'working families'.[76] This was marketed deliberately in terms of '"*your* rights at work", not *union* rights at work'.[77] Unions committed substantial resources to the campaign, both financially and through the allocation of hundreds of activists to local committees.[78] Indeed, according to Ellem, this diversion of resources came at the expense of union organising, which '[fell] off the agenda'.[79]

The Your Rights at Work campaign, in Muir and Peetz's telling: 'was unmatched in Australian political and industrial history for many reasons: its scale and duration; its diversity of activities and technologies; its degree of community support; and its expense'.[80] The campaign succeeded in its goal of unseating the Coalition government in the November 2007 election (and Prime Minister Howard lost his seat in Parliament). The unpopularity of Work Choices and the impact of the campaign against it were widely recognised as pivotal in deciding

[71] There were many more elements of the Workplace Relations Amendment (Work Choices) Act 2005 (Cth), including major constraints on collective bargaining and industrial action: see the special issue (2006) 19:2 *Australian Journal of Labour Law*.

[72] J Fetter, 'Work Choices and Australian Workplace Agreements' (2006) 19:2 *Australian Journal of Labour Law* 210.

[73] See, eg, D Peetz, *Assessing the Impact of 'Work Choices' – One Year On* (Report for the Department of Innovation, Industry and Regional Development, Victoria, 2007).

[74] K Muir, *Worth Fighting For: Inside the Your Rights at Work Campaign* (Sydney, UNSW Press, 2008) 8.

[75] Ibid, 50–52; see also chs 3–5.

[76] Ibid, 58–59, 65–73.

[77] B Ellem, 'Peak Union Campaigning: Fighting for Rights at Work in Australia' (2013) 51:2 *British Journal of Industrial Relations* 264, 273.

[78] K Muir and D Peetz, 'Not Dead Yet: The Australian Union Movement and the Defeat of a Government' (2010) 9:2 *Social Movement Studies* 215, 224; Peetz and Bailey (n 11) 534–35.

[79] Ellem (n 77) 278–79.

[80] Muir and Peetz (n 78) 220; see also R Hall, 'The Politics of Industrial Relations in Australia in 2007' (2008) 50 *Journal of Industrial Relations* 371.

the election outcome.[81] The return of a Labor government under Prime Minister Kevin Rudd saw Combet leave the ACTU for a political career. From that point on, under the leadership of the much lower-profile Jeff Lawrence, the peak union body's major focus was on bedding down the legislation which the Labor Party had pledged to bring forward to abolish Work Choices. Union expectations were high and the new government moved quickly to repeal some of the worst features of Work Choices such as the much-loathed individual workplace agreements.[82] However, Labor's support for a more robust union-orientated reform agenda was qualified: Rudd, unusually for a Labor leader, had no background in the labour movement and had distanced himself from elements of the union leadership.[83] In the lead-up to the election, Labor had moderated its commitments on industrial relations to assuage the business community, promising to maintain flexibility for employers as it restored fairness for workers.[84]

## C. Labor's Fair Work Act Fails to Deliver

The extent to which the ACTU and unions influenced the framing of the Labor government's Fair Work Act 2009 (Cth) (FW Act), has been the subject of some debate. For example, Cooper, Ellem and Wright contend that, in contrast with the Accord era, 'unions struggled to … play the role of, anything beyond a special interest group' and were regarded by the Rudd government as 'only one of the actors engaged in the process of [formulating] public policy'.[85] Similarly, in Muir and Peetz's view, despite their role in the Your Rights at Work campaign, the Labor government treated unions 'in an arm's-length manner, with no more privileges than any number of business groups'.[86] The contents of the resulting legislation may bear these views out, given its only partial support for collective bargaining and retention of previous constraints on industrial action.[87] However, I have argued previously that unions played a central role in framing the FW Act, or at least in ensuring it included certain provisions[88] (such as the low-paid bargaining scheme aimed at enabling award-covered employees to obtain access to collective bargaining, which the LHMU played a key role

[81] Muir and Peetz (n 78) 224–25.

[82] Workplace Relations Amendment (Transition to Forward with Fairness) Act 2008 (Cth): see C Sutherland, 'First Steps Forward (with Fairness): A Preliminary Examination of the Transition Legislation' (2008) 21 *Australian Journal of Labour Law* 137.

[83] C Uhlmann, 'Concerns Rudd moving against unions', *ABC News* (2 July 2007).

[84] K Rudd and J Gillard, *Forward with Fairness: Labor's Plan for Fairer and More Productive Australian Workplaces* (April 2007); K Rudd and J Gillard, *Forward with Fairness: Policy Implementation Plan* (August 2007).

[85] Cooper, Ellem and Wright (n 3) 240–41.

[86] Muir and Peetz (n 78) 226.

[87] See ch 3.

[88] A Forsyth, 'Ten Years of the Fair Work Act: (More) Testing Times for Australia's Unions' (2020) 33:1 *Australian Journal of Labour Law* 122, 126.

in designing[89]). Even so, for many in the union movement, the FW Act was disappointing in its limited re-assertion of collective rights. This assessment formed part of a broader view that the Your Rights at Work campaign had delivered neither the expected legislative dividend, nor a basis for rebuilding the strength of organised labour.[90]

## V. Unions on the Defensive again as the Coalition Returns to Government

By the time the 2010 election came around, workplace relations issues were no longer a focal point, Coalition Opposition Leader Tony Abbott having publicly stated that Work Choices was 'dead, buried and cremated'.[91] The election saw Labor narrowly returned to office under Prime Minister Julia Gillard who, as Minister for Workplace Relations, had overseen the implementation of the FW Act. By September 2013, though, the union movement was again confronted with a conservative government. The Labor Party was voted out of office in the 2013 election, beset by further internal divisions and a leadership change back to Kevin Rudd. Lawrence had been replaced (in 2012) as ACTU Secretary by Dave Oliver, who had to fend off a new round of state hostility. This time, the institutional power of trade unions was the object of the Coalition's regulatory fervour, as a corruption scandal in the Health Services Union provided the justification for establishing the Royal Commission into Trade Union Governance and Corruption.[92] Prime Minister Abbott's government also sought to take on the Construction, Forestry, Mining and Energy Union (CFMEU), through legislation imposing a specific scheme of regulation for unlawful union conduct in the building industry.[93] These were the dominant features of the Coalition's industrial relations agenda in its first term in office[94] and formed the centrepiece of its successful re-election campaign in mid-2016 (under Prime Minister Malcolm Turnbull, who had deposed Abbott the previous year).[95]

[89] See, eg, '20% of workers could gain from low-paid bargaining stream: LHMU', *Workplace Express* (20 November 2008).

[90] Peetz and Bailey (n 11) 537–38; Muir and Peetz (n 78) 226.

[91] L Curtis, 'Abbott sends mixed Work Choices messages', *ABC PM* (19 July 2010).

[92] B Norington, *Planet Jackson: Power, Greed and Unions* (Carlton, Melbourne University Press, 2016); Commonwealth of Australia, *Royal Commission into Trade Union Governance and Corruption* (Final Report, December 2015).

[93] Ultimately enacted in late 2016: Building and Construction Industry (Improving Productivity) Act 2016 (Cth).

[94] The government had given the task of assessing the need for reform of other aspects of industrial relations regulation to the Productivity Commission, which recommended only moderate changes to the FW Act: Productivity Commission, *Workplace Relations Framework: Productivity Commission Inquiry Report* (No 76, 30 November 2015).

[95] D Peetz, 'Industrial Relations Policy and Penalty' in A Gauja, P Chen, J Curtin and J Pietsch (eds), *Double Disillusion: The 2016 Australian Federal Election* (Canberra, ANU Press, 2016) 519.

## VI. Union Decline Intensifies, Spawning Exploration of New Membership Models

### A. Unions have to 'Change, Very Quickly or Die'

Leadership ructions had also surfaced within the ACTU, when Assistant Secretary Tim Lyons (previously an official with the National Union of Workers (NUW)) made an unsuccessful bid in early 2015 for Oliver's Secretary position. Lyons pitched his campaign on the basis that he was 'not interested in party politics' but rather 'outcomes for working people', arguing that unions needed to 'be more active in workplaces and the community'.[96] Although Lyons withdrew from the contest when it became clear he had not garnered sufficient support from key affiliates,[97] his short-lived run for the top job had raised important questions about the ACTU's future direction. The official union membership density figures for 2014, which surfaced in late 2015, triggered particular consternation as they showed a (then) record all-time low of 15 per cent of the workforce.[98] Lyons (by this time, outside the ACTU fold) suggested that the pattern of year-on-year membership loss meant that unions had reached 'an existential moment', and had to 'change, very quickly or die'.[99]

Analysing the 2014 statistics more closely, Peetz indicated that recent membership losses had reversed 'the stabilisation that occurred through most of the 2000s'.[100] In his view, organising efforts were not enough to offset union members departing through retirement and 'a major retention problem amongst relatively new recruits'.[101] Lyons, in collaboration with Troy Burton as directors of the consulting firm Reveille Strategy, contended that unions would struggle to make the traditional 'full service' model of union membership operate sustainably.[102] They presented a range of options, in June 2016, for unions to trial 'new methods of engagement' with 'genuinely transformative' potential.[103] This encouraged placing more responsibility on workers themselves 'to build alternative models to go around legal barriers to organising'.[104] Exploring the capacity of technology based on artificial intelligence and algorithms was, in Burton's

[96] 'ACTU leadership challenger would pursue more "aggressive' agenda', *Workplace Express* (18 February 2015). See also ch 1.

[97] E Hannan, 'ACTU's Tim Lyons to quit after failing to topple Dave Oliver', *Australian Financial Review* (26 February 2015).

[98] ABS, *Characteristics of Employment, Australia, August 2014* (Cat No 6333.0, 27 October 2015).

[99] 'Union density at 15% a "disaster": Experts', *Workforce* (28 October 2015).

[100] D Peetz, 'The ABS Statistics or the Abyss, Statistically?' (Presentation to Queensland Council of Unions Growth Symposium, Brisbane, 14 December 2015) quoted in 'Union Density drop accelerating, as membership decline returns', *Workplace Express* (22 December 2015).

[101] Ibid.

[102] Reveille Strategy, *Transformation vs Adaption: Designing New Forms of Union Organising and Membership* (Research Note, June 2016) 3.

[103] Ibid.

[104] Ibid, 4.

view, critical to helping disparate workers in industries like cleaning form activist groupings around common issues[105] (along the lines of OUR Walmart in the USA).[106]

## B. Constructing 'Tiers to Membership Engagement'

As ACTU Secretary, Oliver addressed the problem of continued membership decline by querying (in February 2016) the approach of 'door-to-door recruitment' and asking unions to consider a range of alternative membership models. This might involve offering workers a choice about membership based on their 'level of engagement, involvement, interest and needs', or 'portable membership' for workers moving in and out of different industries.[107] The foundations for these ideas can be found in a paper by Chris Walton and Erik Locke.[108] They warned that the membership crisis would continue, unless unions adapted the strategy of organising in new areas by moving beyond the (expensive) model of having organisers and industrial officers in the field and a binary approach to membership ('you are either a member or you are not; there is no "half way house" or tiers to membership engagement').[109] The 'new model' they advocated instead, based largely on their work as officials of Professionals Australia[110] and some success in attracting workers like pharmacists to that union, involved several elements. These included: researching the needs, issues and concerns of potential members; using technology to reduce the costs of organising; creating networks among the workforce, initially through social media then following up online or by phone; and offering a variety of membership packages through a 'ladder of engagement'.[111] This could start with adding supporters of union-backed causes (who pay no fees) to a database utilised for campaigns and possible entry into other forms of membership; low-fee members (A$1.00–2.00 per week) who form part of a social media network used to build a presence in non-union areas; mid-range fees (A$300.00–400.00 per year) for members wanting access to a limited range of union services, such as review of contracts or enforcement of minimum wages; through to full-service, full-fee membership (around A$700.00 per year), obligatory for members covered by an enterprise agreement in their workplace.[112]

[105] D Marin-Guzman, 'How "young tech dudes" are decentralising unions with blockchain, AI', *Australian Financial Review* (28 December 2017).

[106] See Reveille Strategy, 'Digital Organising Immersion Training' (undated); and ch 4.

[107] D Oliver, Speech to the ACTU Leadership Forum (Melbourne, 4 February 2016), quoted in 'ACTU's Oliver says the Saints might have the answer', *Workplace Express* (5 February 2016).

[108] Walton and Locke (n 64).

[109] Ibid, 4.

[110] Formerly the Association of Professional Engineers, Scientists and Managers Australia.

[111] Walton and Locke (n 64) 18–19, 22, 33.

[112] Ibid, 15; 'New plan for unions to staunch membership collapse', *Workplace Express* (11 February 2016), noting that average union membership fees in Australia at that time were A$650.00 per year.

Around this time, several unions began experimenting with new grades of membership based on reduced, or no, fees. The NUW introduced a 'community member' category, enabling supporters of its work and campaigns to join the union for A$50.00 per year. NUW Assistant National Secretary Paul Richardson explained that:

> Community membership is not a substitute for industrial membership, it is about building a broad movement for progressive change and linking up union members with community organisations and civil society.[113]

The Media, Entertainment and Arts Alliance (MEAA) established an 'associate member' category, allowing people to join a like-minded community supporting Australia's artistic sector and independent journalism for A$2.00 per week.[114] ACTU Assistant Secretary Scott Connolly said the peak body was 'excited' about the new initiatives of MEAA, NUW and other unions and was expecting positive results from a A$1 million innovation fund for unions to pilot other initiatives.[115] Later in 2016, Connolly indicated that the ACTU's innovation and growth task forces had been examining the approaches of successful membership-based organisations, including the Australian Football League, Hillsong Church, Amnesty International and Greenpeace and online communication forums such as Google Hangouts and LinkedIn.[116]

## C. Unions Can 'Be the Disruptors'

In early 2017, Sally McManus replaced Oliver when he resigned as ACTU Secretary, becoming the first woman to hold that position. A few months later, she told the NexGen2017 Conference that the union movement's 'leaky bucket' (ie, declining membership) could be plugged by enabling unions to recruit 'members for life' irrespective of changing employment or other circumstances.[117] The ACTU had put in place an online membership service to ensure joining a union was as easy as booking an airline flight or an entertainment ticket and would facilitate the automatic transfer of a worker from one union to another when they changed jobs.[118] McManus urged unionists to be open to the use of technology to empower

[113] 'Unions change structures to foster community power base', *Workplace Express* (1 June 2016). In late 2017, the NUW introduced a 'fair go' category of membership (for a joining fee of A$12.00), to enable a group of workers to participate in litigation the union was supporting to recover unpaid wages: 'NUW links with law firm for groundbreaking class action', *Workplace Express* (28 November 2017).

[114] MEAA, 'MEAA Associate Membership'. Available at: www.meaa.org/meaa-associate-membership/. See also 'New "solidarity" membership category for MUA', *Workplace Express* (28 April 2021).

[115] 'Unions change structures to foster community power base', *Workplace Express* (1 June 2016).

[116] 'ACTU seeking to learn from AFL, Hillsong', *Workplace Express* (17 August 2016).

[117] 'Life membership might help unions turn corner: McManus', *Workplace Express* (26 June 2017).

[118] Ibid. See also 'Union membership portal to settle demarcation disputes', *Workplace Express* (15 February 2018); ACTU, 'Join the Movement'. Available at: https://join.australianunions.org.au/.

delegates and members so unions can 'be the disruptors'.[119] The major point of her NexGen2017 speech, though, was to galvanise delegates in support of a shift the ACTU was already making under her leadership: to recreate the success of the Your Rights at Work campaign, using personalised stories of workers' experiences of inequality to highlight the 'broken rules' regulating workplace relations.[120] This time, the union movement's campaign to oust a Coalition government went under the catchcry 'Change the Rules'.

# VII. The 'Change the Rules' Campaign and its Aftermath

## A. Breaking and Changing Unjust Laws

The election of McManus as ACTU Secretary quickly led to a sense of renewed optimism in union ranks, in large part due to her high media visibility and strident agitation for pro-worker legislation. McManus, one of the earliest graduates of Organising Works, deployed skills cultivated as NSW Branch Secretary of the Australian Services Union (ASU) where she had led a successful campaign for equal pay for social and community care workers.[121] On assuming the ACTU's top job (having served as its Campaign Director from 2015), McManus immediately gained national attention in a television interview in which she supported unions breaking laws that are 'unjust'.[122] This marked out the territory which the union movement came to occupy from early 2017 until the federal election of May 2019, through the 'Change the Rules' campaign.[123] Its objective was to expose the deficiencies and unfairness of the FW Act since it commenced operation in 2009, as a basis (once again) for the election of a Labor government that would implement more helpful legislation for unions.

McManus skilfully elevated the prominence of the campaign through her combative communication style, highlighting the problems of income and job insecurity increasingly encountered by many in the Australian workforce.[124] These and other ills arose from the inherent weaknesses of the FW Act, exacerbated by employer 'gaming' of its provisions – for example, to avoid having to engage in collective bargaining with unions.[125] The 'rules' that required 'changing', according

[119] 'McManus calls on unions to disrupt, innovate', *Workplace Express* (26 June 2017).

[120] Ibid.

[121] D Marin-Guzman, 'ACTU chief Sally McManus parlays online support into power', *Australian Financial Review* (4 October 2017).

[122] 'New ACTU boss says it's ok for workers to break "unjust laws"', *ABC 7.30* (15 March 2017).

[123] For a detailed account, see Forsyth (n 88) 132–34.

[124] 'New ACTU leader to push for major overhaul of IR laws', *Workplace Express* (15 March 2017); Marin-Guzman (n 121).

[125] See ch 3.

to the ACTU, included the constraints on sector-wide bargaining, industrial action and union rights of entry.[126] Some tactics were repeated from the Your Rights at Work campaign of a decade earlier, including the heavy use of media advertising to reinforce key messages,[127] a series of big national rallies[128] and targeting of voters in pivotal marginal electorates.[129] These strategies were supplemented by a comprehensive social media campaign, leveraging McManus's large following on Twitter, Facebook and Instagram.[130]

## B. Union Hopes Dashed

The outcome in 2019 was not the same as in 2007. The Labor Party adopted elements of the ACTU critique and some of its proposed solutions.[131] Yet Labor unexpectedly lost the 2019 federal poll as the electorate rejected its ambitious economic policy agenda.[132] This result precipitated a degree of soul-searching about the wisdom of Change the Rules and such a heavy investment by the ACTU in electoral politics.[133] Subsequent assessments credited McManus and ACTU President Michele O'Neill with energising the Australian union movement[134] and placing economic inequality at the forefront of policy discussion.[135] Despite this, Change the Rules failed in its central goal of changing the government:[136] because of the complexity of the arguments the ACTU was trying to make, including its inability to explain the relationship between 'broken' industrial laws and negative outcomes for workers[137] and the 'uncomfortable contradiction' that it was a campaign against Labor's own FW Act.[138] A further factor identified in an

[126] See, eg, 'Bargaining should extend across industries: ACTU', *Workplace Express* (16 April 2018); ACTU, *Congress 2018 Draft Policies and Resolutions* (2018) 30–52; and ch 11.

[127] 'ACTU launches new "change the rules" TV, radio campaign', *Workplace Express* (7 October 2018).

[128] B Schneiders, 'Union movement can't afford to waste goodwill of "staggering" march', *The Age* (9 May 2018); 'Union rally floods Melbourne CBD as tens of thousands march for minimum wage increase', *ABC News* (23 October 2018).

[129] 'Conversations with members crucial in Change the Rules campaign', *Workplace Express* (11 April 2019).

[130] Ibid.

[131] B O'Connor MP, *Wages, Fairness and Inclusive Prosperity* (Speech to the National Press Club, Canberra, 12 December 2018); P Coorey, 'Labor's boost to union power alarms business', *Australian Financial Review* (19 December 2018).

[132] K Murphy, 'Labor loses the unlosable election – now it's up to Morrison to tell us his plan', *The Guardian* (19 May 2019); K Murphy, 'Labor election review blames strategy, adaptability and Bill Shorten for election defeat', *The Guardian* (7 November 2019).

[133] See, eg, D Marin-Guzman, '"I don't get this one": Unions grapple with loss of working-class vote', *Australian Financial Review* (21 May 2019); 'Ex-MP to review unions' election campaign as critics pile on', *Workplace Express* (24 May 2019).

[134] M Phillips, 'Was Change the Rules a failure?', *Medium* (26 May 2019).

[135] D Cahill, 'Change the Rules', *Arena* (June 2019).

[136] Ibid.

[137] See eg, Phillips (n 134); P Karp, 'Election review finds unions had wrong slogan for right message', *The Guardian* (8 August 2019).

[138] Forsyth (n 88) 123; see also D Marin-Guzman, 'ACTU head Sally McManus says Labor's workplace laws sidelined unions', *Australian Financial Review* (6 February 2018).

ACTU-commissioned review of the campaign was that the unions and Labor had been 'out-gunned' by the Coalition's simpler messaging under former marketing executive, Prime Minister Scott Morrison (who had taken over from Turnbull in 2018).[139] As Phillips neatly puts it: 'Inside the union bubble, [Change the Rules] was all that people talked about, but beyond the base it didn't resonate.'[140] For her part, McManus insisted that the ACTU would 'keep talking strongly … on the issues, and that's better rights for working people'.[141] Nevertheless, the outcome of the campaign raised questions as to whether such a central union focus on politics and legal change 'has had its day'.[142]

## C. The Coalition Rounds on Unions (Again)

The Coalition, emboldened by its re-election for a third term, swiftly embarked on yet-another round of state intrusion on the institutional power of unions. A proposed law known by its short-hand title, the Ensuring Integrity Bill, sought to expand the grounds on which union officials could be disqualified from office and on which unions could be deregistered by a court, based on non-compliance with a wide range of laws.[143] The government claimed that, given the privileged position of unions, it was necessary to address 'community concern' about union corruption and 'combat the culture of lawlessness' within some unions.[144] However, Labor Senators echoed the concerns of the ACTU and unions that the bill would 'subject registered organisations to an unprecedented level of political interference'.[145] The Ensuring Integrity Bill was voted down in the Senate in late 2019 and did not pass into law.[146] Yet the debate it engendered in the second half of that year revealed a union movement on the defensive. In the post-election period, the government was also developing a broader, pro-business industrial relations reform agenda.[147] At the start of 2020, just prior to the onset of the COVID-19 pandemic, Australia's unions and the Coalition government were

[139] 'Coalition "swamped" Change the Rules message: Review', *Workplace Express* (8 August 2019).

[140] Phillips (n 134).

[141] D Crowe, '"We'll be the resistance": Unions defend their campaign, vow to take on Morrison', *Sydney Morning Herald* (22 May 2019).

[142] Phillips (n 134). See also chs 1 and 11.

[143] Fair Work (Registered Organisations) Amendment (Ensuring Integrity) Bill 2019, Schs 1 and 2.

[144] Parliament of the Commonwealth of Australia, *Explanatory Memorandum for the Fair Work (Registered Organisations) Amendment (Ensuring Integrity) Bill 2019*, i–ii. This rhetoric revealed that the real target of the Bill was the powerful construction union, although its provisions would apply to all registered unions and employer associations: see, eg, D McCauley, '"We are not the CFMMEU": Nurses plead to be spared from union crackdown', *Sydney Morning Herald* (2 August 2019).

[145] The Senate, Education and Employment Legislation Committee, *Fair Work (Registered Organisations) Amendment (Ensuring Integrity) Bill 2019 [Provisions]* (October 2019) (Labor Senators' Dissenting Report) 63.

[146] B Worthington and A Greenbank, 'Federal government's crackdown on unions rejected by Senate after One Nation sides with Opposition', *ABC News* (28 November 2019).

[147] E Hannan, 'Christian Porter's bid to reshape workplace landscape', *The Australian* (27 June 2019).

locked in a stand-off (not least because the government had re-introduced the Ensuring Integrity Bill into Parliament).[148] As will be shown in Chapter 12, the pandemic transformed that relationship into a cooperative one (at least for a few months) while also hastening the Coalition's opportunistic push for workplace law reform.

## VIII. Conclusion

This chapter has traced the various ways in which Australian unions have sought to rebuild their power and influence over the last 30 years. It showed that, as in the USA, the implementation of strategic organising did not lead to the hoped-for turn around in union membership levels. Australian union leaders have also placed a great deal of faith in electoral politics, through campaigns to remove Coalition governments from office and have sympathetic Labor governments implement favourable labour laws. This strategy was successful in 2007, although the investment did not fully pay off as the Rudd/Gillard Labor governments implemented weak reforms that have failed to stimulate union-based collective bargaining. The second run at this strategy, in 2019, did not produce the electoral outcome that the ACTU and unions expected. The chapter also examined the experimentation by some unions with different approaches to union membership, moving away from the traditional full-fee membership model to connect with some of the hardest workers to organise. The next chapter explores, in greater depth, these kinds of innovations in the shape and accessibility of Australian unions.

[148] D McCauley, 'Porter "absolutely committed" to passing union-busting bill', *Sydney Morning Herald* (29 January 2020).

# 6

# Australian Unions: Innovations, Amalgamations and Organising Beyond the Workplace

## I. Introduction

The last six years have seen some of the most creative experimentation by several Australian unions using new forms of campaigning and activism and a redefinition of the very concept of a 'union'. The clear objective of these efforts is to reach groups of workers who have not traditionally joined unions – but through novel (and in some instances looser) forms of association. Six of these new union prototypes are examined in this chapter, two of them arising from the rejuvenation of one of the world's oldest labour institutions: the Victorian Trades Hall Council (VTHC). The chapter then considers the re-emergence of amalgamations as a union survival strategy, focusing on the motivations for and early experience following two recent mergers. The limited take-up of community-based unionism (in comparison with US unions) is also discussed as a prelude to the examination of one union's efforts to organise and represent workers across the fresh food supply chain.

## II. New Union Models and Digital Prototypes

### A. 'We Have to Show a Whole New Generation Why Unions Are Important'

Under Sally McManus's leadership, the ACTU has adopted other approaches (in addition to the campaign for legal change) to counter membership decline. In late 2019 she stated that the ACTU Executive had 'endorsed a pivot to growth strategy that will change the way we communicate, innovate, support members and campaign into the future'.[1] This would include a particular focus on the entrenched problem of low union membership among younger Australian

[1] 'ACTU looks for growth', *Workplace Express* (6 November 2019).

workers, with union density of only around 8 per cent among the under-25 age group.[2] Announcing the establishment of the Australian Trade Union Institute (ATUI) at the start of 2020, McManus compared the situation in the 1980s, when young people grew up in households where at least one parent was a union member, to the present where: 'We have got to show a whole new generation of Australians why the union movement is important to them.'[3] A paper prepared for the ATUI by Belinda Moore and Chris Walton reinforced this message, highlighting the imperative of unions 'bridg[ing] an ever-widening generational divide' between the 'baby boomers' (who built today's unions but are now retiring) and the 'digital natives' of 'Generation Z'.[4] They recommended that unions tailor specific offerings to attract younger workers who 'crave convenience, impact and personalisation' and 'provide a home for every worker' including the almost 40 per cent of the workforce engaged in insecure work.[5] This would require a shift from 'a traditional service provider operational model' to various 'community platform operating models' (including free membership and flexible 'paid upgrade options').[6] The ACTU Union Innovation Hub has been set up to support unions undertaking these and other kinds of transformation through digital innovation.[7]

## B. Hospo Voice

In 2018, United Voice (UV)[8] launched a 'digital union' called 'Hospo Voice', aimed at attracting millennial workers in the notoriously difficult to organise hospitality industry[9] through a 'Netflix-style membership'.[10] Workers pay A$9.99 per month for access to a range of online tools to deal with the major employment problems that arise in bars, cafés and restaurants.[11] These include 'Pay Checker' and 'Record My Hours' (to counter underpayment); 'Fair Plate' (enabling staff to warn each other about 'dodgy' venues);[12] and the 'Mobilise' app, 'an AI-powered chatbot

[2] Ibid; see also ch 2.

[3] E Hannan, 'Unions target new generation to lift members', *The Weekend Australian* (25–26 January 2020).

[4] B Moore and C Walton, *Rise! Empowering Australian Workers through the Collective Spirit and Collaborative Energy of Unions* (ATUI/Strategic Membership Solutions, 7 May 2020), 10–12.

[5] Ibid, 12–13.

[6] Ibid, 17–18; see also 33–45.

[7] Ibid, 27; ACTU, 'Union Innovation Hub'. Available at: www.uhub.org.au/. See also C Walton, *Guide to Organising and Campaigning with Digital Tools* (ACTU Union Innovation Hub, April 2021).

[8] The LHMU changed its name to UV in 2010. UV then merged with the NUW in 2019 to form the United Workers Union: see Part III below.

[9] B Preiss, 'Hospitality workers offered union membership for $10 a month', *The Age* (21 May 2018).

[10] Hospo Voice, 'Join Now: United We Stand Back Up'. Available at: www.hospovoice.org.au/join.

[11] Ibid.

[12] Hospo Voice, 'Let's Turn the Tables'. Available at: www.hospovoice.org.au/; note, also, the campaign against sexual harassment in the industry, see Hospo Voice, 'Respect is the Rule'. Available at: www.hospovoice.org.au/respect_is_the_rule.

backed by a team of volunteer experts' (which workers can use to obtain quick answers to questions on their employment rights).[13] These digital tools are the first stage in Hospo Voice's 'online to offline' strategy, through which it draws upon online connections with workers to build 'momentum' for attending rallies and union meetings.[14] Hospo Voice uses street protests and campaigning to focus public and media attention on underpayment of award minimum wages by hospitality venues.[15] It helped bring to light underpayments by restaurants run by celebrity chefs including George Calombaris's MAdE Establishment Group and allegations of wage theft at Neil Perry's Rockpool Dining Group and Heston Blumenthal's Dinner by Heston.[16] Hospo Voice's activism has led to the Fair Work Ombudsman (FWO) investigating and bringing enforcement action against several hospitality industry venues[17] and the recovery of unpaid wages for workers.[18]

Hospo Voice also got behind the campaign to criminalise wage theft in Victoria.[19] Once the Victorian legislation was enacted in June 2020,[20] Hospo Voice (which was initially based in that state) set its sights on organising and pushing for similar laws in New South Wales.[21] In October 2020, the union uncovered the alleged underpayment of migrant workers at the Watson's Bay Hotel on Sydney Harbour.[22] Then, in November, Hospo Voice released a research report on the devastating impact of the COVID-19 pandemic on hospitality workers, including the prevalence of insecure work in the sector.[23] Hospo Voice stated in the report that its membership had increased by 76 per cent since February 2020 and that more than 10,000 workers had taken part in its online meetings, protests, petitions

[13] Hospo Voice, 'Unions Mobilise AI to Turn the Tables on Wage Theft in Hospitality' (7 December 2020). Available at: www.hospovoice.org.au/news/unions-mobilise-ai-to-turn-the-tables-on-wage-theft-in-hospitality/, noting that Hospo Voice developed Mobilise in partnership with the ACTU and United for Respect in the USA. See ch 4.

[14] Call Hub, 'The stirrings of Hospo Voice (interview with Communications and Campaigns Director Tim Petterson)'. Available at: https://callhub.io/hospo-voice-callhub-case-study/.

[15] 'Union takes new approach to curbing "wage theft"', *Workplace Express* (4 December 2017); B Knight and M Marozzi, 'Melbourne's Barry café accused of underpaying staff', *ABC News* (23 April 2018); AAP, 'Chinatown restaurant staff got $5/hour, slept in kitchen, union claims', *The Age* (17 July 2019).

[16] ABC, 'George Calombaris's MAdE Establishment underpaid workers $7.8 million', *ABC News* (18 July 2019); 'Rockpool defends new underpayment claims', *Workplace Express* (25 October 2019); B Schneiders, 'Heston Blumenthal, the tax havens and the-ripped off workers', *Sydney Morning Herald* (9 December 2018).

[17] M Marozzi, 'Fair Work Ombudsman launches action against Barry café over underpayment allegations', *ABC News* (25 September 2019); ABC, 'Fair Work Ombudsman investigates timesheet tampering claims at Rockpool Dining Group', *ABC News* (25 October 2019).

[18] 'Hospo Voice claims "stunning victory"', *Workplace Express* (17 October 2019).

[19] 'Unions seeking wage theft laws in Victoria', *Workplace Express* (9 April 2018).

[20] Wage Theft Act 2020 (Vic).

[21] N Bonyhady, 'Sydney hospitality industry under spotlight after Victoria criminalises wage theft', *Sydney Morning Herald* (17 June 2020).

[22] Hospo Voice, '"The Worst Place I Ever Worked": Tell Watsons Bay to Stop Exploiting Migrant Workers'. Available at: www.hospovoice.org.au/petitions/watsons-bay-time-to-pay/.

[23] Hospo Voice, *#RebuildHospo: A Post-COVID Roadmap for Secure Jobs in Hospitality* (November 2020). See ch12.

and surveys.[24] Kimberley and McCrystal consider Hospo Voice to be an important example of organising outside the workplace, in one particular case: 'giving [workers] the collective confidence and strength to demand their legal entitlements, in turn remaking their workplace as a union site'.[25] Having established itself as an effective campaigning organisation, Hospo Voice is turning its attention to the real challenge of using that energy to build an ongoing vehicle for collective strength among hospitality workers.[26]

## C. Hair Stylists Australia

A similar approach to Hospo Voice can be seen in Hair Stylists Australia, a 'union-within-a-union' set up by the Australian Workers' Union (AWU) in early 2017.[27] Like hospitality, the hairdressing industry is beset by widespread underpayments with a high proportion of younger workers employed in small businesses with low union membership.[28] The venture into hairdressing was a major shift for the blue-collar union which traditionally had covered industries such as steel, aluminium, oil and gas production and civil construction. The AWU viewed the establishment of Hair Stylists Australia as an opportunity for membership growth, with its task being 'fundamentally about organising the unorganized' and providing a much-needed voice for exploited workers.[29] Hair Stylists Australia engages with workers mainly online, providing advice and support on workplace rights[30] and access to a jobs board for positions with 'ethical salons'.[31] It has a tiered fee structure reflecting workers' income and seniority in the industry, with different rates for apprentices, qualified hairdressers and sole traders[32] (as 'most hairdressers aspire to become salon owners at some stage'[33]). For the AWU, Hair Stylists Australia signals a transition to organising around professional identity which the union's Assistant National Secretary Misha Zelinsky indicated 'can be

[24] Ibid, 24.

[25] N Kimberley and S McCrystal, 'Contested Spaces: Unions and Employer Controlled Access to Space for Organising under the Fair Work Act 2009 (Cth)' (2020) 33:1 *Australian Journal of Labour Law* 139, 153–54, referring to the Barry café underpayments (see nn 15 and 17).

[26] Hospo Voice, 'How to inspire collective action in the hospo workplace' (15 February 2021). Available at: www.hospovoice.org.au/news/collective-action-in-hospo/. See ch 11.

[27] 'Style makeover as AWU embraces hairdressers', *Workplace Express* (27 February 2017).

[28] 'Union, FWO tackle hairdressing's "cultural problem"', *Workplace Express* (7 August 2018).

[29] 'Style makeover as AWU embraces hairdressers', *Workplace Express* (27 February 2017).

[30] Hair Stylists Australia, 'Support (know your rights at work)'. Available at: https://hairstylistsaustralia.com.au/support/.

[31] Hair Stylists Australia, 'Jobs'. Available at: https://hairstylistsaustralia.com.au/jobs/ and 'Ethical Salons'. Available at: https://hairstylistsaustralia.com.au/ethical-salons/.

[32] Hair Stylists Australia, 'Who Can Join?'. Available at: https://hairstylistsaustralia.com.au/membership/.

[33] AWU National Secretary Daniel Walton, quoted in 'Style makeover as AWU embraces hairdressers', *Workplace Express* (27 February 2017).

very powerful'.[34] On the union's efforts to recruit hairdressers using digital technology, he added: 'the days of sending a person and a car to organise site by site are over'.[35]

## D. Game Workers Unite Australia

Another industry with a high proportion of young, exploited workers – in this instance, often self-employed freelancers – saw the birth of Game Workers Unite Australia (GWUA) in mid-2018.[36] GWUA is the Australian arm of the international Game Workers Unite movement, also to be found in the UK, several other European countries and the USA.[37] The international body was formed in 2016. It took clearer shape following a round table hosted by the International Game Developers Association at the US Game Developers Conference in February 2018 (the meeting was described as pushing a 'union-busting' line which counselled workers against organising).[38] Tim Colwill, a former game developer, helped to launch GWUA and is one of its four volunteer 'moderators' who provide information to game workers about their rights and organise events.[39] In 2018, he explained the rationale for forming GWUA and its objectives in these terms:

> [Game workers traditionally] don't organise or unionise, we're scared, our jobs are so precarious. … All the people coming up have been raised in an era where unions have been, in a very real way, removed from the public consciousness. … Gaming is a very creative field, and it's all about passion and how lucky you are to get this job. But if you're earning less than the minimum wage, you're doing unpaid weekends, you have no superannuation or job security – all the passion in the world won't help you pay your electricity bills. … [However] one of the really important things we can do as a union – we can all come together and say we all agree that we will not do this work for less than this rate.[40]

Somewhat confusingly, GWUA's website states that it 'is not a union': rather, it is a group of unionists working with two established Australian unions with coverage of game workers, the Media, Entertainment and Arts Alliance (MEAA) and Professionals Australia.[40] It is clear, though, that GWUA is seeking to provide

[34] D Marin-Guzman, 'How "young tech dudes" are decentralising unions with blockchain, AI', *Australian Financial Review* (28 December 2017).

[35] Ibid.

[36] 'Video game workers unite to create the industry's first union', *Workforce* (7 June 2018).

[37] Game Workers Unite, 'Get Involved'. Available at: www.gameworkersunite.org/get-involved.

[38] 'Video game workers unite to create the industry's first union', *Workforce* (7 June 2018). See also '"It's very David and Goliath": Inside the growing effort to unionise video game developers', *GeekWire* (9 May 2018); J Weststar and M Legault, 'Why Might a Videogame Developer Join a Union?' (2017) 42:4 *Labor Studies Journal* 295.

[39] GWUA, 'About Us'. Available at: www.gameworkers.com.au/about/.

[40] Ibid.

a collective voice for games developers and others working in the industry (including journalists, streamers, cosplayers and marketing staff).[41] One of the major issues GWUA tries to address is the dedication of game workers that leads to overwork, also described as the 'crunch culture' of the industry.[42] In 2019, a GWUA survey of 258 games developers across Australia showed that one in every five directly employed developers earns less than the award minimum wage of A$51,498 per year.[43] Another survey focused specifically on freelance games developers to produce a database of freelance game-development rates.[44] GWUA is exploring closer links with MEAA and Professionals Australia that would enable it to become a fee-based organisation providing industrial representation and other support to members.[45] Its partnership with Professionals Australia looked to be taking clearer shape in January 2021, when that union confirmed that game developers were among the tech-industry workers it was seeking to prioritise in its organising.[46]

## E. Retail and Fast Food Workers Union

The Retail and Fast Food Workers Union (RAFFWU) is another form of innovative unionism, but with important differences from the examples already considered. RAFFWU was formed in late 2016, in opposition to Australia's second-largest union, the Shop, Distributive and Allied Employees Association (SDAEA).[47] The founding basis of RAFFWU is its position that, over many years, the SDAEA has entered into enterprise agreements with major retailers and fast-food chains, in which organisational rights (including union access to new employees at inductions) have been prioritised over obtaining the best outcomes for a largely young, casualised workforce.[48] The SDAEA denies allegations that it has entered into

[41] J Maxwell, 'Co-op mode: Aussie games devs fight for labour rights', *ScreenHub* (17 August 2019).

[42] A Bogle, 'Video games are a multi-billion-dollar industry: do its workers need a union?', *ABC News* (26 October 2018). See also R Brogan, 'The Digital Sweatshop: Why Heightened Labor Protections Must be Implemented Before Crunch Causes the Backbone of the Video Game Industry to Collapse', *Texas Review of Entertainment and Sports Law*, forthcoming.

[43] GWUA, 'Survey of Australian Games Developers Shows Ongoing Underpayments, Job Security Fears'. Available at: www.gameworkers.com.au/game-developer-survey-release-v2/; directly employed developers made up 50% of the workers surveyed, while 13% were freelancers and 11% contractors.

[44] GWUA, 'GWU Australia Launches New Project to Help Freelance Game Developers'. Available at: www.gameworkers.com.au/gwu-australia-freelancer-rates-survey-launch/.

[45] GWUA, 'Have Your Say in the Future of GWU Australia'. Available at: https://us18.campaign-archive.com/?u=3e0adad9b05d76c26469e8ef2&id=f210dfc898.

[46] See ch1.

[47] A Vos, 'SDA v RAFFWU: A battle at the heart of the Australian union movement', *Medium* (30 June 2019).

[48] B Schneiders and R Millar, 'New union to challenge "shoppies" after massive wages scandal', *The Age* (21 November 2016); D Nicholson, 'Australia's Youngest Union is Organizing Retail and Fast Food Workers', *Jacobin* (11 May 2020).

'sweetheart' deals of this kind with employers.[49] The formation of new unions like RAFFWU is relatively uncommon in Australia, because unions registered under federal law are generally able to successfully object to the registration of another organisation that might fall within their established rights of coverage.[50] RAFFWU has not applied to become a registered organisation under the FWRO Act. Instead, it is an incorporated association under Victorian law and a registered Australian body under the Corporations Act 2001 (Cth), enabling it to operate in all states.[51] Even without registered organisation status, RAFFWU has been able to play an active role in defending its members' interests, particularly by intervening in Fair Work Commission (FWC) proceedings to oppose employer applications (frequently supported by the SDAEA) for approval of enterprise agreements. This is possible because RAFFWU can be appointed as a 'bargaining representative' under the FW Act.[52]

RAFFWU Secretary, Josh Cullinan, first rose to prominence (before the union was formed) as the representative of a lone employee who successfully challenged the approval of a proposed agreement for 77,000 Coles supermarkets employees in May 2016. A Full Bench of the FWC found that the agreement would have disadvantaged some part-time and casual employees,[53] even though it had been voted for by around 90 per cent of staff and had been negotiated with the SDAEA.[54] Cullinan then formed RAFFWU with a number of disaffected SDAEA members, pledging the development of 'a strong successful union led by retail and fast food workers; they haven't had that for decades'.[55] It is not precisely clear how successful RAFFWU has been in attracting members.[56] However, it has achieved

[49] See, eg, N Bonyhady, 'How a controversial union underwent a "quiet revolution"', *Sydney Morning Herald* (26 July 2020).

[50] Under s 19(1)(j) of the Fair Work (Registered Organisations) Act 2009 (Cth) (FWRO Act), there must be no other organisation to which members of an applicant for registration 'could more conveniently belong' and that can 'more effectively represent those members' than the applicant would.

[51] RAFFWU, 'Governance and Finance'. Available at: https://raffwu.org.au/about/governance-finance/, noting that RAFFWU is also an 'industrial association' under the Fair Work Act 2009 (Cth) (FW Act). Industrial associations are not registered organisations under the FWRO Act, but they (and their members) have access to some rights under the FW Act, such as freedom of association protections: see A Stewart, A Forsyth, M Irving, R Johnstone and S McCrystal, *Creighton and Stewart's Labour Law*, 6th edn (Sydney, Federation Press, 2016) 834.

[52] As noted in ch 3, under s 176(1)(c) of the FW Act, an employee can appoint another person as their bargaining representative for a proposed enterprise agreement. Bargaining representatives are able to exercise various rights in the making and approval of an agreement. Bargaining representative status also means that RAFFWU can organise employees to take protected industrial action under the FW Act and represent members under enterprise agreement dispute resolution clauses. However, it cannot exercise certain statutory rights available only to registered unions (including rights of entry to workplaces, and the right to be covered by and to enforce an agreement).

[53] *Hart v Coles Supermarkets Australia Pty Ltd and Bi-Lo Pty Ltd* [2016] FWCFB 2887.

[54] B Schneiders and R Millar, 'Coles workers worse off under deal with shoppies union', *Sydney Morning Herald* (23 May 2015).

[55] Schneiders and Millar (n 48).

[56] As it is unregistered, RAFFWU is not required to report annual membership figures to the Registered Organisations Commission. Nicholson (n 48) states that RAFFWU 'boasts several thousand

some important outcomes for the workers it does represent, among the many cases it has pursued on their behalf.

In 2017, the union obtained termination of expired agreements covering Domino's Pizza outlets, which Cullinan claimed exposed a 'national scandal of underpayment' at the company including the removal of award penalty rates and casual loadings.[57] RAFFWU also opposed the replacement agreement under negotiation between Domino's and the SDAEA, the company ultimately deciding not to conclude an agreement.[58] In 2018–2019, RAFFWU ran a case seeking termination of the expired 2012 agreement covering Woolworths supermarkets, arguing that it left workers up to A$1 billion worse off compared to the General Retail Industry Award.[59] However, this was overtaken by the outcome of the union's parallel effort to block the FWC's approval of a new enterprise agreement for Woolworths staff.[60] A Full Bench of the FWC upheld an earlier decision approving the agreement, finding against RAFFWU's contentions that the company had misled employees in the information it provided ahead of a vote on the SDAEA-negotiated deal.[61]

In contrast, RAFFWU won an important case in 2020, the Federal Court of Australia finding that a McDonald's franchisee in Brisbane had unlawfully coerced employees and misrepresented their right to take toilet breaks.[62] Justice Logan ruled that it was 'a reckless falsehood' for the McDonald's store manager to tell staff, on Facebook, that they would be fortunate to be allowed to use the toilet or take a drink outside the ten-minute break permitted for shifts of four hours or more under the enterprise agreement.[63] In a subsequent decision imposing a penalty of A$82,000 on the franchisee, Justice Logan found that the Facebook post had been aimed at quelling agitation by employees about their right to take breaks and praised RAFFWU for its role in policing the individual rights of workers as a 'service to the national interest'.[64]

paying members' (as of May 2020). In *Retail and Fast Food Workers Union Incorporated* [2021] FWC 3068 at [3], in the course of rejecting the union's application for a ballot to determine whether it had majority employee support for collective bargaining, the FWC noted that RAFFWU claimed to have more than 1,000 members (and represent more than 2,100) out of 103,600 employees at Coles Supermarkets.

[57] B Schneiders and R Millar, 'Pizza driver battles with Domino's, union for pay deal with the lot', *The Age* (21 August 2017); see also 'Agreement for Domino's falls after FWC ruling', *Workplace Express* (1 November 2017), noting that the SDAEA had initiated the agreement termination proceedings but then sought to have them placed on hold until a new agreement could be negotiated with Domino's.

[58] 'Domino's abandons bargaining, plumps for award', *Workplace Express* (26 March 2018).

[59] S Letts, 'Woolworths faces union legal action to scuttle EBA and get $1b in backpay', *ABC News* (23 August 2018).

[60] 'Bench throws out "ersatz" bid to quash Woolies deal', *Workplace Express*, 13 May 2019.

[61] *Retail and Fast Food Workers Union v Woolworths Group Limited and Others* (2019) 289 IR 214, the Full Bench noting at [1] that RAFFWU had acted as bargaining representative for around 105 employees out of 107,000 staff at 1,009 Woolworths stores across Australia.

[62] *Retail and Fast Food Workers Union v Tantex Holdings Pty Ltd* (2020) 299 IR 56.

[63] Ibid at [116]; teenage school students and young university students made up a large proportion of the McDonald's franchisee's workforce.

[64] *Retail and Fast Food Workers Union v Tantex Holdings Pty Ltd (No 2)* (2020) 302 IR 360 at [58], [66]. See also 'McDonald's facing class action over paid breaks', *Workplace Express* (2 October 2020).

## F. Victorian Trades Hall Council

### *(i) The Remaking of the 'Parliament of Labour'*

VTHC was established in 1856, 'making it the first metropolitan peak union body formed in an Australian colony'.[65] The foundation stone for its distinctive building on the northern edge of the Melbourne central business district was laid in 1874.[66] It is 'recognised as the first purpose built trades hall in the world' and has been described as 'the Parliament of Labour'.[67] From a dominant position in the heyday of smaller unions occupying offices in the Trades Hall building, it fell into decline in the aftermath of the wave of union mergers in the late 1980s and early 1990s.[68] Although it played an important role in the opposition to the Kennett Liberal government's 1992 emasculation of state industrial laws and the deregulatory agenda of the Coalition government federally (1996–2007),[69] VTHC was increasingly losing relevance. That was, until Luke Hilakari was elected Secretary in 2014 and began the revitalisation of both the building and the purpose of Trades Hall.[70] The 34-year-old Hilakari brought in a team of younger, energetic staff and transformed VTHC into a campaigning organisation.[71]

This brought early success as Trades Hall mobilised hundreds of public service workers such as nurses, teachers and paramedics to campaign for the election of the Andrews Labor government in Victoria in late 2014.[72] Four years later, the feat was repeated when Hilakari oversaw a social media, door knocking and telephone campaign by unionists which helped secure the state Labor government's landslide re-election. Union members and their families held direct conversations with voters on issues forming part of Labor's 2018 election agenda, including the need for tougher laws on wage theft and workplace deaths.[73] Commenting on the success of this strategy, Hilakari said: 'Trades Hall is all about experimenting, combining new technology, high-quality storytelling and the power of the thousands of people we have in our movement.'[74] A similar approach has been adopted

[65] C Brigden, 'Power and Space in the Victorian Trades Hall Council' in B Ellem, R Markey and J Shields, *Peak Unions in Australia: Origins, Purpose, Power, Agency* (Sydney, Federation Press, 2004) 219.

[66] VTHC, 'Trades Hall History'. Available at: www.weareunion.org.au/history.

[67] Brigden (n 65) 219; see also C Brigden, 'Creating Labour's Space: The Case of the Melbourne Trades Hall' (2005) 89 *Labour History* 125, 126–27, noting the origins of VTHC in the eight-hour day movement in Victoria.

[68] S Green, 'Trade Unions: The new broom in the hall', *Sydney Morning Herald* (11 December 2014).

[69] T Bramble, *Trade Unionism in Australia: A History from Flood to Ebb Tide* (Port Melbourne, Cambridge University Press) 171–72; 'Howard's IR plans find a foe in new Trades Hall head, Brian Boyd', *ABC Radio (The World Today)* (8 March 2005).

[70] Green (n 68); M Phillips, 'Bringing to life the story of the "People's Palace"', *Medium* (9 October 2015).

[71] Green (n 68); A Patty, 'The changing face of trade unions', *Sydney Morning Herald* (13 November 2017).

[72] 'Unions to use Victorian campaign strategy north of the border', *Workplace Express* (2 December 2014).

[73] 'Victorian unions borrow from Bernie Sanders' playbook', *Workplace Express* (26 November 2018).

[74] Ibid.

in recent federal election campaigns, although with less success.[75] Hilakari's rejuvenation of the Victorian labour movement has extended beyond this focus on electoral politics. VTHC seeks to rebuild collective worker power by enabling workers to form different types of attachment to the union movement, including through two dedicated centres for young and migrant workers.

## *(ii) VTHC Young Workers Centre*

The VTHC Young Workers Centre (YWC) was established in September 2015, and officially launched on 24 February 2016 as: 'a one-stop-shop combining education, information, legal assistance, and campaigning to end the exploitation of young people in Victoria'.[76] YWC was initially partly funded by a WorkSafe Victoria grant, enabling it to provide information, advice and support to young workers and educate school children about their rights in the workplace and the role of unions.[77] It is the first specialist community legal centre set up to advise young people on employment issues.[78] Like Hospo Voice, a major aspect of YWC's work has involved exposing wage theft and other forms of exploitation of young workers, and obtaining redress for them through representation and legal proceedings.[79] Its major campaigns have focused on allegations of mistreatment, harassment and bullying of staff in the Mecca cosmetics chain;[80] underpayment of wages and superannuation affecting workers in Pressed Juices stores;[81] and alleged exploitation in the form of extended traineeship arrangements (on low rates of pay) in the Grill'd burger chain.[82]

YWC played a central role in the campaign for wage theft legislation in Victoria, publicising case studies of underpayment and developing legislative proposals for consideration by the state government.[83] Research is another important aspect of YWC's work, including surveys of young workers and submissions to

[75] P Karp, '"Breaking down the myths": blue-ribbon Liberal seats on unions' long target list', *The Guardian* (20 April 2019); T Bramble, 'Unions' pro-Labor electoral strategy a failure', *Red Flag* (20 May 2019). See also ch 5.

[76] YWC, 'How to Launch the Young Workers Centre' (24 February 2016). Available at: www.youngworkers.org.au/launchywc.

[77] P Karp, 'Unions launch Young Workers Centre "to empower" youth against exploitation', *The Guardian* (19 February 2016); see also YWC, 'What is the Young Workers Centre?'. Available at: www.youngworkers.org.au/about.

[78] YWC, *Annual Report 2016–2017*, 4, 10.

[79] YWC recovered over A$1 million for young Victorian workers over its first four years of operation: YWC, *Annual Report 2016–2017*, 10, *Annual Report 2017–2018*, 8, *Annual Report 2018–2019*, 7, *Annual Report 2019–2020*.

[80] D Powell, '"It's all fake": Beauty giant facing bullying claims', *The Age* (17 November 2019).

[81] C Waters, '"We always had to chase": Pressed Juices staff owed wages as stores close', *Sydney Morning Herald* (7 March 2019).

[82] 'Grill'd burger chain accused of keeping young workers in underpaid roles through traineeships', *ABC News* (7 December 2019).

[83] See YWC, *Briefing: Criminalising Wage Theft* (May 2018); K Fitzpatrick, 'Wage Theft and Young Workers' in A Stewart, J Stanford and T Hardy (eds), *The Wages Crisis in Australia: What it is and what to do about it* (Adelaide, University of Adelaide Press, 2018) 174.

federal and state inquiries. This provides intellectual backing for campaigns such as 'Rights for Riders', which exposes the misclassification of food delivery riders working in the gig economy.[84] YWC is not a union, but promotes collective activism through training and outreach programmes including the annual VTHC 'Union Summer' course.[85] Former Director, Keelia Fitzpatrick, described YWC as 'a new approach to engaging young people ... using traditional campaigning tactics like snap protests and recruitment blitzes to build worker power' along with 'new digital tools'.[86] Emulating the YWC model, a Young Workers Centre has been established in Canberra,[87] while a Young Workers Hub has been set up in Brisbane.[88]

### *(iii) Migrant Workers Centre*

The Migrant Workers Centre (MWC) commenced operations in August 2018, with funding from a Victorian government grant of A$2 million.[89] MWC is an incorporated association which initially sub-contracted its establishment and operation to VTHC through an agreement approved by the state government,[90] before becoming an independent non-government organisation with a volunteer board in 2021.[91] MWC's stated role is to '[empower] migrant workers in Victoria to understand our rights, enforce them in our workplaces, and connect with other migrant workers', through education, assistance and collaboration with community partners.[92] The centre also bridges the linguistic and cultural gaps that disadvantage overseas workers: its publications on workplace rights are translated into, and its organisers speak, a range of languages.[93] A major driver for MWC's establishment was to counter the increasing instances of underpayment and other forms of exploitation of temporary visa-holders in Australia. The extent of this problem became clear in 2015, with media coverage of widespread mistreatment of horticultural workers and systemic underpayment in the 7-Eleven convenience store chain.[94] Many federal and state inquiries followed, revealing mounting

[84] See ch 9.

[85] YWC, *Annual Report 2018–2019*, 11; VTHC, 'Union Summer'. Available at: www.weareunion.org.au/unionsummer.

[86] Fitzpatrick (n 83) 183.

[87] See: https://youngworkerscbr.org.au/.

[88] See: http://ywhub.org.au/.

[89] L Henriques-Gomes, '"The big one is underpayment": new centre fights migrant workers' exploitation', *The Guardian* (5 August 2018). Further Victorian government funding took the total amount of support for MWC to A$3.384 million to March 2021: Victorian Auditor-General's Office, *Grants to the Migrant Workers Centre: Independent Assurance Report to Parliament* (February 2021) 2.

[90] Victorian Auditor-General's Office (n 89) 3–4.

[91] Ibid, 13; this shift occurred in response to the Auditor-General's findings (n 89, 5–7) that some MWC staff had been involved in VTHC campaigning in state and federal elections (contravening the terms of the Victorian government grants).

[92] MWC, 'About Us'. Available at: www.migrantworkers.org.au/about.

[93] Ibid; Henriques-Gomes (n 89).

[94] See, eg, ABC TV (4 Corners), *Slaving Away* (4 May 2015); ABC TV (4 Corners), *7-Eleven: The Price of Convenience* (30 August 2015). See also S Huang, 'Sexual assault, lost fingers: exploitation in

evidence of wage theft, health and safety breaches and sexual harassment affecting international students and working holiday makers (overseas backpackers).[95]

MWC focuses on running regular 'Know Your Rights' sessions, 'growing a strong migrant worker led network', and providing industrial representation to migrant workers.[96] It has also tackled the exploitative conduct of migration agents engaged in 'visa fraud', the heightened workplace health and safety risks faced by migrant workers and wage theft affecting international students in the hospitality industry.[97] In addition, MWC has lobbied for effective regulation of the labour hire industry, where illegitimate contractors have taken advantage of vulnerable migrant workers (particularly in the horticulture, meat processing and cleaning industries).[98] MWC wants to ensure that the strong labour hire licensing legislation which emerged from inquiries into the sector in Victoria and Queensland,[99] is not over-ridden by the national labour hire registration framework proposed by the federal Coalition government in 2019.[100] The importance of MWC was most clearly shown through the vital assistance it provided to the many thousands of migrant workers deprived of federal government assistance after the onset of COVID-19.[101] Matt Kunkel, Director of MWC, sums up its guiding philosophy as follows:

> Our centre rejects the divisive politics that blames migrants for suppressing wages or stealing jobs. Instead, we turn our gaze to [the] barriers migrant workers face in full participation in our society.[102]

MWC also aims to build collectivism among the migrant workers it assists. In 2020, a collaboration between MWC and the AWU led to an organising campaign at a Melbourne recycling plant, which saw workers recover significant sums in unpaid wages and obtain more permanent positions.[103] Other union groups

an industry rotten to the core', *Sydney Morning Herald* (11 October 2020), written by MWC Organiser Sherry Huang.

[95] See, eg, Commonwealth of Australia, Senate Education and Employment References Committee, *A National Disgrace: The Exploitation of Temporary Work Visa Holders* (March 2016); FWO, *Harvest Trail Inquiry: A Report on Workplace Arrangements along the Harvest Trail* (November 2018); Australian Government, *Report of the Migrant Workers' Taskforce* (March 2019).

[96] MWC, *2020 Annual Report*, 4; see also 8–21, and MWC, 'Migrant workers recover over $1,000,000 in stolen wages'. Available at: www.migrantworkers.org.au/1_million_stolen_wages.

[97] MWC, *2019 Annual Report*, 12–17.

[98] Industrial Relations Victoria, *Victorian Inquiry into the Labour Hire Industry and Insecure Work: Final Report* (August 2016); S Locke, 'How labour hire villains make millions from Australia's "modern slavery" market', *ABC Rural* (1 November 2017).

[99] Labour Hire Licensing Act 2017 (Qld); Labour Hire Licensing Act 2018 (Vic).

[100] MWC, *Report of the National Conference on Labour Hire Reform* (8 November 2019). See also Australian Government, *Australian Government Response: Report of the Migrant Workers Taskforce* (March 2019); 'Porter sets out "guiding principles" for national labour hire scheme', *Workplace Express* (24 January 2020).

[101] See ch 12.

[102] MWC, *2019 Annual Report*, 5.

[103] MWC, 'Recycling plant workers unionise for their rights'. Available at: www.migrantworkers.org.au/recycling_plant_workers_unionise_for_their_rights. See also MWC, 'Fabrizio's story: the challenges

around Australia have sought to address the specific issues affecting migrant workers. In 2019, Unions NSW provided A$152,000 in funding to establish its Visa Assist partnership with the Immigration Advice and Rights Centre. Union members can access free advice and support on the issues of visa status and citizenship that frequently arise when they challenge their employer on employment concerns like underpayment.[104] This approach is a reversal of MWC's delivery of support and representation to migrant workers, regardless of union membership, as a basis for constructing collective strength.[105]

# III. Back to the Future: A New Wave of Union Mergers

## A. How Could It Go So Wrong? The Construction-Maritime-Textile Unions' Amalgamation

It was noted in Chapter 5 that widespread mergers of Australian unions occurred in the late 1980s–early 1990s, forming a major component of the response of the ACTU and the Labor Government to membership decline. Despite the apparent 'failure' of this as 'a strategy to rebuild or maintain the power of organised labour', interest in a further round of union 'consolidations'[106] emerged from around late 2015. The Construction, Forestry, Mining and Energy Union (CFMEU) announced that it was in merger discussions with, first, the Maritime Union of Australia (MUA)[107] and, then, the Textile, Clothing and Footwear Union of Australia (TCFUA).[108] This could only be viewed as a survival plan for the TCFUA: after many years of job losses in the clothing production industry due to the removal of tariff barriers and offshoring of jobs, it was down to between 4,000 and 5,000 members.[109] The MUA had around 14,000 members but was perceived

facing international students and unionising against wage theft'. Available at: www.migrantworkers.org.au/fabrizios_story, recounting the role of Fabrizio Venturini in organising hospitality workers to form Hospo Voice and as President of NOMIT, the Italian Network of Melbourne (which advises Italian migrant workers on their visa and employment rights and holds joint events with MWC).

[104] 'Migrants joining up to access free visa service, says Unions NSW', *Workplace Express* (15 October 2019); see also Immigration Advice and Rights Centre, 'Visa Assist'. Available at: https://iarc.asn.au/i-need-legal-advice/visa-assist-program/.

[105] Although Unions NSW claims that its approach has also achieved this goal, in that: '[w]hen the offer of free migrant legal services is put forward there is more than 40 per cent uptake for union membership'. See ACTU, *Organising with 2020 Vision: Case Studies of New Approaches to Union Growth and Capacity Building* (Australian Trade Union Institute, 19 November 2020) 52–53.

[106] T Lyons, *The Urge to Merge* (Per Capita, March 2016) 1–2.

[107] 'MUA "here to stay" as it floats merger with CFMEU', *Workplace Express* (16 October 2015).

[108] 'CFMEU and TCFU preparing to merge', *Workplace Express* (26 October 2015).

[109] Ibid; see further I Watson, J Buchanan, I Campbell and C Briggs, *Fragmented Futures: New Challenges in Working Life* (Sydney, Federation Press, 2003) 50–52.

as industrially strong,[110] while the CFMEU – with over 100,000 members – was the dominant partner in the three-way merger.[111]

From the earliest stages of this proposal, employer groups opposed the amalgamation, raising concerns about the 'shallow respect for the law' of the CFMEU and MUA.[112] The Coalition government also sought to counter the merger, pledging (in its 2016 election policy) to subject any future union amalgamations to a: 'public interest test … allow[ing] relevant matters to be taken into account, such as the [merging] organisations' history of compliance with workplace laws.'[113] Once re-elected, the government introduced legislation into Parliament to implement this policy,[114] in what became a race against time to have the proposed new public interest test in place before the FWC had to decide on the amalgamation.[115] After the CFMEU/MUA/TCFUA amalgamation worked its way through the internal processes of the three unions,[116] employer opposition to the plan shifted to the FWC and the courts. There, however, the Australian Mines and Metals Association and the Master Builders Association were repeatedly unsuccessful in thwarting the merger.[117]

It ultimately took effect on 27 March 2018, a day after the Coalition government gave up on obtaining support in Parliament for its proposed public interest test.[118] Speaking of the employer and Coalition efforts to stop the amalgamation, Michael O'Connor, National Secretary of the newly merged Construction, Forestry, Maritime, Mining and Energy Union (CFMMEU) said:

> If they're worried because they think that we will be a more effective voice for fairness, a more effective voice for social justice, a more effective voice for workers' right[s] and human rights, yeah, they should be worried ….[119]

[110] See, eg, 'FWO goes after MUA over 2015 port strikes', *Workplace Express* (9 December 2016); J Oaten, 'Court orders unions to stop blockading Melbourne port as 1,000 containers remain stranded', *ABC News* (27 November 2017).

[111] 'MUA "here to stay" as it floats merger with CFMEU', *Workplace Express* (16 October 2015), also noting the view of MUA National Secretary Paddy Crumlin that his union and the CFMEU were 'like-minded' and would join forces to combat 'ever-pervasive' attacks on workers' entitlements and employment security.

[112] 'Transport unions willing to explore closer relationships', *Workplace Express* (3 March 2016). See also '45 outstanding penalty cases should halt super-merger: Employers', *Workplace Express* (17 January 2018).

[113] Liberal and National Parties, *The Coalition's Commitment to Fairness and Transparency in Workplaces* (June 2016).

[114] Fair Work (Registered Organisations) Amendment (Ensuring Integrity) Bill 2017, sch 4; this was a fore-runner of the Ensuring Integrity Bill which re-emerged in 2019 and 2020 (see ch 5).

[115] Exercising its power under s 73 of the FWRO Act to determine if the amalgamation should be confirmed.

[116] 'Full steam ahead for three-way merger', *Workplace Express* (14 December 2016); 'Members back CFMEU merger with MUA and TCFU', *Workplace Express* (28 November 2017).

[117] See, eg, *Construction, Forestry, Mining and Energy Union; Maritime Union of Australia; and Textile, Clothing and Footwear Union of Australia* [2018] FWC 1017; *Australian Mines and Metals Association; Master Builders Association v Construction, Forestry, Mining and Energy Union* [2018] FWCFB 3710; *Australian Mines and Metals Association v Construction, Forestry, Maritime, Mining and Energy Union* (2018) 268 FCR 128.

[118] 'Super-union to "have a say" in country's future: CFMMEU Secretary', *Workplace Express* (27 March 2018).

[119] Ibid.

In reality, things have not worked out as planned: pre-existing internal CFMEU tensions carried over into the amalgamated organisation. This ultimately led to O'Connor's resignation from his position in November 2020, following a long period of conflict with the Secretary of the Victorian Construction Division, John Setka.[120] Tony Maher, CFMMEU National President, also resigned, signalling that his Mining and Energy Division may seek to withdraw from the union – aided by legislation which the government opportunistically rushed through Parliament making union de-mergers easier to effect.[121] In March 2021, the mining division did just that, applying to the FWC to formally separate from the CFMMEU.[122] Far from the business community's nightmare scenario of an industrially militant CFMMEU wreaking havoc across Australia, within three years the merged union had imploded.[123]

## B. 'Rebuilding Worker Power in this Country': The United Workers Union

In early 2016, it was reported that the Australian Manufacturing Workers' Union (AMWU), with approximately 90,000 members, and the 104,000-strong UV were in discussions about a possible merger.[124] This did not eventuate, however, as the AMWU considered a range of other options for its future.[125] Instead, about 18 months later, UV and the NUW announced their plan to merge into a new 'super union' that would unite 'workers across the country to take power' and 'build a new economy, where every worker counts and where the voice of workers is at the heart of our economic and political system'.[126] The proposal to form the United Workers Union (UWU) would bring together two unions covering industries including: warehousing, logistics and the food supply chain; manufacturing; cleaning; security; aged care and disability care; public and private health care; education (including teachers' aides and early childhood education); and hospitality. Compared with some past union mergers, there seemed to be a more logical fit between UV and the NUW, which had been among the lead innovators

[120] See, eg, A Cooper, 'Setka's CFMMEU branch poached 219 members from rival faction, court told', *The Age* (26 February 2020); 'O'Connor quits leadership of "totally dysfunctional" CFMMEU', *Workplace Express* (5 November 2020).

[121] Fair Work (Registered Organisations) Amendment (Withdrawal from Amalgamations) Act 2020 (Cth); 'CFMMEU mining division might use Porter's law to flee dysfunction', *Workplace Express* (7 December 2020). See also N Bonyhady, 'Labor to back bill allowing unions to split, paves way for CFMMEU to fragment', *Sydney Morning Herald* (7 December 2020).

[122] 'Miners apply for divorce from "tarnished brand"', *Workplace Express* (26 March 2021).

[123] See further D Marin-Guzman, 'The deconstruction of the CFMEU', *Australian Financial Review* (9 December 2020).

[124] 'AMWU and United Voice considering amalgamation', *Workplace Express* (19 February 2016).

[125] Eventually, these included the possibility of a merger with the AWU: D Marin-Guzman, 'AWU in merger talks in battle for survival', *Australian Financial Review* (14 October 2019).

[126] D Marin-Guzman, 'National Union of Workers, United Voice plan to create "new union model"', *Australian Financial Review* (17 August 2017), quoting from the NUW-UV memorandum of understanding on the merger proposal.

in seeking to address falling union membership.[127] In finding that there was the required 'community of interest' between the two unions to enable the proposal to be submitted to ballots of their members, the FWC made some important observations: the NUW and UV shared high numbers of low-paid members and similar proportions of members from migrant backgrounds, in part-time and casual employment, engaged through labour hire arrangements and subject to underpayment and other forms of exploitation.[128]

As the proposal developed, the two unions adopted a bold approach to the structure of the new organisation. The UWU eschewed the traditional state-based branch structure of Australian unions, opting instead for a sectoral organising model and regional constituencies for the election (by members, every four years) of a Members' Convention initially with 500 delegates.[129] The Members' Convention in turn elects a rank-and-file Members' Council (with 50 members) and the merged union's National Executive (made up of 12–24 members).[130] As at early 2019, the NUW had 55,280 members and UV, 100,605; their combined membership created Australia's fourth-largest union.[131] Following the members' vote of 95 per cent in favour of the amalgamation and approval by the FWC,[132] the UWU came into being on 11 November 2019. Its National Secretary, Tim Kennedy, outlined an ambitious project for the new organisation 'to rebuild worker power in this country', both industrially and in the broader political system.[133] Noting the threats presented by climate change, automation and insecure work, Kennedy also stated that the UWU: 'will ensure workers are at the centre of important decisions to be made about these [issues] so that no one is left behind'.[134] The UWU's Rules, under the objective of 'growth and power', commit it to 'constantly innovate, evolve and improve the ability of the Union to reach new groups of workers, through traditional and new organising methods'.[135] The merged union has scored some major victories through an aggressive approach to protected industrial action in support of collective bargaining claims, including a 9 per cent pay increase over three years for manufacturing workers at McCormick

[127] See Part II(B) above; and Part IV below.

[128] *National Union of Workers and United Voice* [2019] FWC 3751 at [27].

[129] 'Latest union marriage vows "radical" structure', *Workplace Express* (26 July 2019); UV and NUW, 'Vote Yes: Big, Strong, United', Annexure A to the FWC's decision in *National Union of Workers and United Voice* [2019] FWC 4411. Under rule 29(a) of the UWU Rules, the number of Convention delegates is determined by dividing the total number of financial members by 300, providing a visible mechanism for ascertaining whether the union is growing in the four years between each Convention. However, UWU has twice delayed holding its inaugural Convention due to the COVID-19 pandemic: 'Merged union's first convention put on ice again', *Workplace Express* (26 May 2021).

[130] 'Latest union marriage vows "radical" structure', *Workplace Express* (26 July 2019); see UWU Rules, rule 30(c)(ii).

[131] 'Blue collar super union plans head to FWC', *Workplace Express* (21 May 2019).

[132] 'UWU set to emerge after FWC backs amalgamation', *Workplace Express* (1 October 2019).

[133] B Schneiders, 'Super union merger could shift Labor to left', *The Sunday Age* (10 November 2019).

[134] D Marin-Guzman, 'New mega union swings Labor to left', *Australian Financial Review* (11 November 2019).

[135] UWU Rules, rule 6(xi).

Foods following a six-week strike leading up to Easter 2021.[136] The UWU also used walkouts to great effect in protecting warehouse and commercial laundry workers against unsafe conditions, among its many actions on behalf of members during the COVID-19 pandemic.[137]

## IV. Campaigning and Organising Beyond the Workplace

Community-based unionism and union coalition-building with other social movement actors have been evident in Australia,[138] although not on the scale of US examples like the Fight for $15 movement.[139] As noted in Chapter 5, landmark episodes like the 1998 waterfront dispute and the pre-2007 election 'Your Rights at Work' campaign saw extensive engagement between unions and community groups with a mutual interest in contesting the Howard government's anti-worker policies. Several Australian unions have built deep connections with aligned community organisations to advance particular causes. The Transport Workers' Union (TWU) has brought organisations like the Concerned Families of Australian Truckies Association, religious leaders and local community activists into its campaign to improve road safety and to persuade policy-makers of the link between safety and fair pay rates for self-employed truck drivers.[140] Similarly, the TCFUA (now part of the CFMMEU[141]) has worked intensively for more than 30 years in community coalitions that gave rise to the FairWear campaign, to obtain stronger regulation of the clothing production supply chain.[142] In a number of prominent industrial

[136] N Bonyhady, 'Maccas sauce workers go on strike as pay talks sour', *Sydney Morning Herald* (25 February 2021); M Merkenich, 'McCormick workers win pay rise, retain conditions', *Green Left* (15 April 2021). For other examples, see N Bonyhady, 'Striking Woolworths workers return to work after 10 per cent pay rise offer', *Sydney Morning Herald* (6 August 2020); UWU, 'Dairy workers in Bendigo win big after 10 days on strike' (15 November 2020). Available at: www.unitedworkers.org.au/dairy-workers-in-bendigo-win-big-after-10-days-on-strike/.

[137] See ch 12.

[138] See, eg, A Barnes and N Balnave, 'Back to Grass Roots: Peak Union Councils and Community Campaigning' (2015) 26:4 *Economic and Labour Relations Review* 577; A Tattersall, 'How Do We Build Power in Coalition? Rethinking Union-Community Coalition Types 12 Years On' (2018) 28:1 *Labour and Industry* 68.

[139] See ch 4.

[140] M Hearn, *Organising Union: Transport Workers Face the Challenge of Change, 1989–2013* (Carlton, Melbourne University Publishing, 2017) 98–102 and ch 13; S Kaine and M Rawling, '"Comprehensive Campaigning" in the NSW Transport Industry: Bridging the Divide Between Regulation and Union Organizing' (2010) 52:2 *Journal of Industrial Relations* 183, 192–95. The Road Safety Remuneration Tribunal, which emerged from these efforts in 2012, fell victim to the more powerful lobbying of industry interests: see M Rawling, R Johnstone and I Nossar, 'Compromising Road Transport Supply Chain Regulation: The Abolition of the Road Safety Remuneration Tribunal' (2017) 39:3 *Sydney Law Review* 303.

[141] See Part III(A) above.

[142] See, eg, R Burchielli, A Delaney and K Coventry, 'Campaign Strategies to Develop Regulatory Mechanisms: Protecting Australian Garment Homeworkers' (2014) 56:1 *Journal of Industrial Relations*

disputes, unions have successfully engaged the wider community in social media-led consumer boycotts of the products and services of the companies they have been entangled with.[143]

In recent years, there has been more evidence of community engagement as a component of union organising for membership growth. The UWU has been at the forefront here, through its organising effort across the fresh food supply chain (formerly known as the Fair Food Campaign).[144] Nelthorpe observes that when the former NUW began this project in around 2015:

> The horticulture industry was long overdue for such a drive and, moreover, the prospect of farmworker unionization raised the possibility of covering horticulture, dairy, and poultry – from farming to processing, warehousing, and distribution – under a single union. If one union were able to organize the whole supply chain, its workers could wield enormous industrial power.[145]

As much as increasing its membership, the UWU's activism has been about righting wrongs for the predominantly migrant workers who have increasingly been exploited in the fields and packing sheds of fruit and vegetable farms and in poultry processing plants.[146] Many of these businesses are suppliers to Australia's two major supermarket operators, Coles and Woolworths, which the union is seeking to hold accountable for underpayments and other forms of mistreatment of workers occurring in the supply chain.[147] In its 2020 submission to the National Agricultural Labour Advisory Committee, the UWU called on the federal Government to recognise 'the significant role that Coles and Woolworths' pricing and purchasing strategies play further down the chain in creating a demand and a market for insecure and underpaid work'; and demanded that the supermarkets 'rais[e] standards … through fair pricing that enables growers to

81. The regulatory solutions adopted have included a formal role for the union in the compliance framework: see, eg, I Nossar, R Johnstone, A Macklin and M Rawling, 'Protective Legal Regulation for Home-based Workers in Australian Textile, Clothing and Footwear Supply Chains' (2015) 57:4 *Journal of Industrial Relations* 585; and Ethical Clothing Australia: https://ethicalclothingaustralia.org.au/.

[143] See, eg, E Woods, 'Unions claim victory as 55 CUB workers return to work', *The Age* (8 December 2016), on the 180-day strike by outsourced beer production workers; '"We'll get better at this", says union leader after boycott win', *Workplace Express* (23 November 2017), on the AMWU's #streetsfree-summer campaign directed at ice-cream manufacturer Unilever.

[144] See J Howe, 'Temporary Migrant Workers and Trade Unions in Australia – A Complex Relationship' in J Tham and C Kelly (eds), *Democracy, Social Justice and the Role of Trade Unions: We the Working People* (London, Anthem Press, 2021) 139, 144–46; UWU, 'Farmworkers' stories'. Available at: https://unitedworkers.org.au/stories/farmworkers/.

[145] T Nelthorpe, 'Organizing Australia's Food Supply Chain', *Jacobin* (25 November 2019); see also E Underhill, D Groutsis, D van den Broek and M Rimmer, 'Organising Across Borders: Mobilising Temporary Migrant Labour in Australian Food Production' (2020) 62:2 *Journal of Industrial Relations* 278, 289. On similar organising efforts internationally, see M Dias-Abey, 'Using Law to Support Social Movement-Led Collective Bargaining Structures in Supply Chains' (2019) 32:1 *Australian Journal of Labour Law* 123.

[146] NUW, *Farm Workers Speak Out!* (July 2019); Nelthorpe (n 145). See also Part II(F).

[147] NUW (n 146) 3–5, 16–18.

meet the true cost of labour compliance over the long term'.[148] One approach to achieving this has been shareholder activism. Working with the Australasian Centre for Corporate Responsibility, the union moved a shareholder resolution at Woolworths' 2017 annual general meeting. This led to the company agreeing: to support the education of workers in its supply chain about their labour rights (including union membership and access to grievance mechanisms); and develop a pre-qualification programme to ensure all labour hire providers to Woolworths comply with labour and human rights.[149]

UWU has advocated for a visa amnesty for undocumented workers in the agricultural sector;[150] supported litigation to help farmworkers recover underpaid wages;[151] and lobbied state and federal governments for stronger regulation (particularly of labour contractors who are instrumental in exploitation).[152] The union has also sought to engage in collective bargaining with agriculture businesses. In partnership with the Vanuatu National Workers Union, UWU supported around 150 workers at a tomato greenhouse in Adelaide to join the union in 2017; defended them against the employer reprisals that followed; and helped them obtain improved conditions.[153] Those workers played a formal role in the process for improving their own wages and conditions, as bargaining representatives under the FW Act.[154] Similar victories, including wage increases of up to A$10.00 per hour, have followed at fresh produce sites in regional Victoria.[155] Under an agreement negotiated by UWU at Coolibah Herbs just outside Melbourne, workers obtained direct employment in permanent positions (rather than insecure jobs through contractors).[156]

In all of these actions to improve the situation of temporary migrant workers in fresh food production, as well as conventional site-by-site organising, the UWU has adopted an approach of 'network collectivism'.[157] It has forged close

[148] UWU, *Submission to the National Agricultural Labour Advisory Committee: National Agricultural Workforce Strategy* (3 August 2020) 4.

[149] Woolworths Group, 'Woolworths reaffirms commitment to improving labour rights in fresh food supply chains' (22 November 2017). See also Howe (n 144) 146–49; C Arup, 'Enforcing Labour Standards in the Supermarket Food Supply Chain' (2019) 32:1 *Australian Journal of Labour Law* 103, 118–19; and 'Coles buys into "safe and fair" produce supply chain', *Workplace Express* (23 May 2019), relating to an agreement reached between Coles and the AWU, SDAEA and TWU.

[150] UWU (n 148) 4, 11–16.

[151] B Schneiders, 'Migrant farm workers launch landmark $10m legal claim', *Sydney Morning Herald* (29 July 2018); B Schneiders, 'Exploited Pacific migrant farm workers settle significant case', *Sydney Morning Herald* (1 August 2019).

[152] NUW (n 146) 13. The NUW played a leading role in the instigation of state-level inquiries which led to the introduction of labour hire licensing laws, see Part II(F).

[153] Nelthorpe (n 145). See also N McKenzie and N Toscano, 'Seasonal Workers Program pickers told if they join a union they'll get no work', *Sydney Morning Herald* (11 March 2017).

[154] See *National Union of Workers; Mr Ram Krishna Sharma; Mr Umed Ali Mahrie; Mr Ejaz Ali v Como Glasshouse No 2 Pty Ltd* [2017] FWC 4025, where the tribunal allowed the union and individual bargaining representatives from the Hazaragi and Nepalese language groups to jointly instigate the process for taking protected industrial action in support of their agreement claims.

[155] Nelthorpe (n 145).

[156] NUW (n 147) 23; see also *Coolibah Herbs Enterprise Agreement 2016* [2016] FWCA 7421.

[157] Underhill et al (n 145) 286, 291.

links with 'ethno-specific social media groups' run by and for Hong Kong, Korean and Taiwanese working holiday visa-holders, as well as churches, the Salvation Army and the Federation of Ethnic Communities Council of Australia (which had formed a broader alliance to combat modern slavery).[158] The social media connections have been particularly important, according to Underhill et al's study, in 'enabl[ing] the [UWU] to reach out to Asian [working holiday makers] irrespective of their workplace location and access to the union'.[159] The union has also engaged organisers and activists from the worker communities to:

> … reflect the ethnic mixing pot of [temporary migrant workers] and refugees found in the food industry workforce, including Sudanese, Somali, Afghan (Hazari), Cambodian, Vietnamese, Taiwanese, Hong Kong Chinese and Myanmar (Rohingya).[160]

The importance of all this is not just that the UWU is taking on the challenge of organising a large segment of the Australian labour market that has been almost completely union free. It is doing it in a way that maximises the involvement of vulnerable migrant workers in their own struggle, leverages the power of their networks and confronts business power at multiple levels (workplace, industry, supply chain). As Caterina Cinanni, UWU Director of Member Power, puts it: 'we can't allow [workers in] parts of the economy to be significantly exploited and turn our backs to it, otherwise we are not doing what unions are meant to do, which is to empower workers to stand up and fight for fairness, dignity and equality'.[161]

## V. Conclusion

Australian unions clearly recognise the need to innovate in order to extend their presence – especially among the young, those working in casual (or other insecure) jobs, migrant workers and others employed in sectors or forms of work where the risk of exploitation is high. The six union prototypes that were examined in this chapter demonstrate the potential for digital and campaign-based membership offerings to help unions connect with hard-to-reach workers. However, as with the examples of alt-labour and similar approaches in the USA, questions remain about the long-term viability and utility of these new forms of unionism (which will be explored further in Chapter 11). The chapter also scrutinised two recent union mergers: one (which produced the CFMMEU) illustrating the difficulties that can arise from internal conflict within a key amalgamation partner; the other (leading to formation of the UWU) an example of carefully chosen union

[158] Ibid, 290–94.
[159] Ibid, 290.
[160] Ibid, 289–90.
[161] M McCarthy, '"We can't afford to pay it": Farmers warn of grocery price rises if unions win horticultural wage hike', *ABC News* (21 June 2018).

partners with closely aligned membership bases and industrial strategies. UWU's whole-of-supply-chain approach to representing workers in fresh food production demonstrates an uplift in Australian adaptation of union coalition-building with other social movement groups. Taking into account all the strategies used by Australian unions to reverse membership decline (considered here and in Chapter 5), the tensions between innovating and relying on law reform are clearly evident – although recent developments suggest that the re-modelling of unions is in the ascendant.

# 7

# The UK: From 'New Unionism' to Indy and Digital Unions

## I. Introduction

This chapter examines how unions in the UK have tackled the challenges of the last 30 years, commencing with the adoption of the US organising model as the Thatcher/Major governments were nearing their denouement in the mid-1990s. The election of the Blair New Labour government brought moderate state support for union recognition, but with it, the promotion of the concept of workplace partnership between employers and unions. After considering the UK union leadership's accommodation of the partnership agenda, the chapter turns to the responses of unions to the austerity measures put in place by the Conservatives since their re-election in 2010, Brexit and the realignment of union-Labour Party relations under Jeremy Corbyn's leadership. This is followed by an exploration of the recent emergence of a more community-based, vibrant and confrontational form of unionism through three examples: the Independent Workers Union of Great Britain (IWGB), United Voices of the World (UVW) and the #McStrike campaign of the Bakers Food and Allied Workers Union (BFAWU). Finally, the chapter discusses the charting of fresh terrain by UK unions and think tanks in their exploration of new membership models and digital experimentation, to broaden the appeal of unions – especially among younger British workers.

## II. The UK Variant of Organising

The devastating effects of the Thatcher era upon UK unions, noted in Chapters 2 and 3, precipitated a search for new thinking about how to counter falling membership levels. By the mid-1990s, as optimism grew among union leaders that the long period of Conservative rule would soon come to an end, attention turned to an organising approach based on the US and Australian models.[1] This formed part of the 'New Unionism initiative' driven by Trades Union Congress (TUC) General Secretary, John Monks, 'a broad-based effort at using a range of

[1] M Simms, J Holgate and E Heery, *Union Voices: Tactics and Tensions in UK Organizing* (Ithaca, Cornell University Press, 2013) 3–4; see further 38–43.

strategies to promote revitalization'.[2] Following exploratory visits to the USA and Australia, the TUC established an Organising Academy in 1998 to train 'specialist organizers' in the 'tactics and ideas' needed to attract workers to a more appealing brand of unionism.[3] Focusing on women, youth and low-paid workers for recruitment, the objectives of organising included assisting unions to expand in existing areas of strength and 'break into new jobs and industries'.[4] As in the US and Australia, organising in the UK involved a shift in priorities away from the traditional approach of servicing union members.[5] This was based on the assumption that union officials 'should never do for workers what they should do for themselves; that the members are "the union" and they must set its agenda by themselves and for themselves'.[6] Organising campaigns would seek to maximise the statutory union recognition procedure for collective bargaining, introduced by the New Labour Government in 1999.[7]

By the mid-2000s, around 200 organisers had been trained through the Organising Academy to take up specialist organising positions with TUC-affiliated unions, many of which also 'encourag[ed] generalist officers to spend more time on recruitment and organising'.[8] Large unions devoting significant resources to new organising included the Transport and General Workers Union (TGWU) (which merged with Amicus in 2007 to form Unite the Union (Unite)), GMB Union (GMB), Union of Shop, Distributive and Allied Workers (USDAW) and Unison (the Public Service Union).[9] The adaptation in the UK of the kind of targeted organising campaigns pioneered by US unions[10] saw British organisers utilising tactics such as 'person-to-person recruitment, workplace mapping, the identification of workplace grievances [as a basis for engaging with potential members], and the principle of like-recruits-like'.[11] Less resort was had to other US-style methods like visiting non-members in their homes and developing closer ties with community groups to advance organising goals.[12] UK organising focused heavily on increasing union membership in areas with rising levels of employment, 'notably private-sector services' including the retail, banking,

[2] Ibid, 18.

[3] Ibid, 4–5; see further 43–53.

[4] P Fairbrother and P Stewart, 'The Dilemmas of Social Partnership and Union Organization: Questions for British Trade Unions', in P Fairbrother and C Yates (eds), *Trade Unions in Renewal: A Comparative Study* (London, Routledge, 2003) 158, 168.

[5] Ibid, 167; see further S de Turberville, 'Does the "Organizing Model" Represent a Credible Union Renewal Strategy?' (2004) 18:4 *Work, Employment and Society* 775, 776–77, 780–82 (questioning the validity of the servicing–organising dichotomy).

[6] G Gall and J Fiorito, 'The Backward March of Labour Halted: Or What is to be Done with "Union Organising"? The Cases of Britain and the USA' (2011) 35:2 *Capital and Class* 233, 235.

[7] E Heery and M Simms, 'Union Organising under Certification Law in Britain', in G Gall (ed), *Union Recognition: Organising and Bargaining Outcomes* (London, Routledge, 2006) 44. See also ch 3.

[8] Ibid, 48–49.

[9] Gall and Fiorito (n 6) 239; see further Simms, Holgate and Heery (n 1) ch 3.

[10] See ch 4.

[11] Simms, Holgate and Heery (n 1) 8–9; see also 132.

[12] Ibid. See Part V below.

telecommunications and printing industries and outsourced public services.[13] Typically, according to Wills:

> Organisers target greenfield sites by leafleting and then meeting with interested workers, prioritising the identification of activists on the inside. Once identified, these activists are the lynchpin of campaigns, working with organisers to recruit and organise from within. When membership levels reach 50%, the union can safely approach the employer to talk about union recognition, and in the event that talks are refused, they can turn to the procedures of the 1999 Employ[ment] Relations Act …[14]

UK unions also pursued 'infill organising' aimed at increasing membership in workplaces where they were already recognised for collective bargaining by employers.[15] Indeed, Heery and Adler maintained that this kind of 'consolidation' of union strength at the workplace level made up 'the bulk of union organizing in Britain'.[16]

Several unions encountered success in their organising initiatives, such as the TGWU and GMB in London casinos (leveraging recognition agreements with large employers to build sectoral membership across multiple workplaces);[17] TGWU in aviation (EasyJet and FlyBe) and logistics (TNT and UPS);[18] and USDAW in the retail sector (including through a partnership agreement with Tesco).[19] In contrast, the implementation of the organising model by the Manufacturing, Science and Finance Union (now also part of Unite) was hampered by the insufficient devotion of resources (including for education, research and communication) to effect a transformational shift in recruitment; and by the absence of engagement with existing members in this project.[20] Overall, as in the USA and Australia, although organising did lead to membership growth in some UK unions, it did not yield the hoped-for reversal of long-term decline. Noting that union membership density fell from 31.4% in 1996 to 27.4% in 2009, Gall and Fiorito contended that the results of organising had 'been disappointing to say the least'.[21] Simms, Holgate and Heery reflected that: 'the investment

[13] Ibid, 120, 122.

[14] J Wills, 'The Geography of Union Organising in Low-Paid Service Industries in the UK: Lessons from the T&G's Campaign to Unionise the Dorchester Hotel, London' (2005) 37:1 *Antipode* 139, 145–46.

[15] Simms, Holgate and Heery (n 1) 124–25.

[16] E Heery and L Adler, 'Organizing the Unorganized' in C Frege and J Kelly (eds), *Varieties of Unionism: Revitalization in a Globalizing Economy* (Oxford, Oxford University Press, 2004) 45, 52.

[17] Simms, Holgate and Heery (n 1) 62–63; M Simms, 'Accounting for Greenfield Union Organizing Outcomes' (2015) 53:3 *British Journal of Industrial Relations* 397, 413–14.

[18] G Daniels, 'In the Field: A Decade of Organizing', in G Daniels and J McIlroy (eds), *Trade Unions in a Neoliberal World: British Trade Unions under New Labour* (London, Routledge, 2009) 254, 259. Compare TGWU's unsuccessful effort to organise for recognition at a major London hotel, explored in Wills (n 14).

[19] Daniels (n 18) 261; Simms (n 17) 411, 415. See also Part III below.

[20] B Carter and R Cooper, 'The Organising Model and the Management of Change: A Comparative Study of Unions in Australia and Britain' (2002) 57:4 *Relations Industrielles/Industrial Relations* 712, 722.

[21] Gall and Fiorito (n 6) 234.

in organizing … has largely enabled unions to hold steady, rather than to expand into growing sectors of the economy'.[22] Daniels more stridently took the view that: 'if we were to measure the turn to organizing on membership numbers alone then it has been an abject failure'.[23] While the limitations of the statutory recognition procedure were no doubt a contributing factor,[24] organising was also hampered by the TUC's simultaneous drive for the adoption of cooperative workplace partnerships with employers.

## III. 'Third Way' Unionism: The Partnership Agenda

The changing institutional context was very significant in the shift to organising in the UK. As Taylor points out, the TUC leader John Monks confronted the reality not only 'that the decline of organised labour was particularly dramatic in Britain between 1980 and 1997', but also that the Conservatives' assault 'and the resulting anti-union climate in the workplace' had pushed many unions 'into retreat'.[25] His New Unionism plan was designed to confront those challenges, including the denigration of trade unions in the Thatcher years, by positioning unions as 'part of the solution' to the nation's problems.[26] This took shape through the TUC's embracing of the continental European notion of social partnership, with Monks offering the prospect of productivity gains for employers that negotiated partnership agreements with unions.[27] The TUC's partnership drive reflected a recognition that there would be a more distant relationship between unions and government under Tony Blair's New Labour than had existed in the 1970s.[28] Government advocacy of workplace partnerships formed a component of its 'Third Way' ethos, which subjugated traditional redistributive objectives of the left to the necessity (and inevitability) of markets, globalisation and competition.[29] In McIlroy's assessment, partnership was a 'device' through which New Labour fostered 'neoliberal trade unionism as an adjunct to management and an instrument of flexibility', consistent with a view of unions as 'labour market lubricators' aligned with the goals of the enterprise.[30]

[22] Simms, Holgate and Heery (n 1) 155. See further J McIlroy and G Daniels, 'An Anatomy of British Trade Unions since 1997: Strategies for Revitalization', in Daniels and McIlroy (n 18) 98, 113–16, 121–22.

[23] Daniels (n 18) 274; see also 266–67.

[24] G Gall, *'Union Organising' and the Health of the Union Movement in Britain* (London, Institute of Employment Rights, 2010) 31. See further ch 3.

[25] R Taylor, *The TUC: From the General Strike to New Unionism* (Basingstoke, Palgrave, 2000) 260.

[26] Ibid, 261.

[27] Ibid, 263–64.

[28] Ibid, 264. See also Fairbrother and Stewart (n 4) 161.

[29] M Upchurch, 'Partnership: New Labour's Third Way?', in Daniels and McIlroy (n 18) 230, 237–40. See further H Collins, 'Is There a Third Way in Labour Law?', in J Conaghan, R Fischl and K Klare (eds), *Labour Law in an Era of Globalization: Transformative Practices and Possibilities* (Oxford, Oxford University Press, 2002) 449.

[30] J McIlroy, 'A Brief History of British Trade Unions and Neoliberalism in the Age of New Labour', in Daniels and McIlroy (n 18) 63, 80, 83.

The government provided £12 million from 1999 to 2004 for joint union-employer projects through a Partnership at Work Fund (later succeeded by the Union Modernisation Fund, which explicitly excluded union recruitment or bargaining activities from eligibility).[31] The then-fashionable concept of 'high performance work systems' – emphasising high trust employee-management relationships, worker participation, job security and productivity – provided the theoretical framing for partnership.[32] This philosophy appeared to have swayed the thinking of many union leaders: the TUC's Partnership Institute, established in 2001, offered 'consultancy services' to assist organisations in developing 'cooperative industrial relations arrangements' founded on 'mutual gains' and similar principles.[33] Partnership agreements were prevalent in the rapidly transforming UK public sector, where 'private finance and private firms' came to play a greater role in the delivery of health, education and other vital services.[34] In the National Health Service (NHS), for example, 'union-management partnership' provided a basis for union and employee influence over the terms on which outsourcing occurred, along with pay and training issues.[35] USDAW utilised partnership agreements with large employers such as Tesco to extract access to new employees at induction and other union security arrangements, in exchange for the union's cooperation with business goals.[36]

Overwhelmingly, the evidence indicated that 'partnership agreements … lopsidedly favoured management'.[37] Partnership enabled (for example) the attainment of multi-skilling of the workforce and greater use of temporary/part-time contracts and other forms of workplace flexibility.[38] In some instances local shop stewards and workers reacted against the imposition of partnership deals.[39] John Monks had tried to explain at the outset that for unions, the goal should be

[31] McIlroy (n 30) 86.

[32] Upchurch (n 29) 232–34. See further T Kochan and P Osterman, *The Mutual Gains Enterprise: Forging a Winning Partnership among Labor, Management and Government* (Cambridge MA, Harvard Business School Press, 1994).

[33] V Badigannavar and J Kelly, 'Partnership and Organizing: An Empirical Assessment of Two Contrasting Approaches to Union Revitalization in the UK' (2011) 32:1 *Economic and Industrial Democracy* 5, 5–6. See further Upchurch (n 29) 235–36; M Terry, Partnership and the Future of Trade Unions in the UK' (2003) 24:4 *Economic and Industrial Democracy* 485.

[34] Badigannavar and Kelly (n 33) 7.

[35] Ibid.

[36] Simms, Heery and Holgate (n 1) 70–74.

[37] G Coderre-La Palme and I Greer, 'Dependence on a Hostile State: UK Trade Unions Before and After Brexit' in S Lehndorff, H Dribbusch and T Schulten, *Rough Waters: European Trade Unions in a Time of Crisis* (European Trade Union Institute, 2018) 259, 265.

[38] M Stuart and M Martínez Lucio, 'Trade Union Representatives' Attitudes and Experiences of the Principles and Practices of Partnership', in M Stuart and M Martínez Lucio (eds), *Partnership and Modernisation in Employment Relations* (London, Routledge, 2005) 101, 113–14. See further J Kelly, 'Social Partnership Agreements in Britain', in Stuart and Martínez Lucio, 188; D Guest and R Piccei, 'Partnership at Work: Mutuality and the Balance of Advantage' (2001) 39:2 *British Journal of Industrial Relations* 207.

[39] Upchurch (n 29) 243, referring to studies of partnership agreements at Blue Circle, Scottish Power, United Distillers, Royal Mail and the Inland Revenue.

'to organize "bad" employers and develop partnership arrangements with "good" employers'.[40] However, the incompatibility between the 'aggressive and adversarial' posture of union organising and the more 'quiescent' stance inherent in partnership,[41] became more apparent over time. Inevitably, so too did the frustration of union leaders, with increasingly vocal criticisms of the partnership agenda emerging by the mid-2000s.[42]

## IV. Back into the Wilderness: Unions Confront Austerity, Brexit and the Legacy of New Labour

The final years of the New Labour government under Prime Minister Gordon Brown brought no significant gains for UK unions, on the contrary (according to McIlroy) '[i]t was neoliberal business as usual'.[43] Once the Conservative party returned to government in 2010 (in coalition with the Liberal Democrats), unions were confronted with a combination of relentless cuts to public expenditure;[44] employment law reforms carrying on the Thatcher tradition (enabled by Blair's Third Way);[45] and ultimately, Brexit. Combating government austerity measures and defending public services became a major focus of union activity from 2010 to 2015, in the form of strikes, large-scale rallies and demonstrations organised by the TUC and unions such as Unison and Unite.[46] The elimination of 500,000 public sector jobs, along with cuts to pensions and the imposition of a pay freeze for public sector workers, 'jolted [unions] into mobilising their societal power resources'.[47] NHS staff took industrial action in 2014, their first strike in more than 30 years, after several years of campaigning against austerity and privatisation in public health care.[48] Austerity continued after the Conservatives were re-elected in their own right in 2015,[49] which also saw an escalation of state hostility through the Trade Union Act 2016.[50] The Brexit referendum in June 2016

[40] Simms, Heery and Holgate (n 1) 18–19.

[41] Daniels (n 18) 255–56; see further Badigannavar and Kelly (n 33).

[42] Upchurch (n 29) 244–45.

[43] J McIlroy, 'Under Stress but Still Enduring: The Contentious Alliance in the Age of Tony Blair and Gordon Brown', in Daniels and McIlroy (n 18) 165, 191.

[44] In response to the 2008 financial crisis: see further S Bach and G Gall, 'Public Service Voice under Strain in an Era of Restructuring and Austerity', in A Bogg and T Novitz (eds), *Voices at Work: Continuity and Change in the Common Law World* (Oxford, Oxford University Press, 2014) 322.

[45] See, eg, B Hepple, 'Back to the Future: Employment Law under the Coalition Government' (2013) 42:3 *Industrial Law Journal* 203; M Martínez Lucio, 'Beyond Consensus: The State and Industrial Relations in the United Kingdom from 1964 to 2014' (2015) 37:6 *Employee Relations* 692, 697–99.

[46] Coderre-La Palme and Greer (n 37) 268–71.

[47] Ibid, 268–69; see also M Bernaciak, R Gumbrell-McCormick and R Hyman, *European Trade Unionism: From Crisis to Renewal?* (European Trade Union Institute, Report 133, 2014) 43.

[48] Coderre-La Palme and Greer (n 37) 270.

[49] See, eg, K Puttick, *The Welfare State, Wages and Work: Disintegration or Renewal?* (London, Institute of Employment Rights, 2019) 5, 10–11.

[50] See ch 3.

presented a significant challenge, in that while union leaders encouraged their members to vote to remain in the European Union (EU),[51] many unionists: 'voted to leave, leading to concerns over the future of employment rights, the competitiveness of internationally exposed industries and racial and ethnic tensions'.[52] Bogg and Ewing maintain that the union leadership failed to counter the concerns of many workers about the over-supply of labour in the UK arising from the EU principle of freedom of movement, through a campaign predicated on the defence of workers' rights derived from EU labour law.[53] The repercussions of the electorate's decision to leave the EU proved calamitous for Labour (and for the unions) three years later.

The year 2015 also marked the election of Jeremy Corbyn to the Labour Party leadership and a consequent realignment of union-Labour relations. This produced a clearer agenda for legal reform to strengthen employment rights and the role of unions. Even before Corbyn's ascension as 'the only anti-austerity candidate' among the leadership contenders,[54] Unite General Secretary Len McCluskey had condemned Blair's as: 'the first Labour government with a huge parliamentary majority which did nothing to touch the fundamentals of wealth and power in our society'.[55] McCluskey became a very influential figure in the Corbyn-led project to overthrow the Labour Party's Blairite modernisers in favour of a more activist-based, authentically left-wing policy programme.[56] Unite under McCluskey had become more industrially militant as he advocated defiance of the mounting legal restrictions on strikes[57] and demanded Labour fix 'trade union law … the great unmentionable of British politics'.[58] Corbyn Labour's 2017 election manifesto therefore proposed 'a 20-point plan for security and equality at work'.[59] It included commitments to repeal the Trade Union Act 2016 and implement a system of sectoral collective bargaining,[60] firming up an earlier Corbyn promise to make

[51] A Bogg and K Ewing, 'The Continuing Evolution of European Labour Law and the Changing Context for Trade Union Organising' (2017) 38:2 *Comparative Labor Law and Policy Journal* 211.

[52] Coderre-La Palme and Greer (n 37) 259.

[53] Bogg and Ewing (n 51) 211–14, observing that the EU social policy agenda had been in retreat for some time and therefore offered a precarious basis for such a campaign. See, further, M Martínez Lucio, A Koukiadaki and I Tavora, *The Legacy of Thatcherism in European Labour Relations: The Impact of the Politics of Neo-Liberalism and Austerity on Collective Bargaining in a Fragmenting Europe* (London, Institute of Employment Rights, 2017).

[54] Coderre-La Palme and Greer (n 37) 277; see also A Murray, *The Fall and Rise of the British Left* (London, Verso, 2019) 151–56.

[55] L McCluskey, 'Can Unions Stay Within the Law Any Longer?' (2015) 44:3 *Industrial Law Journal* 439, 442.

[56] J Watts and T Bale, 'Populism as an Intra-Party Phenomenon: The British Labour Party under Jeremy Corbyn' (2019) 21:1 *British Journal of Politics and International Relations* 99, 104, 106–7, 109; see also E MacAskill, 'Len McCluskey: "If Labour is divided, we're in trouble: Give Jeremy a chance"', *The Guardian* (8 April 2017).

[57] McCluskey (n 55) 443, 445, 447–48. See also J Elgot and R Mason, 'Labour leader refuses to rule out backing industrial action outside the law', *The Guardian* (24 September 2017).

[58] McCluskey (n 55) 440.

[59] Labour Party, *A Fair Deal at Work* (2017).

[60] Ibid.

it 'mandatory for all large employers, with over 250 staff, to bargain collectively with recognised trade unions'.[61]

Corbyn exceeded expectations by steering Labour to a strong (but losing) performance in the 2017 election,[62] bolstering his support among trade unions. He took an equally bold labour law reform policy into the 2019 election.[63] However, by this time, the steadying effect of Boris Johnson's replacement of Theresa May as prime minister combined with Labour's indecisive position on Brexit produced a massive defeat – including the desertion of former Labour voters in pro-Brexit regions of the UK.[64] As Niven observes, Brexit may have been the catalyst, but the 2019 result was the culmination of many years of disenchantment with Labour in its traditional working-class heartlands.[65] The subsequent election of the more moderate Sir Keir Starmer as Labour leader has seen the re-emergence of greater distance between the party and trade unions[66] as the TUC seeks to safeguard the rights of British workers under the UK-EU trade deal arising from Brexit.[67]

## V. Up for a Scrap: Social Movements, 'Indy Unions' and #McStrike

Community engagement and social movement unionism have also featured in the renewal strategies of UK unions, influenced by US practices. However, there has been a certain hesitancy on the part of unions in Britain to 'reorientate their recruitment and organising activities' through engagement with workers outside the workplace.[68] Generally, unions have relied more upon direct approaches to employers in their claims for recognition than coalition building.[69] That said, union coalitions with faith and other community groups have been evident in

[61] D Boffey, 'Corbyn pledges to scrap Blair union laws in favour of collective bargaining', *The Guardian* (30 July 2016).

[62] J Landale, 'Election results 2017: the Jeremy Corbyn factor', *BBC News* (9 June 2017); see also Murray (n 54) 168, 186–89.

[63] Labour Party, *It's Time for Real Change: The Labour Party Manifesto 2019* (2019) 59–64. Labour's 2017 and 2019 policies were buttressed by reform proposals developed by the UK Institute of Employment Rights: see ch 11.

[64] See, eg, L McCluskey, 'Brexit is the reason Labour lost – here is how it can win again', *Huffington Post UK* (13 December 2019).

[65] A Niven, 'The Labour Party's Spectacular Defeat Had Been Coming for Decades', *New York Times* (20 December 2019).

[66] See, eg, L Goodall, 'Unite decides to cut Labour affiliation money amid frustrations', *BBC News* (7 October 2020); S Rodgers, 'Bakers Union plans to consult members on staying affiliated to Labour', *LabourList* (20 November 2020); J Stone, 'Keir Starmer opposes strike action by teachers and says they may have to work during holidays', *The Independent* (22 February 2021).

[67] TUC, *The TUC's Ten-Point Plan to Protect Jobs, Rights and Public Services After Brexit* (2021).

[68] P James and J Karmowsaka, 'British Union Renewal: Does Salvation Really Lie beyond the Workplace?' (2016) 47:2 *Industrial Relations Journal* 102, 103; see also Wills (n 14) 154.

[69] C Frege, E Heery and L Turner, 'The New Solidarity? Trade Union Coalition-Building in Five Countries', in Frege and Kelly (n 16) 137, 146; see also Simms, Holgate and Heery (n 1) 136.

campaigns focused upon ending poverty through the 'Living Wage', including the activism of the London Citizens group,[70] now undertaken nationally by Citizens UK.[71] Unite has led the way in forging social movement links through its Justice for Cleaners campaign[72] and the support of the union's hotel and restaurant branch for the Justice for Domestic Workers campaign.[73] The union introduced a community membership category in 2011, 'open[ing] its membership to people not in paid employment such as students, retirees, claimants and carers'.[74] Unite has also employed dedicated community organisers and established community branches of the union in cities including Liverpool and Sheffield, campaigning on local issues such as reduced health services and nursery closures and, on occasion, enlisting the support of this wider membership base in industrial action.[75] GMB operated a specialist branch and learning centre for Polish migrant workers in Southampton from 2006 until 2012.[76] The Transport Salaried Staffs Association built an alliance of environmental, transport user and disability activist groups and the National Union of Rail, Maritime and Transport Workers, into the Together for Transport campaign to protest cuts to train services and the jobs of rail workers.[77] These and other examples reflect the closer integration of UK unions and civil society groups precipitated by the need to combat austerity.[78]

Using many of the community-based, direct-action tactics of US alt-labour groups like the Fight for $15 movement,[79] the more innovative forms of unionism to emerge recently in the UK are the independent, grass-roots unions seeking to mobilise low-paid workers. Two significant examples are IWGB, formed in 2012 'by a group of Hispanic cleaners as a breakaway from Unite and Unison';[80]

[70] J Holgate, 'An International Study of Trade Union Involvement in Community Organizing: Same Model, Different Outcomes' (2015) 53:3 *British Journal of Industrial Relations* 460, 466–68. See further J Holgate and J Wills, 'Organising Labor in London: Lessons from the Living Wage Campaign', in L Turner and D Cornfield (eds), *Labor in the New Urban Battlefields: Local Solidarity in a Global Economy* (Ithaca, ILR Press, 2007) 211.

[71] See Citizens UK, 'Who we are'. Available at: www.citizensuk.org/about-us/who-we-are/ and 'The campaign for a real living wage'. Available at: www.citizensuk.org/campaigns/the-campaign-for-a-real-living-wage/. On the development of the Living Wage in the context of the UK National Minimum Wage, see Puttick (n 49) ch 4; for the currently applicable minimum rates, see: www.gov.uk/national-minimum-wage-rates.

[72] M Tapia and L Turner, 'Union Campaigns as Counter-Movements: Mobilizing Immigrant Workers in France and the United Kingdom' (2013) 51:3 *British Journal of Industrial Relations* 601, 608–10.

[73] Z Jiang and M Korczynski, 'When the "Unorganisable" Organize: The Collective Mobilization of Migrant Domestic Workers in London' (2016) 69 *Human Relations* 813, 821.

[74] M Simms, J Holgate and C Roper, 'The Trades Union Congress 150 Years On: A Review of the Organising Challenges and Responses to the Changing Nature of Work' (2019) 41:2 *Employee Relations* 331, 339. For a detailed account and assessment of the 'Unite Community' membership initiative, see J Holgate, 'Trade Unions in the Community: Building Broad Spaces of Solidarity' (2021) 42:2 *Economic and Industrial Democracy* 226.

[75] J Holgate, 'Community Organising in the UK: A "New" Approach for Trade Unions?' (2015) 36:3 *Economic and Industrial Democracy* 431, 443.

[76] James and Karmowsaka (n 68) 103, 106–13.

[77] Holgate (n 75) 444–45.

[78] See Part IV above.

[79] See ch 4.

[80] J Temperton, 'The biggest legal crisis facing Uber started with a pile of vomit', *Wired* (13 June 2018).

and UVW, set up in 2014.[81] Between them, IWGB and UVW 'organise the most vulnerable of [the UK's] immigrant workers', including outsourced and bogus self-employed 'cleaners, carers, couriers, bar staff and security guards'.[82] In mid-2018, IWGB had around 2,500 members,[83] increasing this to 4,623 by the end of 2019.[84] At the same point in time, UVW had 3,510 members.[85] Yet the influence of both unions extends well beyond these membership figures, as they have combined lively campaigning and strategic legal cases to obtain some significant outcomes for their members. IWGB campaigns are worker-led, Parfitt explaining that: 'New members compile their own demands … while organisers provide guidance and head office provides legal support.'[86] The approach of both unions is 'scrappier' than the norm.[87] The robust resistance of businesses in the sectors they cover means that: 'The IGWB and UVW place more stress on strikes and other kinds of collective action than most other unions.'[88] The tactics of these 'indy unions' also borrow from OUR Walmart[89] in seeking to 'raise labour standards through the threat of reputational damage' to employers.[90] Roberts illustrates the style of these two unions in the context of the IGWB's campaign at the University of London in 2018:

> … outside the [university's] art deco Senate House, in Bloomsbury, a Latin American wake-up call is blasting away. Horns are blown, samba music bellows, empanadas and coffee are supplied, while the one-day strikers – among them cleaners, porters and receptionists – wave enthusiastically to the car drivers who honk support. *This is protest as carnival.*[91]

The IWGB's action in conjunction with UVW through the 'Back in House' campaign succeeded in obtaining the University of London's reversal of outsourcing, bringing many workers into direct employment and ending zero-hours contracts.[92] A similar campaign and nine-day strike by UVW members at St Mary's Hospital

[81] S Parfitt, 'Two tiny but mighty trade unions offer UK a better way to "take back control"', *The Conversation* (11 July 2018). See, further, J Shenker, *Now We Have Your Attention: The New Politics of the People* (London, The Bodley Head, 2019) ch 3.

[82] Parfitt, ibid.

[83] Y Roberts, 'The tiny union beating the gig economy giants', *The Guardian* (1 July 2018).

[84] IWGB, 2019 Annual Return to the Certification Officer.

[85] UVW, 2019 Annual Return to the Certification Officer.

[86] Parfitt (n 81); see also J Benfield, 'The workers will see you now: organising with the IWGB', *Notes from Below* (16 July 2018).

[87] I West-Knights, 'How a new breed of trade union is leading the fight for precarious workers', *New Statesman* (23 October 2019).

[88] Parfitt (n 81).

[89] See ch 4.

[90] A Wood, 'It's a matter of time: can Deliveroo deliver collective bargaining for the gig economy?', *Oxford Internet Institute Blog* (16 August 2016). Available at: www.oii.ox.ac.uk/blog/its-a-matter-of-time-can-deliveroo-deliver-collective-bargaining-for-the-gig-economy/.

[91] Roberts (n 83), emphasis added.

[92] Ibid, tracing the origins of the campaign to IWGB's fight over many years for London Living Wage rates, sick and holiday pay and pensions for outsourced University of London workers. See also J Hayns, 'We are not the dirt we clean', *Jacobin* (17 May 2017).

London in 2019 resulted in the Imperial College Healthcare NHS Trust ending its outsourcing of cleaners, porters and catering staff through Sodexo, improving pay and conditions for 1,200 workers across five of the Trust's hospitals.[93] UVW claimed this result was 'a historic turning point in … labour relations in the English NHS', as contracted-out workers had for the first time '"done the impossible"' by obtaining direct employment in an NHS Trust.[94] IWGB has also challenged the gig economy's sham self-employment model on behalf of private hire car drivers and food delivery workers, placing it 'at the forefront of "test" litigation on employment status and thereby public policy'.[95] The union now has eleven branches, including newer ones covering yoga instructors[96] and game workers.[97] The formation of the latter demonstrates the attraction of the IWGB model for workers wanting to collectivise based on their identity, Woodcock highlighting that, by the end of 2018:

> In under a year, many videogame workers had gone from not knowing what a union was – but knowing that managers did not want them to join one – to forming their own union. Joining the IWGB provided the opportunity for them to preserve aspects of their own organization and the branding they had developed, while establishing a legal trade union structure.[98]

Most importantly, IWGB and UVW have given marginalised, precarious workers – large numbers of whom are women – a voice for the first time in their lives. Shenker goes so far as to claim that in contrast to the conventional assessment of the weakness of organised labour in the UK: 'The reality is that labour militancy hasn't died at all. It is simply playing out on fresh terrain, and fizzing with life as it does so.'[99]

In addition to the indy unions, Shenker's contention is based on the 'McStrike' campaign led by BFAWU.[100] In September 2017, 40 workers at two McDonald's

[93] B Staton, 'NHS trust brings workers in-house after industrial action', *Financial Times* (31 January 2020). See also the video documentary of the UVW members' action at St Mary's Hospital, 'United Voices', *The Guardian* (August 2020). Available at: www.theguardian.com/politics/ng-interactive/2020/aug/12/united-voices-outsourced-key-workers-fighting-for-equal-rights-video.

[94] UVW, 'Campaigns: St Mary's Hospital'. Available at: www.uvwunion.org.uk/en/campaigns/st-marys-hospital/.

[95] M Ford and T Novitz, 'There is Power in a Union? Revisiting Trade Union Functions in 2019', in A Bogg, J Rowbottom and A Young (eds), *The Constitution of Social Democracy: Essays in Honour of Keith Ewing* (Oxford, Hart Publishing, 2020) 261, 270–71. See further chs 9–10.

[96] IWGB, Yoga Teachers' Union. Available at: https://yogateachersunion.co.uk/; see also R Booth, 'UK's first yoga union fights for fairer share of £900m-a-year industry', *The Guardian* (4 February 2021).

[97] IWGB, 'We are the IWGB Game Workers', at: www.gwu-uk.org/.

[98] J Woodcock, 'Organizing in the Game Industry: The Story of Game Workers Unite U.K.' (2020) 29:1 *New Labor Forum* 50, 55.

[99] Shenker (n 81) 82–83. See also S Eason, 'Amid TUC decline, Britain's radical unions grow', *Freedom News* (21 December 2017); K Rogers, 'Precarious and Migrant Workers in Struggle: Are New Forms of Trade Unionism Necessary in Post-Brexit Britain?' (2017) 41:2 *Capital and Class* 336; D Però, 'Indie Unions, Organizing and Labour Renewal: Learning from Precarious Migrant Workers' (2020) 34:5 *Work, Employment and Society* 900.

[100] Shenker (n 81) 83–89.

stores in London took industrial action over safety and sexual assault concerns, low pay and the prevalence of zero-hours contracts, the strike soon spreading to other parts of the country.[101] Organised predominantly through social media using the hashtag #McStrike, a movement 'inspired by' the Fight for $15 was under way with striking workers supported by protesters at rallies outside Parliament and McDonald's head office in London.[102] According to BFAWU, McDonald's workers 'on low wages – with no guarantee of hours … [felt] as if they [had] no alternative but to take action' in support of a £10 per hour minimum wage and recognition of their union.[103] May Day 2018 saw further strikes at several of the fast-food chain's UK stores.[104] This was followed by a national day of action on 4 October 2018, bringing together McDonald's workers and those in other parts of the food sector (including TGI Fridays restaurants, JD Wetherspoon pubs and Uber Eats).[105]

The McStrike movement yielded agreement from McDonald's to a minimal increase in hourly rates for workers in early 2018 (from £7.60 to between £8.00–10.00 per hour for those aged over 25 and proportionate increases for younger staff; the UK minimum wage at the time was £7.50 per hour).[106] It also carried symbolic significance, in that a multinational corporation, emblematic of US anti-unionism, discovered that young, vulnerable workers were willing to unionise and go out on strike for the first time. Yet Wood has questioned the disempowering effects, for the workers, of what was essentially a social media-driven mobilising campaign and called for unions like BFAWU to build on this through 'greater organising activity'.[107] The parallel collective action at the Wetherspoons pubs has proved to be a more fertile basis for sustained unionisation (at least at two sites, in Brighton) and improvements in pay and working conditions.[108]

## VI. 'An Alternative to Simply not being Present': New Membership Models and Digital Experiments

In the last five years, the TUC and union-aligned think tanks have produced numerous reports examining the path forward for UK unions and identifying

[101] B Quinn, 'McDonald's set for more strikes as action spreads across Britain', *The Guardian* (19 November 2017).

[102] A Wood, 'Beyond Mobilisation at McDonald's: Towards Networked Organising' (2020) 44:4 *Capital and Class* 493, 493, 496.

[103] BFAWU, 'McStrike'. Available at: www.bfawu.org/mcstrike.

[104] 'McDonald's workers strike in protest of zero-hours contracts', *Institute of Employment Rights* (4 May 2018).

[105] Wood (n 102) 496–97; 'McDonald's, UberEats and Wetherspoon workers strike over pay', *BBC News* (4 October 2018).

[106] B Chapman, 'McDonald's workers "over the moon" about pay rise but vow to fight on for living wage', *The Independent* (4 January 2018).

[107] Wood (n 102) 400. See ch 11.

[108] C Cant and J Woodcock, 'Fast Food Shutdown: From Disorganisation to Action in the Service Sector' (2020) 44:4 *Capital and Class* 513, 514–16, 519; see also J Canady, 'Lessons from McStrike',

examples of innovation in union renewal.[109] Tait's 2017 report for the Fabian Society and Community Union's joint initiative, the Changing Work Centre,[110] laid out 'a plan for a trade union membership renaissance' – by tackling 'the major but not insurmountable challenge' of attracting the millions of private sector workers who are not union members.[111] The report found (based on survey and focus group data) that private sector workers were generally supportive of the role of trade unions, but felt that unions were distant from their working lives and 'not for me' or not representative of workers' diverse backgrounds.[112] However, non-unionised workers indicated they would be prepared to join a union if provided with 'evidence of how it could help them [personally]' and that it represented 'value for money' (among other factors).[113] Tait outlined 11 recommendations for unions to reverse 40 years of falling membership through 'a mixture of reflection and modernisation', including: providing workers with a compelling case for joining the union linked to positive stories of winning gains for members; offering discount membership rates for workers under 35 and those in workplaces where the union is not recognised; enabling prospective members to obtain instant membership coverage when a workplace problem arises (rather than union membership being 'a form of insurance' against a problem that might emerge in the future); and investing in technology 'to develop new tools and resources that can help make the organisation of hard-to-reach workers more economically viable'.[114]

Brock's 2019 report, also for the Changing Work Centre, zeroed in on the UK's 4.8 million self-employed workers (of which only 7% are union members) and maintained that: 'There is no reason that the growth in self-employment in the UK could not be developed into a new culture of self-employed worker trade unionism.'[115] To achieve this, unions have to overcome the absence of a traditional workplace for many self-employed workers by organising digitally, including through the use of 'WorkerTech' tools that 'help produce a sense of community across geographic distance'.[116] Successful examples of this approach include the

*Workers' Liberty: Reason in Revolt* (11 September 2019). Available at: www.workersliberty.org/story/2019-09-11/lessons-mcstrike.

[109] In addition to the reports considered in the following discussion, see Unions 21, *Roadmap to Renewal: A Manifesto for Change* (April 2018); P Willman, A Bryson and J Forth, *New Model Unions: Options for the 21st Century* (Unions 21, August 2019). See also K Schoemann, 'Digital Technology to Support the Trade Union Movement' (2018) 6 *Open Journal of Social Sciences* 67.

[110] See: https://community-tu.org/changing-work-centre/.

[111] C Tait, *Future Unions: Towards a Membership Renaissance in the Private Sector* (The Changing Work Centre, November 2017) 10–11.

[112] Ibid, 20–31.

[113] Ibid, 31–34.

[114] Ibid, 35, 39–47. See also ch 11.

[115] J Brock, *Getting Organised: Low-Paid Self-Employment and Trade Unions* (The Changing Work Centre, May 2019) 4, 11.

[116] Ibid, 11–12. See further Inline Policy, *Understanding the Emergence of WorkerTech: How New Businesses and Platforms Support Independent Workers* (undated), available at: www.inlinepolicy.com/understanding-workertech.

TUC's WorkSmart app aimed at recruiting young workers into unions (see below) and OUR Walmart's WorkIt app in the USA.[117] Brock argued the self-employed 'are running a one-person business and unions need to identify a package of support that helps them in this endeavour', for example services that help self-employed workers to deal with taxation compliance, sickness and injury cover and retirement planning.[118]

Digital transformation is also a major theme of Coatman's 2020 report for the TUC, examining the lessons of its WorkSmart project: 'a programme of research and innovation to explore how the union movement can better reach young workers'.[119] WorkSmart was part of a major campaign to rebuild the UK's unions undertaken by the TUC in 2018, its 150th anniversary year.[120] TUC General Secretary, Frances O'Grady, stated that: '[W]e've begun to prototype a model of trade unionism that appeals to young workers and is tailored to their lives.'[121] The TUC sought to address 'a gap in the union offer' in failing to make available 'the kind of digital experiences young people are used to' like Netflix and Spotify, contributing to the low level of membership among those aged 20–29.[122] Within this age bracket, the TUC's initiative targeted what it describes as 'young core workers': those on low to median wages, not in full-time education, and working in the private sector (particularly retail, hospitality and social care) for companies 'with enough other staff to form a collective' (ie, 50 or more employees).[123] Among these workers, the barriers to engaging with unions include highly insecure work, employers pitting workers against each other, a sense of futility and negative associations with unions (for example, that they are 'ineffective, irrelevant, bureaucratic, hierarchical and unrepresentative of wider society, as they are seen as older, white and male').[124] Through in-depth consultation with younger workers, the TUC developed the WorkSmart app, providing:

> … a personalised, mobile-first experience, with bite-size content, that's ready when [young workers] are, in accessible language ….
>
> …

[117] Brock (n 115) 13–14; see also ch 4.

[118] Ibid, 17; at 18, Brock noted the success of unions covering freelancers in the creative industries in negotiating collective agreements and providing services that address the unique issues of these self-employed professionals. This includes the professionals' union Prospect, explored further in S Ferns, 'How do unions eat the digital elephant? One bite at a time', in C Tait and T Phibbs (eds), *A New Collectivism: How Private Sector Trade Unions Can Innovate and Grow* (Fabian Society, December 2017) 20. See also ch 10.

[119] C Coatman, *The Missing Half Million: How Unions Can Transform Themselves to be a Movement of Young Workers* (TUC, January 2020) 4.

[120] K Carberry, 'Working Together' in Tait and Phibbs (n 118) 14, 15; TUC, 'Building stronger unions', available at: www.tuc.org.uk/building-stronger-unions.

[121] F O'Grady, 'Introduction', in Tait and Phibbs (n 118) 4.

[122] Coatman (n 119) 5, noting that 14.1% of this age group were union members in 2019 (and only 7.5% in the private sector).

[123] Ibid, 10.

[124] Ibid, 17. See also S O'Connor, 'Trade unions strive to stay relevant by wooing the young', *Financial Times* (18 September 2017).

> … WorkSmart offers rights information, presented as top ten lists, in quizzes and as tools, eg a salary checker …. There are also more subtle mechanisms, eg polls, where young workers can see the aggregate results of how others feel to build a sense that they are not alone.[125]

This construction of a bridge to collectivism is the key point of WorkSmart. Coatman found that in the TUC's pilot of the app from June 2018 to March 2019, young workers who 'were not drawn to union branding and logos' became 'receptive to hearing about unions' once they had formed a relationship with a brand they trusted.[126] As Simms, Holgate and Roper observe in their consideration of WorkSmart, after using the app to engage workers around a workplace issue or problem:

> Like all organising, the trick is then to use that issue as a jumping off point to broaden the conversation and introduce new possibilities; including union membership. It is explicitly an effort to move organising activity into a digital space ….[127]

In 2019, the TUC established the TUC Digital Lab to develop 'strategic principles for unions in approaching digital transformation' and to run best practice workshops and pilot projects.[128] Its February 2021 report examined how mainstream UK unions are using technology to meet the challenge presented by 'disruptors', including the new independent unions and an array of campaigning, advisory and activist organisations.[129] One example is Community's partnership with Labour Xchange, a platform that matches self-employed workers with businesses.[130] The workers are guaranteed UK Living Wage pay rates, and gain access to Community-provided advice and information on the Labour Xchange portal if they opt to become associate members of the union free of charge: 'This helps introduce the union to these workers, who can choose to upgrade to full union membership at self-employed rates.'[131] Community invested £40,000 in seed funding for Labour Xchange, which also has mechanisms to steer workers and the businesses engaging them towards more permanent forms of work.[132] The TUC Digital Lab report warns that while unions 'need to be wary about getting into new areas solely focused around providing services to individuals', this can be 'the first step to[wards] a collective approach'.[133] It recommends experimentation

[125] Coatman (n 119) 21–23. See also www.getworksmart.co.uk/; and chs 4 and 6.
[126] Ibid, 24–26.
[127] Simms, Holgate and Roper (n 1) 338–39.
[128] TUC Digital, 'A digital lab for the trade union movement'. Available at: https://digital.tuc.org.uk/a-digital-lab-for-the-union-movement/. See also TUC Digital, 'TUC digital health-check (Self-assessment tool for unions)'. Available at: https://digital.tuc.org.uk/tuc-digital-healthcheck/.
[129] TUC Digital, *Unions and Digital Disruption* (February 2021) 7–10.
[130] Ibid, 13. See also www.labourxchange.uk/.
[131] TUC Digital (n 129) 14.
[132] Brock (n 115) 23; R Wright, 'Gig economy app seeks to balance UK workers and employers', *Financial Times* (22 February 2019).
[133] TUC Digital (n 129 above) 15.

with digital offerings, including 'sub-brands or spin-off unions', based on the idea that:

> Where the normal union model isn't working for particular situations, we need to consider ways to offer different models of organising, around the core values of unionism, *as an alternative to simply not being present in that area.*[134]

## VII. Conclusion

The organising model has not saved UK unions, any more than it did in its homeland, the USA, or in another export recipient, Australia. In the British context, organising's successes were constrained by the concurrent pursuit of workplace partnerships – a road to nowhere, in terms of union revitalisation. While UK unions have been buffeted by decades of confrontation from the state and employers, it was noted in Chapter 2 that membership numbers have been inching back upwards during the last few years.[135] There are other reasons for optimism. As this chapter has shown, there is a bolder, more confident form of unionism emerging in the UK, embodied by IWGB, UVW and #McStrike.[136] There is also the promise, not yet fully realised but explored in the union and think tank discussion papers examined here, of what Simms, Holgate and Roper have called 'a digital revolution in the [labour] movement'.[137] Experiments like the TUC's WorkSmart app provide a connection point with workers who have tended to evade unions, but more needs to be done to develop these into mechanisms for workers to build and exercise collective power.[138]

[134] Ibid (emphasis added).
[135] See also R Wright, 'Niche trade unions buck trend of falling membership', *Financial Times* (25 June 2019); and ch 12.
[136] See also chs 9 and 10.
[137] Simms, Holgate and Roper (n 1) 338.
[138] See ch 11.

# 8

# Italian Unions: Fighting for the Marginalised

## I. Introduction

It was shown in Chapter 2 that Italian unions have not experienced the extent of decline that has beset their counterparts in the USA, the UK and Australia. For this and other reasons, the strategies adopted by Italian unions to preserve and grow their membership have differed markedly from those of unions in the other three countries. Given the close links between unions and the Italian state, the provision of services to members has featured prominently (for example, through the *patronati* offices which assist workers in accessing welfare schemes, along with union-run taxation and legal advocacy services).[1] Social movement unionism has generally not been as visible in the Italian context as in the other three countries (although there are now stronger signs of its emergence, as discussed in Part V below). Focused lobbying for legal reform has not preoccupied the Italian unions, given the more favourable institutional and regulatory context in which they operate.[2]

Probably the major distinctive feature of the path taken by Italian unions over the last 30 years is that, as was observed in Chapter 1, the US organising model has not formed a central component of union renewal efforts. Writing at a time when organising by US, UK and Australian unions was reaching its peak, Heery and Adler observed that Italian unions had not (for the most part) engaged in similar 'campaigns to extend membership to non-union enterprises'.[3] This was partly attributable to the (traditionally) integral position of the main union confederations as 'authoritative social partners' recognised by the state, 'thereby reducing their need to rely on internal sources of strength, developed through organizing'.[4] As we saw in Chapters 2 and 3, the principal source of institutional strength of

[1] L Frangi and M Barisione, 'Are You a Union Member? Determinants and Trends of Subjective Union Membership in Italian Society (1972–2013)' (2015) 21:4 *Transfer* 451, 456; S Leonardi, 'Trade Unions and Collective Bargaining in Italy during the Crisis', in S Lehndorff, H Dribbusch and T Schulten, *Rough Waters: European Trade Unions in a Time of Crisis* (European Trade Union Institute, 2018) 87, 103–4.

[2] See ch 3.

[3] E Heery and L Adler, 'Organizing the Unorganized' in C Frege and J Kelly (eds), *Varieties of Unionism: Revitalization in a Globalizing Economy* (Oxford, Oxford University Press, 2004) 45, 55–56.

[4] Ibid, 60.

Italian unions is their central role in collective bargaining, with national collective agreements for each industry establishing 'the threshold of reference' for decent minimum working conditions.[5] This is supplemented by the second channel of workplace-based representation through RSAs and RSUs. These structures are thought to act as 'functional equivalents [to organising] that allow unions to secure legitimacy, control resources, and represent their members', although without necessarily increasing membership.[6]

Instead of US-style organising, Italian unions have increasingly sought to advance a 'more inclusive unionism' by targeting vulnerable worker groups in which there may be 'potential growth in terms of stronger representation and membership'.[7] Three major areas of focus have been migrant workers; 'the constant and strong mobilisation against precarious work';[8] and the logistics sector, which has seen an upsurge in union activism in recent years. Each of these is examined closely in this chapter, beginning with precarious work and, in particular, the efforts of unions to represent and build strength among agency workers. Another significant site of mobilisation on the part of Italian unions and self-organised worker groups, the gig economy, is explored in Chapters 9 and 10.

## II. Specialist Unions for Precarious Workers – And Challenging Agency Work

Liberalisation of labour market regulation in Italy from the 1980s led to fixed-term contracts, self-employment (both false and genuine) and sub-contracting '[becoming] more accessible for firms willing to compete on labour costs'.[9] By 2009, while the use of part-time and fixed-term work was largely in line with the European Union (EU) average, self-employment (at around 17 per cent of the national workforce) was well above EU levels.[10] Self-employment in Italy reached 23 per cent in 2015, compared with the EU average of 14 per cent.[11] Zero-hours contracts (*lavoro a chiamata*) have proliferated since they were first legalised in 2003.[12] In the early stages of the evolution of atypical forms of work in Italy,

[5] Leonardi (n 1) 109.

[6] Heery and Adler (n 3) 65; see also 59.

[7] Leonardi (n 1) 105.

[8] Ibid; see also L Zamponi and M Vogiatzoglou, 'Contentious Labour in Italy and Greece: Movements and Trade Unions in Times of Precarity and Austerity' in M Wennerhag, C Fröhlich and G Piotrowski (eds), *Radical Left Movements in Europe* (Farnham, Ashgate, 2017) 82, 89–91.

[9] V Pulignano, L Gervasi and F de Franceschi, 'Union Responses to Precarious Workers: Italy and Spain Compared' (2016) 22:1 *European Journal of Industrial Relations* 39, 42.

[10] Ibid; see also A Murgia and G Selmi, '"Inspire and Conspire": Italian Precarious Workers between Selforganization and Self-advocacy' (2012) 4:2 *Interface* 181, 183.

[11] A Murgia and V Pulignano, 'Neither Precarious nor Entrepreneur: The Subjective Experience of Hybrid Self-Employed Workers' (2019) *Economic and Industrial Democracy* (advance access), 3, 7.

[12] S Gasparri, P Ikeler and G Fullin, 'Trade Union Strategy in Fashion Retail in Italy and the USA: Converging Divergence between Institutions and Mobilisation' (2019) 25:4 *European Journal of Industrial Relations* 345, 350.

the major union confederations (CGIL, CISL and UIL)[13] moved from outright opposition to non-standard employment to various forms of engagement with the concerns of precarious workers.[14] Unions came to defend the rights of these workers 'through the national level social dialogue' (for example, seeking to extend social security benefits to fixed-term and agency staff) and 'political bargaining … directed at reducing the economic incentive to use atypical contracts'.[15] In addition, from the late 1990s, Italian unions set up dedicated organisations for temporary workers, agency staff, the 'bogus' (or dependent) self-employed, freelancers and others engaged in atypical work.[16] Three significant examples are CGIL's NIDiL (*Nuova Identitá di Lavoro*), FELSA (*Federazione Lavoratori Somministrati Autonomi ed Atipici*) established by CISL, and UILTemp: as Regalia explains, 'unions of an entirely new kind' in that their membership is based on 'a specific type of employment contract' rather than workers being engaged in a particular sector.[17]

According to Durazzi, the formation of these specialist unions reflects a 'general organizational principle' that atypical worker representation is best advanced at two levels: at the horizontal level of the workers' status (to meet the common demands that inevitably arise from such status), combined with the vertical level of the sector (linking atypical workers to the broader collective bargaining and political agenda of the industry-wide unions).[18] Leonardi observes that the 'atypical unions' have contributed to overall membership growth, NIDiL reaching almost 94,000 members by 2016; and combined with FELSA and UILTemp, an increase from 85,000 members in 1998 to 205,000 in 2016.[19] Marino et al suggest that these unions have the common objective of 'increas[ing] employment protection granted to self-employed, semi-autonomous and temporary workers through collective bargaining and shop-floor representation', although through different routes.[20] For example, NIDiL has sought to restrict the contractual options available to companies (such as staff-leasing), while FELSA and UILTemp have pursued more of 'an individual servicing model' to assist workers

[13] See ch 2.

[14] S Marino, M Bernaciak, A Mrozowicki and V Pulignano, 'Unions for Whom? Union Democracy and Precarious Workers in Poland and Italy' (2019) 40:1 *Economic and Industrial Democracy* 111, 122.

[15] Ibid.

[16] Leonardi (n 1) 105; M Bernaciak, R Gumbrell-McCormick and R Hyman, *European Trade Unionism: From Crisis to Renewal?* (European Trade Union Institute, Report 133, 2014) 21.

[17] I Regalia, 'Italian Trade Unions: Still Shifting between Consolidated Organizations and Social Movements?' (2012) 23:4 *Management Revue* 386, 398. See also Pulignano et al (n 9) 44–45; Murgia and Selmi (n 10) 184–85; and the websites of NIDiL (www.nidil.cgil.it/), FELSA (www.felsa.cisl.it) and UILTemp (www.uiltemp.it/).

[18] N Durazzi, 'Inclusive Unions in a Dualized Labour Market? The Challenge of Organizing Labour Market Policy and Social Protection for Labour Market Outsiders' (2017) 51:2 *Social and Policy Administration* 265, 271–72.

[19] Leonardi (n 1) 105.

[20] Marino et al (n 14) 120.

in dealing with specific problems.[21] However, in collective bargaining, each of these three unions has worked in tandem with their respective confederations to improve protections for atypical workers (especially in 'fostering their transitions to permanent employment').[22]

Agency work is a particular form of precarious work in respect of which the union confederations and their atypical worker offshoots have all been active. The broader move towards promoting flexible work took the form of specific legislation relating to agencies in 1997 (known as the Treu reform).[23] Law 196/1997 removed the former ban on agency work, replacing it with a narrower prohibition on the engagement of low-skilled workers through agencies but allowing the engagement of agency staff to meet genuine, temporary business needs.[24] Sectoral collective agreements could make provision for further permitted situations of agency staff use; and, in all cases, the principle of 'equal treatment' applied so that agency workers would receive the same pay and conditions as permanent employees.[25] The 2003 Biagi reform (Law 276/2003) gave additional impetus to agency work, establishing rules for its deployment including registration requirements that agencies must meet to be able to operate; permitting businesses to use agency workers 'for technical, productive, organisational or replacement reasons'; and retaining the principle of equal treatment.[26] Subsequent labour law changes 'lifted the remaining legislative limits to employers' use of agency work and the obligation to justify it'.[27] The net effect of all this relaxation of regulation was to

[21] Ibid, 121. On NIDiL's various strategies for representing atypical workers, see further H Choi and A Mattoni, 'The Contentious Field of Precarious Work in Italy: Political Strategies, Actors and Coalitions' (2010) 13 *Working USA: The Journal of Labor and Society* 213, 217, 219–22.

[22] Marino et al (n 14) 123; see also Pulignano et al (n 9) 45–46. Note also the collective agreement for call centre workers signed by FELSA and NIDiL with the call centre employers' association in June 2016: see O Razzolini, *Collective Action for Self-Employed Workers: A Necessary Response to Increasing Income Inequality* (Centre for the Study of European Labour Law 'Massimo D'Antona', Working Paper 155/2021) 14.

[23] Marino et al (n 14) 117.

[24] C Benassi and L Dorigatti, 'The Political Economy of Agency Work in Italy and Germany: Explaining Diverging Trajectories in Collective Bargaining Outcomes', in V Doellgast, N Lillie and V Pulignano (eds), *Reconstructing Solidarity: Labour Unions, Precarious Work, and the Politics of Institutional Change in Europe* (Oxford, Oxford University Press, 2018) 124, 133.

[25] Ibid. On the application and effects of the equal treatment principle, see V Pulignano and A Signoretti, 'Union Strategies and National Institutions and the Use of Temporary Labour in Italian and US Plants' (2016) 54:3 *British Journal of Industrial Relations* 574, 581–82.

[26] MA Tranfaglia, 'Agency Work and its Regulatory Challenges: Lessons Learnt Through a Comparative Overview of Australian and Italian Approaches' in J Howe, A Chapman and I Landau (eds), *The Evolving Project of Labour Law: Foundations, Development and Future Research Directions* (Sydney, Federation Press, 2017) 206, 211–12.

[27] C Benassi, L Dorigatti and E Pannini, 'Explaining Divergent Bargaining Outcomes for Agency Workers: The Role of Labour Divides and Labour Market Reforms' (2019) 25:2 *European Journal of Industrial Relations* 163, 174. These were Law 24/2012 implementing the European Directive on Agency Work of 2008, and the Jobs Act 2015, moderated to some extent by the Dignity Decree (Law 87/2018): for a detailed exposition of the Italian legal position, see MA Tranfaglia, *A (Functional-Purposive) Comparative Analysis of the Protection of Workers Involved in Triangular Work Arrangements through*

massively increase the number of Italian workers engaged through intermediaries, from just under 15,000 in 1998 to around 675,000 in 2016.[28]

Soon after the liberalisation facilitated by the 1997 Treu reform, the three atypical worker unions (NIDiL, FELSA and UILTemp) negotiated a sectoral collective agreement covering agency work which included: income support for workers in situations of sickness, maternity or unemployment; welfare benefits (eg, childcare, healthcare); and access to training.[29] Around the same time, the metal unions obtained provisions in their sectoral agreement to 'slow down' the take-up of agency work, for example through a provision setting an upper quota of 8 per cent of a company's workforce.[30] Ceilings of this kind became common in industry-wide agreements covering all sectors in the 2000s.[31] Over time, according to Benassi and Dorigatti, collective agreements have shown a gradual weakening in the levels of protection afforded to agency workers.[32] For example, a rule in the 2008 agency work sectoral agreement requiring a worker to be permanently hired on completion of 42 months' continuous employment was removed in the 2014 agreement.[33] A similar provision in the 2008 metalwork sectoral agreement was retained in the next bargaining round, but another provision requiring businesses to provide the rationale for using agency workers was removed.[34] Benassi and Dorigatti illustrate further that (starting in the 2000s) the metal employers' association *Federmeccanica* has maximised the increasing flexibility granted by the law, and a level of division among the metalworker union affiliates of the major confederations, to dilute the collective agreement measures dealing with agency workers.[35] In contrast, Burroni and Pedaci consider that collective bargaining over the period spanning the 2008 and 2014 agency work sectoral agreements led to the enhancement of job stability, welfare, training and pension benefits for Italian temporary workers.[36] In the last few years, the prevalence of agency work

*Labour Providers in Australia and Italy* (Unpublished PhD Thesis, University of Melbourne, November 2020) ch 5.

[28] Benassi, Dorigatti and Pannini ibid, 166. See also Durazzi (n 18) 270.

[29] Benassi and Dorigatti (n 24) 128, 134. See also L Burroni and M Pedaci, 'Collective Bargaining, Atypical Employment and Welfare Provisions: The Case of Temporary Agency Work in Italy' (2014) 101 *Stato e Mercato* 169, 176–80, considering the retention and expansion of various welfare measures in more recent bargaining rounds; Durazzi (n 18) 274–77.

[30] Benassi and Dorigatti (n 24) 128, 134.

[31] Durazzi (n 18) 273.

[32] Ibid, 128–29, 136–38.

[33] Ibid, 128; see also Burroni and Pedaci (n 29) 175.

[34] Benassi and Dorigatti (n 24) 128–29.

[35] Ibid, 137–38. Compare Pulignano and Signoretti (n 25) 585, 590, exploring the success of metalworker unions in obtaining the inclusion of temporary workers in job rotation, overtime and access to permanency, through local negotiations at one Italian automotive plant.

[36] Burroni and Pedaci (n 29) 187–88. See also Durazzi (n 18) 266, 277–78; and, demonstrating the constraints on agency work obtained through local-level bargaining in two Italian manufacturing firms, C Benassi and L Dorigatti, 'Out of Sight, Out of Mind: The Challenge of External Work Arrangements for Industrial Manufacturing Unions in Germany and Italy' (2020) 34:6 *Work, Employment and Society* 1027, 1033–34.

in the logistics sector has formed part of the basis for the main union confederations' mobilisation targeting Amazon.[37]

## III. Italian Unions and Migrant Workers

In the context of hardening societal views towards migrants stoked by 'xenophobic elements of the [*Lega Nord*] constituency',[38] unions in Italy have demonstrated levels of solidarity and inclusiveness that led them to be considered 'among the most open to immigrants in Western countries'[39] and certainly within Europe.[40] These efforts (particularly from the mid-1990s to the late 2000s) included public advocacy in coalition with non-government organisations to oppose government reforms undermining migrants' rights; offering various forms of welfare and support to migrant workers (for example in relation to work permits, health and housing issues); and then gradually bringing these and other concerns into local and sectoral collective bargaining agreements.[41] Some unions established self-organised sections, such as the *Comitati Migranti* or *Coordinamenti Migranti* within CGIL and dedicated offices for the provision of services to migrant workers.[42] Unions also ran national-level anti-racism campaigns, although these did not directly address racism and discrimination at the workplace level ('arguably … in an attempt to avoid confrontational issues in a period of increasing support for the Lega Nord among rank-and-file union members'[43]). The various endeavours of CGIL, CISL and UIL to organise migrant workers had some success in increasing membership: by 2013, around 35 per cent of migrants in regular employment were members of one of the confederations (equating to

[37] See Part IV below.

[38] M Evangelista, 'Italy in Crisis: Epper si muove', in M Evangelista (ed), *Italy from Crisis to Crisis: Political Economy, Security, and Society in the 21st Century* (Abingdon, Routledge, 2018) 3, 17.

[39] L Frangi, T Zhang and R Banerjee, 'Constructing Inequalities: Tenure Trajectories of Immigrant Workers and Union Strategies in the Milan Construction Sector' (2020) *British Journal of Industrial Relations* (advance access) 2.

[40] M Rinaldini and S Marino, 'Trade Unions and Migrant Workers in Italy: Between Labour and Social Rights', in S Marino, J Roosblad and R Penninx (eds), *Trade Unions and Migrant Workers: New Contexts and Challenges in Europe* (Cheltenham, Edward Elgar Publishing, 2017) 266.

[41] Ibid, 266–67, 273–76. See also M Ambrosini, D De Luca and S Pozzi, 'Immigrants and Trade Unions in Italy: What Prospects for Mobility and Careers? A Reflection Starting from the Role of Union Delegates', in M Espinoza-Herold and M Contini (eds), *Living in Two Homes: Integration, Identity and Education of Transnational Migrants in a Globalised World* (Bingley, Emerald Publishing Limited, 2017) 61, 63–64; S Marino, 'Trade Union Inclusion of Migrant and Ethnic Minority Workers: Comparing Italy and the Netherlands' (2012) 18:1 *European Journal of Industrial Relations* 5, 12–14.

[42] Rinaldini and Marino (n 40) 275; Ambrosini, De Luca and Pozzi (n 41) 66–68. See also D De Luca, S Pozzi and M Ambrosini, 'Trade Unions and Immigrants in Italy: How Immigrant Offices Promote Inclusion' (2018) 60:1 *Journal of Industrial Relations* 101; and (for example) CGIL Bergamo, *Ufficio Migranti*. Available at: www.cgil.bergamo.it/index.php/migranti.

[43] Rinaldini and Marino (n 40) 277. See also G Zazzara, '"Italians First": Workers on the Right Amidst Old and New Populisms' (2018) 93 *International Labour and Working-class History* 101; P Goodman and E Bubola, 'The Chinese roots of Italy's far-right rage', *New York Times* (5 December 2019).

7.2 per cent of total union membership).[44] In 2016, foreign workers accounted for 9.3 per cent of overall membership.[45]

In Rinaldini and Marino's view, while there was a discernible 'cooling off' in the major union confederations' 'investment in terms of resources and effort' on behalf of migrant workers from the late 2000s,[46] representation of these workers has continued and can be seen in several 'new initiatives and campaigns'.[47] One of the most important has been that combating the exploitation of foreign workers in the agricultural sector, in which it is estimated that 400,000 irregular workers are engaged in tomato, fruit, grape and olive harvesting (concentrated in southern Italy).[48] D'Onofrio illustrates the plight of these workers, mostly migrants from Africa and Eastern Europe, as follows:

> The majority of [them] live in poor conditions within makeshift slums built by workers themselves along the countryside. The system of hiring day laborers is managed by informal intermediaries called *Caporali*, and the farm work is carried out in sweatshop working conditions: bad health and safety conditions, with a lack of labor, social and human rights.[49]

He explains that the FLAI-CGIL union (agri-industry workers' federation affiliated with CGIL) has sought to address this exploitation through both national and local-level strategies: the former, through strikes and demonstrations aimed at pressuring the Italian Department of Agriculture to adopt a policy response, ultimately achieved through legislative requirements introduced in 2016; and the latter through more direct action, such as the 'street union squads' deployed to make contact with workers on farms and inform them of their employment rights during the summer harvest in the province of Foggia.[50] Another significant

[44] Rinaldini and Marino (n 40) 281.

[45] De Luca, Pozzi and Ambrosini (n 42) 107.

[46] Rinaldini and Marino (n 40) 267; see further 278–80.

[47] Ibid, 281.

[48] G D'Onofrio, *Firms, Labour, Migrations and Unions within Tomato Value Chain in Southern Italy* (Milano, Ledizione LediPublishing, 2020) 59. See also T Jones and A Awokoya, 'Are your tinned tomatoes picked by slave labour?', *The Guardian* (20 June 2019).

[49] D'Onofrio (n 48) 59 (footnote omitted); see further ch IV. See also M Perrotta and D Sacchetto, 'Migrant Farmworkers in Southern Italy: Ghettoes, *Caporalato* and Collective Action' (2014) 1:5 *Workers of the World* 75, 80–88, detailing the role of the *caporali* or gangmasters in perpetuating the exploitation of migrant seasonal harvest workers. Another significant site of exploitation (of a predominantly Chinese-background workforce) is the garment production industry in the Tuscan town of Prato: see E Menegatti, 'Mending the Fissured Workplace: The Solutions Provided by Italian Law' (2015) 37 *Comparative Labor Law and Policy Journal* 91, 110–12; D Max, 'The Chinese workers who assemble designer bags in Tuscany', *The New Yorker* (9 April 2018); Goodman and Bubola (n 43). On union attempts to recruit and represent these workers, see L Munkholm, *Re-Inventing Labour Law Enforcement: A Socio-Legal Analysis* (Oxford, Hart Publishing, 2020) ch 5.

[50] D'Onofrio (n 48) 104–5; see also the description of FLAI-CGIL's *sindicato di strada* strategy in B Staunton, '"A worker is a worker": The trade unions organising migrants across Europe', *Equal Times* (27 February 2020). Available at: www.equaltimes.org/a-worker-is-a-worker-the-trade?lang=en#.YEmjOrhVc2w. The legislation curbing farmworker exploitation is Law 199/2016, which included new penal sanctions (substantial fines and imprisonment for up to six years) directed at the *carporali* and others engaged in illicit labour brokering: see Unauthored, 'Contrast to the exploitation of labour

element of FLAI-CGIL's localised action has been to support migrant workers to build their own representation system, by training delegates within the worker settlements so they have the skills to take on 'the responsibility of pushing workers to denounce exploitation'.[51] Yet D'Onofrio is critical of FLAI-CGIL's commitment of scant resources to its farmworker campaign.[52]

More encouraging is the approach of the independent union USB (*Unione Sindacale di Base*) in: 'organising and unionising the workers along the entire agri-food chain, "from field to table"'.[53] Through a whole-of-supply-chain strategy aligning the common interests of workers, farmers and consumers, USB has led regional and national demonstrations following farmworker deaths and continued revelations of exploitation (although D'Onofrio suggests that this effort, too, 'has failed to substantially improve workers' conditions'[54]). USB also led farmworker protests (a 'strike of the invisibles') following the Italian government's introduction, in May 2020, of temporary six-month work permits for undocumented workers.[55] Another independent union, SI Cobas, has played a very important role in the logistics sector, becoming 'the "migrants' union" par excellence' based on 'conflictual action inspired by class solidarity'.[56]

## IV. Building (Rank-and-File) Union Strength in the Logistics Sector

The Italian logistics sector has been an increasingly productive site for worker activism – especially by independent unions – over the last decade or so. The ingredients for this outburst have included the high proportion of migrant workers engaged in logistics and warehousing and a concentration of major global distribution and retail companies (including Amazon, TNT Express, DB Schenker and IKEA) in or near the Po Valley.[57] This region, as Curcio describes:

> … functions as a huge logistics space suited for the just-in-time capitalist valorisation process. It represents the heart of the circulation of goods in Italy and Europe.

in agriculture: the Italian legislation', FLAI-CGIL/Fondazione Metes (7 March 2019). Available at: www.fondazionemetes.it/italian-laws-against-work-exploitation-agriculture.

[51] D'Onofrio (n 48) 106. On the importance, and actual experience, of integrating migrant workers within the delegate networks and formal structures of Italian unions, see Ambrosini, De Luca and Pozzi (n 41).

[52] D'Onofrio (n 48) 106–7, 111–12.

[53] Ibid, 108–9.

[54] Ibid, 109–11.

[55] 'Foggia migrant farmworkers protest against "lack of rights"', *ANSA.it (English edition)* (25 May 2020); see also R Hughes, 'New migrant worker rights in Italy just another form of exploitation?', *Forbes* (16 May 2020).

[56] S Battistelli and P Campanella, 'Subcontracting Chain and Working Conditions in Italy: Evidence from the Meat and Food Industry' (2020) 27:2 *Studies on Labour Law and Social Policy* 135, 143.

[57] A Curcio, 'Italy: The Revolution in Logistics', in D Azzellini and M Kraft (eds), *The Class Strikes Back: Self-Organised Workers' Struggles in the Twenty-First Century* (Chicago, Haymarket Books, 2017) 259, 261.

> Milan, Piacenza, Bologna, as well as Verona and Padua are its epicentres, the nodal points connected by the harbours of Genoa … and Venice …. The whole [system of] import-export between the Middle East and North Africa passes through here.[58]

She also illustrates that many of the logistics firms, as well as taking advantage of the unique positioning of this region, have utilised a 'subcontracted labour force', engaged through cooperatives, to avoid labour and social security regulations.[59] As the cooperatives are not subject to national collective agreements, the conditions are created for the exploitation of a low-skilled workforce of which around 98 per cent are migrants.[60] These outcomes are consistent with the more general 'expansion of precarious work' in the performance of functions like parcel delivery and warehousing (not only in Italy), as these are increasingly situated as 'integrative parts of a sector with systemic importance in ensuring the smooth functioning of global supply chains'.[61] In the Italian context, the utilisation of cooperatives to distance logistics companies from the workers performing labour has given rise to piece-rate payment systems, up to 12-hour working days and close monitoring of work performance.[62] This has also been a de-unionisation strategy, which has seen the core workforce in many unionised warehouses replaced (since the 2000s) by sub-contracted staff.[63]

According to Benvegnú, Haidinger and Sacchetto, the main Italian union confederations have focused mostly on core/white-collar workers in the logistics sector and neglected the large body of migrant workers engaged as 'porters'.[64] In their view, this reflects a broader 'inertia and slowness to adapt to the dynamic economic of logistics' on the part of the mainstream unions, which have long regarded warehousing and storage 'as auxiliary activities to the factory, where the core of production takes place'.[65] Newer, grassroots unions have stepped in to fill the vacuum, providing 'legal and organizational support to [the workers']

[58] Ibid. See also N Cuppini, M Frapporti and M Pirone, 'Logistics Struggles in the Po Valley Region: Territorial Transformations and Processes of Antagonistic Subjectivation' (2015) 114:1 *South Atlantic Quarterly* 119.

[59] Curcio (n 57) 261–62; see also C Benvegnú, B Haidinger and D Sacchetto, 'Restructuring Labour Responses and Employment in the European Logistics Sector: Unions' Responses to a Segmented Workforce', in Doellgast, Lillie and Pulignano (n 24) 83, 85–86, 89–90. On the link between cooperatives and exploitative or precarious working conditions in other economic sectors, see F Ianuzzi and D Sacchetto, 'Outsourcing and Workers' Resistance Practices in Venice's Hotel Industry: The Role of Migrants Employed by Cooperatives' (2020) *Economic and Industrial Democracy* (advance access); G Borraccino and A Gentile, 'Trade Unions and Self-Organised Groups of Educational Workers in Italy' (2019) 7:2 *Critical and Radical Social Work* 215.

[60] Curcio (n 57) 262; see also 263–67, detailing the intimidation, violence and racist treatment directed towards the warehouse workers in Emilia-Romagna who are predominantly from Northern African countries (including Egypt, Morocco and Tunisia).

[61] Benvegnú, Haidinger and Sacchetto (n 59) 83.

[62] Ibid, 90; see further R Cillo and L Pradella, 'New Immigrant Struggles in Italy's Logistics Industry' (2018) 16:1 *Comparative European Politics* 67, 75–76.

[63] Benvegnú, Haidinger and Sacchetto (n 59) 91.

[64] Ibid, 88.

[65] Ibid, 94–95 (although note the role played by the union confederations at Amazon, see further below).

struggles', in particular SI Cobas and ADL Cobas.[66] SI Cobas is a 'militant workers' union', formed in 2010 to represent migrant workers not only in logistics but also in the transport, food, hospitality and cleaning sectors.[67] One of SI Cobas's earliest interventions was in 2012–2013, when it assisted TNT warehouse workers, frustrated by the lack of support from CGIL, with a blockade to support the application of the sectoral collective agreement at the sites.[68] SI Cobas operates across the country,[69] while its 'sister union' ADL Cobas is focused on the Veneto region[70] with a presence also in other parts of northern and central Italy.[71] Curcio elucidates that these unions have responded to the unmet needs of logistics workers by 'following the initiative of workers themselves. From 2011 onwards, they have rapidly expanded into many warehouses … '.[72] Direct action, including blockades and picket lines, have been organised through open worker assemblies, where collective decisions on tactics 'are based on the workers' knowledge of the production and distribution cycle'.[73]

Although there are difficulties for unions in accessing workers 'in outsourced links of the logistics chain', opportunities are also presented by the nature of just-in-time production and distribution: workers can cause damage by disrupting the supply chain (especially during peak periods).[74] Deployment of this power to interrupt the flow of commerce has been a common feature of many of the disputes in the Italian logistics sector over the last 10 years. According to Curcio: 'it was especially when workers managed to materially damage the companies that they dared more and found the courage to ask for better wages and conditions'.[75] By blockading the entrances to warehouses at critical times, workers (with the support of SI Cobas and ADL Cobas) have been able to pressure companies into negotiating – and have obtained improvements in pay and conditions (including sickness payments), application of the national collective agreement and reinstatement of dismissed co-workers.[76] A collective agreement struck by SI Cobas with

[66] Ibid, 88. The cobas or 'base unions' in Italy (*comitati di base*) have their origins in the factory councils (*consigli di fabbrica*) which emerged during the Hot Autumn of 1969 as avenues through which workers challenged the authority of the established union confederations. These evolved into various base union organisations during the 1980s, which now operate as independent unions: see Unauthored, 'The Base Unions in Italy', *Struggles in Italy* (2013). Available at: https://strugglesinitaly.wordpress.com/work/the-base-unions-in-italy/. See also G Gall, 'The Emergence of a Rank-and-File Movement: The Comitati di Base in the Italian Worker's Movement' (1995) 19:1 *Capital and Class* 9; and Part III above.

[67] R Luzzi and J Canady, 'Regrouping the far left in Italy', *Workers' Liberty* (20 November 2019). Available at: www.workersliberty.org/story/2019-11-20/regrouping-far-left-italy. See also ch 9.

[68] Curcio (n 57) 270–71.

[69] See http://sicobas.org/#.

[70] Curcio (n 57) 271. See further Ianuzzi and Sacchetto (n 59) 14.

[71] See https://adlcobas.it/.

[72] Curcio (n 57) 271.

[73] Ibid, 271–72; see also Cillo and Pradella (n 62) 77.

[74] Benvegnú, Haidinger and Sacchetto (n 59) 92; see also R Cillo and L Pradella, 'Strike Friday at Amazon.it', *Jacobin* (29 November 2017).

[75] Curcio (n 57) 268; see also 269.

[76] Benvegnú, Haidinger and Sacchetto (n 59) 93, 98–99; Curcio (n 57) 268. See also Unauthored, 'Ditching the fear! Warehouse workers struggles in Italy and their wider significance', *libcom.org*

several large logistics firms in February 2015 included job security measures such as the requirement 'to directly employ workers and to hire those already employed in a warehouse in the case of a contractual change'.[77] Despite being met at times with a repressive response from the state (including a strong police presence at many of the blockades)[78] and from employers,[79] unions like SI Cobas and ADL Cobas have been critical in enabling some of Italy's most marginalised workers to contest their precarity. As Benvegnú, Haidinger and Sacchetto conclude:

> Small, rank-and-file Italian unions were less institutionally constrained [than mainstream unions], and thus able to develop new social and informal strategies. The grassroots character of [these] unions in warehousing allowed them to deploy workers' associational power in such a way as to make best use of their strategic position in the logistics supply chain.[80]

Mainstream unions have not been completely absent from this field. In fact, FILCAMS-CGIL, FISASCAT-CISL and UILTUCS (the divisions of the three major confederations covering commerce, services, hotel and tourism workers) succeeded in obtaining a collective agreement for Amazon workers in 2018. In contrast with the use of cooperatives by other logistics firms, Amazon supplements its permanent Italian workforce with temporary staff sourced through agencies (their numbers swelling considerably in peak sales periods).[81] The oppressive working conditions in Amazon fulfilment centres globally, noted in Chapter 1, are clearly evident in Italy. Writing in 2017, Cillo and Pradella maintained that at the company's Piacenza warehouse:

> … the average worker is thirty years old, but up to 80 percent suffer from health problems thanks to the intensity of work, its extremely fast pace, and the repetitive tasks. Management constantly checks workers with metal detectors to prevent theft, and employees must ask their foremen for permission to go to the toilet.[82]

Amazon's antipathy toward unions has also been on display. Cattero and D'Onofrio have highlighted the 'hostile attitudes' and 'many obstacles' to unionisation imposed by the company at its sites in Italy.[83]

(12 July 2015). Available at: https://libcom.org/blog/ditching-fear-warehouse-workers-struggles-italy-their-wider-significance-12072015.

[77] Cillo and Pradella (n 74).

[78] Unauthored (n 76); Cillo and Pradella (n 62) 78. See also Curcio's account of the bitter dispute at the Granarolo company's dairy plant in Bologna in early 2014 (n 57, at 259–60, 263–65, 272–74).

[79] See, eg, E Milanesi, 'Coca-Cola used tasers against Adl Cobas workers', *Il Manifesto* (31 March 2017).

[80] Benvegnú, Haidinger and Sacchetto (n 59) 84; see also Cuppini, Frapporti and Pirone (n 58) 132.

[81] B Cattero and M D'Onofrio, 'Organizing and Collective Bargaining in the Digitized "Tertiary Factories" of Amazon: A Comparison Between Germany and Italy', in E Ales, Y Curzi, T Fabbri, O Rymkevich, I Senatori and G Solinas (eds), *Working in Digital and Smart Organizations: Legal, Economic and Organizational Perspectives on the Digitalization of Labour Relations* (Cham, Palgrave Macmillan, 2018) 141, 156.

[82] Cillo and Pradella (n 74). See also, Reuters Staff, 'Italian officials inspect working conditions at Amazon hub', *Reuters* (8 December 2017).

[83] Cattero and D'Onofrio (n 81) 156–58.

Nevertheless, CGIL, CISL and UIL have sought to build solidarity among the Amazon workforce, commencing with a 'Black Friday' strike at the Castel San Giovanni (Piacenza) hub in November 2017, supported by SI Cobas.[84] The action also targeted the major agencies, like Adecco, Manpower and Gi Group, which supply temporary workers to Amazon.[85] The strike led to negotiations and the announcement, in May 2018, that Amazon had concluded a collective agreement with FILCAMS-CGIL, FISASCAT-CISL and UILTUCS for the Piacenza warehouse (which would operate subject to the applicable national collective contract).[86] The agreement, voted up by almost 70 per cent of the workers, provided for night work to be on a voluntary basis and paid at 25 per cent above the normal hourly rate; and new scheduling arrangements to ensure fairness in the allocation of weekend work (with workers having at least four free weekends over an eight-week period).[87] This was widely celebrated as 'the first-ever direct agreement between unions and [Amazon] anywhere in the world'.[88]

The company immediately put paid to any notion that similar agreements would follow elsewhere, reasserting its view that 'a direct relationship with employees is the most effective way to answer their needs'.[89] Even so, Cillo and Pradella considered that the 2017 'Amazon walkout' illustrated 'that a new labor movement is growing in Italy, reacting to working conditions that are worsening by the day'.[90] While much of the activity in the logistics sector has been taken up by independent unions, the growing demand from workers that the traditional unions play their part produced a significant outcome in the Amazon collective agreement. The main union confederations have subsequently organised more widespread actions against Amazon, such as the strike across its supply chain on 22 March 2021, to protest the working conditions of warehouse staff and delivery service drivers.[91]

## V. Conclusion

The traditionally strong position of Italian unions within the national social partnership and collective bargaining infrastructure and at the workplace level, has meant that they have not generally pursued US-style organising as a path to

[84] Cillo and Pradella (n 74 above).

[85] Ibid.

[86] A Sciotto, 'Amazon bows to the unions: new shifts and higher wages', *Il Manifesto* (23 May 2018).

[87] Ibid. See also UNI Global Union, 'First-ever agreement between Amazon and unions halts inhumane work hours in Italy' (23 May 2018).

[88] UNI Global Union (n 87); on the background of contested relations between unions and Amazon at the Castel San Giovanni hub, see Cattero and D'Onofrio (n 81) 157–58.

[89] Sciotto (n 86).

[90] Cillo and Pradella (n 74).

[91] A Giuffrida, 'Italians urged to boycott Amazon to support day of strikes', *The Guardian* (23 March 2021).

membership growth. Instead, Italy's main union confederations have focused their attention on specific groups of workers most in need of collective representation, including migrants and those engaged in various forms of precarious work. Independent rank-and-file unions have come to play a progressively influential role, contesting exploitative and contingent work in circumstances where the mainstream unions have, at times, failed to act.[92] The independent or base unions are also far more radical, free of the political connections of CGIL, CISL and UIL and are therefore more willing to resort to the weapon of national strikes to progress their demands.[93]

Alongside the rise of grassroots unions has come a greater affinity between organised labour and other social movement actors. Historically, Italian unions formed connections with organisations focused on the protection of the environment and immigration issues, but these were not central to revitalisation attempts.[94] The institutional security enjoyed by Italian unions meant there was 'less incentive for unions to seek alliances with other institutions in civil society' and 'less need to borrow the power of other movements'.[95] However, the loosening of that institutional power in the period since the global financial crisis has seen unions 'moving toward social unionism … and embracing a notion of social solidarity stretching beyond the industrial relations arena'.[96] This shift can be seen in, for example, the involvement of CGIL, CISL and UIL as founding partners of the Alliance against Poverty, 'a network of civil society organisations' formed in 2013 to campaign for better income protection for the unemployed and low-wage workers;[97] in the coalitions formed by grassroots unions in the logistics sector with groups advocating for migrants' rights and student activists;[98] and in the national protests organised by the main union confederations, SI Cobas and a broad range of church and community groups against the 2018 'security decree' of the *Lega*/M5S government (which imposed extensive new restrictions on migrant and refugee entry into Italy).[99]

[92] In addition to logistics (see Part IV above), see the discussion of the actions of grassroots unions in the education sector, in Borraccino and Gentile (n 59) 221–27; and in hotels, in Ianuzzi and Sacchetto (n 59) 17–18.

[93] See, eg, Unauthored, '21st October: a day of general strike', *Struggles in Italy* (24 October 2016). Available at: https://strugglesinitaly.wordpress.com/2016/10/24/en-21st-october-a-day-of-general-strike/.

[94] C Frege, E Heery and L Turner, 'The New Solidarity? Trade Union Coalition-Building in Five Countries', in Frege and Kelly (n 3) 137, 138, 147, 152, 184–85.

[95] Ibid, 153.

[96] N Durazzi, T Fleckenstein and S Lee, 'Social Solidarity for All? Trade Union Strategies, Labour Market Dualization, and the Welfare State in Italy and South Korea' (2018) 46:2 *Politics and Society* 205, 214.

[97] Ibid, 214–17. Note also the role of unions in *Campagna Puliti Abiti* (the Italian section of the global Clean Clothes Campaign), see www.abitipuliti.org/; Clean Clothes Campaign, *Can you earn a living wage in fashion in Italy?* (Report, 2014); Clean Clothes Campaign, 'Italian factory conditions deteriorate' (23 January 2015). Available at: https://cleanclothes.org/news/2015/01/23/italian-factory-conditions-deteriorate.

[98] Benvegnú, Haidinger and Sacchetto (n 59) 97–98; Unauthored (n 76).

[99] See, eg, R Gonnelli, 'Italy rises up against racist policies of far-right government', *Il Manifesto* (26 October 2018); R Chiari, 'Workers march to Piazza Duomo in protest of the "Salvini decree"',

This greater openness to social movement activism has not generally taken the form of US-style campaigns to improve working conditions, like the Fight for $15 movement. Yet, the tactics deployed in those kinds of campaigns, including street protests and the strategic use of social media, have become part of the armour of some Italian unions. One effort of FILCAMS-CIGL even looked, in many respects, like an organising drive based on the US model: the union's successful attempt to sign up workers and collectively bargain on their behalf at Abercrombie & Fitch's main retail store in Milan.[100] In this endeavour, FILCAMS-CIGL:

> … arranged meetings and assemblies with workers (during the day for cashiers and shop assistants, during the night for warehouse workers); it exceptionally set a low membership fee for zero-hours workers (a lump sum of €30), rather than the typical 1 percent of monthly salary; it developed campaigns at the community level on key issues for retail workers, without directly targeting any specific employer but involving the media through initiatives like *Noi i diritti li socializziamo* (we socialize rights), with leaflets, sit-ins and flashmobs in the town centre.[101]

Through these and other collective actions over a period of some years, FILCAMS-CIGL 'became the main union actor at A&F' and achieved 55 per cent union density among permanent and zero-hours contract workers.[102] Some of the tactics that were utilised in this campaign have been more clearly visible in the actions of Italian unions and self-organised worker activists to collectivise the gig economy – as we shall see in the next two chapters.

*Il Manifesto* (21 January 2020). See also A Giuffrida, 'Italian government approves Salvini bill targeting migrants', *The Guardian* (25 September 2018); Jones and Awokoya (n 48).

[100] Gasparri, Ikeler and Fullin (n 12) 350–52.

[101] Ibid, 350–51.

[102] Ibid, 351–52.

# 9

# Unions and the Gig Economy: Advocacy, Campaigning, Mobilising

## I. Introduction

The advent of the gig economy is the latest challenge to the representative role of unions presented by employers' interposition, over a much longer period, of various business models to distance themselves from responsibility for their workforce.[1] The provision of services to consumers via an electronic platform or 'app' has enabled global gig economy players to maintain the pretence that they do not employ any of the millions of workers who carry out the work that is critical to their operations. These platforms have engaged in a masquerade on a grand scale, conjuring up legal and contractual structures to misclassify workers as self-employed, independent contractors. Thus, gig workers are denied protection under laws regulating minimum wages, working hours, health and safety and many other rights commonly associated with employment status. In addition, this 'contracting model' generally precludes workers from fully exercising the right to freedom of association. This is because access to collective bargaining through a trade union is (in many labour law systems) dependent on categorisation as an 'employee' or a 'worker'.

This and the next chapter examine how unions and self-organised platform workers have sought to contest this newest iteration of precarious work, innovating and adapting to build solidarity among a new breed of workers. As Shenker observes:

> … organised resistance by digitally outsourced workers has erupted repeatedly on the streets of major cities in recent years, usually beginning in the back alley spots where delivery riders are encouraged by their apps to congregate and then fanning out rapidly through WhatsApp networks, word of mouth and some technological trickery.[2]

Before turning to consider the advocacy, campaigning and mobilisation efforts of unions on behalf of platform workers, the next parts of this chapter provide an overview of the nature and effects of the gig economy in the USA, the UK, Australia and Italy – and some of the obstacles it presents to unionisation.

[1] See chs 1 and 2.
[2] J Shenker, 'Rise App!', *The Guardian Weekly* (6 September 2019) 40, 43.

## II. Overview of the Gig Economy in the Four Countries

The gig economy has many other names: the sharing economy, the on-demand economy, the app economy and what Srnicek has called 'platform capitalism'.[3] For purposes of this book, I use the term 'gig economy' to refer to the group of companies that Srnicek describes as 'lean platforms'. That is, 'asset-less companies' (other than the key asset of 'software and data analytics') which:

> … operate through a hyper-outsourced model, whereby workers are outsourced, fixed capital is outsourced, maintenance costs are outsourced … All that remains is a bare extractive minimum – control over the platform that enables a monopoly rent to be gained.[4]

As Scholz explains, these types of businesses 'function as brokers of services through an app', connecting 'people who are looking for work and others who try to get things done'.[5] Typical examples of platforms of this nature are those matching consumers and workers performing transportation services (eg, Uber, Lyft, Ola, Didi); food delivery services (eg, Uber Eats, Deliveroo, Foodora, DoorDash, Menulog, Postmates, Grubhub, Glovo, Just Eat); and domestic and skilled services like gardening, furniture assembly/removal, cleaning, marketing, advertising and translating (eg, TaskRabbit, Airtasker, Whizz, Fiverr, Upwork, Freelancer).[6] More recently, platforms have also started operating in the personal care services sector including aged, disability and child care (eg, Mable, Le Cicogne, Care.com and UberCare).[7]

Gig economy work occupies a small but growing proportion of the labour market in the economies of each of the four countries. Data from the US Bureau of Labor Statistics indicated that, in May 2017, 1.6 million American workers were performing 'electronically mediated work', equating to 1 per cent of total employment.[8] Other sources suggest that the extent of gig work in the USA is

[3] N Srnicek, *Platform Capitalism* (Cambridge, Polity Press, 2017) 36–37.

[4] Ibid, 75–76.

[5] T Scholz, *Uberworked and Underpaid: How Workers are Disrupting the Digital Economy* (Cambridge, Polity Press, 2017) 45.

[6] See, eg, T Haipeter, D Owczarek, M Faioli and F Iudicone (eds), *Don't Gig Up: Final Report* (Fondazione Giacomo Brodolini and Partners, 2020) 1, 6; N James, *Report of the Inquiry into the Victorian On-Demand Workforce* (Melbourne, Victorian Government, 2020) 11, 33–34; V De Stefano and A Aloisi, *Digital Age: Employment and Working Conditions of Selected Types of Platform Work – National Context Analysis, Italy* (European Foundation for the Improvement of Living and Working Conditions, 2018) 2–3. See also R O'Farrell and P Montagnier, *Measuring Platform Mediated Workers* (OECD Digital Economy Papers No 282, April 2019) 5–7.

[7] James (n 6) 33–34, 88–92; De Stefano and Aloisi (n 6) 3; B Wray, 'Towards the Uberisation of Care? Interview with Alisa Trojansky', *Brave New Europe* (4 October 2020). See further F Flanagan, 'Theorising the Gig Economy and Home-based Service Work' (2019) 61:1 *Journal of Industrial Relations* 57; F Macdonald, *Individualising Risk: Paid Care Work in the New Gig Economy* (Cham, Palgrave Macmillan, 2021).

[8] US Bureau of Labor Statistics, 'Electronically Mediated Employment' (28 September 2018). Available at: www.bls.gov/cps/electronically-mediated-employment.htm; see also Srnicek (n 3) 80.

considerably higher.[9] The incidence of gig work across the Australian economy is not entirely clear. However, a national survey of over 14,000 workers carried out for the Victorian government's On-Demand Work Inquiry found (as at 2019) 7.1 per cent of respondents were currently working or seeking to work for digital platforms, while 13.1 per cent had done so at some point.[10] In the UK, the 2017 Report of the Taylor Review into Modern Working practices drew upon Chartered Institute of Personnel and Development data indicating that 1.3 million people (or 4 per cent of those in employment) were working in the gig economy.[11] Data prepared for the European Commission Collaborative Economy and Employment Project showed that for the UK, 1.6 per cent of those surveyed in 2018 relied on gig work as their main source of working hours and income; 5.7 per cent relied on gig work as a secondary source of work/income; 3.5 per cent used it marginally; and 2 per cent, sporadically.[12] The equivalent measures for Italy were 0.9 per cent of those surveyed using gig work as their main source of work/income; 3.9 per cent secondarily; 2.5 per cent marginally; and 1.5 per cent sporadically.[13] Another 2018 survey indicated that between 700,000 and 1,000,000 workers (or 2.6 per cent of the Italian working-age population represented in the survey) were gig workers.[14]

## III. The Mirage of Liberating Work in the Gig Economy

Scholz observes that through platform work: 'People who are in dire need of extra income can become amateur chefs, painters, furniture assembly experts, personal assistants, or cabbies.' However, he adds: 'These one-off gigs are mostly low-paid.'[15] This points to the essence of the lean platform model, pioneered by Uber and since adopted by many others. Kessler describes Uber's portrayal of itself, from the outset, as 'a technology company rather than a transportation company' and its deliberate structuring of arrangements with drivers as independent contractors rather than employees: '[relieving] the company from government-mandated

[9] See, eg, G Iacurci, 'The gig economy has ballooned by 6 million people since 2010. Financial worries may follow', *CNBC* (4 February 2020).

[10] James (n 6) 31, referring to P McDonald, P Williams, A Stewart, R Mayes and D Oliver, *Digital Platform Work in Australia: Prevalence, Nature and Impact* (University of Adelaide and University of Technology Sydney, 2019).

[11] M Taylor, G Marsh, D Nicol and P Broadbent, *Good Work: The Taylor Review of Modern Working Practices* (2017) 25, referring to Chartered Institute of Personnel and Development, *To Gig or Not to Gig? Stories from the Modern Economy* (Survey Report, March 2017).

[12] M Urzì Brancati, A Pesole, E Férnandéz-Macías, *New Evidence on Platform Workers in Europe: Evidence from the Second COLLEEM Survey* (JRC Science for Policy Report, Luxembourg, Publications Office of the European Union, 2020) 15–16.

[13] Ibid.

[14] De Stefano and Aloisi (n 6) 3, referring to the online survey carried out by the Fondazione Rodolfo DeBenedetti in May 2018.

[15] Scholz (n 5) 43.

employer responsibilities in most countries'.[16] In this way, Uber forced onto drivers the responsibility for providing not only their own vehicle and fuel but also for health insurance, taxes and whether they took breaks: 'An Uber driver, in other words, was as close to a piece of code as Uber could find.'[17]

Precise language is deployed in the contracts drawn up by the platforms to buttress the fiction that they do not employ a single soul. Uber drivers are 'valued "partners"',[18] Deliveroo riders are 'independent suppliers'[19] (or 'Roomen' and 'Roowomen' and part of 'the Roo community'[20]), Grubhub drivers are 'Delivery Service Providers',[21] while both TaskRabbit and Airtasker call workers 'taskers'.[22] DoorDash delivery riders are 'dashers', the platform sticking to this label even when speaking of a Melbourne rider who was tragically killed while making a food delivery.[23] Prassl neatly labels the platforms' linguistic twists and turns as 'doublespeak'.[24] Cunningham-Parmeter describes this as 'the language of platform exceptionalism … the notion that the distinctive nature of on-demand work warrants distinct legal treatment'.[25] This connects to another striking feature of how platforms have developed, identified by Rosenblat: their crafting of a narrative of glamorised, freelance-style work which would especially appeal to tech-savvy millennials.[26] This is a calculated effort to:

> … project a higher social status onto work that has long been associated with lower-status workers. … The gig economy tech-washes this work into something more culturally desirable, but the passion and sharing rhetoric reinforce an older idea that [these] workers … aren't entitled to a living wage or labor protections.[27]

In these and many other ways, the platforms have latched onto technology and innovation and the (supposed) attraction of flexibility and entrepreneurship to the putative self-employed worker, as ruses for exploitation.[28]

[16] S Kessler, *Gigged: The Gig Economy, the End of the Job and the Future of Work* (London, Random House, 2018) 17.

[17] Ibid, 7–8.

[18] H Palmer, 'An Uber Driver Writes', *Futures of Work Forum* (19 November 2018).

[19] S Butler, 'Deliveroo accused of "creating vocabulary" to avoid calling couriers employees', *The Guardian* (6 April 2017).

[20] Deliveroo, *Deliveroo Rider Community*. Available at: https://au.roocommunity.com/.

[21] K Cunningham-Parmeter, 'Gig-Dependence: Finding the Real Independent Contractors of Platform Work' (2019) 39:3 *Northern Illinois University Law Review* 379, 390.

[22] Ibid, 391; Airtasker, *Meet some Taskers!*. Available at: www.airtasker.com/.

[23] N Zhou, 'Food delivery driver Chow Khai Shien the third gig economy worker to die in a month in Australia', *The Guardian* (27 October 2020).

[24] J Prassl, *Humans as a Service: The Promise and Perils of Work in the Gig Economy* (Oxford, Oxford University Press, 2018), ch 2 (especially 42–45). See also S Harnett, 'Words Matter', in D Acevedo (ed), *Beyond the Algorithm: Qualitative Insights for Gig Work Regulation* (Cambridge, Cambridge University Press, 2020) 169.

[25] Cunningham-Parmeter (n 21) 390 (footnote omitted).

[26] A Rosenblat, *Uberland: How Algorithms Are Rewriting the Rules of Work* (Oakland, University of California Press, 2018) 34–38. See also Kessler (n 16) ch 6; J Tolentino, 'The Gig Economy Celebrates Working Yourself to Death', *The New Yorker* (22 March 2017).

[27] Rosenblat (n 26) 37.

[28] A Tassinari and V Maccarrone, 'Riders on the Storm: Workplace Solidarity among Gig Economy Couriers in Italy and the UK (2020) 34:1 *Work, Employment and Society* 35, 44; see also Prassl (n 24) 45–46.

Over time, the gulf between the myth and the reality of gig work has become ever-more apparent. Typical problems experienced by gig workers include:

> … low pay or non-payment, a lack of work or overwork, irregular hours, constant pressure from customer ratings, the risk of sudden "deactivation" by the platform algorithm … and reduced social and employment protections.[29]

The unilateral imposition of independent contractor arrangements is at the root of these ills: 'major insecurities stem from the "(bogus) self-employed worker" status'.[30] This has also been described as the 'misclassification business model' of gig companies, through which they 'want it both ways: to act like employers [by exerting significant control over the workers] but not to be held accountable as such'.[31] In 2020, the Inquiry into On-Demand Work in the State of Victoria finally called this business model out, finding that in Australia:

> While there are a small number of notable exceptions, the arrangements established by the platforms with the workers are usually consciously framed to avoid an employment relationship arising between the worker and the platform.[32]

Much of the academic writing on the gig economy has focused on the employment law categorisation of gig workers as contractors[33] and the search for alternative solutions including an intermediate category sitting between employees and the genuinely self-employed.[34] Only in recent years has greater attention been paid to the collective dimensions of platform work.

## IV. Enter, the Unions …

In many countries (including those considered in this study) unions have increasingly sought to assert their role as the representative voice of workers in the platform economy, despite significant obstacles. The designated status of these workers as contractors rather than employees is an immediate barrier to union organisation, precluding their access to collective bargaining[35] and discouraging

[29] S Joyce, D Neumann, V Trappmann and C Umney, *A Global Struggle: Worker Protest in the Platform Economy* (European Trade Union Institute Policy Brief No 2/2020) 1.

[30] Ibid.

[31] National Employment Law Project, *Rights at Risk: Gig Companies' Campaign to Upend Employment as We Know It* (25 March 2019) 2.

[32] James (n 6) 16.

[33] See further ch 10.

[34] See, eg, M Cherry and A Aloisi, 'A Critical Examination of a Third Employment Category for On-Demand Work' in N Davidson, M Finck and J Infranca (eds), *Cambridge Handbook on the Law of the Sharing Economy* (Cambridge, Cambridge University Press, 2018) 316. See also ch 11.

[35] See, eg, E Kennedy, 'Employed by an Algorithm: Labor Rights in the On-Demand Economy' (2017) 40 *Seattle University Law Review* 987. Competition law rules also impose constraints on collective bargaining by independent contractors: see chs 10 and 11.

many from even choosing to seek collective representation.[36] According to Vandaele et al, younger gig workers, such as those engaged in food delivery, are less likely to appreciate the worth of unions (although they may consider joining if the presence and value of unions was clearer to them).[37] De Stefano and Aloisi point to further formidable blocks to union organising: the difficulty of building 'class consciousness' among workers who are usually geographically dispersed and who worry about retaliation if their union involvement is discovered.[38] Antipathy is another barrier, demonstrated by the outright refusal of most platforms to engage with unions.[39] This stance is taken to the extreme in the form of elaborate union-busting tactics, including the establishment of limp worker voice forums and the sponsorship of tame 'company unions':[40] a long-standing business strategy used to sideline effective representation of workers' interests through independent trade unions.[41]

Yet the nature of platform work also provides unique opportunities for organising and the deployment of innovative resistance tactics. Vandaele has considered the 'disruptive capacity' of on-demand food couriers in western European cities, including the ability of riders to turn the technology through which they are managed into tools of communication and mobilisation.[42] He has also explored their use of 'discursive power ... to debunk the platforms' narrative about entrepreneurship' and 'ideationally [frame] direct action against [them] in such a way that it resonates in the public discourse'.[43] Zamponi highlights the potential for food delivery riders in Italy to latch onto the image crafted by the platforms – of young riders embodying 'an idea of smartness, coolness, and modernity, spiced with techno-enthusiasm and environmental sensitivity' – and use this to gain support from the media and the public.[44] Far from the notion of

[36] S Kaine and E Josserand, 'The Organisation and Experience of Work in the Gig Economy' (2019) 61:4 *Journal of Industrial Relations* 479, 487.

[37] K Vandaele, A Piasna and J Drahokoupil, *Algorithm Breakers are not a Different 'Species': Attitudes towards Trade Unions of Deliveroo Riders in Belgium* (European Trade Union Institute, Working Paper 2019.06) 4, 14, 19–21, 30–32.

[38] De Stefano and Aloisi (n 6) 20. See also H Johnston and C Land-Kazlauskas, *Organizing On-Demand: Representation, Voice and Collective Bargaining in the Gig Economy* (Conditions of Work and Employment Series No. 94, Geneva, International Labour Office, 2018) 3–4; R Page-Tickell and J Ritchie, 'Presence and Pretence: Trade Unions and the Gig Economy', in R Page-Tickell and E Yerby (eds), *Conflict and Shifting Boundaries in the Gig Economy: An Interdisciplinary Analysis* (Bingley, Emerald Publishing Limited, 2020) 63, 78–80.

[39] J Prassl, *Collective Voice in the Platform Economy: Challenges, Opportunities, Solutions* (Report to the European Trade Union Confederation, 2018) 14.

[40] Ibid, 14–15. See also Part V(B) below.

[41] See, eg, J Pencavel, 'Company Unions, Wages and Work Hours' (2003) 12 *Advances in Industrial and Labor Relations* 7.

[42] K Vandaele, *Will Trade Unions Survive in the Platform Economy: Emerging Patterns of Platform Workers' Collective Voice and Representation in Europe* (European Trade Union Institute, Working Paper 2018.05) 15–16.

[43] Ibid, 16.

[44] L Zamponi, 'Bargaining with the Algorithm', *Jacobin* (June 2018); see also Part V(D) below.

a union backwater, Joyce et al claim that 'platform work has rapidly emerged as one of the most vibrant and exciting areas of labour organising'.[45]

For trade unions and other worker representative groups, there has been no one single strategy to organise and represent workers in the gig economy. The US AFL-CIO's approach encompasses legal cases to challenge misclassification, developing alliances to provide services to and lobby on behalf of gig workers and campaigning for regulatory reform.[46] These avenues and more have been pursued in the other three countries. In Australia, unions have brought legal test cases challenging gig workers' status, while also utilising survey and other data as bases for both organising and public advocacy. Several UK unions have devoted much effort to grass-roots organising off the back of worker-led movements, in combination with litigation. In Australia, the US, the UK and Italy, union groups have also tried to negotiate better pay and conditions for these workers through various forms of collective bargaining. These and other strategies to collectivise gig work – including the emergence of online forums, spontaneous protests and self-organised worker groups – are examined in detail in the following part and the next chapter. The focus is predominantly on gig work in the rideshare and food delivery markets, as these are the areas in which collective action has been predominant. Union representation of gig workers in the context of the COVID-19 pandemic is explored in Chapter 12.

## V. Exposing the Reality of Gig Work as a Basis for Advocacy, Campaigning and Mobilising

### A. Australia

Trade unions in Australia have shone a spotlight on the devastating impact of the platforms' imposition of contractor status on their workers. The Transport Workers' Union (TWU) has led these efforts, engaging dedicated organisers for the food delivery sector, and working with the Young Workers Centre (YWC)[47] through the Delivery Riders Alliance. Their #Rights4Riders campaign[48] has focused on the exploitation of food delivery riders and drivers working for Deliveroo, Uber Eats, Menulog, DoorDash, Foodora (until it vacated the Australian market in August 2018[49]) and other platforms. The campaign aims to improve 'safety, pay,

[45] Joyce et al (n 29) 1; see also K Vandaele, 'Collective Resistance and Organizational Creativity among Europe's Platform Workers: A New Power in the Labour Movement?', in J Haidar and M Keune (eds), *Work and Labour Relations in Global Platform Capitalism* (Cheltenham, Edward Elgar, 2021), forthcoming.

[46] Johnston and Land-Kazlauskas (n 38) 5.

[47] See ch 6.

[48] TWU, '#Rights4Riders'. Available at: www.twu.com.au/on-demand/the-fight-for-rights4riders/; YWC, 'Rights for Riders'. Available at: www.youngworkers.org.au/rights4riders.

[49] See ch 10.

conditions and job security', to be achieved by riders 'joining with other riders to stand up for your rights'.[50] YWC also provides practical information, for example on where riders stand if they are injured or their bike is damaged, regularity of payment and minimum shift periods.[51]

The Delivery Riders Alliance has undertaken regular surveys of food delivery workers, revealing a consistent pattern of underpayment, intrusive surveillance and inadequate safety protections.[52] For example, a survey released in September 2020 showed that the average wage for riders/drivers was just A$10.42 per hour; 88 per cent had noticed a decrease in delivery payments over time; and 36 per cent had been injured while working (and of those, 81 per cent did not receive any support from the company they worked for).[53] Eighty-seven per cent of respondents thought they should have access to rights such as superannuation, sick leave, penalty rates and a minimum wage; and 90 per cent wanted their interests to be represented collectively.[54] In July 2020, the Victorian On-Demand Work Inquiry confirmed many of the concerns identified by unions when it found that:

> Food delivery platforms do not employ delivery workers. They are emphatic that an employment-based model would not be compatible with their systems. … [These] platforms provide 'low-leveraged' workers with access to flexible jobs with low barriers to entry; especially young people, students and visa workers. But the roles appear to provide, on average, less income per hour than the casual minimum wage (considering costs).[55]

As well as the #Rights4Riders campaign, the TWU has represented food delivery workers in many other ways (considered further in Chapter 10). Of particular note was its strong public criticism of the platforms' business model in the wake of a series of rider deaths in late 2020.[56] Stating that the riders had died 'without these

[50] YWC, 'Rights for Riders FAQ'. Available at: www.youngworkers.org.au/rights4ridersfaq.

[51] Ibid.

[52] In addition to the survey discussed here, see YWC, *Young Workers Centre Submission: Inquiry into Corporate Avoidance of the Fair Work Act* (January 2017); S Bright and A Fitzgerald, *Snapshot: On-Demand Food Delivery Riders* (TWU/YWC, 2018); Delivery Riders Alliance, *It's Even Worse Than You Think. Snapshot: On-Demand Food Delivery Riders* (November 2019).

[53] Delivery Riders Alliance, *Food Delivery Driver/Rider Survey* (September 2020); over 200 riders responded to the survey, including those working for Uber Eats, Deliveroo, Menulog, DoorDash, Yello, Easi, Sherpa and Hungry Panda (with many riders working for multiple apps).

[54] Ibid. On the extent to which Australian gig workers miss out on superannuation entitlements, see James (n 6) 131–37; McDonald et al (n 10) 81.

[55] James (n 6) 79 (references omitted). See further C Goods, A Veen and T Barratt, '"Is your gig any good?" Analysing Job Quality in the Australian Platform-based Food Delivery Sector' (2019) 61:4 *Journal of Industrial Relations* 502; Anonymous, '"By Tuesday, I'm sitting on $31.08": a week in the life of a Melbourne food delivery worker', *The Guardian* (1 November 2020).

[56] In September 2020, two riders (Dede Fredy and Xiaojun Chen, who worked for Uber Eats and Hungry Panda respectively) were killed in road accidents within a week of each other: N Bonyhady and T Rabe, '"Gut wrenching": Sydney delivery rider deaths spark anger', *Sydney Morning Herald* (3 October 2020); N Bonyhady, 'Delivery rider's widow mourns as injuries in the sector leap up', *Sydney Morning Herald* (9 November 2020). A third rider (Chow Khai Shien, who worked for Door Dash) died in late October: Zhou (n 23). This was followed by the deaths of another two riders in the space of just three days in November (Bijoy Paul and IK Wong, who both worked for Uber Eats): N Bonyhady,

companies even blinking',[57] TWU National Secretary Michael Kaine urged the federal government to investigate the workplace safety standards adopted by the platforms and establish 'an independent tribunal which [gig] workers can turn to for the rights and protections they need'.[58] Similar tragedies in 2019 had prompted the TWU to instigate processes for representing Deliveroo riders under occupational health and safety legislation.[59]

The TWU has also devoted extensive efforts to representing rideshare drivers. This has again involved utilising the results of driver surveys to highlight the exploitative arrangements imposed by Uber, Didi, Ola, Taxify and other platforms.[60] Self-organised rideshare driver groups have also proliferated. These include: the Rideshare Drivers Network (formerly Rideshare Driver Co-operative), a private Facebook group set up in February 2018[61] which has done joint advocacy work with the TWU;[62] the Ride Share Drivers Association of Australia (RSDAA), established in March 2016 to build unity among drivers, protect their rights and lobby for improved regulation of the rideshare industry;[63] and RideShare Drivers United (RSDU), an online forum for Uber, Didi, Ola and other rideshare drivers formed in June 2016, offering free membership with around 7,000 members based mainly in Australia and the USA.[64] Of these, RSDU is the group which most closely approximates a traditional union, using the language of 'collaboration and collective actions' and '[uniting] drivers

'Uber Eats rider killed in Sydney's south identified as Bangladeshi student Bijoy Paul', *Sydney Morning Herald* (22 November 2020); N Zhou, 'NSW government announces taskforce to investigate food delivery deaths', *The Guardian* (24 November 2020). On the minimal safety protections subsequently put in place by Uber Eats (eg, providing riders with lights, reflective vests and phone holders), see N Bonyhady, 'Uber lifts safety game for Australian streets in world first', *Sydney Morning Herald* (28 February 2021).

[57] J Om, A McDonald and A Prihantari, 'Online food delivery deaths prompt calls for better worker's [sic] compensation for gig economy workers', *ABC News* (9 February 2021).

[58] C Wilson, 'The Transport Workers Union has called for the federal government to act after the death of a fifth food delivery rider in just 2 months', *Business Insider* (24 November 2020); see ch 11.

[59] See ch 10.

[60] See, eg, TWU and Rideshare Driver Co-operative, *Rideshare Driver Survey* (24 October 2018); N Zhou, 'Australian rideshare drivers found to be earning $12 an hour and at risk of harassment and assault', *The Guardian* (15 November 2020). See further J Stanford, *Subsidising Billionaires: Simulating the Net Incomes of UberX drivers in Australia* (Australia Institute, Centre for Future Work, March 2018); James (n 6) 93–99.

[61] Rideshare Drivers Network, see: www.facebook.com/groups/ridesharedrivercooperativevic/.

[62] See TWU and Rideshare Driver Co-operative (n 60).

[63] RSDAA, 'About Us'. Available at: https://rsdaa.org.au/about-us/. RSDAA portrays its members as drivers who are running independent small businesses. In one submission, the group stated that it does not seek to have drivers recognised as employees, but wants their contracts subjected to Australian law (rather than, eg, Uber's contracts which are governed by the law of The Netherlands): RSDAA, *Submission on Point-to-Point Transport (Taxis and Hire Vehicles) Regulation 2017 (NSW)* (9 May 2017) 5. However, RSDAA has also suggested that Uber's designation of drivers as contractors needed to be questioned as they 'could possibly fall under the categorisation of casual employees': RSDAA, 'Unfair Dismissal Claims'. Available at: https://rsdaa.org.au/unfair-dismissal-claims/.

[64] RSDU, 'Welcome Driver!'. Available at: http://ridesharedriversunited.com/.

anywhere in the world with fellow drivers right next door, to help change our situation right here right now!'.[65]

RSDU organised a strike and protest of Uber drivers in Melbourne on 11 April 2017, claiming that between 1,200 and 1,500 drivers took part.[66] Further mass 'log-offs' occurred in Australian capital cities on 5 and 22 August 2018.[67] At that time, RSDU was demanding that Uber pay its drivers for the actual time and distance they drive (rather than according to an upfront pricing model) and introduce a 12-hour limit on drivers' work-days.[68] RSDU is run by 'Max B', an Uber driver who conceals his identity out of concern that he will be removed from the app.[69] He told the Victorian On-Demand Work Inquiry that because platforms can 'deactivate drivers for no reason, most drivers prefer not to publicly disclose their identities when making a complaint or discuss their issues in public'.[70] Max B says that 'Uber never consults drivers',[71] implying that it also does not deal with RSDU. This is consistent with Uber's position that it communicates with 'driver and delivery partners' through newsletters, roundtables and focus groups[72] and with its general disinclination to engage with labour groups globally.

## B. USA

Unions in the USA have also been very active in revealing the detrimental effects of rideshare platform work through research and public advocacy. Gig Workers Rising is a campaign group aimed at organising and improving work for app and platform-based rideshare drivers[73] (supported by the Teamsters and SEIU[74]). In August 2019, it published a research report in collaboration with Human Impact Partners which showed that 'ride-hail' drivers working for Uber and Lyft in northern California: were subject to decreasing levels of income over time (as the platforms increased the commission rates they take from drivers' fares); felt significant stress arising from the constant threat of deactivation from the app (for example, if they rejected drive requests for any reason); and experienced

[65] Ibid.

[66] 'Uber drivers signal further strikes after Melbourne "log-off"', *Workplace Express* (12 April 2017).

[67] S Thomsen, 'Uber drivers are holding another nationwide strike in Australia today', *Business Insider* (22 August 2018). Australian rideshare drivers also participated in a world-wide stop-work on 8 May 2019, including a large protest outside Uber's Melbourne headquarters: see D Ziffer and D Malaish, 'Uber drivers stage global protest over pay and conditions', *ABC News* (8 May 2019).

[68] AAP, 'Uber drivers log off in Australia-wide protest against low fares', *The Guardian* (6 August 2018).

[69] P Hatch, 'Uber drivers feel "pay cut" pinch as rivals grow', *The Age* (30 July 2018).

[70] RSDU, *Submission prepared by Max B. – for Ride Share Drivers United, Inquiry into the On-Demand Workforce in Victoria* (undated) 4.

[71] AAP (n 68).

[72] Uber, *Submission: Inquiry into the Victorian On-Demand Workforce* (2019) 11–12.

[73] Gig Workers Rising, 'About us'. Available at: https://gigworkersrising.org/get-informed.

[74] R Cohen, 'A California Bill could transform the lives of gig workers. Silicon Valley wants labor's help to stop it', *The Intercept* (18 July 2019).

'the psychological toll of working for an algorithm' including constant monitoring by the platforms and social isolation.[75] Numerous other studies have documented the sub-minimum wages and other forms of ill-treatment experienced by US rideshare drivers.[76]

However, rideshare driver representation in the USA has been compromised by competition between drivers' groups and established unions, stoked at times by the platforms. For example, in California, there are three major groups:[77] Rideshare Drivers United (RDU), the Mobile Workers Alliance, in addition to Gig Workers Rising. According to Dubal, RDU is 'the only grassroots, worker-led association of Uber/Lyft drivers' with over 5,000 members as at May 2019, while the other two groups are supported by unions.[78] In the context of public debate over a new legislative proposal to regulate the gig economy in California in 2019,[79] it was reported that SEIU officials in that state had discussed with Uber and Lyft the prospect of forming a drivers' association – but with the premise that their classification as independent contractors would be retained.[80] However this position was not endorsed by the SEIU's national-level leadership. Rather, 'the union supported full employee status [for rideshare drivers], including the California bill that would enshrine it'.[81] Seeking to foment 'deep rancor within the labor ranks and set unions against one another'[82] was but one in the multitude of tactics deployed by the rideshare platforms to resist the proposed Californian legislation.

In New York City, at least three different union groups have sought to play a representational role: the International Brotherhood of Electrical Workers (IBEW), which in 2016 applied to the NLRB to commence the process for a unionisation vote after it signed up several hundred Uber drivers at La Guardia airport;[83]

[75] M Ockenfels-Martinez and L Farhang, *Driving Away Our Health: The Economic Insecurity of Working for Lyft and Uber* (Human Impact Partners and Gig Workers Rising, August 2019) 6–7, 9–10, 12–15.

[76] See, eg, S Waheed, L Herrera, A Gonzalez-Vasquez, J Shadduck-Hernández, T Koonz and D Leynov, *More Than a Gig: A Survey of Ride-hailing Drivers in Los Angeles* (UCLA Labor Center, 30 May 2018); J Berg and H Johnston, 'Too Good to Be True? A Comment on Hall and Kreuger's Analysis of the Labor Market for Uber's Driver-Partners' (2019) 72:1 *Industrial and Labor Relations Review* 39; V Dubal, 'An Uber Ambivalence: Employee Status, Worker Perspectives, and Regulation in the Gig Economy', in Acevedo (n 24) 33; F Manzo and R Bruno, *On-Demand Workers, Sub-Minimum Wages: Evidence from Transportation Network Provider Trips in the City of Chicago* (Illinois Economic Policy Institute/University of Illinois Project for Middle Class Renewal, 19 January 2021).

[77] Dubal ibid, 52.

[78] Ibid, 53. See also RDU, 'Rideshare Drivers United'. Available at: www.drivers-united.org/; N Scheiber and K Conger, 'Far-flung ride-hailing drivers find unity and power with an app', *New York Times* (21 September 2019). Note that RDU is different from RSDU, the Australian-based organisation with the same name; see Part V(A) above.

[79] See ch 10.

[80] N Scheiber, 'Debate Over Uber and Lyft Drivers' Rights in California Has Split Labor', *New York Times* (29 June 2019).

[81] Ibid.

[82] Ibid.

[83] S Greenhouse, 'On Demand, and Demanding Their Rights', *The American Prospect* (Summer 2016); see also A Chen, 'An Uber Labor Movement Born in a La Guardia Parking Lot', *The New Yorker* (8 February 2016).

the New York Taxi Workers Alliance (NYTWA), 'a membership-based' organisation that 'strongly identifies as a union',[84] formed in 1998 and now with 21,000 members among NYC's yellow taxi and rideshare drivers;[85] and the Independent Drivers Guild (IDG), an offshoot of the International Association of Machinists and Aerospace Workers (Machinists Union), which commenced operating in 2016 under an agreement struck with Uber.[86] The IBEW 'backed off after the Machinists launched their [organising] drive',[87] leaving the IDG and NYTWA to fight out their 'turf war' in NYC.[88]

IDG has focused its efforts on lobbying regulatory authorities, including New York's Taxi and Limousine Commission (TLC), for improvements in drivers' pay, conditions and safety protections, as well as caps on the numbers of licensed rideshare operators and opposition to the city's traffic congestion tax.[89] One of the major successes IDG claims is the TLC's December 2018 decision to implement a US$17.22 per hour minimum wage (after expenses) for drivers working for Uber, Lyft and other platforms, raising the average pay for 77,000 drivers by around US$9,600 per year.[90] However, observers such as Dubal have questioned the extent to which IDG can take credit for this achievement, which 'was heavily championed by the [NYTWA] who pushed for the ordinance to apply to *all* drivers in the sector (not just app-based drivers)'.[91] Dubal also zeroes in on a deeper concern about IDG – its lack of independence – noting that under their 2016 agreement:

> Uber pays an undisclosed sum to the Machinists [Union] – which uses the money to fund the … IDG. The IDG has not been elected by workers …. After [its] formation, the worker association agreed (for a period of five years) not to contest the status of drivers and not to go on strike.[92]

In its defence, IDG argues that it is attempting to 'get [drivers] organised' and change the basis on which the rideshare industry operates 'without worrying about the employee-independent contractor thing for now'.[93] James Conigliaro of the Machinists Union suggests that 'this is the best model … because it achieves immediate results', including support for drivers and 'a seat at the table with Uber managers'.[94] However, there is no getting around the fact that under

[84] Johnston and Land-Kazlauskas (n 38) 11.
[85] NYTWA, 'Drivers Serve the World. We Serve the Drivers'. Available at: www.nytwa.org/.
[86] Greenhouse (n 83).
[87] D Wiessner and D Levine, 'Uber deal shows divide in labor's drive for role in "gig economy"', *Reuters* (23 May 2016).
[88] Greenhouse (n 83).
[89] Johnston and Land-Kazlauskas (n 38) 6; IDG, 'Campaigns'. Available at: https://drivingguild.org/current-campaigns/ and 'News'. Available at: https://drivingguild.org/news/.
[90] S Ghaffary, 'New York City has set the nation's first minimum pay rate for Uber and Lyft drivers', *Vox* (4 December 2018).
[91] V Dubal, 'Gig Worker Organizing for Solidarity Unions', *Law and Political Economy Blog* (19 June 2019), emphasis in original.
[92] Ibid. See also N Scheiber, 'Uber has a union of sorts, but faces doubts on its autonomy', *New York Times* (12 May 2017).
[93] Johnston and Land-Kazlauskas (n 38) 6.
[94] Greenhouse (n 83).

its pact with Uber, the Machinists Union has given up both a critical feature of independent trade unionism (the right to organise and take collective action) *and* pressuring the company about the issue at the heart of gig economy exploitation (misclassification). IDG therefore takes on the guise of a tame 'company-influenced "worker association"'.[95] In contrast, NYTWA has supported a national rideshare driver protest and log-off timed to coincide with Uber's initial public offering on 8 May 2019,[96] which extended globally; campaigned forcefully for the minimum rates set by the TLC in 2018; and instituted several legal actions against Uber.[97] The Executive Director of NYTWA, Bhairavi Desai, has stated that it aims 'someday to win a union representation election for Uber drivers in New York'.[98] She is unequivocal about the association's nearer-term goals, which include:

> ... to upend a business model that has unleashed so much poverty across the driver workforce. ... We want to send Uber and its Wall Street investors a message that we're going to keep up our agitation and strikes until the business model recognizes its fundamental flaws. So concretely, we want drivers to come out of poverty and to win job security.[99]

## C. UK

In the UK, the GMB Union (GMB) – an established union with over 620,000 members[100] – has channelled significant energy towards organising drivers engaged by Uber and other rideshare platforms.[101] GMB has regularly publicised the likely losses of earnings experienced by drivers under Uber's fee and commission structures, as part of the legal case challenging misclassification that has been the major feature of its representative strategy.[102] In 2015, GMB calculated that the highest-paid Uber drivers in London were making only £5.68 per hour (once their operating costs were deducted), 15% less than the UK national minimum wage.[103] A few years later, GMB estimated that Uber's UK drivers had missed out on around £18,000 each as a result of their misclassification

[95] Dubal (n 91). See also H Johnston, 'Workplace Gains beyond the Wagner Act: The New York Taxi Workers Alliance and Participation in Administrative Rulemaking' (2018) 43:2 *Labor Studies Journal* 141, 157–58; Kennedy (n 35) 1009.

[96] J DeManuelle-Hall, 'Strike by Drivers Disrupts Uber Launch', *Labor Notes* (31 May 2019).

[97] See ch 10.

[98] Greenhouse (n 83).

[99] F Garza, 'Bhairavi Desai on Why the Uber and Lyft Strikes Are the Future of Labor', *Jezebel* (8 May 2019). In food delivery in NYC, note the similarly robust aims and efforts of Los Deliveristas Unidos, an organising group supported by the Workers Justice Project, see: www.losdeliveristasunidos.org.

[100] GMB, 'GMB Union: On your side'. Available at: www.gmb.org.uk/.

[101] GMB, 'Taxi for Uber'. Available at: www.gmb.org.uk/campaign/taxi-uber.

[102] See ch 10.

[103] GMB, 'New Uber drivers pay down by £1 per hour'. Available at: http://archive.gmb.org.uk/newsroom/new-uber-drivers-pay-down-by-one-pound.

as contractors.[104] The United Private Hire Drivers (UPHD) Branch of the Independent Workers Union of Great Britain (IWGB)[105] also represents private hire drivers working for any operator, aiming to build 'real collective power' among these workers.[106] In October 2018, UPHD organised what was described as the 'first coordinated national strike' for British Uber drivers, encouraging the platform's customers 'not to cross a "digital picket line"'.[107] Participants in the 24-hour strike rallied in London (outside Uber's head office), Birmingham and Nottingham, protesting against the company's inadequate safety protections for drivers, arbitrary deactivations from the app and low pay.[108] This was followed by UK rideshare drivers' participation in the global day of action against Uber on 8 May 2019, again invoking the digital picket line.[109] IWGB also supported two of the claimants in the misclassification test case against Uber noted earlier, at least until those claimants (Yaseen Aslam and James Farrar) formed a new organisation in 2020: the App Drivers and Couriers Union (ADCU).[110] ADCU provides legal assistance and representation to private hire drivers and a support network for couriers and fast food delivery riders, claiming to be the 'only truly independent trade union representative 100% dedicated to you and to the industry we share'.[111]

Food delivery platform work has been an even richer source of union activism in the UK gig economy, mostly driven by IWGB but with origins in self-organised worker movements. This began with a protest in August 2016 by London delivery riders in response to Deliveroo's alteration of payment arrangements from an hourly rate to piecework rates.[112] The riders' collective log-out evolved into a six-day 'strike', attracting media attention[113] as: '[t]hey held mass gatherings outside the company's offices, flying pickets around the city to raise visibility, and coordinated reputational attacks against Deliveroo's social media pages'.[114] Traditional union tactics were combined with tech-era messaging as consumers were called upon to support: 'an immediate and total #boycott of #slaveroo! Make your own dinner! Donate to the strike fund instead!'.[115] Deliveroo rider Callum

[104] J Brock, *Getting Organised: Low-Paid Self-Employment and Trade Unions* (The Changing Work Centre, May 2019) 27.

[105] See ch 7.

[106] UPHD, 'Join the UK's union for Private Hire Drivers'. Available at: https://uphd.org.uk/.

[107] B Quinn, 'Uber UK strike: users urged not to cross "digital picket line"', *The Guardian* (9 October 2018).

[108] Ibid.

[109] 'Uber drivers strike over pay and conditions', *BBC News* (8 May 2019).

[110] ADCU, 'About us'. Available at: www.adcu.org.uk/about-us.

[111] ADCU, 'App Drivers and Couriers Union'. Available at: www.adcu.org.uk/.

[112] Tassinari and Maccarrone (n 28) 42.

[113] See, eg, H Osborne and S Farrell, 'Deliveroo riders strike again over new pay structure', *The Guardian* (15 August 2016).

[114] Tassinari and Maccarrone (n 28); see also Shenker (n 2) 43.

[115] A Wood, 'It's a matter of time: can Deliveroo deliver collective bargaining for the gig economy?', *Oxford Internet Institute Blog* (16 August 2016). Available at: www.oii.ox.ac.uk/blog/its-a-matter-of-time-can-deliveroo-deliver-collective-bargaining-for-the-gig-economy/.

Cant recounts the story of its UK managing director addressing a rowdy group of protestors, responding to their requests for pay increases through collective bargaining with the standard line:

> "That is a dialogue we will have individually." … For the first time [though], … [he was] face-to-face with organized couriers …. The thousands of dots on the map, spread all over London, [were] showing that they [were] real people with real power.[116]

The strike achieved some success, as 'the company eventually agreed not to unilaterally impose the new payment system, instead starting an opt-in trial with one month of guaranteed wages'.[117] Although 'only a partial victory' in that new riders would be subject to Deliveroo's per-drop payment system, the London 'strike was the beginning of something' much bigger.[118]

IWGB's support for the London protestors laid the ground for 'a longer-term campaign for unionisation' which has spread across the UK.[119] Regular 'flash strikes' and other protest actions have since been taken by food delivery riders in cities including Bristol, Nottingham, Cheltenham, Birmingham, Manchester, Cardiff and Brighton.[120] Cant explains that, given very low pay rates, long periods of (unpaid) time waiting for food orders and the lack of accident insurance coverage: 'it's no surprise that we started to get organised'.[121] This began with riders circulating the 'Rebel Roo', a bulletin about the campaign for improved wages and conditions and meeting with IWGB in early 2017 to form a 40-rider assembly.[122] It produced a set of demands, including a living wage, a freeze on new hires (to create more work for existing riders) and no victimisation of union activists. Deliveroo agreed only to hold off on new recruits, so the riders' assembly ramped up their campaign, gaining media coverage through an ITV investigation of Brighton riders' working conditions and support from the Labour Party.[123] Although strikes by the riders sent the Deliveroo app into 'meltdown', they were unable to get the company to budge from its resistance to granting any concessions or engaging in collective negotiations.[124] Another Deliveroo rider, Paul Shanks, recounts that:

> … what caused me to start getting involved with organising was the realisation that if we didn't start to do something about it, Deliveroo would drive our pay down until they found the riders' bottom limit.[125]

[116] C Cant, *Riding for Deliveroo: Resistance in the New Economy* (Cambridge, Polity Press, 2019) ix.
[117] Tassinari and Maccarrone (n 28) 42.
[118] Cant (n 116) x.
[119] Tassinari and Maccarrone (n 28) 42–43.
[120] P Shanks, 'Resisting exploitation and building power: the Deliveroo workers fighting back', *Bright Green* (12 February 2019); T Cork, 'Deliveroo riders to stage Valentine's Day flash strike in Bristol', *Bristol Post* (14 February 2019); T Falls, 'Work as a Deliveroo courier: our work, our struggles and the future', *Futures of Work Forum* (19 December 2018).
[121] C Cant, 'I'm a Deliveroo rider. Collective action is the only way we'll get a fair deal', *The Guardian* (31 March 2017).
[122] Ibid; see further Cant (n 116) 107–9, 113–14.
[123] Cant (n 121).
[124] Cant (n 116) 116–17; see also 128.
[125] Shanks (n 120).

He helped mobilise Deliveroo and Uber Eats couriers in Bristol to take part in a strike in October 2018 (simultaneously with gig workers in more than ten cities around the UK). Out of this, the riders formed the Bristol Couriers Network and affiliated with IWGB.[126]

IWGB's representation of these workers is now undertaken by its Couriers and Logistics Branch, through a campaign called 'Deliveroo Riders RooVolt'. It seeks to connect 50,000 riders around the country and offers coordinated assistance to riders (for example, following unfair termination from the app) through a 'WhatsApp Hotline'.[127] In the lead-up to Deliveroo's flotation on the London Stock Exchange in April 2021, IWGB provided riders' invoicing data to investigative journalists who revealed that one in three riders were paid less than the UK national minimum wage for those aged over 25.[128] Another major component of IWGB's plan to unionise the food delivery platform work is its legal case seeking to establish collective bargaining rights for these workers under UK law, accompanied by employment rights litigation.[129] In addition to IWGB, grassroots food delivery worker mobilisation in the UK is supported by the Industrial Workers of the World Couriers Network and United Voices of the World, both of which have organised protest actions in recent years.[130]

## D. Italy

Italy has seen a similar pattern of development of self-organised food delivery worker activism to the UK, although this has not been seized upon by established unions to the same extent. Razzolini notes that Italian food delivery riders have generally been sceptical of traditional unions, 'prefer[ring] to create new unions characterized by a strong occupational consciousness and job-related identity'.[131] Foodora's implementation of a payment-by-delivery system (replacing an hourly rate) in September 2016 kick-started a protest by around 300 riders in Turin on 8 October. Their other concerns included having to meet their own bicycle repair and internet costs, the company's imposition of non-employee status and its victimisation of rider activists.[132] The Turin 'proto-strike' involved riders

[126] Ibid.

[127] 'Deliveroo Riders RooVolt. Your union. Your choice'. Available at: https://ridersroovolt.com/.

[128] E Mellino, C Boutaud and G Davies, 'Deliveroo riders can earn as little as £2 an hour during shifts, as boss stands to make £500m', *The Bureau* (25 March 2021). Available at: www.thebureauinvestigates.com/stories/2021-03-25/deliveroo-riders-earning-as-little-as-2-pounds; see also K Rawlinson, 'Deliveroo riders planning strike across England over pay and conditions', *The Guardian* (7 April 2021).

[129] See ch 10.

[130] See, eg, Tassinari and Maccarrone (n 28) 43; '"Flamme rouge": Reflections on the IWW Couriers Network' (22 March 2020). Available at: https://libcom.org/news/flamme-rouge-reflections-iww-couriers-network-22032020.

[131] O Razzolini, *Collective Action for Self-Employed Workers: A Necessary Response to Increasing Income Inequality* (Centre for the Study of European Labour Law 'Massimo D'Antona', Working Paper 155/2021) 5, 7–8 (footnote omitted).

[132] Tassinari and Maccarrone (n 28) 43; A Tassinari and V Maccarrone, 'The mobilisation of gig economy couriers in Italy: Some lessons for the trade union movement' (2017) 23:3 *Transfer* 353, 354.

engaging in a mass log-off (aimed at limiting Foodora's ability to meet customer orders), negative social media commentary about the company, and:

> … visible protests around the city with their bikes and flags, holding "flying pickets" that went through restaurants and squares handing out flyers to restaurant owners and members of the public, inviting them to boycott the app.[133]

As a result of the protest, Foodora held a meeting with several riders' representatives, giving some ground through a small increase in the new delivery rate but rejecting their other demands.[134] Some riders paid a heavy price for their involvement in the campaign to improve their conditions, as their contracts with Foodora were not renewed.[135]

However this spontaneous, worker-led movement, with some support from the grassroots union SI-Cobas,[136] evolved to encompass further protest actions against Foodora, Deliveroo and other platforms in cities including Milan, Bologna and Rome over the following years.[137] Groups with names like Deliveroo Strike Raiders and Deliverance Milano have made deft use of tactics like 'flash-mobs', online tools (such as petitions and alternative rating systems for the apps) and private groups on Facebook and WhatsApp to organise and publicise collective actions.[138] The technology instrumental to the riders' labour is therefore turned back on the platforms through snap strikes and log-offs.[139] Riders have also maximised the opportunity for constructing new manifestations of the collective which are presented by the location of their work, as Chesta, Zamponi and Caciagli explain:

> Public spaces like streets and squares function as the place in which riders work and also get in touch with one another. While new jobs are hidden, private and atomised, the city dimension is what makes it evident that the virtual (on-line) relations of production are still relations of capitalistic production and accumulation … Thus, urban space gives people the occasion and the physical place to activate new forms of unionism.[140]

Over time, traditional unions have come to engage more closely with the self-organised rider collectives, resulting in some advances in regional and national-level regulation of food delivery work. For example, in 2018, CGIL, CISL and UIL combined with the worker-organised Riders Union Bologna to negotiate

[133] Tassinari and Maccarrone (n 132; 2017 article) 354.

[134] Ibid, 355.

[135] Tassinari and Maccarrone (n 28) 43.

[136] Ibid. SI-Cobas has emerged to fill the gap left by the three main union confederations in representation of platform workers: De Stefano and Aloisi (n 6) 20; see also ch 8.

[137] Zamponi (n 44). See also R Chesta, L Zamponi and C Caciagli, 'Labour Activism and Social Movement Unionism in the Gig Economy: Food Delivery Workers Struggles in Italy' (2019) 12:3 *Partecipazione e Conflitto* 819, 833–34; A Foti, 'The Italian riders [sic] strike was a historic day', *Brave New Europe* (24 March 2021).

[138] De Stefano and Aloisi (n 6) 21–22. See also www.facebook.com/strikeraidersunited/ and /www.facebook.com/deliverancemilano/.

[139] Chesta, Zamponi and Caciagli (n 137) 833–34.

[140] Ibid, 824 (references omitted); see also 829–30.

a 'Charter of fundamental digital workers' rights within an urban setting' with the Bologna City Council and a food delivery platform based in the city.[141] The Charter includes provisions for fixed hourly wage rates as set down in national collective agreements, compensation for overtime work and public holidays, formal notification (with reasons) for excluding workers from a platform, accident and sickness insurance, freedom of association and the right to strike.[142] Chesta, Zamponi and Caciagli argue that the connections forged between groups like Riders Union Bologna and local student organisations and youth clubs amount to a form of social movement unionism.[143] Similarly, Razzolini views the Bologna Charter as an example of a union-community social coalition, in which the 'municipality acted as an intermediary' by seeking to persuade platforms 'voluntarily … to apply fair labor standards to food delivery riders'.[144] Local initiatives to provide advice and information for riders, and improved protections for platform workers more broadly, have been adopted in Milan and Lazio respectively.[145] The main union confederations have also obtained the inclusion of a 'rider' classification in the national collective bargaining agreement for the logistics service sector, so that working conditions can be negotiated for these workers (including wage levels, insurance and social security measures).[146]

The various outcomes achieved by mainstream unions, according to De Stefano and Aloisi, illustrate how they 'appear to support initiatives of platform workers rather than to go into competition with them'.[147] However the separation between traditional unions and self-organised collectives became a focal point in 2018, when the Lega/M5S Government proposed a decree to increase protections for food delivery platform workers[148] as an element of its 'public commitment to combat precariousness for the younger generations'.[149] Zamponi contends that the government deliberately chose to negotiate with self-organised worker groups rather than the main union confederations, providing 'an unquestionable piece of recognition for the [riders'] movement'.[150] In the end, the proposed law

[141] Zamponi (n 44); S Liebman and A Aloisi, 'The Labor Rights of Riders and other Gig Workers' (30 July 2018). Available at: www.viasarfatti25.unibocconi.eu/notizia.php?idArt=19849.

[142] De Stefano and Aloisi (n 6) 20–21. See also Vandaele (n 42) 17, noting that major platforms like Deliveroo, Foodora and JustEat did not sign the Bologna Charter.

[143] Chesta, Zamponi and Caciagli (n 137) 836–38.

[144] Razzolini (n 131) 13. Note also the Bologna City Council's ethical deliveries initiative, *Consegne Ethiche*. Available at: https://consegnetiche.it/chi-siamo/.

[145] De Stefano and Aloisi (n 6) 21. On the Lazio law establishing rights for digital workers, see also Haipeter et al (n 6) 20; S Borelli, 'Italy', in I Daugareilh, C Degryse and P Pochet (eds), *The Platform Economy and Social Law: Key Issues in Comparative Perspective* (European Trade Union Institute, Working Paper 2019.10) 63, 68.

[146] De Stefano and Aloisi (n 6) 18, 21.

[147] Ibid.

[148] De Stefano and Aloisi (n 6) 13.

[149] A Aloisi, *A Fascinating Chapter in the "Gig" Saga: How to Deliver Decent Work to Platform Workers in Italy?* (European Commission Mutual Learning Programme, Peer Review on Platform Work, September 2020) 2.

[150] Zamponi (n 44).

(which would have given workers the right to minimum hourly payments and to disconnect from their apps) was not implemented due to strong opposition from the platforms.[151] Instead, the government proposed another statute including a framework of minimum standards for self-employed riders (to apply if collective bargaining on their behalf did not produce an agreement within one year). This legislation was passed in November 2019.[152]

## VI. Conclusion

This chapter has provided an overview of the gig economy, including its growth in each of the four countries. It highlighted the construction by platforms globally of a narrative of freedom and flexible work, in contrast to the reality of widespread exploitation of gig workers through the imposition of presumed self-employed status. The chapter then turned to consider the roles increasingly being played by unions, and self-organised worker collectives, in mobilising rideshare drivers and food delivery workers to contest their precarity. Despite significant obstacles, collective representation in each nation – through research, public advocacy, campaigning, and organisation of driver/rider strikes and protests – has magnified awareness of the true situation of platform work. It has also helped many gig workers to obtain improvements in their conditions. These efforts have paved the way for unions to launch (or support) legal challenges to gig worker misclassification and to engage in collective bargaining with the platforms, both of which are considered in detail in Chapter 10.

[151] Aloisi (n 149) 2–3. See also J Politi, 'Di Maio takes aim at Italy's gig economy', *Financial Times* (19 June 2018), quoting the CEO of Foodora Italy stating that the government's 'demonisation of technology is incredible, it's almost medieval' and was intended to drive digital platforms out of the country; F Nespoli, 'How Di Maio seduced and abandoned the riders', *Vogon Today* (4 October 2020). Available at: www.vogon.today/startmag/how-di-maio-seduced-and-abandoned-the-riders/2020/10/04/.

[152] Aloisi (n 149) 3, referring to Law No 128/2019 (amending Decree 101/2019). See also ch 10.

# 10

# Unions and the Gig Economy: Misclassification Test Cases and Collective Bargaining

## I. Introduction

The gig economy's contracting model is vigorously defended by the platforms in the face of any efforts to challenge it in the courts or subject it to new forms of regulation. Misclassification test cases have been common in Australia, the US, the UK, Italy (and indeed across the world).[1] In this chapter, the more significant cases and decisions are considered in detail, emphasising the role played by trade unions not only in supporting platform workers to contest their work status in the courts but also in defending their rights in other contexts (including public discourse about regulation of the gig economy). The chapter then examines the endeavours of trade unions in all four countries to collectively bargain on behalf of gig workers. This covers several examples of agreements entered into by unions with platforms (in which the contractor status of the workers is left undisturbed); attempts by unions to extend collective bargaining rights to these workers through test cases and changes to legislation; and other forms of collective representation utilised by unions (such as that available under workplace health and safety law).

## II. 'Litigating the Digital Platform Model':[2] Legal Challenges to the Misclassification of Gig Workers

### A. Australia

In Australia, early test cases challenging independent contractor categorisation were brought by unrepresented Uber drivers. They were unsuccessful in their

[1] See generally J Moyer-Lee and N Kountouris, 'The "Gig Economy": Litigating the Cause of Labour' in International Lawyers Assisting Workers Network, *Taken for a Ride: Litigating the Digital Platform Model* (Issue Brief, March 2021) 6.

[2] Ibid.

attempts to bring unfair dismissal claims, having been cut off from the Uber app for receiving low passenger ratings and allegedly breaching Uber's community standards.[3] Under Australian law, employees are distinguished from contractors through a common law test which considers the true nature of the working relationship by reference to a range of factors. These include: the extent of control exercised over or by the worker; the manner and timing of payment; responsibility for taxation deductions; and whether the worker provides their own tools or equipment, is able to delegate work performance to others, or may offer their services to other parties.[4] This test applies for purposes of protective labour regulation, such as the minimum wages and conditions set out in industry-level awards and provisions of the Fair Work Act 2009 (Cth) (FW Act) relating to collective bargaining and unfair dismissal.[5]

In the early Uber decisions, the Fair Work Commission (FWC) dismissed the drivers' arguments that they were really employees. The tribunal placed considerable store on the apparent freedom of drivers to log on and off from the Uber app. Further, the necessary wages-work bargain was not present where drivers were not compelled to perform work (even once they logged onto the app).[6] The same analysis was adopted by the Fair Work Ombudsman (FWO) in the conclusion of its two-year examination into Uber's relationship with its drivers. The enforcement agency reached the view that this 'is not an employment relationship' because 'drivers are not subject to any formal or operational obligation to perform work'. Therefore, the FWO would not be taking any compliance action against Uber.[7] This was an unsatisfactory finale to an investigation which could have shed much more public light on a central player in the Australian gig economy.[8]

Over time, the Transport Workers' Union (TWU) has become more involved in gig worker classification challenges. In 2018, the union supported Foodora delivery rider, Josh Klooger, in a successful unfair dismissal claim.[9] The FWC accepted that Foodora exercised significant control over the work of its riders, including through a 'batching' system which allocated delivery jobs based on performance metrics.[10] The tribunal was even prepared to overlook the fact that Klooger operated a substitution scheme through which other riders occasionally performed

[3] *Kaseris v Rasier Pacific V.O.F.* (2017) 272 IR 289; *Pallage v Rasier Pacific Pty Ltd* [2018] FWC 2579; *Suliman v Rasier Pacific Pty Ltd* [2019] FWC 4807.

[4] See, eg, *Stevens v Brodribb Sawmilling Co Pty Ltd* (1986) 160 CLR 16; *Hollis v Vabu Pty Ltd* (2001) 207 CLR 21.

[5] The FW Act definitions of 'employer' and 'employee' in s 12 are based on the ordinary (ie, common law) meaning of these terms.

[6] See the decisions at n 3 above.

[7] FWO, 'Uber Australia investigation finalised', *Media Release* (7 June 2019).

[8] See, eg, A Patty, 'Fair Work watchdog hiding details behind Uber knockback decision', *Sydney Morning Herald* (11 November 2019).

[9] *Klooger v Foodora Australia Pty Ltd* (2018) 283 IR 168.

[10] Ibid, [73]–[74].

his delivery duties, because this had been approved by Foodora management.[11] The FWC concluded that Klooger:

> … was, despite the attempt to create the existence of an independent contractor arrangement, engaged in work as a delivery rider/driver for Foodora as an employee of Foodora.[12]

He was, therefore, able to bring an unfair dismissal claim and was awarded A$15,559 in compensation. The tribunal accepted he had been dismissed for his public activism contesting the working conditions of Foodora riders (including an appearance on national television[13]) and not for breaching the company's intellectual property rights as it had claimed.[14]

In June 2018, the FWO indicated it would bring enforcement proceedings against Foodora, alleging breaches of the FW Act prohibition of sham contracting[15] (that is, misrepresenting an employment relationship as an independent contracting arrangement[16]). However, just two months later, the company announced it was departing Australia so it could 'focus on other markets [with] a "higher potential for growth"'.[17] By entering into voluntary administration, Foodora temporarily held off the FWO's legal action against it.[18] However, the company's decision sent the TWU into overdrive in seeking recompense for over 5,000 riders left without a job. It soon emerged that Foodora had been in possession of opinions from federal and NSW taxation authorities that its riders were employees, and the company had substantial outstanding debts for unpaid tax and superannuation.[19] Foodora's administrators also concluded that it was likely the company's former food delivery riders had been casual employees, who were therefore owed more than A$5 million in unpaid entitlements. But Foodora's German parent company, Delivery Hero, offered a settlement of just A$3 million to creditors, including the tax authorities.[20] The TWU reluctantly recommended that riders accept the offer,

[11] Ibid, [79]–[87].

[12] Ibid, [102].

[13] D Marin-Guzman, 'Foodora fires courier for refusing to quit workers' chat group', *Australian Financial Review* (14 March 2018).

[14] *Klooger v Foodora Australia Pty Ltd* (n 9), [111]–[113], [138].

[15] D Tran and M Marozzi, 'Online food delivery company Foodora facing legal action over alleged underpayment of staff', *ABC News* (12 June 2018).

[16] FW Act, s 357; see eg, *Fair Work Ombudsman v Quest South Perth Holdings Pty Ltd* (2015) 256 CLR 137. The TWU is pursuing a sham contracting case under this provision on behalf of a Deliveroo rider, Jeremy Rhind: A Patty, '"It's not fair. It's not right": Rider takes Deliveroo to court', *Sydney Morning Herald* (28 August 2019).

[17] J Taylor, 'Foodora is pulling out of Australia after accusations it underpaid workers', *Buzzfeed News* (3 August 2018).

[18] 'Landmark gig economy cases up in the air', *Workplace Express* (20 August 2018).

[19] D Chau, 'Foodora fallout: ATO comes after failed food delivery company for unpaid taxes', *ABC News* (28 August 2018); D Marin-Guzman, 'Mystery of the three "unofficial" Foodora directors', *Australian Financial Review* (21 September 2018).

[20] N Zhou, 'Foodora Australia admits riders owed $5m were "more likely than not" employees', *The Guardian* (9 November 2018).

which eventually led to 1,700 riders receiving around 30 per cent of the amounts they had claimed (with more than 3,800 riders receiving nothing).[21] The FWO ultimately abandoned its proceedings against Foodora, noting that the company's exit from Australia should provide a warning to other businesses that they may not be sustainable if they cannot comply with Australian workplace laws.[22] For the TWU, the episode illustrated 'the orgy of greed in the gig economy'.[23]

In another major test case, an Uber Eats driver (Amita Gupta, represented by her husband) failed at first instance in her unfair dismissal claim.[24] Gupta had been removed from the Uber Eats app (according to her husband, because she was 10 minutes late completing a delivery). However, the FWC determined that she was not an employee: even though Uber Eats exercised 'soft control' over her work (including through customer performance ratings) she was free to choose her working hours and whether to accept or refuse deliveries.[25] Although the TWU supported Gupta's appeal, a Full Bench of the FWC also ruled that Gupta was an independent contractor.[26] The majority members of the Full Bench found she had chosen not to take up the freedom to branch out into developing her own delivery business (even though they had acknowledged she had no real means of doing so).[27] The third member reached the extraordinary conclusion that there was no commercial relationship at all between Gupta and Uber Eats,[28] allowing the platform to take advantage of the multi-party services agreement it imposed on her to maintain the pretence that she simply worked for herself. The TWU also backed Gupta's further appeal to the Full Federal Court of Australia. The parties settled the case in late 2020, after a hearing in which judges asked penetrating questions about whether Uber Eats' contracts reflected the true nature of its relationship with food delivery workers.[29] Uber Eats then rolled out new contracts for its delivery workers from 1 March 2021, under which riders have a direct relationship with the platform (although purportedly, still not as employees).[30]

Finally, in May 2021, the FWC found in favour of another TWU-backed food delivery rider, Diego Franco, who obtained orders for reinstatement and payment of lost wages following his unfair dismissal by Deliveroo.[31] The tribunal concluded

[21] 'Failed food delivery platform coughs up $2.3m for former riders', *Workplace Express* (10 May 2019).

[22] A Patty, 'Fair Work watchdog drops legal case against Foodora', *Sydney Morning Herald* (21 June 2019).

[23] 'Failed food delivery platform coughs up $2.3m for former riders', *Workplace Express* (10 May 2019).

[24] *Gupta v Portier Pacific Pty Ltd; Uber Australia Pty Ltd T/A Uber Eats* [2019] FWC 5008.

[25] Ibid, [87]–[90].

[26] *Gupta v Portier Pacific Pty Ltd; Uber Australia Pty Ltd T/A Uber Eats* (2020) 296 IR 246.

[27] Ibid, [68], [72].

[28] Ibid, [78], [81]–[82].

[29] C Prosser, 'Uber settles out of court with driver who alleged unfair dismissal for late delivery', *ABC News* (30 December 2020).

[30] J Taylor, 'Uber Eats accused of using new contract to exploit Australian delivery riders', *The Guardian* (29 January 2021).

[31] *Franco v Deliveroo Australia Pty Ltd* [2021] FWC 2818.

that Franco had been Deliveroo's employee, as he 'was not carrying on a trade or business of his own'.[32] In contrast to the 'apparent freedoms' in the working relationship, Deliveroo could 'exercise a significant level of control' over Franco and other riders – including through 'an extraordinarily vast repository of data relating to [their] performance and activities'.[33] The fact that Franco could engage in 'multi-apping' (working for competitors of Deliveroo at the same time) did not disturb the tribunal's overall conclusion that he was an employee.[34] The platform's termination of his services by e-mail, for alleged delivery delays, was considered to be 'perfunctory [and] callous'.[35] Deliveroo foreshadowed an appeal against the decision.[36]

## B. USA

In the USA, many legal challenges have been brought against the classification of gig workers as contractors who fall outside different forms of employment regulation,[37] with some involvement on the part of unions. There is a vast range of federal and state laws regulating minimum employment standards and collective bargaining, each with their own definitions of employment – and varying interpretations of these provisions by federal and state courts. As a result, 'there is no uniform test for distinguishing employees from independent contractors', but the approaches adopted in legislation and judicial decisions generally 'apply different variants of either an agency test or an economic realities test'.[38] The relatively narrow agency test focuses mostly on who has control over the work undertaken by the worker (or the right to exercise such control).[39] The economic realities approach, applied for purposes of the Fair Labor Standards Act 1938 (FLSA),[40] considers control alongside a broader range of factors. These include how the worker is paid, the level of skill involved in performing the work, whether the

[32] Ibid, [139].

[33] Ibid, [107], [110]–[111].

[34] Ibid, [115]–[118], [139].

[35] Ibid, [144], [146], [150].

[36] N Bonyhady, 'Deliveroo loses landmark case as sacked driver ruled an employee', *Sydney Morning Herald* (18 May 2021).

[37] It is not possible to do justice to this voluminous case law here. See, eg, M Cherry, 'Beyond Misclassification: The Digital Transformation of Work' (2016) 37 *Comparative Labor Law and Policy Journal* 577; K Cunningham-Parmeter, 'Gig-Dependence: Finding the Real Independent Contractors of Platform Work' (2019) 39:3 *Northern Illinois University Law Review* 379.

[38] K Stone, 'Unions and On-demand Work in the United States' in J López López (ed), *Collective Bargaining and Collective Action: Labour Agency and Governance in the 21st Century?* (Oxford, Hart Publishing, 2019) 101, 106.

[39] Ibid, 106–7.

[40] The legislation setting the federal minimum wage and regulating overtime pay and child labour: see D Weil, *The Fissured Workplace: Why Work Became So Bad for So Many and What Can Be Done to Improve It* (Cambridge MA, Harvard University Press, 2014) 21.

services provided are integral to the business and whether the worker is liable for profit or loss or is able to exercise judgment or initiative.[41]

A class action commenced in 2013, on behalf of almost 400,000 Uber drivers, sought to establish various employee entitlements codified in the California Labor Code.[42] In the course of this litigation, a judge of the Federal District Court in San Francisco ruled that the drivers 'are Uber's presumptive employees' and rejected as 'fatally flawed' Uber's argument that it is 'merely a technological intermediary between potential riders and potential drivers'.[43] A settlement claim was reached in April 2016 on terms including a payment of US$100 million to the drivers; Uber also committed to recognise a driver association and deactivate drivers from the app only with just cause.[44] However, the settlement was rejected by the Federal District Court as unfair and inadequate.[45] In a later decision, the Ninth US Circuit Court of Appeals upended the ability of the plaintiffs to proceed with a class action, ruling that the arbitration clauses in Uber's driver contracts precluded such proceedings.[46] This meant that many thousands of drivers had to pursue individual arbitration claims.[47] A much smaller group of drivers (not subject to the contractual arbitration clauses) could proceed with the class action, which was settled for $US20 million in March 2019.[48]

The legal status of the drivers was not resolved in the Californian Uber case, but has been considered in several other contexts. In April 2019, the General Counsel of the National Labor Relations Board (NLRB) issued a memorandum in response to charges brought in regional NLRB offices alleging breaches of the NLRA, including that Uber unlawfully assisted or dominated a labour organisation representing drivers in New York City.[49] In the memorandum, recommending dismissal of the charges, the General Counsel concluded that Uber drivers are independent contractors and therefore are not covered by the NLRA's protections against unfair labour practices, because:

> The drivers had significant entrepreneurial opportunity by virtue of their near complete control of their cars and work schedules, together with freedom to choose log-in locations and to work for competitors of Uber.[50]

[41] Stone (n 38) 107; see also Weil, ibid,184–85, comparing differing approaches to the economic realities test applicable under the FLSA, and under the Occupational Health and Safety Act, 1970 and National Labor Relations Act, 1935 (NLRA)).

[42] E Kennedy, 'Employed by an Algorithm: Labor Rights in the On-Demand Economy' (2017) 40 *Seattle University Law Review* 987, 1005; *O'Connor v Uber Technologies, Inc.*, No 211, (ND Cal, 11 March 2015) (Order Denying Defendant Uber Technologies, Inc's Motion for Summary Judgment) 1.

[43] *O'Connor v Uber Technologies, Inc* ibid, 1, 10, 13, 15.

[44] Kennedy (n 42) 1007–8.

[45] Ibid, 1008; J Wong, 'Uber v drivers: judge rejects "unfair" settlement in US class action lawsuit', *The Guardian* (19 August 2016).

[46] *O'Connor v Uber Technologies, Inc.*, Ninth Circuit Case No 16-15595 (25 September 2018), relying on the US Supreme Court decision in *Epic Systems Corp v Lewis*, 138 SCt 1612, 200 LEd2d 889 (2018).

[47] A Hawkins, 'Uber scores a big win in legal fight to keep drivers as independent contractors', *The Verge* (25 September 2018).

[48] M Dickey, 'Uber agrees to pay drivers $20 million to settle independent contractor lawsuit', *Techcrunch* (13 March 2019).

[49] United States Government, National Labor Relations Board, Office of the General Counsel, *Advice Memorandum* (16 April 2019).

The General Counsel's opinion was significant in signalling that the agency charged with enforcing rights to organise and bargain collectively considered they did not apply to Uber drivers – and other gig economy workers might similarly be excluded.[51] The NLRB's position is likely to shift, however, under the new General Counsel installed by President Biden[52] and the implementation of his policy to counter misclassification of gig workers by adopting the Californian 'ABC test' of employment status.[53]

As for union involvement in misclassification challenges, the New York Taxi Workers Alliance (NYTWA) has brought a number of cases in which it has successfully assisted Uber drivers to establish employee status for purposes of New York state's unemployment insurance scheme.[54] In June 2016, NYTWA initiated a class action claiming that Uber had misclassified drivers as contractors in breach of the minimum wage and overtime provisions of the FLSA,[55] which was settled.[56] Unions were not behind a pivotal case in California, leading to an April 2018 decision establishing a new test for determining employment status – but they have been at the centre of the political ruptures arising from it. In *Dynamex Operations West, Inc v Superior Court of Los Angeles*,[57] the Supreme Court of California determined that on-demand couriers (providing deliveries to customers of stores like Home Depot) were employees for purposes of that state's minimum wage and benefits orders. This conclusion was based on the application of what the court called the ABC test[58] for differentiating between employees and independent contractors. Under this test, a worker is presumed to be an employee unless three factors are present:

(a) 'that the worker is free from the control and direction of the hirer in connection with the performance of the work, both under the contract for the performance of such

[50] Ibid, 5. See N Scheiber, 'Uber drivers are contractors not employees, Labor Board says', *New York Times* (14 May 2019).

[51] L Mishel and C McNicholas, 'Uber drivers are not entrepreneurs', *Economic Policy Institute* (20 September 2019).

[52] See ch 4.

[53] J Biden, 'The Biden Plan for Strengthening Worker Organizing, Collective Bargaining, and Unions'. Available at: https://joebiden.com/empowerworkers/; the ABC test is discussed below. See also N Bose, 'Exclusive: U.S. Labor Secretary throws his support behind classifying gig workers as employees', *Reuters* (30 April 2021).

[54] H Johnston and C Land-Kazlauskas, *Organizing On-Demand: Representation, Voice and Collective Bargaining in the Gig Economy* (Conditions of Work and Employment Series No 94, Geneva, International Labour Office, 2018) 5–6; D Rubinstein, 'Uber loses a "precedential" victory, and some New York drivers win "employee" status', *Politico* (18 July 2018). See also *Matter of Lowry (Uber Tech Inc-Commissioner of Labor)* (2020) 189 AD3d 1863; and ch 12.

[55] S Greenhouse, 'On Demand, and Demanding Their Rights', *The American Prospect* (Summer 2016).

[56] 'Uber cuts $195k deal with 7 NYC cab drivers in wage suit', *Law360* (13 March 2019).

[57] 416 P3d 1, 36 (Cal 2018) ('*Dynamex*').

[58] The court noted (*Dynamex*, page 7 of the unreported decision) that the ABC test was already in use in various contexts in other jurisdictions. See further Cunningham-Parmeter (n 37) 408–10; R Sprague, 'Using the ABC Test to Classify Workers: End of the Platform-Based Business Model or Status Quo Ante?' (2020) 11:3 *William and Mary Business Law Review* 733, 748.

> work and in fact'; (b) 'that the worker performs work that is outside the usual course of the hiring entity's business'; and (c) 'that the worker is customarily engaged in an independently established trade, occupation, or business of the same nature as the work performed for the hiring entity'.[59]

The *Dynamex* ruling was immediately thought to carry huge implications for the gig economy, potentially automatically re-casting workers for platforms such as Lyft, Uber and Postmates as employees.[60] Then, in December 2018, Democratic Assemblywoman Lorena Gonzalez introduced a bill into the Californian legislature to codify and clarify the application of *Dynamex* ('Assembly Bill 5', known as 'AB5').[61]

This fundamental threat to their contracting model triggered a massive counter-campaign from the platforms. AB5 proposed that 'a person providing labor or services for remuneration shall be considered an employee unless the hiring entity demonstrates' that the three conditions set out in the *Dynamex* ABC test are satisfied.[62] However, AB5 also set out a long list of exemptions from this presumption of employment status, including securities brokers, investment advisers, real estate licensees and people engaged in direct sales.[63] In response to AB5, the CEOs of Uber and Lyft penned an op ed in the *San Francisco Chronicle*, offering:

> … to work with legislators and labor groups to find a different solution [than AB5] that preserves drivers' ability to work independently if they choose to do so while improving the quality and security of their work.[64]

They also pledged to 'give workers more of a say in the decisions affecting their lives and livelihoods' by 'forming a new driver association, in partnership with state lawmakers and labor groups'.[65] The platforms lobbied Californian legislators, seeking a deal for AB5 exemptions in exchange for a set of basic driver protections.[66] They were offering a few token improvements in drivers' conditions, to preclude harder-edged regulation.

[59] *Dynamex* (page 7 of the unreported decision; see also 66–67, 76, noting that the burden rests on the hiring entity to establish the existence of the three factors in the ABC test).

[60] See, eg, L DePillis, 'California ruling puts pressure on Uber, Lyft and other gig economy employers', *CNN Money* (3 May 2018).

[61] California Legislative Information, *AB-5 Worker Status: Employees and Independent Contractors* (Assembly Bill No 5, 3 December 2018). Available at: https://leginfo.legislature.ca.gov/faces/billNavClient.xhtml?bill_id=201920200AB5. See the critiques of AB5 in Unidentified student author, 'California Adopts the ABC Test to Distinguish Between Employees and Independent Contractors' (2020) 133:7 *Harvard Law Review* 2435; S Prince, 'The AB5 Experiment – Should States Adopt California's Worker Classification Law?', *American University Business Law Review*, forthcoming.

[62] AB5, section 3(a).

[63] Ibid, section 3(b).

[64] D Khosrowshahi, L Green and J Zimmer, 'Open Forum: Uber, Lyft ready to do our part for drivers', *San Francisco Chronicle* (12 June 2019).

[65] Ibid.

[66] B Sachs and S Block, 'Will California Legislate Fairness for Gig Workers?', *On Labor* (9 September 2019); K Conger and N Scheiber, 'California passes landmark bill to remake gig economy', *New York Times* (11 September 2019).

As the debate over AB5 intensified in the summer of 2019, the platforms ratcheted up their opposition. Uber and Lyft descended into classic union-busting.[67] Evidence emerged that drivers felt pressured by the companies into signing a petition against AB5 through e-mails and in-app messages.[68] Drivers were recruited to attend a protest rally, with some of their costs met by the 'I'm Independent Coalition' (a lobby group funded by the California Chamber of Commerce).[69] Union groups likewise marshalled and supported drivers to attend rallies in support of AB5.[70] The bill was passed by the State Senate and signed into law by Governor Gavin Newsom in September 2019, taking effect on 1 January 2020.[71]

The platforms then shifted to a legal strategy. Uber and Postmates sought, but were denied in February 2020, a preliminary injunction to hold off the enforcement of AB5 pending a full trial of their claim (arguing that the legislation breaches the Californian and US constitutions).[72] In refusing the injunction, a judge of the US District Court for the Central District of California rejected the companies' argument that AB5 unfairly targeted gig economy operators for regulation. Rather, the new law 'furthers the State's legitimate interest in addressing misclassification' of platform workers'.[73] In May 2020, the Californian Attorney-General commenced proceedings against Uber and Lyft with the aim of enforcing AB5.[74] On 22 October 2020, the Court of Appeals for the State of California upheld a preliminary injunction restraining the rideshare platforms from continuing to classify drivers as independent contractors in breach of AB5.[75]

In the meantime, the platforms had adopted a political strategy to derail AB5. In late 2019, the 'Protect App-Based Drivers and Services' campaign (funded by Uber, Lyft and DoorDash) initiated a referendum proposal exempting the platforms from AB5, to be voted on at the November 2020 elections.[76] This triggered more aggressive tactics from the platforms, this time to persuade the electorate to support their ballot proposal known as 'Proposition 22' (or more commonly,

[67] See also ch 9.

[68] S Ghaffary, 'Some Uber and Lyft drivers say they were misled into petitioning against their own worker rights', *Vox* (27 June 2019).

[69] J Bhuiyan, 'Uber and Lyft drivers were paid up to $100 to demonstrate against bill', *The San Diego Union-Tribune* (15 July 2019).

[70] Ibid; C Said and D Gardner, 'Gig-work bill passes Senate committee as crowds rally for and against it', *San Francisco Chronicle* (10 July 2019); K Paul, 'California Uber and Lyft drivers rally for bill granting rights to contract workers', *The Guardian* (27 August 2019).

[71] Conger and Scheiber (n 66).

[72] *Olsen, et al v State of California, et al.* CV 19-10956-DMG (RAOx), 10 February 2020.

[73] Ibid, 8–13.

[74] K Conger, 'California sues Uber and Lyft, claiming workers are misclassified', *New York Times* (5 May 2020).

[75] *The People v Uber Technologies, Inc. et al* A160701, A160706, City & County of San Francisco Super Ct No CGC-20-584402, 22 October 2020.

[76] A Campbell, 'Uber and Lyft have launched a campaign to avoid government regulation in California', *Vox* (29 October 2019); D Kerr, 'Uber, Lyft, DoorDash's gig worker ballot initiative heads to voters in November', *cnet.com* (27 February 2020).

'Prop 22').[77] As well as the relentless bombardment of drivers with in-app messages,[78] Uber, Lyft, Postmates, Instacart and DoorDash spent more than US$200 million on advertising in support of Prop 22.[79] Protests against Prop 22 were organised by Gig Workers Rising and Rideshare Drivers United (RDU),[80] the Service Employees International Union and Unite Here.[81] However, all of this opposition was to no avail: on 3 November 2020, Prop 22 was passed by a 58 per cent majority of ballots cast.[82] Despite the result, labour groups affirmed their willingness to continue fighting for platform workers' rights and to resist the attempts foreshadowed by the companies to use Prop 22 as a stalking horse for obtaining laws thwarting gig work regulation in other US states.[83]

## C. UK

The GMB Union (GMB) and the Independent Workers Union of Great Britain (IWGB) have been at the forefront of litigation contesting the misclassification of gig workers. In contrast to the Australian and US legal position, based on the binary distinction between employee and independent contractor, UK law provides for the intermediate category of 'worker' as a 'qualifying category' for a limited range of employment rights (including the national minimum wage and regulation of working time).[84] The employee–contractor divide is still the main basis for determining whether most protective employment regulation applies,

[77] In addition to the AB5 exemption, under Prop 22, drivers engaged by the platforms would obtain certain benefits including a 120% minimum wage 'guarantee' (but only for driving time, not time between trips), health care subsidies (for those who drive over 25 hours per week) and access to occupational accident insurance: S Harnett, 'Prop. 22 explained: Why gig companies are spending huge money on an unprecedented measure', *KQED News* (26 October 2020). See, further, M Cherry, 'Proposition 22: A Vote on Gig Worker Status in California' (2021) *Comparative Labor Law and Policy Journal* (Dispatch No 31).

[78] A Hawkins, 'Uber and Lyft had an edge in the Prop 22 Fight: their apps', *The Verge* (4 November 2020).

[79] A Sammon, 'How Uber and Lyft Are Buying Labor Laws', *The American Prospect* (5 October 2020).

[80] K Paul, 'Prop 22 explained: how California voters could upend the gig economy', *The Guardian* (15 October 2020).

[81] V Irwin, 'Organized labor fights Uber and Lyft's Prop. 22', *SF Weekly* (16 October 2020).

[82] K Paul and J Wong, 'California passes Prop 22 in a major victory for Uber and Lyft', *The Guardian* (4 November 2020).

[83] Ibid; 'Uber, Lyft could expand new California gig economy model to other states, experts say', *Yahoo News* (5 November 2020). See (more generally) R Smith and M Pinto, 'Rewriting the Rules: Gig Companies' Drive for Labor Deregulation', in D Acevedo (ed), *Beyond the Algorithm: Qualitative Insights for Gig Work Regulation* (Cambridge, Cambridge University Press, 2020) 189. Note also that, since Prop 22 took effect, drivers have raised concerns that the benefits they were supposed to obtain have not materialised: see, eg, M Sainato, '"A slap in the face": California Uber and Lyft drivers criticize pay cuts under Prop 22', *The Guardian* (16 May 2021).

[84] M Freedland and J Prassl, *Employees, Workers and the "Sharing Economy": Changing Practices and Concepts in the United Kingdom* (University of Oxford, Legal Research Paper Series No 19/2017, March 2017) 11.

resting on 'a series of common law tests such as control, economic reality and mutual obligation' to distinguish dependent or subordinate relationships from the independent or autonomous.[85] However, the 'worker' classification has provided the most fruitful basis for establishing the coverage of minimum labour standards for those working in the gig economy[86] and a vehicle for arguments seeking to establish collective bargaining rights.[87]

GMB, IWGB and the App Drivers and Couriers Union (ADCU) all backed the longest-running litigation, a case against Uber seeking to establish that five of the platform's drivers were entitled to minimum wages and paid leave (under the National Minimum Wage Act 1998 and Working Time Regulations 1998 respectively).[88] This requires that the drivers are 'workers' for purposes of those laws, where 'worker' is defined to include (as well as an individual working under a contract of employment) an individual who works under:

> any other contract … whereby the individual undertakes to do or perform personally any work or services for another party to the contract whose status is not by virtue of the contract that of a client or customer of any profession or business undertaking carried on by the individual.[89]

The claimants succeeded, first, before the London Central Employment Tribunal. In October 2016 it found that the drivers fell squarely within the 'worker' definition, as they 'are recruited and retained by Uber to enable it to operate its transportation business'.[90] The Tribunal also observed that: 'The notion that Uber in London is a mosaic of 30,000 small businesses linked by a common "platform" is to our minds faintly ridiculous.'[91] On appeal, the Employment Appeal Tribunal (EAT) upheld the first-instance decision. In its November 2017 ruling, the EAT rejected Uber's argument that it was simply an agent facilitating a contractual relationship

[85] J Prassl, *The Concept of the Employer* (Oxford, Oxford University Press, 2015) 2. See further L Mason, 'Locating Unity in the Fragmented Platform Economy: Labor Law and the Platform Economy in the United Kingdom' (2020) 41:2 *Comparative Labor Law and Policy Journal* 329, 332–33, noting that UK courts (in applying the common law tests) consider factors including whether there is remuneration in exchange for work, the level of control exercised over the performance of work, whether the worker has taken on any risk, the extent of the worker's integration into the enterprise and the existence of a personal obligation to work.

[86] And for ostensibly self-employed workers engaged outside platform work: see eg, *Pimlico Plumbers Ltd and another v Smith* [2018] UKSC 29.

[87] See Part III(C) below.

[88] S Fredman and D Du Toit, 'One Small Step Towards Decent Work: *Uber v Aslam* in the Court of Appeal' (2019) 48:2 *Industrial Law Journal* 260, 261.

[89] National Minimum Wage Act 1998, s 54(3)(b); Working Time Regulations 1998, reg 2 (definition of 'worker'); see also Employment Rights Act 1996, s 230(3)(b). Workers for these purposes are commonly referred to as 'limb (b) workers'.

[90] *Aslam v Uber BV* [2017] IRLR 4, at para [93].

[91] Ibid, at para [90]. See further E McGaughey, 'Uber, the Taylor Review, Mutuality and the Duty Not to Misrepresent Employment Status' (2019) 48:2 *Industrial Law Journal* 180, 193–95.

between driver and passenger. Rather, the contracts were between Uber and drivers 'whereby the drivers personally undertook work for Uber'.[92]

Uber struck out again, before the Court of Appeal, a majority of judges confirming (in December 2018) that each of the claimant drivers was working for the platform 'as a "limb (b) worker"'.[93] The majority considered there was 'a high degree of fiction in the wording' of the contractual documents entered into between Uber and the drivers, which could not paper over the fact that Uber 'enforces [significant] control over the drivers' to protect its position as a licensed private hire vehicle operator in London.[94] Further, drivers are 'working': at the latest, from the moment they accept any trip through the Uber app; and even before that, when they are waiting for a booking and are at Uber's disposal (because they are required to accept a high proportion of trips under penalty of being logged off from the app).[95] The Court of Appeal's ruling affirmed the entitlement of Uber's drivers to the minimum wage, work breaks and paid holidays.[96]

However, that decision was the subject of a further appeal by Uber to the UK Supreme Court. In its judgment handed down on 19 February 2021, the Supreme Court determined conclusively that the drivers are 'workers' for purposes of the relevant statutory definitions.[97] This was based on factors including that: their remuneration was fixed by Uber, which 'dictated' the contractual terms; although drivers could choose when and where to work, true choice was constrained (for example, by Uber's monitoring of the level of a driver's acceptance or cancellation of trip requests); Uber exercised considerable control over the performance of services by drivers, via its chosen technological platform and the passenger ratings system (the latter described in the judgment as 'a classic form of subordination that is characteristic of employment relationships').[98] The Supreme Court also affirmed the view that drivers were 'workers' from the time that they logged onto the Uber app in London.[99] After a four-year legal tussle, the drivers – supported by their unions – had finally won basic rights at work. In the aftermath of this decision, Uber announced that it would ensure its 70,000 London drivers receive

[92] *Uber BV, Uber London Ltd, Uber Britannia Ltd v Aslam, Farrar, Dawson and others* (EAT, Appeal No UKEAT/0056/17/DA), para [106].

[93] *Uber BV, Uber London Ltd, Uber Britannia Ltd v Aslam, Farrar, Dawson and others* [2019] IRLR 257, [2019] ICR 845, para [71].

[94] Ibid, paras [90]–[91]; see Fredman and Du Toit (n 88) 265–68, 270, noting the influence of the UK Supreme Court decision in *Autoclenz Ltd v Belcher* [2011] ICR 1157 on the Court of Appeal's capacity to disregard the artificiality of the contractual terms imposed on drivers by Uber, and 'appreciat[e] the social reality beyond the contract'.

[95] *Uber BV, Uber London Ltd, Uber Britannia Ltd v Aslam, Farrar, Dawson and others* (n 93), paras [103]–[104], noting, however, that Uber may be able to establish that a driver was not at its disposal (and therefore was not working for it) if the driver also had a rival app switched on while waiting for trips on the Uber app.

[96] See further A Davies, 'Wages and Working Time in the "Gig Economy"' (2020) 31 *King's Law Journal* 250.

[97] *Uber BV and others (Appellants) v Aslam and others (Respondents)* [2021] UKSC 5, para [119].

[98] Ibid, paras [94]–[99].

[99] Ibid, para [130].

the minimum wage, holiday pay and pension entitlements – although they would only be paid for the time spent driving (not the time between trips).[100] This was followed by Uber reaching a recognition agreement with GMB.[101]

IWGB has brought several other cases, including a minimum wage and paid holidays claim on behalf of 50 Deliveroo riders which it settled for 'a material sum' in June 2018.[102] A more significant outcome, in establishing the legal rights associated with 'worker' status, came through IWGB's series of successful Employment Tribunal cases against the courier company CitySprint.[103] In one of the decisions, the finding that courier Mags Dewhurst was a 'worker' entitled to the statutory minimum wage was reached in part on the basis that CitySprint had its couriers 'on circuit' all day with only short breaks (in keeping with its '"all hands to the pump" ethos').[104] These cases were coupled with parallel efforts by IWGB to affirm the rights of gig workers to access the statutory recognition procedure for collective bargaining.[105] Similarly, GMB has pursued the twin track of employment rights litigation and collective bargaining, including its successful minimum wage claims against mini-cab company Addison Lee[106] and courier firm Hermes[107] and the negotiation of a collective agreement for Hermes drivers.[108]

## D. Italy

In Italy, several cases have been initiated – by gig workers themselves and, in some instances, by trade unions – seeking to establish legal rights for those engaged through platforms. The most significant litigation involved a claim pursued by six Foodora riders, arguing they had been misclassified and wrongfully dismissed in retaliation for protesting against the platform's introduction of piece rate payments.[109] The Italian legal position on categorisation is probably the

[100] 'Uber "willing to change" as drivers get minimum wage, holiday pay and pensions', *BBC News* (17 March 2021). See also S Butler, 'Just Eat to offer 1,500 Liverpool couriers minimum hourly rate and sick pay', *The Guardian* (21 April 2021).

[101] See Part III(C) below.

[102] S Butler, 'Deliveroo couriers win six-figure payout in employment rights case', *The Guardian* (29 June 2018).

[103] See, eg, 'Bike courier wins "gig" economy employment rights case', *BBC News* (7 January 2017); IWGB, 'IWGB wins worker status and rights for "gig economy" CitySprint couriers once and for all' (6 August 2020). Available at: https://iwgb.org.uk/post/iwgb-wins-worker-status-and-rights-for-gig-economy-citysprint-couriers-once-and-for-all.

[104] *Dewhurst v CitySprint UK Ltd* (ET case no 2202512/2016, 5 January 2017), paras [14], [84]–[87].

[105] See Part III(C) below.

[106] *Addison Lee Ltd v Lange* (UKEAT/0037/18/BA).

[107] *Leyland and others v Hermes Parcelnet Ltd* (ET decision, 22 June 2018).

[108] See Part III(C) below.

[109] V De Stefano and A Aloisi, *Digital Age: Employment and Working Conditions of Selected Types of Platform Work – National Context Analysis, Italy* (European Foundation for the Improvement of Living and Working Conditions, 2018) 12; A Aloisi, '"With Great Power Comes Virtual Freedom": A Review of the First Italian Case Holding that (Food-Delivery) Platform Workers are not Employees' (2018) *Comparative Labor Law and Policy Journal* (Dispatch No 13). See also ch 9.

most complex of the four countries examined in this study. Traditionally, the law maintained a strict distinction between employees (who 'have been granted full protection' by employment laws) and self-employed workers (who were denied any statutory safeguards).[110] Employees are those engaged to perform intellectual or manual work under the direction and control of an entrepreneur,[111] as compared with those undertaking services or tasks without any subordination to the principal party.[112] While 'the employment contract has been the sole mean[s] of access' to rights under the law and collective agreements, as Del Conte and Gramano observe: 'there has always been a degree of uncertainty in the [legal] definition of employee'.[113] The blurring of categories arising from new technologies and forms of work organisation has inevitably led to exploration of regulatory solutions, including a possible intermediate classification to cover the 'gray area' between employee and contractor.[114] The status of self-employed workers was addressed in provisions introduced by the Renzi government's 2015 Jobs Act[115] and subsequent reforms in 2019, noted below.

In 1973, a new sub-category of self-employment known colloquially as 'co.co.co' was introduced for purposes of civil dispute resolution, expediting cases involving workers who engage in continuous and coordinated collaboration with a principal (but not involving subordination).[116] The co.co.co. category, encompassing the 'semi-subordinate worker, legally autonomous but economically dependent', has come to make up a large proportion of the 17% of Italian workers in self-employment.[117] The Foodora delivery riders in the aforementioned case had been engaged on this basis, under standard contracts providing they were 'free' to apply to undertake each specific delivery (or not) and were paid at the rate of €5.60 per hour.[118] At first instance, the Employment Tribunal of Turin ruled (in May 2018) that because they could decide when they would work, and accept or refuse shifts, the riders were not subordinate to the business's power to command

[110] M Del Conte and E Gramano, 'Looking to the Other Side of the Bench: The New Legal Status of Independent Contractors under the Italian Legal System' (2018) 39:3 *Comparative Labor Law and Policy Journal* 579, 580.

[111] Ibid, 583–84, referring to Italian Civil Code, art 2094; see also 585–586, noting the subsidiary factors indicating an employment relationship (developed through case law) including defined working hours, performance of work at the business's premises and the worker's use of tools provided by the employer. See further S Borelli, 'Fitting the Panoply in a Binary Perspective: The Italian Platform Workers in the European Context' (2020) 41:2 *Comparative Labor Law and Policy Journal* 365, 371–75.

[112] Del Conte and Gramano (n 110) 583–86, referring to Italian Civil Code, art 2222. See also M Cataudella, 'Types of Worker and Employment Contract' in F Carinci and E Menegatti, *Labour Law and Industrial Relations in Italy: Update to the Jobs Act* (Milano, Wolters Kluwer Italia, 2015) 1, 6.

[113] Del Conte and Gramano (n 110) 580–81.

[114] Ibid, 581–82.

[115] Ibid, 583.

[116] Ibid, 587, referring to the Code of Civil Procedure, art 409; see also Borelli (n 111) 372.

[117] V Pulignano, L Gervasi and F de Franceschi, 'Union Responses to Precarious Workers: Italy and Spain Compared' (2016) 22:1 *European Journal of Industrial Relations* 39, 42. See also Del Conte and Gramano (n 110) 588–89; and ch 7.

[118] Aloisi (n 109).

and therefore were not employees.[119] Pizzoferrato argues that this decision overlooked the limitations on the workers' freedom imposed by 'incisive control and monitoring' and prescriptive requirements of their work performance, with sanctions applied for 'behaviours not liked by the company'.[120] Aloisi elaborates upon this critique, suggesting that 'the judge in Turin decided the case by looking at the rear-view mirror' and applying:

> … the same reasoning made thirty years ago for delivery couriers on mopeds, even though technological progress and the regulatory framework have taken significant steps forward.[121]

In January 2019, the Turin Court of Appeal confirmed the Employment Tribunal's finding that the Foodora riders could not be considered employees, yet also determined that they were not properly to be viewed as self-employed.[122] Rather, the 'riders belong[ed] to a third type of relationship between self-employment and subordinated employment'.[123] According to Aloisi, the Turin Court 'applied the 2015 provisions that extend employment protection to (nominally independent) self-employed workers whose personal activity is unilaterally organised by the principal'.[124] This is a reference to the Jobs Act's attempt to reduce the grey zone between self-employed and subordinate workers, through a provision granting traditional employment protections to those engaged to provide exclusively personal work in continuous collaboration with a principal (where the latter organises the method of work performance and the time and place of work).[125] Nevertheless, in the Foodora ruling, the Turin Court only extended *some* employment protections to the riders (those relating to wages and health and safety).[126] Other protections did not apply, for example that against dismissal (because the riders' contracts were considered to naturally expire on the completion of each task).[127]

The matter was finally determined in a further appeal to the Italian Supreme Court, which ruled in January 2020 that the riders fell within the category of

[119] A Pizzoferrato, 'Platform Workers in the Italian System' (2019) 12:1 *Italian Labour Law E-Journal* 93, 94, referring to Tribunal of Turin, Judgment No 778 (7 May 2018).

[120] Ibid, 94–95.

[121] Aloisi (n 109 above).

[122] F Pedroni, 'Appeal court deems Foodora riders self-employed with certain workers' rights', *International Law Office* (13 March 2019). Available at: www.internationallawoffice.com/Newsletters/Employment-Immigration/Italy/Stanchi-Studio-Legale/Appeal-court-deems-Foodora-riders-self-employed-with-certain-workers-rights, referring to the Court of Appeal of Turin judgment (4 February 2019). See also M Biasi, 'The On-Demand Work (Mis)classification Judgments in Italy. An Overview' (2019) 12:1 *Italian Labour Law E-Journal* 49, 55.

[123] Pedroni (n 122).

[124] A Aloisi, *A Fascinating Chapter in the "Gig" Saga: How to Deliver Decent Work to Platform Workers in Italy?* (European Commission Mutual Learning Programme, Peer Review on Platform Work, September 2020) 4.

[125] Del Conte and Gramano (n 110) 590, referring to art 2 of Decree 81/2015.

[126] Aloisi (n 124) 4.

[127] Biasi (n 122) 56.

'"collaborations organized by the principal"' established under the Jobs Act.[128] Certain characteristics of the work relationship (including requirements that riders deliver orders within 30 minutes, arrive at a meeting point at the start of each shift and confirm various steps in the food ordering and delivery process) justified the Supreme Court's conclusion that the riders – although self-employed contractors – were '"etero-organizzati", a concept that literally translates to "organised from the outside"'.[129] The riders (and all workers whose work is organised by the other party in this way) were thus entitled to the benefit of all labour and employment protections.[130] This effect has essentially been achieved by a statutory amendment in 2019, which clarified that the Jobs Act provision extends to all workers engaged by digital platforms 'if their work is organized by the platform'.[131] Another part of this amendment applies specifically to self-employed riders, conferring upon them 'the right to a minimum wage set forth by national collective agreements' covering logistics.[132]

Although not directly involved in the Foodora litigation, unions were central to another case in which Deliveroo's algorithmic management tool was challenged on grounds of discrimination. The CGIL-affiliated unions NIDiL, FILCAMS-CGIL and FILT-CGIL brought the case in the Labour section of the Court of Bologna, arguing that the algorithm used to offer shifts to Deliveroo riders based on a ranking of 'reliability' was discriminatory.[133] The Court decided in favour of the riders, finding (in a December 2020 ruling) that in failing to take into account a rider's reason for having to cancel a pre-booked shift via the app, Deliveroo's algorithm discriminated against those with legitimate reasons for not working (such as illness or caring responsibilities).[134] Seeing past the platform's contention that 'Frank' (the algorithm) was blind or objectively neutral, so it could not engage in discrimination, the court ordered Deliveroo to pay €50,000 to the claimant riders.[135] NIDiL also supported a legal challenge by a rider for the Glovo food delivery platform

[128] O Razzolini, *Collective Action for Self-Employed Workers: A Necessary Response to Increasing Income Inequality* (Centre for the Study of European Labour Law 'Massimo D'Antona', Working Paper 155/2021) 4, referring to Court of Cassation, Judgment No 1663 (24 January 2020).

[129] M Sideri, 'Employed or self-employed? The Italian Supreme Court gives new clarity on delivery riders', *Ius Laboris – Global HR Lawyers* (4 March 2020); see also Borelli (n 111) 378.

[130] A Aloisi and V De Stefano, 'Delivering employment rights to platform workers', *La Rivista il Mulino* (31 January 2020). Available at: www.rivistailmulino.it/news/newsitem/index/Item/News:NEWS_ITEM:5018.

[131] Ibid; see also Aloisi (n 124) 3, referring to Law No 128/2019 (amending Decree 101/2019).

[132] Razzolini (n 128) 13–14; see also ch 9 and Part III(D) below.

[133] B Wray, 'Italian union hails court victory over "discriminatory" Deliveroo algorithm', *Brave New Europe* (8 January 2021). Available at: https://braveneweurope.com/ben-wray-italian-union-hails-court-victory-over-discriminatory-deliveroo-algorithm.

[134] G Geiger, 'Court rules Deliveroo used "discriminatory" algorithm', *Vice* (6 January 2021); Moyer-Lee and Kountouris (n 1) 25–26, referring to the Bologna Court's decision in Case No 2949/2019 (31 December 2020).

[135] Wray (n 133). For further insights into how 'Frank' operates, see C Cant, *Riding for Deliveroo: Resistance in the New Economy* (Cambridge, Polity Press, 2019) 44–45, 49–50; *Franco v Deliveroo Australia Pty Ltd* [2021] FWC 2818, [13]–[14], [19], [62].

who was disconnected from access to the app.[136] This occurred supposedly due to a delay in transferring money received from customers, but also followed the rider's participation in a television programme in which he criticised the platform's working conditions and failure to provide COVID-19 protective equipment.[137] The Tribunal of Palermo decided in November 2020 that the rider, putatively self-employed and paid a 'per-drop' fee and lump sum for riding/waiting, was rather (at law) an employee.[138] In reaching this conclusion the judge considered that the rider's 'freedom' to turn on the app (and therefore work, or not) was subject to the reality that he was closely integrated in Glovo's business; and that any autonomy was outweighed by robust managerial tools of surveillance and work allocation through an algorithm.[139] The 'de-platforming' of the rider was found to be retaliatory and void.[140] Aloisi maintains that the decision represents an 'important step forward', as the finding of employment status:

> … was made possible by a detailed analysis of the factual circumstances of the job performance and by a modern understanding of 'subordination' that does not fit the archetype of physical supervision over the worker's shoulders.[141]

This apparent interruption of the business model of food delivery platforms was bolstered by the February 2021 decision of the Italian Labour Inspectorate and a Milan tribunal. They jointly ordered Uber Eats, Glovo, Just Eat and Deliveroo to re-engage 60,000 riders as coordinated, continuous workers – and pay €733 million in fines (or face criminal proceedings).[142] The order arose from an investigation into health and safety breaches by the platforms.[143] The Deliverance Milano riders group welcomed the decision, stating that it was: 'a very heavy blow to the platform narrative, … based on false autonomy and the abuse of occasional work, on the denial of any right and the infringement of laws and contracts'.[144] This development followed Uber Italy being placed into temporary receivership by a Milan court in 2020 based on concerns over the exploitation of Uber Eats riders and a prosecutor's subsequent notification to ten Uber Eats managers of likely indictments on alleged gangmastering and taxation offences.[145] The intense scrutiny of

[136] A Ribaudo, 'Rider vince la causa contra Glovo: assunto a tempo indeterminato', *Corriere della Sera* (23 November 2020).

[137] A Aloisi, 'Demystifying Flexibility, Exposing the Algorithmic Boss: A Note on the First Italian Case Classifying a (Food Delivery) Platform Worker as an Employee' (2021) *Comparative Labor Law and Policy Journal* (Dispatch No 35).

[138] Ibid, referring to Tribunal of Palermo, Case No 3570/2020 (21 November 2020).

[139] Ibid.

[140] Ibid.

[141] Ibid; see also Razzolini (n 128) 4.

[142] L Cater, 'Italy demands €773m in fines from food delivery platforms', *Politico* (25 February 2021).

[143] Ibid; 'Food delivery firms must hire 60,000 riders – prosecutor', *ANSA.it (English edition)* (24 February 2021).

[144] Cater (n 142).

[145] 'Ten face indictment on Uber Italy gangmaster case', *ANSA.it (English edition)* (12 October 2020). See also L Tondo, 'Uber Eats in Italy investigated over alleged migrant worker exploitation', *The Guardian* (14 October 2020); Borelli (n 111) 380–81; and ch 8.

how Italian food delivery platforms operate, and a growing legal reckoning, is at least partly attributable to the efforts of trade unions and self-organised worker collectives.

## III. 'Staying United to Reverse the Race to the Bottom': Collective Bargaining in the Gig Economy

### A. Australia

The peak union body in the state of New South Wales – Unions NSW – has contested the mistreatment of workers engaged through Airtasker, a platform matching 'job-posters' with people to perform home-based tasks such as cleaning, maintenance, repairs and removal. In 2017, Airtasker's CEO Tim Fung claimed that: 'If we're doing a great job of crafting a great working environment for the people on our platform, then hopefully a union is not necessary.'[146] However, the emerging evidence suggested otherwise. Unions NSW had released a research report in 2016, finding that serious safety risks arose from workers performing trades-qualified work in private homes (via Airtasker), without any scrutiny as to whether they held the required trade qualification or licence; and that the platform's recommended hourly rates for various tasks were below award minimum pay rates (once Airtasker's 15% fee was deducted from payments to workers).[147] Kate Minter, then-research director at Unions NSW, explained that the union body used the 2016 report as a springboard for negotiations 'regarding how to better protect workers hired through the platform.'[148] Minter further noted that Unions NSW opted to seek these improvements '[i]n the absence of clear legal protections and entitlements' for workers engaged through Airtasker.[149] That is, it was accepting the workers' designation as independent contractors,[150] and seeing what could be achieved within those constraints.

The agreement Unions NSW reached with Airtasker in 2017 was hailed as 'a world first' for the gig economy,[151] although there were also critics of its shortcomings. Under the deal, the platform committed to posting recommended pay rates

[146] A Uribe, 'Gig economy workers don't need a union: Airtasker chief', *Australian Financial Review* (15 August 2017).

[147] Unions NSW, *Innovation or Exploitation? Busting the Airtasker Myth* (2016). See also K Gregory, 'Airtasker: Unions raise safety concerns over "gig economy" cowboys', *ABC News* (9 March 2018).

[148] K Minter, 'Negotiating Labour Standards in the Gig Economy: Airtasker and Unions New South Wales' (2017) 28 *The Economic and Labour Relations Review* 438, 449.

[149] Ibid.

[150] Although see also ibid, 442: 'the fact that price, payment and access to work are governed by an intermediary for-profit company should raise immediate and serious questions about the legitimacy of the application of the independent contractor classification to this form of work.'

[151] D Taylor, 'Airtasker agrees to minimum working conditions for "gig economy" contractors', *ABC News* (2 May 2017).

on its website reflecting minimum award wage rates applicable to the type of work being performed; and to develop safety guidelines that would assist Airtasker, job-posters and workers to ensure compliance with their obligations under NSW work health and safety legislation.[152] Airtasker would also work with Unions NSW and insurance providers to develop optional personal injury coverage for workers and a dispute resolution process for workers and job-posters through the FWC.[153] Unions NSW itself recognised the limitations of the agreement, Minter conceding that the recommended minimum pay rates 'cannot be enforced' and lack the 'full, formal protection' of 'the complete set of labour standards available to other workers'.[154] Kaine highlighted a key element of Airtasker's system that would likely undermine the Unions NSW agreement:

> Airtasker's business model is based on workers 'bidding' for work. As they can only 'win' a job by submitting the lowest bid, workers are pitted against each other in a reverse auction. This system seems directly opposed to creating a minimum wage.[155]

In practice, the agreement has resulted in some improvements to the situation of workers engaged via the site, including 'better income' and access to injury protection insurance.[156]

A collective agreement can only be made under the FW Act between an employer and its employees[157] (based on the common law employee/independent contractor distinction[158]). The Unions NSW-Airtasker agreement was, instead, made outside the formal system of employment regulation. The TWU has also adopted this approach, reaching an accord in July 2020 with a new entrant to the Australian market, US food delivery platform DoorDash. The main thrust of the agreement was to provide additional protections to drivers in response to the COVID-19 emergency.[159] However, it also included this rare statement from a platform operator (all the more remarkable coming from one of the arch enemies of gig work regulation in California[160]):

> DoorDash recognizes that collective representation from workers through regular dialogue and engagement with the TWU is valuable to identify, discuss, and resolve issues of general and specific concern and enhance food delivery work in the emerging gig economy.[161]

[152] Minter (n 148) 446–47, 449.

[153] Ibid, 447–49.

[154] Ibid, 450.

[155] S Kaine, 'All care and no responsibility: Why Airtasker can't guarantee a minimum wage', *The Conversation* (3 May 2017).

[156] 'Technology won't protect workers from themselves: Airtasker', *Workplace Express* (4 May 2018), noting the comments of Unions NSW Secretary Mark Morey on the first 12 months' operation of the agreement.

[157] See ch 3; the ability to take lawful industrial action is similarly confined.

[158] See Part II(A) above.

[159] See ch 12.

[160] See Part II(B) above.

[161] *TWU-DoorDash COVID-19 Response* (July 2020).

The TWU's Michael Kaine indicated that the agreement would be used to push for a 'charter … about the way we try and move standards in DoorDash and across the industry. … This is a good step in trust'.[162] The union has since organised protests by Hungry Panda riders which led to the platform reversing unilateral pay reductions, providing injury/death insurance and reinstating two sacked riders (through an informal agreement reached in March 2021).[163] In April, Menulog announced it would conduct a trial of direct employment for its delivery riders, and work with the TWU and FWC to develop a specialised award for food delivery work.[164]

The TWU has pursued an additional path to build collectivism among platform workers: work health and safety (WHS) regulation. Australian WHS statutes typically provide for the election of health and safety representatives (HSRs) upon the request of 'workers' in one or more 'work groups'[165] (for these purposes, 'worker' means a person who carries out work in any capacity, including as an employee or contractor[166]). This process includes the obligation of the 'person conducting the business or undertaking', a broad concept which takes in the employer or occupier of the work site,[167] to facilitate the determination of the relevant work group(s) through negotiations between the workers concerned and their representatives.[168] In late 2019, a group of Deliveroo riders (supported by the TWU) requested that the platform commence the formation of work groups and election of HSRs under the WHS legislation in NSW. This followed the deaths of four Australian food delivery riders in the course of their work in 2019, the union raising concerns that Deliveroo riders received no training and inadequate protection from collisions, heat stress and other risks.[169] Deliveroo had (not long before the NSW riders made their request) established its own 'rider panel' consisting of ten workers appointed by the company, to advise it on safety issues and develop initiatives with management.[170] The TWU alleged the panel was nothing more than a 'smoke-screen', with riders who had previously agitated about safety concerns overlooked by Deliveroo.[171]

[162] N Bonyhady, 'First step: Union strikes coronavirus deal with delivery giant DoorDash', *Sydney Morning Herald* (28 July 2020).

[163] TWU, 'Historic win for gig workers: Hungry Panda increases pay, reinstates sacked workers' (16 March 2021). Available at: www.twu.com.au/press/historic-win-for-gig-workers-hungry-panda-increases-pay-reinstates-sacked-workers/.

[164] L Henriques-Gomes, 'Menulog announces pivot towards "employment model" for all couriers within coming years', *The Guardian* (12 April 2021).

[165] See, eg, Work Health and Safety Act 2011 (NSW) (WHS Act), s 50.

[166] WHS Act, s 7.

[167] Ibid, s 5.

[168] Ibid, ss 51–52.

[169] TWU, *Deliveroo Riders Invoke Tough Work Health & Safety Laws* (1 November 2019). Available at: www.twu.com.au/press/deliveroo-riders-invoke-tough-workplace-health-safety-laws/. On the series of further rider deaths in 2020, see ch 9.

[170] D Marin-Guzman, 'Deliveroo sets up gig economy's first rider advisory panel', *Australian Financial Review* (15 October 2019).

[171] Ibid.

The platform then dug in to resist the attempt by workers and the union to activate the NSW legislation. Deliveroo had 14 days from the date of the riders' request to elect HSRs, to commence negotiations over the composition of work groups.[172] After that, agreement had to be reached 'within a reasonable time'.[173] It emerged in February 2020 that Deliveroo disputed the union's proposal to form small, geographic work groups to represent the various types of safety hazards encountered by riders in different parts of Sydney.[174] The platform argued, instead, that a single work group for all riders across NSW would be appropriate, while also asserting that the statutory provisions for electing HSRs for work groups: '[do] not readily apply to the flexible nature of our relationship with independent contractors engaged to provide delivery services'.[175] The TWU therefore requested the WHS regulatory agency, SafeWork NSW, to appoint an inspector[176] to investigate both the dispute over work groups and the union's allegation that Deliveroo had unlawfully discriminated against a rider involved in instigating the WHS process.[177] On 7 May 2020, the TWU posted an update on Twitter indicating that SafeWork NSW had 'provided Deliveroo with a notice forcing it to comply' with the WHS legislation. On 5 June, the union reported (also on Twitter) that Deliveroo had appealed against this decision. Nevertheless, by early January 2021, the union was claiming a big win: the election of seven Deliveroo HSRs under the WHS Act: 'the first such representatives ever elected at a gig economy company despite [HSRs] being commonplace at most workplaces'.[178]

## B. USA

In the USA, where the challenges facing unions seeking to collectively bargain for employees are formidable,[179] bargaining on behalf of those putatively engaged as contractors in the gig economy is an even tougher ask. It was noted in Chapter 3 that independent contractors are excluded from the NLRA's coverage.[180] Further (as discussed earlier in this chapter), the Trump-era NLRB regarded Uber drivers as falling outside the legislation.[181] Some US unions have therefore sought legislative support for modified forms of collective bargaining for platform workers.[182]

[172] WHS Act, s 54(3)(a)(i).
[173] Ibid, s 54(3)(b).
[174] 'TWU seeks SafeWork intervention at Deliveroo', *Workplace Express* (27 February 2020).
[175] Ibid.
[176] Under WHS Act, s 54(1).
[177] In contravention of WHS Act 2011, ss 104–106.
[178] TWU, 'win for delivery riders as first safety reps elected' (5 January 2021). Available at: https://twunsw.org.au/press/win-for-delivery-riders-as-first-safety-reps-elected/.
[179] See chs 2, 3 and 4.
[180] See, further, R Gorman, M Finkin and T Glynn, *Cox and Bok's Labor Law: Cases and Materials* 16th edn (St Paul, Foundation Press, 2016) 61–65.
[181] See Part II(B) above.
[182] In addition to the Seattle example considered here, the Independent Drivers Guild and New York State AFL-CIO supported proposed legislation (the Right to Bargain Act) allowing unions

In 2015, the App-Based Drivers Association (formed with the support of a Teamsters Union local) successfully lobbied the Seattle City Council to introduce an ordinance allowing rideshare drivers to unionise and engage in collective bargaining, despite remaining classified as independent contractors.[183] Not surprisingly, this initiative met with resistance from the platforms.[184] The Council relied upon its regulatory powers in relation to for-hire vehicles and taxis under the Seattle Municipal Code to introduce the ordinance and rules supporting it. Under these provisions, drivers who met specified minimum driving periods for defined 'driver coordinators' (eg, Uber, Lyft) would be eligible to choose an 'exclusive driver representative' (EDR).[185] A union or other advocacy body (meeting the requirements of being democratically organised, with experience in concluding agreements with employers or contractors) could petition the Council to be designated as the EDR for a group of drivers; the Council would certify such a union or advocacy body as the EDR if satisfied that a majority of eligible drivers wanted to be represented by that organisation.[186] The certified EDR could then bargain with the rideshare companies over issues such as 'vehicle standards, safe driving practices, the nature and amount of payments to be made, [and] minimum hours of work'; interest arbitration would be available if agreement could not be reached; and any resulting agreement would be legally binding (after clearing a compliance review by the Council).[187]

However, in early 2016, before the Seattle ordinance had much of an opportunity to operate, the US Chamber of Commerce (acting on behalf of the rideshare industry) challenged its validity in a federal court action, arguing two main grounds: that local and state governments were pre-empted from enacting collective bargaining measures covered by federal law (the NLRA); and that the Seattle ordinance breached the prohibition in the Sherman Antitrust Act, 1890 of collective negotiations by independent contractors (which, in antitrust terms,

representing rideshare and delivery workers to obtain exclusive negotiating rights with Uber, Lyft and other platforms – but on the condition that various existing worker protections and the right to strike or protest would not apply and contractor status would remain unchallenged. The proposal drew heavy criticism from NYTWA and many other union groups (at the time of writing, it was unclear if the law would proceed). See, eg, J Valasquez and C Aponte, 'Support for gig worker union bill in New York collapsing after scrutiny', *The City* (25 May 2021); S Greenhouse, 'Unionized but impotent? Row erupts over gig workers' labor proposal', *The Guardian* (27 May 2021).

[183] S Greenhouse, *Beaten Down, Worked Up: The Past, Present, and Future of American Labor* (New York, Alfred A Knopf, 2019), 230; N Wingfield and M Isaac, 'Seattle will allow Uber and Lyft Drivers to form unions', *New York Times* (14 December 2015). The Ordinance Relating to Taxicab, Transportation Network Company, and For-Hire Vehicle Drivers (Ordinance No 124968), was passed by the Council on 14 December 2015: D Iglitzin and J Robbins, 'The City of Seattle's Ordinance Providing Collective Bargaining Rights to Independent Contractor For-Hire Drivers; An Analysis of the Major Legal Hurdles' (2017) 38:1 *Berkeley Journal of Employment and Labor Law* 49, 54–55.

[184] See, eg, M Nickelsburg, 'Uber GM says service may leave Seattle if landmark union law is implemented', *Geekwire* (24 March 2017).

[185] Kennedy (n 42) 1011–12; Stone (n 38) 111.

[186] Ibid, 1013; Ibid.

[187] Stone, ibid, 111–12.

would be regarded as price-fixing or an illegal cartel).[188] The case wound its way through the US courts, the Ninth Circuit Court of Appeals ruling in May 2018 in favour of the Chamber of Commerce's antitrust argument (although not the NRLA pre-emption objection).[189] This outcome led to the Seattle City Council modifying its collective bargaining ordinance to limit bargaining over pay rates.[190] The litigation challenging the original ordinance was withdrawn in April 2020.[191] By then, the Council had turned to alternative regulatory tools under the guise of the mayor's 'Fare Share' scheme, including ordinances directly setting minimum hourly rates for rideshare drivers (modelled on the New York Taxi and Limousine Commission's 2018 law);[192] and providing drivers with the right to contest any unwarranted deactivation from a rideshare app.[193] The attempt at collective regulation in Seattle further demonstrates the bind in which gig workers are placed by the imposition upon them of independent contractor status: stuck outside collective bargaining law, and rendered powerless by antitrust (or competition) law. Paul and Vaheesan highlight the paradoxical situation in which rideshare platforms are permitted under antitrust law to set prices for hundreds of thousands of drivers: 'When Uber engages in price coordination, it's legal. When gig workers do, they're considered to be acting collusively.'[194]

## C. The UK

As mentioned earlier in this chapter, as well as their role in test cases, GMB and IWGB have pursued various avenues of collective bargaining on behalf of gig workers. IWGB has sought to affirm the rights of Deliveroo riders to utilise the statutory union recognition procedure under Schedule A1 of the Trade Union and Labour Relations (Consolidation) Act 1992 (TULRCA). As Chapter 3 detailed,

[188] Kennedy (n 42) 1013 (and see further 1014–35); Stone ibid, 112. See also Iglitzin and Robbins (n 183) 55–71; C Garden, 'The Seattle Solution: Collective Bargaining by For-Hire Drivers and Prospects for Pro-Labor Federalism' (2017) 12 *Harvard Law and Policy Review Online* 1, 9–13.

[189] *Chamber of Commerce v City of Seattle* 890 F3d 769 (9th Cir 2018); see Unidentified student author, '*Chamber of Commerce v City of Seattle*: Ninth Circuit Holds Collective Bargaining Ordinance Not Subject to State Action Immunity' (2019) 132 *Harvard Law Review* 2360.

[190] M Steinbaum, 'Antitrust, the Gig Economy, and Labor Market Power' (2019) 82 *Law and Contemporary Problems* 45, 60.

[191] K Schofield, 'Legal challenge to Seattle Uber driver's collective bargaining ordinance ends', *Seattle City Council Insight* (10 April 2020). Available at: https://sccinsight.com/2020/04/10/legal-challenge-to-seattles-uber-drivers-collective-bargaining-ordinance-ends/.

[192] Seattle.gov, *Transportation Network Company Minimum Compensation Ordinance* (undated). Available at: www.seattle.gov/laborstandards/ordinances/tnc-legislation/minimum-compensation-ordinance; N Scheiber, 'Seattle passes minimum pay rate for Uber and Lyft drivers', *New York Times* (29 September 2020). See also ch 9.

[193] Seattle.gov, *Transportation Network Company Driver Deactivation Rights Ordinance* (undated). Available at: www.seattle.gov/laborstandards/ordinances/tnc-legislation/driver-deactivation-rights-ordinance.

[194] S Paul and S Vaheesan, 'Make Antitrust Democratic Again!', *The Nation* (12 November 2019). See further S Paul, 'Uber as For-Profit Hiring Hall: A Price-Fixing Paradox and Its Implications' (2017) 38:2 *Berkeley Journal of Employment and Labor Law* 233.

Schedule A1 enables a trade union to seek recognition for collective bargaining on behalf of a group of workers in a bargaining unit. For these purposes, a 'worker' is defined (in addition to a person working under an employment contract) as an individual who works: 'under any other contract whereby he [or she] undertakes to do or perform personally any work or services for another party to the contract who is not a professional client of his [or hers]'.[195] Although defined slightly differently to the limb (b) worker concept which applies under the UK minimum wage and working time laws,[196] the TULRCA worker concept (similarly) extends the operation of the union recognition procedure beyond those working as employees. Whether it extends to platform workers, like those delivering food for Deliveroo, is the central issue in the IWGB's recognition test case.

In late 2016, the union applied to the Central Arbitration Committee (CAC) to be recognised for collective bargaining in respect of riders working for Deliveroo in the Camden and Kentish Town zone in London. In a November 2017 decision, the CAC determined that the riders could not be the subject of a claim for recognition as they are not 'workers' as defined in TULRCA.[197] In the CAC's view, clauses in the riders' contracts enabling them to substitute the carrying out of food delivery tasks to other riders meant that they are not personally obliged to perform any work or services.[198] The CAC found this right of substitution to be genuine, and accepted the evidence that some riders had exercised the right in practice (although most had not).[199] The freedom of riders 'to substitute at will' was considered 'fatal to the Union's claim'.[200] The CAC even overlooked the possibility that the contractual substitution clauses were drafted with the purpose of precluding the riders being classified as workers,[201] an 'aspect of the reasoning that is particularly troubling' according to Atkinson and Dhorajiwala.[202] In reaching its conclusion that the riders are not workers for purposes of a claim for union recognition, the CAC also rejected the union's argument that section 296(1)(b) of TULRCA should be interpreted in light of the right of freedom of association in Article 11 of the European Convention on Human Rights (ECHR).[203]

On IWGB's application for judicial review of the CAC's decision, the only review ground which the High Court was prepared to consider was that relating to the import of Article 11 of the ECHR.[204] In December 2018, the High Court also

[195] TULRCA, s 296(1)(b).

[196] See Part II(C) above.

[197] *Independent Workers Union of Great Britain v RooFoods Ltd T/A Deliveroo* [2018] IRLR 84.

[198] Ibid, para [100].

[199] Ibid, paras [78]–[80], [100].

[200] Ibid, paras [101]–[102].

[201] Ibid, para [99].

[202] J Atkinson and H Dhorajiwala, '*IWGB v RooFoods*: Status, Rights and Substitution' (2019) 38:2 *Industrial Law Journal* 278, 292 (see further 292–95).

[203] *Independent Workers Union of Great Britain v RooFoods Ltd T/A Deliveroo* (n 197), para [104].

[204] *R (on the application of The Independent Workers Union of Great Britain) v Central Arbitration Committee and RooFoods Ltd t/a Deliveroo* [2018] EWHC 3342 (Admin), para [3].

ruled against the IWGB. The union argued that a restriction on the right to obtain statutory recognition under Schedule A1, TULRCA amounts to a restriction on the right to collective bargaining under Article 11(1).[205] However, the High Court found that only those working in an employment relationship enjoy the rights provided by Article 11(1) (including 'the right collectively to bargain');[206] and as the Deliveroo riders are not in such a relationship, they do not have Article 11(1) rights.[207] Further, even if they enjoyed such rights, any interference with Article 11(1) imposed by the requirement of personal performance (to determine whether someone is a worker under section 296(1)(b) of TULRCA) 'achieves a fair balance between the competing interests' and is therefore permissible within Article 11(2).[208] On this point, the High Court concluded that:

> Any interference with Art. 11(1) is of a limited nature. The personal service obligation does not prevent Riders from belonging to the Union if they choose to do so, or prevent the making of voluntary arrangements. All it precludes is the compulsory mechanism provided by Schedule A1 of the 1992 Act.[209]

Bogg contends that the High Court's reasoning on Article 11: 'is mistaken. The interference with the Riders' freedom of association is very far-reaching, because worker status in UK law is the gateway to the most basic freedom of association protections'.[210] He identifies a range of rights under UK law which (consequently) are not available to riders, including the right to participate in strike action, so that: 'the denial of worker status represents a complete negation of [the riders'] freedom of association'.[211] IWGB's appeal against the High Court's decision was heard by the UK Court of Appeal in February 2021.[212]

IWGB *was* able to establish the right to recognition from The Doctors Laboratory (TDL), a company that provides delivery services for the National Health Service. TDL purportedly engages its couriers as independent contractors and refused the union's August 2017 request for recognition under Schedule A1 of TULRCA.[213] It does not seem that TDL argued the same point as Deliveroo (that the couriers

[205] Ibid, para [29] (art 11(1) provides that: 'Everyone has the right … to freedom of association with others, including the right to form and to join trade unions for the protection of his [or her] interests.')

[206] Ibid, para [36].

[207] Ibid, paras [33], [39].

[208] Ibid, para [55] (under art 11(2), restrictions on the exercise of art 11(1) rights must be 'necessary in a democratic society' for reasons including 'the protection of the rights and freedom of others').

[209] Ibid, para [46].

[210] A Bogg, 'Taken for a Ride: Workers in the Gig Economy' (2019) 135 *Law Quarterly Review* 219, 220.

[211] Ibid, 223. See also Atkinson and Dhorajiwala (n 202) 282–90; A Aloisi, '"A Worker is a Worker is a Worker": Collective Bargaining and Platform Work, the Case of Deliveroo Couriers' (2019) 5:1 *International Labor Rights Case Law Journal* 36.

[212] No decision had been handed down at the time of writing.

[213] *Independent Workers Union of Great Britain v The Doctors Laboratory Limited* (TUR1/1016/2017), para [1].

are not 'workers' within s 296(1)(b)). Instead, TDL disputed the composition of the employee bargaining unit for purposes of determining the recognition application and argued that a ballot should be held to prove that IWGB had majority support among the employees.[214] However, the CAC was satisfied on the evidence that 55.63 per cent of the 108 workers in the ultimately agreed bargaining unit were union members and made a declaration of recognition in favour of IWGB (without the need for a ballot).[215] In June 2019, proposed strikes by TDL workers were cancelled after IWGB secured a collective agreement including the option of hourly (rather than by delivery) payment for couriers, and additional payments for expenses and night work.[216] TDL courier Alex Marshall (who went on to become President of IWGB) trumpeted the outcome: 'This victory shows that by staying united and campaigning together it is possible to reverse the race to the bottom inherent in the business models of [gig platforms].'[217]

In early 2019, GMB negotiated a deal with parcel delivery firm Hermes, under which the company's 15,000 self-employed couriers receive a guaranteed minimum rate of £8.55 per hour and holiday pay.[218] The union built on its successful claim in 2018 establishing that Hermes couriers are 'workers' for purposes of the National Minimum Wage Act[219] to land the agreement, known as the '"self-employed plus" deal'.[220] Drivers can continue under their previous terms and conditions, or opt into the agreement to obtain the minimum hourly pay rate, up to 28 days' paid leave and full representation by GMB (which is recognised for these purposes by the company) – with the catch that drivers opting in are required to follow certain routes set by Hermes.[221] Most public commentary reflected the view that the Hermes agreement was an important breakthrough in challenging the flawed (self-employment) basis of gig work,[222] although there was some disquiet that a union would be party to an 'opt in or out' model of employment rights.[223] Even stronger concerns were raised about GMB's recognition agreement with Uber, announced in May 2021 in the wake of the UK Supreme Court's affirmation of

[214] Ibid, paras [3]–[4], [8]–[9].

[215] Ibid, paras [11]–[16]. See also M Ford and T Novitz, 'There is Power in a Union? Revisiting Trade Union Functions in 2019', in A Bogg, J Rowbottom and A Young (eds), *The Constitution of Social Democracy: Essays in Honour of Keith Ewing* (Oxford, Hart Publishing, 2020) 261, 276.

[216] 'IWGB reaches historic pay deal with NHS contractor TDL and calls off strikes' (21 June 2019). Available at: https://iwgb.org.uk/post/5d0c844ddd65b/iwgb-reaches-historic-pay-deal.

[217] Ibid.

[218] S Butler, 'Hermes to offer gig economy drivers better rights under union deal', *The Guardian* (4 February 2019); J Brock, *Getting Organised: Low-paid self-employment and trade unions* (The Changing Work Centre, May 2019) 30.

[219] See Part II(C) above.

[220] Brock (n 218) 30.

[221] A Chakelian, 'Hermes couriers win holiday pay – but what does it mean for the UK's gig economy?', *New Statesman* (4 February 2019).

[222] See, eg, J Cox, 'Hermes is now delivering on workers' rights. Is the gig economy changing?', *The Guardian* (5 February 2019); S O'Connor, 'Gig economy agreements promise a brighter future for trade unions', *Financial Times* (26 February 2019).

[223] O'Connor (n 222); Chakelian (n 221).

Uber drivers' rights as limb (b) workers.[224] Under the deal, GMB gains access to drivers at Uber 'hubs', quarterly meetings with management and the right to represent drivers if they are removed from the app.[225] However, rival unions ADCU and IWGB questioned whether GMB would engage in genuine collective bargaining with Uber, including over the critical issue of drivers being paid from the time they log on (in accordance with the Supreme Court's decision).[226]

## D. Italy

In contrast to the legal systems of Australia, the USA and the UK, under Italian law (as Borelli explains):

> … the right to collectively bargain and the right to strike are guaranteed [not only to employees but] also to own-account self-employed workers (i.e. workers that have not engaged any employees to work for them).[227]

It was mentioned in Chapter 9 that the main Italian union confederations had a rider classification added to the national collective agreement for transport and logistics. This provision was included in 2017, but does not seem to have stimulated collective bargaining with mainstream unions over riders' working conditions by the major food delivery platforms.[228] Instead, the businesses negotiated (through a lobbying organisation called Assodelivery) an agreement with the right-wing UGL (*Unione Generale del Lavoro*), described by Mará and Pulignano as a '"yellow" union'.[229] The agreement covering Uber Eats, Deliveroo, Glovo and Just Eat, revealed in September 2020, provides riders with some safety protections and access to training, but is premised on their categorisation as self-employed.[230] The main confederations rejected the agreement, CGIL maintaining that no collective agreement should be entered into that does not recognise riders as employees.[231] De Stefano's criticism was perfectly apt: 'This is going to be the first

[224] See Part II(C) above.

[225] S Butler, 'Uber agrees union recognition deal with GMB', *The Guardian* (27 May 2021).

[226] B Wray, 'Grassroots unions question the value for drivers in GMB's formal recognition agreement with Uber', *Brave New Europe* (27 May 2021).

[227] Borelli (n 111) 386; see also ch 3.

[228] Aloisi (n 124) 4. However, note that Laconsegna (a smaller platform based in Florence) concluded an agreement with CGIL and CISL affiliates in 2019 providing riders with minimum pay rates for all hours worked and other employment-like benefits: F Meta, 'Riders, a Firenze il primo contratto nazionale', *cor.com* (10 May 2019). Available at: www.corrierecomunicazioni.it/lavoro-carriere/riders-arriva-il-primo-contratto-nazionale-firenza-apripista/.

[229] C Mará and V Pulignano, 'Collective voice for platform workers: riders' unions struggles in Italy', *Social Europe* (10 December 2020).

[230] Ibid; Aloisi (n 124) 3.

[231] M Hekkilä and P Tamma, 'Delivery companies unveil labor deal with Italian far-right union', *Politico* (16 September 2020).

collective agreement that *deprives* workers of rights.'[232] According to Aloisi, the Assodelivery-UGL agreement was, in fact, aimed at avoiding the 2019 legislation establishing a collective bargaining framework for self-employed riders engaged by platforms.[233] Under that law, if the social partners could not conclude an agreement by November 2020, minimum standards (including wages as per applicable national collective agreements, extra pay for work at night or in poor weather, health insurance coverage and protection against arbitrary disconnection) would operate in respect of food delivery riders' contracts.[234] Oddly, Just Eat later withdrew from Assodelivery, admitting that the deal provided for piece-work payment rates.[235] Apparently responding to the February 2021 order of prosecuting authorities,[236] Just Eat agreed to hire approximately 4,000 riders as direct employees.[237] This formed part of an agreement reached with CGIL, CISL and UIL under which Just Eat riders would receive the minimum wage and other conditions accorded by the national logistics collective agreement.[238]

## IV. Conclusion

This and the previous chapter have demonstrated that, without unions, the gig economy would simply have been an uncontested 'free for all', where platforms could invoke technological disruption as a ruse for exploitation and get away with it. Instead, unions and self-organised worker groups have held them to account, responding to the desire of rideshare drivers and food delivery riders for collective voice, representation and power. The union project in the gig economy, in its many manifestations, is also a major exemplar of the innovation and adaptation which this book argues is essential to union revitalisation. The next chapter turns to analysis of these and other lessons for unions from the examination of their responses to membership decline in the four country studies (Chapters 4–8) and their efforts in the gig economy – along with the reforms needed to strengthen collective worker representation.

[232] Quoted in ibid (emphasis added). See also M Marenco, 'Contesting the gig economy: food delivery riders in Italy', *Futures of Work* (2 December 2020). Available at: https://futuresofwork.co.uk/2020/12/02/contesting-the-gig-economy-food-delivery-riders-in-italy/.

[233] Aloisi (n 124) 3, referring to Law No 128/2019 (amending Decree 101/2019).

[234] Ibid. See also ch 9.

[235] S Galeotti, 'Dopo l'annuncio che assumerà i rider Just Eat esce da Assodelivery. E ammette: "Il ccnl firmato con Ugl prevede pagamento a cottimo"', *Il Fatto Quotidiano* (11 November 2020); Mará and Pulignano (n 229).

[236] See Part II(D) above.

[237] 'Just Eat to add 4,000 workers on new contract terms in Italy', *Reuters* (31 March 2021).

[238] Ibid.

# 11

# What is the Future of Unions and Worker Representation? What Changes are Needed in Labour Laws?

## I. Introduction

This book has examined the many ways in which trade unions in the US, the UK, Australia and Italy have responded to falling membership levels since the 1980s and the roles being played by newer worker representative groups. It was outlined in Chapter 1 that the book aims to use these detailed accounts of union renewal efforts in each country and the exploration of unions in the gig economy to identify how union revitalisation can be achieved. That analysis is presented in Part II of this chapter. It identifies eight themes arising from comparative assessment of the various union strategies considered in the earlier chapters, highlighting steps that unions need to take – along with issues and questions they need to address – to rebuild collectivism into the future. Chapter 1 also considered the tension over whether union revival plans should prioritise the innovations which unions need to pursue themselves or obtaining more favourable labour laws. While maintaining that legal reform will not, in itself, fix organised labour's problems, it was indicated that this book would argue for changes in the law to maximise the capacity for workers to build and utilise collective power. Options for reform in eight essential areas are presented in Part III of this chapter.

## II. A Pathway to Union Revitalisation

### A. Organising is Necessary but Not Enough

As Chapters 4 to 7 have shown, the US organising model formed the cornerstone of union responses to membership decline in that country and in Australia and the UK from the 1990s. However, it was also demonstrated that, in each instance, organising has not provided the hoped-for panacea. Union membership levels have continued to fall in all three countries. Despite this, strategic organising remains the primary method through which unions in the US, the UK and Australia pursue membership growth. In the US, organising drives using the National Labor Relations Act (NLRA) process of recognition elections, or union-employer neutrality deals, are still very common and are pursued on a large scale. Among many other recent examples,[1] in April 2021 nurses voted 1001:750 in favour of recognising the Maine State Nurses Association/National Nurses United at Maine Medical Center,[2] the biggest successful National Labor Relations Board (NLRB) election since 2018.[3] Organising remains a major priority for the TUC and the UK's major unions, with recent successes utilising the statutory recognition procedure for the GMB Union,[4] Unite[5] and the entertainment division of Prospect Union[6] (among others). More interesting in the UK context is the newer brand of organising by IWGB and UVW, combining grass-roots mobilisation of low-paid workers with efforts to access the statutory recognition procedure for collective bargaining.[7] Similar forms of activism through independent unions have also been seen recently in Italy (where, as Chapter 8 indicated, US-style organising has not generally featured prominently).

Australian unions continue to organise, utilising the founding strategy of identifying issues of concern in the workforce; moving workers to discussion of changing their situation with help from activists; then formulating action 'to exercise the power to win'.[8] Although this formula is now more than 30 years old, the methods and tactics of organising have evolved. Increasingly, unions are embracing digital tools, like the Australian Services Union (SA-NT Branch)'s organising of local council staff via online petitions and events on LinkedIn; UWU's use of peer-to-peer messaging platforms in recruitment campaigns; and the creation of private Facebook groups to build membership among retail workers (SDAEA) and pharmacists (Professionals Australia).[9] Other unions have adapted organising to zero in on new worker groups. The NSW Nurses and Midwives' Association

[1] See Jonah Furman's 'Who Gets the Bird? (The week in US unions)' updates. Available at: https://whogetsthebird.substack.com/; and Cornell University ILR School's 'Labor Action Tracker', which monitors US strikes and protests (including those in support of union organising drives). Available at: https://striketracker.ilr.cornell.edu/.

[2] E Keller, 'Maine Medical Center nurses vote to form first-ever union', *News Center Maine* (29 April 2021).

[3] '2,000 Maine nurses unionize in big win for labor', *Law 360* (30 April 2021).

[4] *GMB and Mears Facilities Management* (TUR1/1157/2020); *GMB and Dyer Engineering Ltd* (TUR1/1188/2020).

[5] *Unite the Union and Loganair Limited* (TUR1/1166/2020); *Unite the Union and Wates Property Services Ltd* (TUR1/1202/2021).

[6] *Bectu a sector of Prospect and Whitechapel Gallery* (TUR1/1195/2020).

[7] See, eg, *United Voices of the World and OCS Group UK Limited* (TUR1/2019) (where recognition was ultimately granted after the employer had disputed the bargaining unit and contested the conduct of a postal ballot rather than one held at the workplace; the union also brought unsuccessful complaints of unfair practices against the employer); on IWGB's union recognition case against Deliveroo, see ch 10.

[8] B Moore and C Walton, *Rise! Empowering Australian Workers through the Collective Spirit and Collaborative Energy of Unions* (ATUI/Strategic Membership Solutions, 7 May 2020) 54.

[9] ACTU, *Organising with 2020 Vision: Case Studies of New Approaches to Union Growth and Capacity Building* (Australian Trade Union Institute, 19 November 2020) 10–15, 22–26.

refined a longer-term strategy of recruiting student nurses, by providing information on the graduate recruitment process and transition to a nursing career (through webinars and e-mails) as students near the end of their courses. Using a marketing automation tool (Salesforce) to offer repeated opportunities to convert from free student membership to full membership on commencement of work, the union signed up 65% of the 2020 graduating group (1,637 new members).[10]

This reflects the success of the Australian Nursing and Midwifery Foundation (ANMF) more generally. It is Australia's largest union, with 250,959 members in 2017 (an 84.1% increase on its membership in 2003).[11] By the end of 2020, it had grown to 284,699 members.[12] ANMF has achieved this by obtaining excellent conditions for its members through enterprise bargaining,[13] lobbying for mandated nurse–patient ratios and forging a professional identity for nurses and midwives. Membership of the union forms an integral part of that identity: the union acts as the channel for members to access the training and continuing professional development courses necessary for career progression.[14] ANMF's blending of professional and education services with organising, collective bargaining and protecting the industrial rights of members is a gold standard. Not all unions will be in a position to emulate the ingredients of this success, but they have to try. As Chapters 5 and 6 noted, even Chris Walton (one of the architects of the Australian organising project) has come to the view that *more* than organising is required if unions are to rebound. Unions need to supplement organising with novel membership offerings, campaigns and opportunities to participate in the labour movement.

## B. Change it Up: The Old Union Proposition doesn't Work for Generation Z

Chapters 6 and 7 set out the extensive efforts of unions in Australia and the UK to appeal to younger workers. Innovations have included the (digital) reconception of the very concept of a union (eg, Hospo Voice), dedicated organisations (eg, VTHC's Young Workers Centre) and the provision of union services through technology (eg, TUC's WorkSmart app, Hospo Voice's Mobilise app). These initiatives reflect the reality that the conventional union model is not attractive to many

[10] Ibid, 56–57.

[11] Parliament of Australia, Department of Parliamentary Services, *Trends in Union Membership in Australia* (Research Paper Series, 2018–19, 15 October 2018) 5.

[12] ANMF, Annual Return to the Registered Organisations Commission (5 May 2021).

[13] See, eg, 'Victorian nurses retain nurse:patient ratios after long bargaining campaign', *Workplace Express* (16 March 2012); '"Hero" nurses on track for 3% pay hikes', *Workplace Express* (13 August 2020).

[14] See, eg, ANMF, 'Education and Resources'. Available at: www.anmf.org.au/education; and Australian Nursing and Midwifery Journal, 'Learning and Career Hub'. Available at: https://anmj.org.au/learning-career/.

younger workers, as shown in their very low rates of unionisation.[15] The imperative of reversing this trend is underscored by Visser's contention that:

> Getting more young people into unions is the key to any strategy of union renewal. Revitalisation requires that, at a minimum, unions must aim [to] double the current union density rate of young people, until the age of 30, raising the average from the present 11 to 22 percent.[16]

How to achieve this is not so straightforward. In the Australian context, Moore and Walton suggest it requires more than simply 'starting a Facebook page' or a dedicated group for young members (unconnected to other parts of the union).[17] In their view, young workers will only join if the union 'can demonstrate tangible outcomes that justify [their] investment of time and/or money', either for the worker 'or around a cause they wish to advance'.[18] The potential for alignment between unions and the values held by many younger people is explored by Cha, Holgate and Yon. They argue that unions should actively engage with issues that young people are concerned about – not only their often precarious working conditions, but also 'housing, tax avoidance by large companies, immigration and racial and environmental justice'.[19] For example, the 'Fast Food Rights' campaign of BFAWU in the UK used '"tax-shaming"' of large multi-national companies to engage young workers (via social media) in protests about zero-hours contracts and low pay at McDonalds.[20] In the view of these authors, unions can tap into the desire of young people to act against structural inequality, as an 'entry point' which helps remove traditional barriers between unions and younger workers and 'bring[s] them into the union movement'.[21]

This kind of engagement does seem to present unions with an important opportunity to reach younger workers, but it needs to be built upon with more concerted measures. Unions have to communicate 'using a language, visuals and messages that [appeal] to young people',[22] recognising that technological devices and social media are the default *modi operandi* for Generations Y and Z. Recalling the views of young UK workers about the remoteness and unrepresentativeness

[15] See ch 2.

[16] J Visser, *Trade Unions in the Balance* (ILO/ACTRAV Working Paper, International Labour Organization, 2019) 68 (the average figures Visser refers to are those across the countries examined in his study). See also J Cha, J Holgate and K Yon, 'Emergent Cultures of Activism: Young People and the Building of Alliances Between Unions and Other Social Movements' (2018) 45:4 *Work and Occupations* 451, 460.

[17] Moore and Walton (n 8) 11; see also B Carneiro, *Trade Unions and Facebook: The Need to Improve Dialogue and Expand Networks* (ETUI Policy Brief, No 5 2018).

[18] Moore and Walton (n 8) 12.

[19] Cha, Holgate and Yon (n 16) 460.

[20] Ibid, 450–51, 453–54. BFAWU's campaign developed into #McStrike; see ch 7.

[21] Ibid, 459; see also 452, 457. See further M Tapia and L Turner, 'Renewed Activism for the Labor Movement: The Urgency of Young Worker Engagement' (2018) 45:4 *Work and Occupations* 391, 400.

[22] K Vandaele, 'Trade unions and young workers: how to overcome the disconnect?', *Medium* (31 August 2017). See also J Jansson and K Uba, *The Untapped Possibilities of YouTube as a Trade Union Tool* (ETUI Policy Brief, No 7 2018).

of traditional unions (see Chapter 7), the make-up of a union's staff should be reconsidered. Are there enough young, diverse, energetic officials and activists that potential recruits can relate to? Going even further, can the union (or part of it) be reconceived in a digital form that makes young workers think 'they've really made an effort to connect with me'? Is there a range of options for becoming a member or forming a relationship with the union short of full membership,[23] reflecting in particular the high concentration of young people in temporary or insecure work?[24] Union leaders have to ask themselves these questions because (as Moore and Walton put it) if young workers do not find 'a responsive, innovative, socially aware organisation' in a union, 'they will look elsewhere' or start their own network.[25] We have seen this occurring in the self-mobilisation of (predominantly young) food delivery riders in Italy and the UK.[26] There is much evidence that young workers *want* to take collective action, as seen in the global 'School Strike for Climate' movement. Unions need to transform that activism into a willingness to collectivise in the workplace.

## C. 'What Happens After the Campaign Ends?' Making the Campaigning or Digital Union Sustainable

This book has examined several examples of new forms of campaigning by unions, including those carried out through alliances with other social movement groups, to advance the interests of workers – like the Fight for $15 in the US, which inspired the #McStrike in the UK. It has also considered a number of digital union models, like Australia's Hospo Voice and OUR Walmart/United for Respect in the US, which adopt direct action tactics of the kind pioneered by the Fight for $15. These fresh manifestations of collective action offer some of the most promising signs of vibrancy in labour activism in the four countries. They have achieved significant gains, such as the minimum wage increases extracted from large corporations and through changes to state/local laws by the Fight for $15. Hospo Voice has drawn attention to endemic underpayments and exploitation in Australian cafés and restaurants and contributed to the successful campaign for wage theft laws. YWC has assisted young workers across several industries to recover stolen wages and (working with the TWU) pressed back hard against the gig economy.

However, some criticisms of the Fight for $15 campaign, OUR Walmart/United for Respect and #McStrike were noted in Chapters 4 and 7: that they

[23] See Part II(D) below.

[24] M Simms, D Eversberg, C Dupuy and L Hipp, 'Organizing Young Workers Under Precarious Conditions: What Hinders or Facilitates Union Success' (2018) 45:4 *Work and Occupations* 420, 425–26.

[25] Moore and Walton (n 8) 13.

[26] See ch 9.

have not moved beyond social media campaigns (attracting considerable media attention and shaming some employers into moderate improvements in working conditions) and have not resulted in workers being organised into unions on any appreciable scale. In this vein, Fisk asks: '[W]hat happens after the campaign ends? Enduring worker power requires some form of institutionalization.'[27] Mundlak poses the question in these terms:

> … how do alternative institutions of workers' voice negotiate changes in wages, working conditions, social security and ensure dignity at work, rather than do bits and pieces (ensuring compliance with minimum statutory rights, or affecting political change on macro political matters)?[28]

These issues have been the subject of extensive debate in US literature considering the sustainability of alt-labour. Compa contends that worker centres, OUR Walmart 'and other Alt-labor groups are exciting initiatives' but they have 'not solved the test of creating stable, mass, dues-paying organizations'.[29] He adds that: 'painless digital organizing cannot prevail when workers hear only from managers and supervisors at work, while their defenders are online'.[30] Another common criticism is that alt-labour groups have only obtained 'traction' through the substantial support of 'Old-labor'.[31] Fisk repositions the alt-labour/traditional union dynamic in more positive terms, noting that the #RedForEd strikes in 2018 saw teachers' unions providing resources for 'publicity, media relations and organizing' that contributed to 'the revival of movement activism'.[32] Reiterating many of the concerns already considered, Matthew Ginsburg (Associate General Counsel at the AFL-CIO) focuses on the question of 'organizational stability':

> At the end of the day, workers must pay for their own organizations. A plan for organizational self-sufficiency is thus fundamental to any proposal for … a new labor movement.[33]

He also highlights the inability of sectoral campaigns like the Fight for $15 'to negotiate a collective bargaining agreement with any particular employer'.[34] For Ginsburg, given the mass 'concentration of unorganized workers in the [US]' in

[27] C Fisk, 'Sustainable Alt-Labor' (2020) 95:1 *Chicago-Kent Law Review* 7, 17.

[28] G Mundlak, *Organizing Matters: Two Logics of Trade Union Representation* (Cheltenham, Edward Elgar Publishing, 2020) 225.

[29] L Compa, 'Careful What You Wish For: A Critical Appraisal of Proposals to Rebuild the Labor Movement' (2015) 24:3 *New Labor Forum* 11.

[30] Ibid, 12; see also T Juravich, 'Constituting Challenges in Differing Arenas of Power: Worker Centers, the Fight for $15, and Union Organizing' (2018) 43:2 *Labor Studies Journal* 104, 113.

[31] Compa (n 29) 9. See also M Crain and K Matheny, 'The "New" Labor Regime' (2017) 126 *Yale Law Journal Forum* 478, 483–84; M Oswalt, 'Alt-Bargaining' (2019) 82:3 *Law and Contemporary Problems* 89, 134.

[32] Fisk (n 27) 18 (footnote omitted).

[33] M Ginsburg, 'Nothing New Under the Sun: "The New Labor Law" Must Still Grapple with the Traditional Challenges of Firm-Based Organizing and Building Self-Sustainable Worker Organizations' (2017) 126 *Yale Law Journal Forum* 488, 494.

[34] Ibid, 497.

private sector employers like Walmart, Amazon and T-Mobile: 'there is no realistic path towards rebuilding labor's voice in society that does not begin with organizing key firms in industries with significant existing union density'.[35]

In contrast,[36] Andrias defends endeavours like the Fight for $15 as necessary responses to the limitations of the US labour law framework (and fissured work arrangements), utilising 'sectoral, social bargaining' but without 'abandoning worksite organization'.[37] She acknowledges the self-sufficiency concern identified by alt-labour critics, observing that without 'the promise of membership dues via exclusive bargaining agreements with particular employers, or another source of funding, the [SEIU] cannot sustain [Fight for $15's] efforts indefinitely'.[38] However, from Andrias's perspective, the shift towards a social bargaining approach is groundbreaking. It extends the reach of the state's influence over labour regulation by: 'position[ing] government as a co-negotiator in determining workers' material conditions … , while moving unions more squarely into the public policy space'.[39] This also entails a reconsideration of union purpose.[40] Rather than advocating simply on behalf of their own members, unions thus become 'social actors empowered to advance the interests of workers generally'.[41] Similarly, Rosenblum contends that: 'The Fight for $15 is transformational as long as it's understood not as an end goal but rather as an on-ramp to a much greater struggle and a powerful vision of a just society'.[42] According to Juravich:

> … unions need to look beyond alt-labor efforts instrumentally as simply incubators for new organising campaigns. Instead, support for alt-labor needs to continue and grow dramatically, not because it will necessarily yield more union members but because it is a way to fight injustice, which needs to remain at the core of what unions stand for.[43]

These polarised positions reflect the extremity of the challenge facing US labour, presenting a (flawed) choice: between the purity of the legislative organising process (in practice, accessible to a dwindling proportion of workers) and a promised land of campaigning, activist-based worker representation. In reality, for the labour movement in the US and the other countries considered here, both options are viable and their simultaneous pursuit will strengthen the overall position of workers. Providing 'institutional leverage' through the ability to engage in collective bargaining[44] would be an important enhancement of the power that

[35] Ibid, 488.

[36] See also ch 4 for extensive consideration of the views of the proponents of alt-labour, community-based unionism and similar approaches.

[37] K Andrias, 'The New Labor Law' (2016) 126 *Yale Law Journal* 2, 47; see also 32–33, 78.

[38] Ibid, 93.

[39] Ibid, 68; see also 63.

[40] See further Part II(D) below.

[41] Ibid, 58.

[42] J Rosenblum, 'Fight for $15: Good Wins, but Where did the Focus on Organizing Go?' (2017) 42:4 *Labor Studies Journal* 387, 391.

[43] Juravich (n 30) 114.

[44] Fisk (n 27) 9–10.

campaign-based or digital union protypes (of the kind examined in this book) are able to exercise.[45]

The incubator role of established unions – like VTHC's support of YWC and MWC, the AWU establishing Hair Stylists Australia, and UWU's underwriting of Hospo Voice – is a model that works. More unions should sponsor this kind of experimentation. Hospo Voice has given underpaid hospitality workers a taste of how collectivism can help them fight back against exploitation. Will they move in significant numbers from paying $A9.99 per month in dues, to full UWU membership? Can Hospo Voice evolve from campaigning and holding hospitality employers to account for wage theft, to become a strong workers' organisation which negotiates wages and conditions and enforces safety laws? It is unclear, but before too long, the UWU leadership will have to make a judgment as to whether the union's continued investment of resources is worth it. Another emerging approach is shown by Game Workers Unite Australia: the fledgling union was started by a core group of activists providing free information and advice to workers online; it then sought to partner with a mainstream union to provide industrial representation and services on a fee-paying basis.

It is also important to note the examples of newer, campaign-orientated unions like IWGB and UVW in the UK, and SI Cobas in Italy who *have* developed into durable, membership-based bodies. They all perform a range of traditional union functions and obtain effective outcomes for their members but they are not like conventional unions. In many respects they are more vibrant, member-led, confrontational and (therefore) appealing to marginalised workers. RAFFWU in Australia and gig economy unions like NYTWA in the US further illustrate the potential for moving alt-labour groups from a transitional to a more permanent footing. They also demonstrate (along with IWGB) that litigation is another reliable tool for obtaining 'big justice' for workers of the kind more commonly associated with traditional unions.[46] IWGB is successfully segmenting its offering by creating new branches to fit the identity of the workers it aims to attract (eg, game developers, yoga teachers, cycling instructors, nannies, couriers) – a clever strategy from the upstart union to secure its longevity.

## D. A Broader Purpose than Simply Increasing Membership Numbers … and a Less Rigid Concept of 'Membership'

The question of union purpose was touched upon in Part II(C) above. In response to the critiques of alt-labour and social bargaining, Andrias and others contend that unions have a broader role than just looking after their members, as advocates

[45] Including, as Andrias urges (n 37, 78–89), through sectoral bargaining; see further Part III(B) below.

[46] Juravich (n 30) 113.

for fairness on behalf of all workers. Among the many functions of trade unions identified by Ewing – including individual and collective workplace representation functions, and the provision of services and benefits to members[47] – is the regulatory function: 'a process of rule-making that extends beyond their members'.[48] This regulatory role can take the form of multi-employer collective bargaining, or (overlapping with the government and public administration functions of unions) obtaining favourable legislation from the state.[49] Ewing viewed the regulatory function of unions as: 'perhaps the most important … this being the most visible manifestation of the trade union role in promoting fairness and social justice not only at work but within the economy as a whole'.[50] The necessity of unions taking on the mantle of champions for *all* workers, especially the disempowered, is illustrated by many of the examples of union action considered in this study.[51] But where does this leave union *membership*?

Membership numbers and density have been the traditional yardsticks for measuring the influence of unions, and their decline.[52] On that basis, only a substantial lift in these measures would be evidence that unions were turning things around. Visser has this to say on the matter: 'There is more to unions and unionism than membership and it would be wrong to reduce union power in any given country, industry or enterprise to the share of unionized workers.'[53] He adds, though, that 'membership remains a critical resource' and the 'best way [for unions] to secure independence from other social forces and actors'.[54] Mundlak suggests that in a world of 'identity politics' and social change through protest movements, '[p]erhaps membership is no longer feasible' – but concludes that it remains necessary 'to fund organizing, servicing, retention, negotiations, monitoring and political action'.[55] On the contrary, Moore and Walton emphatically assert that:

> People do not care how many members you have. They care about the positive outcomes you create. …
>
> [R]ecruiting and retaining members is not a union's core purpose. Instead, membership is one of many tools that can assist a union to achieve its core purpose.

[47] KD Ewing, 'The Function of Trade Unions' (2005) 34:1 *Industrial Law Journal* 1, 3–4.

[48] Ibid, 4.

[49] Ibid, 4–5.

[50] Ibid, 13; see also at 13–15, where Ewing noted the increasing obstacles to unions' capacity to fulfil this regulatory function in the UK. See further M Ford and T Novitz, 'There is Power in a Union? Revisiting Trade Union Functions in 2019', in A Bogg, J Rowbottom and A Young (eds), *The Constitution of Social Democracy: Essays in Honour of Keith Ewing* (Oxford, Hart Publishing, 2020) 261, 279–84.

[51] This broader function of unions is particularly illustrated by their responses to the COVID-19 pandemic: see ch 12.

[52] See ch 2, including the consideration of different measures for assessing the strength of unions in Italy.

[53] Visser (n 16) 11.

[54] Ibid.

[55] Mundlak (n 28) 224, 227; see also 228.

> … Workers join [unions] and organise so that they have a voice in their workplaces, industry and society. They join to create a better life.[56]

Back in 2012, then-NUW (now UWU) official Godfrey Moase stated the position in almost exactly the same terms: 'A union is about workers coming together to exercise direct power in their workplace, industries and communities.'[57] Moase emphasised the importance of membership as an indication of the willingness of a group of workers to unite in their own interests. Indeed, he considered that membership: 'is the vehicle which creates the power necessary to win the change they want to see'.[58] However, his conception of membership formed part of a transition he urged from 'representational' to 'direct' unionism – from the conventional model which sees union officials acting as the advocates of the (passive) rank-and-file through legal processes like collective bargaining, to one where 'working people [are] actively grabbing hold of their own destiny and struggle'.[59] Moase's direct union would offer a 'continuum of membership' including options for campaign subscribers, community members, minority members (those able to access services but not covered by a union agreement) and bargaining members (those covered by a union agreement or working towards one).[60]

This proposal is similar to the 'ladders of engagement' through new membership categories introduced by several Australian unions since 2016, including community membership and the low or part-fee options offered by Hospo Voice and Hair Stylists Australia (see Chapters 5–6). Think-tanks and unions in the UK have considered and trialled similar experiments in moving away from the conventional full-fee union membership model (see Chapter 7). All these examples, alongside other initiatives to reach younger workers,[61] demonstrate a diversity of avenues through which unions are striving to form connections with people who have not traditionally engaged with them. This might look something like Freeman and Rogers' concept of 'open source unionism', a central aspect of which (according to Oswalt) was 'counting anyone interested in working with the union on a workplace or community issue as a genuine "member"'.[62] As we saw in Chapter 4, bargaining for the common good has seen US education unions extending their vision of their core constituency beyond teachers to include students, parents and the wider community – and expanding their bargaining agenda to ensure better funding of public education is placed alongside improvements in employment conditions.

[56] Moore and Walton (n 8) 22.

[57] G Moase, 'A New Species of Shark: Towards Direct Unionism' (2012) 4:2 *Interface: A Journal for and About Social Movements* 280, 288.

[58] Ibid, 287.

[59] Ibid, 280, 284–86.

[60] Ibid, 289–91.

[61] See Part II(B) above.

[62] M Oswalt, 'Improvisational Unionism' (2016) 104:3 *California Law Review* 597, 634, discussing R Freeman and J Rogers, 'Open Source Unionism: Beyond Exclusive Collective Bargaining' (2002) 5 *Working USA: The Journal of Labor and Society* 8, 13.

At a practical level, a critical mass of full-fee paying members will be essential to the viability of most unions. But there must also be a preparedness to allow workers to form looser attachments to the union that reflect the extent to which they want to (or can afford to) engage. Unions might be more willing to do this, if the problem of non-member free-riding was properly addressed.[63]

## E. Keep Reaching for the Hardest to Organise Workers, in the Toughest Areas of the Economy

This book reinforces the importance of unions doing (as Visser argues) the hard work of attempting to mobilise groups such as migrants, youth and precarious workers.[64] These are all areas where unions have enjoyed some success despite the difficulties they face. It has been shown (in Chapters 4–8) that this can take a range of different forms: (i) VTHC's establishment of YWC and housing of MWC; (ii) the dedicated union offshoots for atypical workers set up by the major Italian union confederations (NIDiL, FELSA and UILTemp), making a significant contribution to overall union membership growth; (iii) the emergence of independent unions in Italy (SI Cobas, ADL Cobas) and the UK (IWGB, UVW) aimed specifically at low-paid, predominantly migrant workers in outsourced jobs or subject to other forms of fissuring; (iv) union organising and representation efforts directed at exploited farmworkers in Italy (FLAI-CGIL, USB) and Australia (UWU's multifaceted strategy to lift labour standards for workers across the fresh food supply chain); and (v) the alliances forged between unions and social movements in the US (in particular, the Fight for $15 movement, providing millions of workers including those from Black, Hispanic and migrant communities with wage increases for the first time). Many of these examples, along with the #RedForEd teachers' strikes in the US and self-organised food delivery rider protests in Italy and the UK, also show that workers will not simply wait for mainstream unions to act. When a tipping point of oppression is reached, workers take the initiative and start organising protests, flash-mobs, log-offs and strikes online – often with the support of the new independent unions. The lesson, for traditional unions, is to pay close attention to the needs of these workers, organise and guide them to action.

Unions also need to continue exerting a presence in economic sectors where the odds are stacked against them (and workers). This is demonstrated by the work of the base unions in the Italian logistics sector – and, of course, the gig economy, where unions in all four countries have played a vital role. This is not only an opportunity for unions to engage with a growing pool of potential members. It is also vital that the gig economy's business model (the assumption of the worker's

[63] See Part III(I) below.
[64] Visser (n 16) 68–69. See also ch 1.

contractor status and therefore displacement from employment protections) is challenged and overturned. If platforms can get away with this inversion of the traditional employment law order, there is a risk that this will eventually become the norm across nations and economies: a race to the bottom by businesses to avoid employment regulation. Only unions have the power and resources to meaningfully contest the gig economy. The actions of the many unions and self-organised worker groups detailed in Chapters 9 and 10 have started to erode the platforms' contracting model: highlighting the exploitation this brings through campaigning and advocacy for gig workers, landmark test cases challenging misclassification, collective bargaining and its proxies. It cannot be overstated how much it must mean to a London Uber driver to have the UK Supreme Court declare that they are entitled to basic employment rights. There is a signalling effect at play here as well: a message is sent to other gig workers, 'you *can* win if you band together' – and to the platforms, 'we *will* hold you accountable'.

## F. There is No Union Recovery in Partnership, Company Unionism … or Internal Union Conflict

It is clear from several examples considered in this book that unions are mistaken if they believe their future lies in cooperation or partnership with management. The pursuit of workplace partnerships by UK unions in the New Labour era, driven by the TUC, demonstrates the futility of that approach most starkly (see Chapter 7). The partnership agenda did not lead to any overall increase in union membership and resulted in agreements with employers that compromised the interests of workers. Further, partnership was an instrument utilised by New Labour to accommodate the only form of unionism it considered palatable: one that was subservient to the interests of business and the economy more generally. It was therefore surprising to see, among the recommendations in Tait's 2017 report for the Changing Work Centre in the UK,[65] a call for 'a new industrial partnership between government, unions and business'.[66] Part of the rationale for this is the suggestion that within firms, 'having business on side can make it easier for unions to organise' through access to the workforce facilitated by the employer.[67] Yet those very kinds of arrangements entered into by USDAW, in the heyday of Third Way partnership, also involved the accommodation of business interests.[68] Similar concerns about enterprise agreements made with employers by the SDAEA in Australia were the motivating factor in the formation of rival

[65] C Tait, *Future Unions: Towards a Membership Renaissance in the Private Sector* (The Changing Work Centre, November 2017); see ch 7.

[66] Ibid, 53.

[67] Ibid.

[68] See ch 7.

union, RAFFWU.[69] Chapter 4 showed that the neutrality deals negotiated by US unions, to get around the fraught NLRA recognition process, also carry some risk of prioritising management objectives. While Australian union leaders wielded significant political influence under the 1980s-early 1990s Accord agreements with successive Labor Governments, this eventually entailed the embracing of a productivity-oriented business agenda. It also saddled unions with the system of enterprise-based bargaining that has increasingly constrained workers' collective power (see Chapter 5). Social partnership of the kind practised in Italy only functions effectively for unions in a context of deep entrenchment of their role (along with employer associations) in an established national-level framework.

Other instances of 'soft' unionism amounting to no more than feeble attempts to obtain outcomes for workers were highlighted in the examination of the gig economy in Chapters 9 and 10. IDG's agreement with Uber in the US, under which it is partly funded by the platform in exchange for giving up on contesting misclassification of drivers and striking, is crass complicity in union-busting. Rival unions raised valid concerns about the authenticity of GMB's recognition agreement with Uber in the UK. UGL's collective agreement with the Assodelivery body representing Italian food delivery platforms preserved a central tenet of rider exploitation, the assumption of self-employed status, without sufficient improvements in working conditions. This is not to say that unions should not try to negotiate collective agreements on behalf of gig workers notionally categorised as self-employed, such as those reached between GMB and Hermes, TWU and DoorDash, and Unions NSW and Airtasker.[70] However, in seeking to play this role, unions must ensure their primary objective is the betterment of the workers they represent, rather than simply ousting another union at the behest of a platform. Legitimate unions have to be constantly vigilant for these and other 'divide and rule' strategies from management, like Deliveroo's hand-picking of 'rider panel' members to fend off the TWU's pursuit of authentic health and safety representation under NSW legislation. These kinds of tactics were also seen in the political lobbying by platforms to stymie gig economy regulation in California, successfully enveloping thousands of gig workers in a campaign that was contrary to their own interests.

There may occasionally be circumstances where a level of cooperation with business and government is necessary, such as the COVID-19 pandemic. As we will see in Chapter 12, the ACTU and major Australian unions accommodated urgent employer requests to vary employment regulations so businesses could adjust their operations when the pandemic began. Union leaders then got drawn into a broader government-driven industrial relations reform process, yielding no benefits for workers. This reveals that cooperation of this kind can only be temporary and not part of a longer-term strategy for the recovery of unions. Business groups and conservative governments will always take advantage of union goodwill, reverting to their deregulatory agenda when the crisis passes.

[69] See ch 6.
[70] See also Part III(H) below.

Several instances of conflict between and within union groups have been considered in this study: the group of Change to Win unions splitting from the AFL-CIO in the mid-2000s; the splintering of divergent forces within OUR Walmart, eventually producing United for Respect; the internal problems within the CFMEU which caused the construction-maritime-textile unions' merger (into the CFMMEU) to unravel; and the competition between various worker organisations in the US to represent rideshare drivers, opportunistically stoked by the platforms. In most of these cases, unions and other collectivist groups have prioritised their own political and institutional interests over those of the workers. This almost always plays into the hands of business interests, conservative political forces and others who do not wish unions (or workers) well.

## G. The Bolder 'Strike-Ready' Union

'We don't need to innovate. … We can fight, and we can win.'[71] That is the conclusion Jane McAlevey reaches, based on her involvement in successful US organising drives in recent years. For McAlevey, it is imperative that US unions keep winning organising campaigns in sectors like health care, education and other 'strategic sectors made up of enough workers who are hard to replace, and … have a moral authority in mission-driven work', to widen their appeal to non-unionised workers.[72] She points to the Marriott hotel workers' strike in 2018, the joining up of striking teachers and bus drivers in West Virginia in 2018 and the Los Angeles teachers' strike in early 2019,[73] arguing that when workers build 'strike-ready' organisations, 'they win'.[74] Chapter 4, having examined the #RedForEd teachers' uprising, noted that it had formed part of a small upsurge in industrial action by US workers.[75] In the UK and Italy, many workers – particularly those in low-paid, oppressive work, who may consider they have nothing to lose – are joining unions and movements that are more willing to take on employers directly than some traditional unions (see Chapters 7[76] and 8). What is more, they are succeeding in bringing an end to outsourcing and other forms of fissured work. While strikes have often been pursued in defiance of legal restrictions, in the case of UWU in Australia it has been a matter of developing a confrontational stance within the limits of the legislation regulating collective bargaining and industrial

[71] J McAlevey, *A Collective Bargain: Unions, Organizing, and the Fight for Democracy* (New York, Harper Collins, 2020) 245.

[72] Ibid, 197; see also 160.

[73] Ibid, 241.

[74] Ibid, 235.

[75] For more recent examples see, eg, A Press, 'Hunts Point workers went on strike and won', *Jacobin* (23 January 2021); E Goldberg, '"They're trying to bully us": N.Y.U. graduate students are back on strike', *New York Times* (30 April 2021); and see, again, Cornell University's 'Labor Action Tracker' (n 1).

[76] See also Strike Map UK. Available at: https://strikemap.wordpress.com/about-us/.

action (see Chapter 6). As will be seen in Chapter 12, unions have led frequent walkouts to protest unsafe working conditions in the COVID-19 pandemic. The circumstances of the current moment support the reassertion of economic power by workers through their unions ('the power to stop production'[77]), supported by greater capacity to engage in lawful strike action.[78] Further, as Loomis urges, this more aggressive posture needs to be directed not only at business: '... workers have to take control over their own destiny in order to give themselves power. No *government* is going to do anything for workers if workers do not demand it first.'[79]

## H. The Digital Picket Line and the Digital Union

There has been much consideration in this book of unions exploring how they can maximise technology to reach new groups of workers. The peak union bodies in Australia and the UK have recently established, respectively, the ACTU Union Innovation Hub and TUC Digital Lab, to support unions in their exploration and trialling of digital organising and WorkerTech. Hospo Voice, GWUA, the Fight for $15 and OUR Walmart/United for Respect illustrate the re-imagining of unionism in digital form and campaigning via the internet and social media to build worker power. Online organising and communication have become even more essential to unions in the COVID-19 pandemic.[80] The study has also examined the use of technology by workers and unions to contest exploitation and develop collective strength in the gig economy. The platforms have sold technology to workers as a liberating force (the flexibility, 'be your own boss' trope), then utilised their apps to exercise high levels of control (algorithmic allocation of work, monitoring, customer ratings). Yet gig workers have been able to turn this automated oppression back on the platforms, using their smartphones to organise action and fight back through WhatsApp and Facebook groups.

The future for unions is digital: in terms of what a union looks like, in the ways it communicates with and provides access to workers and in the tactics it deploys. At the same time, it must be seen that digital tools are simply *new ways of forging connections between workers* – connections that, in the past, were formed through union halls, workers' clubs, *case del popolo* and workers' education organisations like Mechanics Institutes, community and sporting groups and churches. As in the past, *the next step* – after workers are brought together digitally or otherwise – is the decision *to take collective action together*. The mobilisation of workers from online to offline action was seen, for example, in the US #RedForEd teacher strikes in 2018; and in the protests by rideshare and food delivery riders in all four

[77] Juravich (n 30) 113.

[78] See Part III(F) below.

[79] E Loomis, *A History of America in Ten Strikes* (New York, The New Press, 2018) 224 (emphasis added).

[80] See ch 12.

countries, online and in the streets, coordinating local and global log-off strikes and urging customers and supporters not to cross digital picket lines. So, I return to the point made in the last part of Chapter 1: combining technology with the best traditions of unionism is critical to the survival of the labour movement in all four countries examined in this book.

# III. Reforming Labour Law to Empower Workers and Unions to Win

## A. Introduction

It was seen in Chapters 4, 5 and 7 that unions in the US, Australia and the UK have placed considerable store in electoral politics, lobbying and campaigning to secure legal reform. In the run-up to national elections in Australia and the UK in 2019, unions focused heavily on re-installing Labor/Labour governments, but without success. The labour laws of both countries therefore remain heavily weighted against workers and unions, while in the US, reform to address the even greater shortcomings of the NLRA has proven totally elusive. Obtaining a more supportive legal and institutional environment is therefore a necessary component of union recovery strategies – complementing the other approaches discussed in Part II above. The situation in Italy is different: law reform has not been such a priority, because Italian unions operate in a more favourable legal setting and draw their strength primarily from collective bargaining. The examination of reform options in this Part therefore focuses overwhelmingly on the changes needed to maximise the collective power of workers under US, UK and Australian law – including improvements that could be made by looking to Italian law. In some areas – including regulation of the gig economy, the right to strike and countering free-riding by non-unionists – the reform options discussed have potential application in all four countries.

## B. Multi-Employer Bargaining

It was shown in Chapter 3 that the labour laws of the US, UK and Australia generally only allow collective bargaining at the level of the enterprise. In each country, the law has not kept pace with fissured work arrangements through which businesses interpose other entities, to distance themselves from the responsibilities of direct employment. Unions are unable to organise around and bargain with the host business in an agency/labour hire arrangement, multiple employers across industries, or lead businesses at the summit of supply chains. These limitations have contributed to falling levels of collective bargaining coverage in each of these countries. In contrast, in Italy, collective bargaining has long been conducted at the national level for agreements covering each industry (with only a minimal role in recent years for firm-level negotiations). Bargaining coverage remains very high. This reflects a more general phenomenon: for example, Schnabel's international study shows that countries which allow multi-employer bargaining at sectoral or national level have collective bargaining coverage rates of between 50 and more than 90 per cent, compared with 11 to 34 per cent in systems based around establishment or company-level bargaining.[81]

Italy's system of coordinated, sectoral collective bargaining has evolved over a long period, through a strong tradition of social partnership in which the roles (and legitimacy) of trade unions and employer associations have been accepted. This could not be emulated in the very different industrial relations and economic systems of the US, the UK or Australia.[82] Nevertheless, the labour laws of these three countries must be altered to permit unions to bargain beyond the direct employer, with business entities who exercise significant economic power over workers' wages and conditions. Various reform proposals to expand bargaining rights in this way have been articulated in each country in recent years.[83] McAlpine and Roberts' proposal for multi-employer bargaining in Australia was mentioned in Chapter 1. They outlined a framework in which a bargaining electorate, made up of at least 2,000 employees, could be formed across a large enterprise or 'an industry, or an occupation, a supply chain or some combination of these, usually within a defined geographic area'.[84] A ballot would be held among workers in that electorate on whether to establish bargaining for a 'common or multi-employer agreement'.[85] As part of the ACTU's Change the Rules campaign from 2017 to 2019, Sally McManus argued that 'workers should be able to choose the group or the scope of how they bargain and that should fit the modern economy'.[86] However, the ACTU did not provide any details about its proposed framework for multi-employer bargaining.[87]

[81] C Schnabel, *Union Membership and Collective Bargaining: Trends and Determinants* (University of Erlangen-Nuremberg, Labor and Socio-Economic Research Center, LASER Discussion Papers, No 121, 2020) 23–24. See also J Visser, *Wage Bargaining Institutions – From Crisis to Crisis* (European Commission, Economic Papers 488, April 2013) 9–12; OECD, *Negotiating Our Way Up: Collective Bargaining in a Changing World of Work* (Paris, OECD Publishing, 2019) 44–46.

[82] The same applies in respect of the Italian system of workplace-level representation through RSAs and RSUs (see chs 2, 3 and 8). On the difficulty of transplanting works council-like structures from dual channel to single channel worker representation systems, see A Forsyth, 'The "Transplantability" Debate Re-Visited: Can European Social Partnership Be Exported to Australia?' (2006) 27:3 *Comparative Labor Law and Policy Journal* 305. Compare S Block and B Sachs, *Clean Slate for Worker Power: Building a Just Economy and Democracy* (Harvard Law School, 2020) 33–34.

[83] The following discussion and that in Part III(C) below, develop some ideas set out in T Kennedy, B Redford, R Burns and A Forsyth, 'Rebuilding Worker Power in Australia through Multi-Employer Bargaining' (2021) *Labour and Industry*, forthcoming.

[84] K McAlpine and S Roberts, *The Future of Trade Unions in Australia* (Paper for the Association of Industrial Relations Academics of Australia and New Zealand Conference, Canberra, 9 February 2017) 7.

[85] Ibid, 7–8.

[86] 'Wages fix about bargaining "where the power is": ACTU', *Workplace Express* (7 June 2017); see Ch 5.

[87] See ACTU, *Congress 2018 Draft Policies and Resolutions* (ACTU D No 153/2018) 39–40, mostly reiterating the arguments for moving beyond enterprise bargaining.

The British Labour Party's 2017 and 2019 general election commitments on sectoral collective bargaining were supported by two papers by the UK Institute of Employment Rights (IER).[88] The second of these, published in 2018, outlined a sectoral bargaining system in which the Secretary of State for Labour would designate trades, industries or occupations constituting the relevant sectors.[89] Bargaining would take place through National Joint Councils made up of representatives of workers and employers. These Councils would be established following a request by a union or at the Secretary of State's initiative based on specified criteria; and the Secretary of State could designate employer representatives if the employers in a sector refused to participate.[90] Priority sectors for setting up National Joint Councils included those with a 'public interest in protecting vulnerable workers' (eg, adult social care, child care, hotels, fast food, retail, agriculture and cleaning).[91]

Chapter 1 touched on the Harvard Labor and Worklife Programme's 'Clean Slate for Worker Power' report (in the context of its digital picket line proposal). The 2020 report also recommended 'the establishment of a system of sectoral bargaining for all [US] firms', in which unions 'would bargain – on behalf of all workers in a sector – with employer associations'.[92] This would occur through 'sectoral bargaining panels', set up by the Secretary of Labor at the request of a union with at least 5,000 members or 10 per cent membership across the relevant sector (whichever is lower).[93] So, for example, 'unions representing fast food workers nationally could secure wage and benefit gains across the fast food industry'.[94] A subsequent report of the Clean Slate project outlined options for implementing sectoral bargaining through a vertical approach (eg, for the green energy industry) or horizontally (ie, across the economy but only in relation to specific subjects of bargaining such as automation or scheduling).[95] The proposed Protecting the Right to Organize Act (PRO Act), discussed in Chapter 4, does not include any provision shifting the focus of bargaining under the NLRA beyond the enterprise.[96]

[88] KD Ewing, J Hendy and C Jones (eds), *A Manifesto for Labour Law: Towards a Comprehensive Revision of Workers' Rights* (Liverpool, Institute of Employment Rights, 2016); KD Ewing, J Hendy and C Jones (eds), *Rolling Out the Manifesto for Labour Law* (Liverpool, Institute of Employment Rights, 2018); see also ch 7.

[89] Ewing, Hendy and Jones (n 88; 2018) 20–21.

[90] Ibid, 18–20. See also K Ewing and J Hendy, 'New Perspectives on Labour Law – Trade Union Recognition and Collective Bargaining' (2017) 46:1 *Industrial Law Journal* 23, 38–40.

[91] Ewing, Hendy and Jones (n 88; 2018) 20.

[92] Block and Sachs (n 82) 39.

[93] Ibid, 41.

[94] Ibid, 39; see also 38.

[95] Clean Slate for Worker Power, *Principles of Sectoral Bargaining: A Reference Guide for Designing Federal, State and Local Laws in the U.S.* (Harvard Labor and Worklife Program, May 2021) 6–8.

[96] A provision in an earlier version of the PRO Act required the Government Accountability Office to report on options for sectoral bargaining in the US, but this was omitted from the 2021 version: see B Magner, 'Breaking down the PRO Act', *Labor Law Lite* (19 January 2021). Available at: https://brandonmagner.substack.com/p/breaking-down-the-pro-act.

Barenberg has argued that 'indirect employers' with the capacity to exercise 'sufficient bargaining power' over the direct employer of particular workers should be required to engage in collective bargaining with US unions.[97] This would address the difficulties he identified in union efforts to bargain under the NLRA with various kinds of 'disintegrated employers', including: employers and other firms in a single-product supply chain; production and distribution networks (eg, those utilised by major retailers); 'hub and spoke' systems covering the suppliers of services to a lead firm (eg, building owners who contract with cleaning, security and insurance firms); and 'pyramid' arrangements (eg, a fast food brand operating a chain of franchise stores).[98] Barenberg proposed the extension of bargaining obligations to indirect employers primarily through an expanded definition of 'employer' under the NLRA, and by empowering the NLRB to designate single-employer bargaining units as multi-employer units where necessary 'to provide "the maximum potential for worker empowerment"'.[99] Further, he contended:

> Legal reform should authorize worker organizations to designate a multi-employer unit not only on the basis of supply-chain, network, hub-and-spoke wheel, or pyramid, but also on the basis of industry, occupation, and/or geography.[100]

There are many options available for configuring multi-employer collective bargaining and complexities to consider in its implementation within the labour law systems of the US, the UK and Australia. However, several key principles should apply. First, workers must have control over the level at which bargaining occurs, and the ability to bargain (as the ACTU puts it) wherever the locus of employer power is – whether that be with the direct employer at enterprise level if workers so choose, with the manufacturing plant that brings in workers from multiple labour hire agencies, or with the major supermarkets at the apex of the food supply chain (along with the supplier firms within that chain). Secondly, workers' preferences need to be assessed based on achievable thresholds of employee support, through methods other than a ballot (see Part III(C) below). Thirdly, decisions about the scope of multi-employer bargaining should not be placed in the hands of a government figure or department (as proposed by the IER and Clean Slate). Rather, existing state institutions should be adapted for this purpose. In Australia, for example, the Fair Work Commission (FWC) already plays an important role in overseeing the collective bargaining process (including the scope of proposed agreements where this is disputed).[101] It could,

[97] M Barenberg, *Widening the Scope of Worker Organizing: Legal Reforms to Facilitate Multi-Employer Organizing, Bargaining and Striking* (Roosevelt Institute, 2015) 15–16.

[98] Ibid, 3–7.

[99] Ibid, 26, 28–29.

[100] Ibid, 31.

[101] See Fair Work Act 2009 (Cth) (FW Act), ss 238–39; in the US and the UK, the NLRB and the CAC respectively are involved in bargaining unit determination.

therefore, be entrusted with determining the shape of multi-employer bargaining units, through the application of carefully developed statutory tests.[102] Fourthly, those statutory criteria should partly be directed at the consideration of workers' preferences – but there should be a residual capacity to allow multi-employer bargaining based on its necessity to improve the wages and conditions of particular workers. In framing this statutory gateway to multi-employer bargaining, the lessons of Australia's failed experiment with the low-paid bargaining stream must be taken into account. As discussed in Chapter 3, the FW Act established tests for accessing multi-employer bargaining that were too stringent and unnecessarily balanced the needs of low-paid workers with business objectives. A simpler approach is proposed by the IER: an assessment of whether no effective sectoral-level bargaining is already occurring in a particular industry or is not presently sufficient to establish minimum wages and conditions for the whole sector.[103] Finally, it is critical that multi-employer bargaining be mandatory – both through the requirement that employers participate in it[104] and the legally binding effects of collective agreements once they are made.[105]

## C. Realistic Thresholds for Affirming the Right to Bargain, through Non-Ballot Methods

Another major shortcoming of the US, the UK and Australian labour law systems, revealed in Chapter 3, is their majoritarian foundation for establishing the right to bargain – supposedly resting on democratic principles. Especially in the US and the UK, the contest to determine workers' true preferences has been perverted through a permissive approach to employer anti-union tactics. Effectively countering these is considered further in Part III(D) below. But the concept of majoritarianism itself needs to be reconsidered, especially in the context of multi-employer bargaining, where the difficulty of securing majority employee support increases with the size and dispersion of the employee constituency. In the IER's sectoral bargaining system, there would be no employee threshold necessary to trigger the right to bargain. Rather, a union could simply request the Secretary of

[102] There is a potential risk in this approach, in that appointments to the FWC have become politicised in recent years with new members mostly coming from employer/conservative ranks (see, eg, 'ACTU to push Labor to review FWC's "stacked" deck', *Workplace Express* (26 April 2019); P Coorey, 'Former Liberal MP Sophie Mirabella appointed to plum Fair Work post', *Australian Financial Review* (23 March 2021)). That risk is greatly heightened in the context of the NLRB in the US (see W Gould, 'Politics and the Effect on the National Labor Relations Board's Adjudicative and Rulemaking Processes' (2015) 64 *Emory Law Journal* 1051), but does not seem to be evident with respect to the composition and functioning of the CAC in the UK (see 'Membership of the Central Arbitration Committee'. Available at: www.gov.uk/government/organisations/central-arbitration-committee/about/membership).

[103] Ewing, Hendy and Jones (n 88; 2018) 18.

[104] Andrias (n 37) 79.

[105] Ewing and Hendy (n 88; 2018) 37–38.

State to start the process on application of the statutory criteria, while Clean Slate specified a threshold of the lower of 5,000 union members or 10% membership in the sector (as noted above). A recent proposal in New Zealand for industry-level bargaining through 'fair pay agreements' set a representation test of 10 per cent union membership (or 1,000 members in the sector); *or* the satisfaction of a public interest test with reference to specified factors (eg, the presence within an industry or occupation of low pay or low worker bargaining power).[106]

The idea of centring the right to bargain on its necessity to enhance workers' negotiating position, rather than majoritarian considerations, has considerable merit. As outlined in Part III(B) above, it should be included as an option for the establishment of multi-employer bargaining. At the same time, meeting *realistic* thresholds of employee support can provide unions with legitimacy, both among the workforce and in obtaining outcomes from employers. Setting the level of these thresholds is difficult, but as a guiding principle the extent of required employee support could *decrease* as the proposed level of bargaining *widens*. So, for example, the threshold to trigger enterprise-level bargaining at a KFC store would be 40 per cent of the employees in that workplace; for bargaining across all the stores in a KFC franchise chain, 2,000 employees; and across the fast-food sector, 1,000 employees. The thresholds in the multi-employer configurations are expressed numerically, rather than as a percentage, to reduce the prospect of employer manipulation of the constituent group (as a basis for challenging whether the union has met the required threshold). These sample proposed thresholds recognise the barriers to organising workers across disparate work groups and locations in a multi-employer structure and the certainty of continued employer resistance. They would level the playing field, which has for so long been tilted heavily in employers' favour.

It is also clear from the US and UK experience that methods other than ballots must be utilised to assess employee preferences. As was shown in Chapter 3, ballot-based systems create too many opportunities for employer interference. In the UK, the IER suggested that once a union establishes 10% support to trigger single-employer bargaining, it need only show it has likely support from 'a majority in the bargaining unit (expressed by union membership or in another convincing way)' to secure recognition.[107] Clean Slate proposed that the required level of

[106] New Zealand Ministry of Business, Innovation and Employment, *The Proposed Fair Pay Agreement System* (undated) 2. Available at: www.mbie.govt.nz/business-and-employment/employment-and-skills/employment-legislation-reviews/fair-pay-agreements/; New Zealand Ministry of Business, Innovation and Employment, *Fair Pay Agreements: Approval to Draft* (Cabinet Paper, 7 May 2021) 6. Despite significant business opposition, Prime Minister Jacinda Ardern's Labour government is proceeding with legislation to implement this new system in early 2022: see J Walls, 'Unions v businesses: Fair pay agreement news staunchly divides factions', *New Zealand Herald* (7 May 2021); 'NZ's Fair Pay Agreements "biggest change in decades"', *Workplace Express* (11 May 2021).

[107] Ewing, Hendy and Jones (n 88; 2018) 30. This would improve on the current system where too much statutory discretion is placed in the hands of the CAC to avoid granting recognition without a ballot: see ch 3.

union membership for setting up a sectoral bargaining panel could 'be shown by a membership card or petition, physical or online'.[108] The proposed PRO Act would allow certification of a union for collective bargaining in the US based on card-check, if employer unfair labour practices have interfered with an employee vote. It would be preferable to permit the simpler card-check method, as President Biden's 2020 election policy proposed, without having to prove illicit employer intent.[109] Under Australia's FW Act, signed employee petitions are generally accepted to establish majority support. Non-ballot methods like petitions and card-check can reliably be utilised to evidence the required level of employee support for collective bargaining, whatever its scope.

## D. Union Access to the Workforce and the Right of Free Communication

The examination of the legal framework in the US and UK demonstrated that ballot-based recognition systems work even more against employees, where the law limits union access to the workplace and prioritises the free speech rights of employers. The free exchange of ideas in the battle for workers' hearts and minds becomes a one-way contest, largely controlled by the employer.[110] These concerns would be lessened if ballots were replaced by less demanding forms of establishing employee support.[111] However, even if petitions or card-check were utilised, there would remain a period during which the union is seeking to win over the workforce – and the employer is aiming to suppress unionisation. Unions must therefore have access to workers and the right to counter anti-union communications from the employer, which can be developed from among the following options.

The Italian Workers' Statute offers one model, through its provisions allowing union representatives to hold workplace meetings with employees (including some during working time) and to distribute information to the workforce.[112] To address the primacy of employer speech, Clean Slate and the PRO Act propose that US employers be prohibited from requiring workers to attend captive audience meetings during union organising drives.[113] Another approach is to require the employer to give the union equal time for communication with the

[108] Block and Sachs (n 82) 41; see also Clean Slate for Worker Power (n 95) 14.

[109] See ch 4, including its consideration of card-check as proposed in the Employee Free Choice Act in 2008–2009.

[110] Although it was noted in ch 3 that the 2004 amendments to Sch A1 of the Trade Union and Labour Relations (Consolidation) Act 1992 (TULRCA) had made some improvements in facilitating union access during recognition campaigns.

[111] See Part III(C) above.

[112] See ch 3.

[113] Block and Sachs (n 82) 50–51; Magner (n 96).

workforce, premised upon fair access arrangements.[114] Australia provides a statutory framework of union rights of entry to the workplace for organising and recruitment purposes. It was noted in Chapter 3 that these rights are significantly limited (including notice and permit requirements) and that employers have been able to confound their practical utility (by generating disputes over the workplace location for union meetings). The ACTU, in its Change the Rules campaign, pushed for the imposition of 'a positive obligation on employers and occupiers of premises to … facilitate worker access to union representation in all areas of the workplace', without unions having to provide notice of intended entry.[115]

The IER proposed that full-time officers and lay representatives of an independent trade union in the UK have a reasonable right of access to workers at their workplace.[116] Access would be 'both physical and electronic (such as by e-mail or social media)'; and would be permitted for recruiting members, encouraging workers to support recognition of the union, or consulting them on agreement negotiations (among other objectives).[117] Clean Slate argued that US union organisers be given 'the ability to meet with workers at work', including 'the right to access non-work areas' to meet with employees (once support for the union has reached 25 per cent) and 'access to the names and contact information of all workers in a workplace'.[118] In addition, Clean Slate explored the notion of 'digital access', including the recommendation that workers be able 'to use the full panoply of employer technology – Slack, Google Docs, [etc] – to be in contact with co-workers during non-work time'.[119]

## E. Countering Anti-Union Conduct by Employers

Employer strategies to prevent workers from unionising have been illustrated throughout this book. Vigorous anti-unionism takes many forms, including the union-busting industry that evolved in the US and was exported to the UK; the new techniques developed by Australian employers, exploiting loopholes in the FW Act's moderate support for collective bargaining; and other strategies adopted by employers in all four countries, often involving sponsorship of tame 'company unions'. Both the US and the UK proscribe employer unfair labour practices, but as we saw in Chapter 3, these provisions have proven to be of limited practical utility. More effective legal remedies to counter these practices are needed. Clean Slate noted that typical employer tactics, like dismissing union activists or scaring the

[114] K Andrias and B Rogers, *Rebuilding Worker Voice in Today's Economy* (Roosevelt Institute, 2018) 22–23.

[115] ACTU (n 87) 36–37.

[116] Ewing, Hendy and Jones (n 88; 2018) 28.

[117] Ibid.

[118] Block and Sachs (n 82) 50.

[119] Ibid, 53; see, also, at 54, proposals for employer-facilitated 'digital meeting space[s]'.

workforce into voting the union down by threatening relocation, are already illegal under the NLRA – but are not subject to sufficient sanctions. Clean Slate supported the PRO Act's proposals to substantially increase the penalties for these and other employer violations of the NLRA (ie, civil penalties of up to US$50,000 or double that for repeat breaches).[120] The IER proposed the prohibition of employer 'anti-union practices designed to frustrate either (a) organising, or (b) recognition activity', defined as follows:

> … where the employer has intimidated, threatened, harassed or subjected to detriment one or more workers (including threats that jobs are at risk, or by awarding or promising a benefit to one or more workers which it withholds … from others …).[121]

Further, the employer would have to disprove that it engaged in the conduct complained of, and the CAC – on finding the employer committed an unfair labour practice – could order it to recognise the union automatically.[122]

Protections against employer anti-union conduct of more general application apply under Australian and Italian law. Under the FW Act, these form part of the 'general protections' in Part 3-1 (mentioned briefly in Chapter 3). Union delegates and members are protected from adverse treatment in the workplace (eg, dismissal, disciplinary action) taken by an employer because of their union affiliation or involvement. Specifically, an employer must not take 'adverse action' against an employee or an independent contractor,[123] because he or she is an officer or member of an industrial association[124] or engages in 'industrial activity'.[125] Industrial activity includes establishing a union, organising or promoting lawful union activity, representing the views or claims of a union, or seeking to be represented by a union.[126] Workers, or unions representing them, can seek remedies for breaches of these protections including: uncapped compensation; the imposition of civil penalties upon the offending employer; and injunctions.[127] In practice, however, these protections have been rendered largely nugatory, because the High Court of Australia has given priority to the motivations asserted by employers as to their true reasons for taking adverse action against unionists. So, for example, an employer avoided liability by demonstrating it had dismissed an employee who held an 'anti-scab' sign on a picket line, not because he had engaged in industrial activity, but because the sign was considered offensive and his behaviour contravened a workplace conduct policy.[128]

[120] Ibid, 51–52; Magner (n 96).

[121] Ewing, Hendy and Jones (n 88; 2018) 30.

[122] Ibid.

[123] FW Act, s 342.

[124] Ibid, s 346(a).

[125] Ibid, s 346(b).

[126] Ibid, s 347(b); see also s 341(1)–(2) (protections against adverse action due to the exercise of 'workplace rights').

[127] A Stewart, A Forsyth, M Irving, R Johnstone and S McCrystal, *Creighton and Stewart's Labour Law* 6th edn (Sydney, Federation Press, 2016) 687–89.

The ACTU has criticised the tendency of Australian courts to 'read down the [general protections] provisions by applying a test that allows employers to avoid liability too easily'.[129] The peak body proposed instead a set of 'positive rights' for delegates to represent workers and engage in broader union activity and for workers to be represented by and participate in the union. This would be reinforced by a test for breach of these provisions 'based on the effect on the workplace rights of the conduct in question'.[130] This is the approach taken under Article 28 of the Italian Workers' Statute.[131] This provision has enabled unions to contest employer infringements of the Statute's positive framework of freedom of association protections, through court proceedings to injunct a wide range of anti-union conduct. Article 28, under which Italian courts focus on the effect of the employer's impugned conduct (rather than whether the employer intended to subvert workers' rights to engage in union activity or strikes), could therefore provide a starting point for developing more robust unfair labour practice provisions under US, UK and Australian law.

## F. Freeing Up the Right to Strike

In contrast to the more liberal approach to strike activity in Italy, we saw in Chapter 3 that the legal limits placed on industrial action in the US, the UK and Australia have contributed to declining collective bargaining coverage. Removing these constraints and instituting stronger rights for workers to engage in strikes and other forms of collective action is imperative. As Clean Slate put it in the US context:

> Workers' ability to deploy effectively their most important economic weapons – strikes, walk outs, pickets, and boycotts – is critical to creating a system that produces not just a seat at the table but also the ability to influence the outcome of what happens at the table.[132]

Accordingly, Clean Slate recommended that workers be provided with the right to direct these various forms of collective action, not only at their legal employer but also 'any entity that they believe has the power to set the terms and conditions of their employment'.[133] This would overcome employer fissuring

[128] *Construction, Forestry, Mining and Energy Union v BHP Coal Pty Ltd* (2014) 253 CLR 243; see also *Board of Bendigo Regional Institute of Technical and Further Education v Barclay* (2012) 248 CLR 500. These cases turned on the court's assessment of whether the employer had taken adverse action 'because of' a prohibited reason (see, eg, FW Act, s 346); for these purposes, the employer has the onus of proving it did not act for such a reason (s 361(1)).

[129] ACTU (n 87) 36.

[130] Ibid.

[131] See ch 3.

[132] Block and Sachs (n 82) 56.

[133] Ibid, 58.

strategies, complementing the expanded scope of bargaining (see Part III(B) above). It would also permit secondary action, which reform advocates in Australia and the UK have likewise called for.[134] Ending the ability of employers to permanently replace striking workers is considered essential in the US context.[135] UK law prohibits replacement workers being sourced through labour hire firms, while in Italy, employers' utilisation of temporary strike-breakers is considered likely to breach the Workers' Statute protections of union rights. In Australia, unions have objected to the complex statutory rules for taking lawful industrial action – including the secret ballot requirements and the many opportunities the law provides for employers to prevent such action or to end it on so-called 'public interest' grounds.[136] Rather than amending these provisions it is necessary, as the IER has suggested in relation to the heavy procedural restrictions applicable under UK law, to 'start again'.[137]

In creating a new framework of positive industrial action rights,[138] Clean Slate's proposal to allow workers and unions to use cyberspace to appeal for wider support should be implemented.[139] The law must allow workers and unions to deploy digital picket lines. Take the example, from Chapter 1, of the New Yorker Union's use of a digital picket line to gain support from the magazine's readers, politicians and the public for its virtual walkout during the pandemic (by boycotting the New Yorker's online festival). If this occurred in Australia, organising and maintaining the digital picket line would be unlikely to be considered protected industrial action under the FW Act (and therefore would not be immune from liability). In part, this is because regular picketing does not fall within the legislation's definition of 'industrial action' (and therefore cannot be 'protected').[140] Employers could therefore seek remedies including injunctions and damages, to deal with a digital picket line that interferes with the target business or has other tortious effects.[141] The legal rules in Australia, as well as those in the US, the UK and even Italy, would need to be reformulated to permit the use of digital picket lines.

[134] ACTU (n 87) 43–44; Ewing, Hendy and Jones (n 88 above; 2016) 53–54.

[135] See, eg, the PRO Act discussed in Magner (n 96); Andrias and Rogers (n 114) 35; Block and Sachs (n 82) 61; J Getman, 'The Central Role of the Right to Strike', in R Bales and C Garden (eds), *The Cambridge Handbook of U.S. Labor Law for the Twenty-First Century* (Cambridge, Cambridge University Press, 2020) 291.

[136] See ch 3; and ACTU (n 87) 43; 'Re-energised unions push Labor on right to strike', *Workplace Express* (29 June 2018).

[137] Ewing, Hendy and Jones (n 88 above; 2016) 54–55.

[138] See further ibid, 51–52.

[139] See ch 1.

[140] FW Act, s 19; *Davids Distribution Pty Ltd v National Union of Workers* (1999) 91 FCR 463. See further P McCabe, 'Picket Lines and the Principle of Legality' (2020) 33:2 *Australian Journal of Labour Law* 209.

[141] See Stewart et al (n 127) 959–60. A digital picket line may also give rise to liability on the part of the union, its officers and members, consumers and/or other participants, under the boycott provisions of the Competition and Consumer Act 2010 (Cth); these are explained in Stewart et al (loc cit) 964–70.

## G. Bringing Gig Workers within Employment and Labour Law Protections

Chapters 9 and 10 illustrated that categorisation lies at the heart of the gig economy's ability to exploit workers in all four countries. In addition to extensive litigation challenging worker misclassification, the platforms' contracting model has precipitated a search for regulatory solutions. It was shown in Chapter 10 that employment and labour laws in Australia, the US and UK extend their full protection to those categorised as employees, through various formulations of common law tests. These tests apply a range of indicia such as control and economic reality to assess the level of a worker's dependence on the business engaging them. In the UK, the intermediate category of worker (sitting between employee and independent contractor) provides a gateway to a limited range of employment rights. In Italy, the position is more complex, with categories including employees (in subordinated employment); those providing exclusively personal work in continuous collaboration with a principal (who organises the work); and the self-employed.

We saw, through the examination of legal challenges to their categorisation as independent contractors/self-employed in the UK and Italy, that intermediate categories have been an important basis for extending protections to gig workers. However, this approach devalues employment rights: workers with employee-like characteristics are deemed worthy of only *some* protections, and difficult choices must be made about what their confined basket of rights should contain.[142] A third or intermediate category also enables businesses, as Stewart and McCrystal put it, to: 'disenfranchise existing employees through reclassification or manipulation of their legal status'.[143] Even more pointedly, Cherry and Aloisi suggest that '[t]hree categories create more room for mischief than two'.[144] A third category is often proposed by the platforms themselves, to create the appearance of granting workers 'benefits' (like sick pay and injury insurance) but without thereby allowing them to fall into the employee category.[145]

A better option, examined extensively in academic scholarship and by policy makers in recent years, is to expand the definition of the existing category of employees who are subject to the full coverage of employment and labour laws.[146]

[142] See, eg, M Cherry and A Aloisi, '"Dependent Contractors" in the Gig Economy: A Comparative Approach' (2017) 66 *American University Law Review* 635, 677–80; A Stewart and S McCrystal, 'Labour Regulation and the Great Divide: Does the Gig Economy Require a New Category of Worker?' (2019) 32:1 *Australian Journal of Labour Law* 4, 12–15. For a defence of the UK's intermediate worker category (although arguing it should be renamed 'dependent contractor') see M Taylor, G Marsh, D Nicol and P Broadbent, *Good Work: The Taylor Review of Modern Working Practices* (2017) 35.

[143] Stewart and McCrystal ibid, 19.

[144] Cherry and Aloisi (n 142) 677; see also 666, 675.

[145] See, eg, A Patty, 'A "third way": the controversial push for a new type of worker', *Sydney Morning Herald* (16 February 2019).

[146] This option is also preferable, in my view, to the TWU/federal Labor Opposition's proposal to expand the FWC's powers to make orders setting minimum standards for 'employee-like' workers

A selection of these proposals is considered here. In 2018, Stewart, Stanford and Hardy proposed that the definition of 'employee' in the FW Act be widened as follows:

> Anyone who agrees to supply their personal labour should be presumed to be an employee, unless there is clear evidence that they have a genuinely independent business of their own.[147]

This heads in the direction of the 'entrepreneurship approach' to clarifying 'work status' recommended in the 2020 report of the Victorian government's On-Demand Work Inquiry:

> Genuinely self-employed, autonomous business people should operate under commercial arrangements. Workers who operate as part of another's business or enterprise should be covered by protections and entitlements provided by labour regulation.[148]

This approach is informed by a number of Australian court decisions in the last decade or so (outside the context of gig work). In these cases, the determination of whether the relevant workers were employees or contractors was resolved by considering factors such as their autonomy/self-reliance or subservience/economic dependence, in the course of assessing whether they were performing work as entrepreneurs operating their own businesses.[149]

As discussed in Chapter 10, the 'ABC test' has been adopted in some US jurisdictions, creating a presumption of employment status unless a worker: is free from the hirer's control and direction in the performance of work; performs work outside the normal course of the hirer's business; *and* is usually engaged in an independent trade or business of the same kind as the work carried out for the hirer. In May 2021, Lord Hendy QC introduced the Status of Workers Bill into the House of Lords, proposing a single employment status under UK laws.[150]

in Australia: see T Rabe and N Bonyhady, '"Exploitation, plain and simple": Labor's plan to protect delivery riders', *Sydney Morning Herald* (26 November 2020). See further M Rawling and J Riley Munton, *Proposals for Legal Protections for On-Demand Gig Workers in the Road Transport Industry* (A report prepared for the Transport Education Audit Compliance Health Organisation by UTS Faculty of Law, January 2021) 43–49.

[147] A Stewart, J Stanford and T Hardy, 'Conclusion: Wages and Inclusive Growth' in A Stewart, J Stanford and T Hardy (eds), *The Wages Crisis in Australia: What it is and what to do about it* (Adelaide, University of Adelaide Press, 2018) 277, 291. See also the proposal for 'a default presumption of employment status' under US law in Cherry and Aloisi (n 142) 682–84.

[148] N James, *Report of the Inquiry into the Victorian On-Demand Workforce* (Melbourne, Victorian Government, 2020) 192.

[149] See, eg, *On Call Interpreters and Translators Agency Pty Ltd v Federal Commissioner of Taxation (No 3)* (2011) 214 FCR 82; on this and other relevant cases, see Stewart and McCrystal (n 142 above) 8. For more recent judicial consideration see, eg, *Construction, Forestry, Maritime, Mining and Energy Union v Personnel Contracting* (2020) 297 IR 269.

[150] Status of Workers Bill, at: https://bills.parliament.uk/, proposing amendments of relevant provisions of TULRCA and the Employment Rights Act 1999. Part of the motivation for this Bill was the Johnson Conservative Government's failure to bring forward a promised Employment Bill clarifying

The Bill defines both 'worker' and 'employee' as an individual who seeks to be engaged by another to provide labour, is so engaged or was so engaged; 'and is not, in the provision of that labour, genuinely operating a business on his or her own account'. An 'employer' for these purposes is a person or entity engaging the worker, 'who substantially determines terms on which the worker is engaged at any material time'.[151] A 'contract of employment' is:

> … a contract of service or apprenticeship, or any other contract whereby an individual undertakes to do or perform any work or services for another party to the contract whose status is not by virtue of the contract that of a client or customer of any profession or business or undertaking carried on by the individual, and any reference to a worker's contract must be construed accordingly.[152]

Further, the business which contests a claim that it is the employer in legal proceedings must show it is not the employer, and that the person providing labour is not an employee or worker.[153] Finally, Menegatti has proposed that (for purposes only of the right to minimum wages) all those engaged in 'personal work relations' should be covered, that is 'everyone who personally performs any work or service for another party', regardless of whether they are under the employer's control and integrated into its business or are self-organised.[154]

Any of these proposed reformulations of the definition of 'employee' (and related concepts) would bring more gig workers within employment and labour protections under US, UK, Australian or Italian law. It will be recalled from Chapter 10 that Uber, Lyft and other platforms spent over US$200 million on a campaign to overturn the AB5 statute enshrining the ABC test in Californian law, assuming it would have deemed the workers on those platforms to be employees.[155] Lord Hendy QC's proposal would likely capture a wider range of platform workers as it dispenses with any consideration of control or subordination.[156] The other essential component of his proposal is to shift the burden to establish employment

the tests for employment status in response to the Taylor Review (see Taylor et al, n 142; HM Government, *Good Work Plan* (December 2018) 26–29): IER, 'New Bill will abolish insecure work' (26 May 2021). Available at: www.ier.org.uk/press-releases/new-bill-will-abolish-insecure-work/.

[151] Status of Workers Bill, ibid.

[152] Ibid.

[153] Ibid.

[154] E Menegatti, 'A Fair Wage for Workers On-demand via App,' in E Ales, Y Curzi, T Fabbri, O Rymkevich, I Senatori and G Solinas (eds), *Working in Digital and Smart Organizations: Legal, Economic and Organizational Perspectives on the Digitalization of Labour Relations* (Cham, Palgrave Macmillan, 2018) 67, 79.

[155] Note that both Clean Slate and the PRO Act propose adoption of the ABC test for purposes of determining the 'employees' who would be covered by a recast NLRA: see Block and Sachs (n 82) 25–26. For further consideration of the utility of the ABC test, see R Sprague, 'Using the ABC Test to Classify Workers: End of the Platform-Based Business Model or Status Quo Ante?' (2020) 11:3 *William and Mary Business Law Review* 733, 750–59; K Dau-Schmidt, 'The Problem of "Misclassification" or How to Define Who Is an "Employee" under Protective Legislation in the Information Age', in Bales and Garden (n 135) 140, 144–46; and (for a UK comparative perspective) S Deakin, 'Decoding Employment Status' (2020) 31:2 *King's Law Journal* 180, 191–93.

[156] See also Ewing, Hendy and Jones (n 88 above; 2018) 36–37.

status from the worker to the platform, which the Victorian On-Demand Inquiry also recommended (along with 'a fast-tracked and inexpensive determination' process).[157] A *presumption of employment* would mean those with the least power and resources (gig workers) no longer have to pursue legal action against global giants of the platform economy, to establish basic rights at work.

## H. Collective Bargaining Rights for Gig Workers

It was outlined in Chapter 10 that collective bargaining in the US and Australia is limited to employees, thus excluding those categorised as independent contractors in the gig economy. In the UK, collective bargaining may be engaged in by employees and those in the intermediate worker category, but Deliveroo has (to date) successfully prevented its riders from meeting the worker definition and being able to bargain. Italy differs from the other three countries in extending both the right to collectively bargain and the right to strike to those categorised as own-account, self-employed workers. However, European Union competition laws restrict the collective bargaining and collective action rights of the self-employed in Italy and in the UK.[158] Independent contractors are similarly constrained by Australian competition regulation.[159] Seattle's collective bargaining ordinance was used to illustrate the bind in which platform workers are placed under US law: excluded from collective bargaining under the NLRA and precluded, by antitrust law, from negotiating together.

Chapter 10 also revealed that, despite these limits, unions in all four countries have sought to engage in various forms of collective negotiation on behalf of gig workers. In some instances, such as Unions NSW's agreement with Airtasker and TWU's with Door Dash, only limited gains were made, but establishing a collective basis for discussions was an achievement in itself. GMB's 'self-employed plus' deal with Hermes and IWGB's collective agreement with The Doctors Laboratory realised more tangible benefits for workers. All these examples – along with IWGB's litigation seeking statutory recognition rights for UK Deliveroo riders and TWU's efforts to utilise NSW work health and safety legislation – indicate that unions are responding to the desire of platform workers for collective representation. For the many that have independent contractor status imposed on them and the few who may well be genuinely self-employed, competition law rules should not preclude them from coming together to bargain.

[157] James (n 148) 193, 197.

[158] A Aloisi and E Gramano, 'A Solution in Search of a Problem? Collective Rights and the Antitrust Labor Exemption in Italy', in S Paul, S McCrystal and E McGaughey (eds), *Labor in Competition Law* (Cambridge, Cambridge University Press, forthcoming, 2022); L Mason, 'Locating Unity in the Fragmented Platform Economy: Labor Law and the Platform Economy in the United Kingdom' (2020) 41:2 *Comparative Labor Law and Policy Journal* 329, 339. See further N Countouris, V De Stefano and I Lianos, 'The EU, Competition Law and Workers' Rights' in Paul, McCrystal and McGaughey (ibid).

[159] Rawling and Riley Munton (n 146) 41; James (n 148) 173.

A recent reform of Australian competition law offers the basis for a solution.[160] Under the Competition and Consumer Act 2010 (Cth), collective negotiations by independent businesses may give rise to liability for price-fixing or reducing competition in a market. However, in late 2020, the Australian Competition and Consumer Commission (ACCC) made a class exemption, allowing independent contractors and businesses with annual turnover of less than A$10 million to bargain collectively with suppliers or customers (by providing a collective bargaining class exemption notice to the ACCC).[161] Businesses or contractors wanting to use the class exemption to negotiate over terms and conditions and rates can appoint a bargaining representative, which can include a trade union (although a union cannot initiate the process).[162] This new mechanism in Australian law opens up the capacity for gig workers (and their unions) to negotiate with platforms over pay rates, rest periods, safety standards and managerial control through algorithms. However, as Hardy and McCrystal point out, the ACCC class exemption has important limitations: it is a voluntary process and there is no right to take collective or boycott action.[163] While acknowledging its potential utility in the context of platform work,[164] they conclude that: 'the exemption does not go far enough to ensure that the purported benefits of collective bargaining can be realised in practice'.[165] These constraints would need to be addressed, for this regulatory option to provide gig workers classified as independent contractors with an effective right to bargain.

## I. Addressing the 'Free-Rider' Problem

A final matter, which can only be considered briefly here, is the 'free-rider' problem. In each of the four countries, collective agreements negotiated by unions apply to all workers in the relevant bargaining unit. This includes non-members, who thereby obtain the benefits of union organisation at the workplace for free.[166] Further, the laws of each nation limit or prohibit unions imposing 'agency', 'fair share' or 'bargaining services' fees on non-unionists to overcome free-riding. In Italy, such an arrangement would likely fall foul of Article 15 of the Workers'

[160] See also Clean Slate's proposal to allow collective bargaining by independent contractors under US law: Block and Sachs (n 82) 26.

[161] Competition and Consumer (Class Exemption – Collective Bargaining) Determination 2020.

[162] ACCC, *Explanatory Statement: Competition and Consumer (Class Exemption – Collective Bargaining) Determination 2020.*

[163] T Hardy and S McCrystal, 'Bargaining in a Vacuum? An Examination of The Proposed Class Exemption for Collective Bargaining for Small Businesses' (2020) 42:3 *Sydney Law Review* 311, 313, 335–36.

[164] 'Bargaining go-ahead a "big step forward" for gig workers', *Workplace Express* (23 October 2020).

[165] Hardy and McCrystal (n 163) 332.

[166] See, eg, G Orr, 'Agency Shops in Australia? Compulsory Bargaining Fees, Union (In)Security and the Rights of Free-Riders' (2001) 14 *Australian Journal of Labour Law* 159.

Statute, which protects workers' rights to freedom of and from association.[167] Australian law bans unions from making a claim for a 'bargaining services fee'[168] (and precludes a provision for the imposition of such a fee from being included in an enterprise agreement[169]). UK law does not include such an explicit prohibition, but does protect a non-union worker against detriment from an employer to enforce a requirement that the worker make some form of payment (such as a deduction from remuneration).[170] In the US, agreements between unions and employers for the imposition of fair share or agency fees on non-unionists are prohibited in the 27 states that have enacted 'right to work' laws[171] and in the public sector nationally.[172] Overturning these various restrictions and prohibitions would recognise that the benefits won by unions through collective bargaining 'have the character of public goods'.[173] Unions should be able to prevent non-members from obtaining those benefits without paying for them. Offering workers a choice between union membership and paying an agency or fair share fee would ensure unions meet the transaction costs of collective bargaining and build collective strength in workplaces (as workers would have less incentive to opt out of union membership).[174]

# IV. Conclusion

This chapter has outlined both a pathway to revitalisation for unions and the legal changes that will help them get there. As I have maintained throughout the book, law reform is not the end goal for unions – it is one element of a plan to rebuild their strength. Technological innovation is another fundamental component of how unions must transform in years to come. Further re-imagining of organising and campaigning, including the use of digital tools, will enable unions to attract younger workers – without whom there is no 'future of unions'. Linkages with aligned social movement organisations will continue to fortify union efforts

[167] T Treu, *Labour Law in Italy* 3rd edn (Alphen aan den Rijn, Wolters Kluwer, 2011) 149; see ch 3.

[168] FW Act, s 353.

[169] Ibid, ss 12 (definition of 'objectionable term') 186(4) and 194(b).

[170] TULRCA, s 146(3)–(4), interpreted in *Samuel v London Bus Services Ltd* (ET Case No 3202466/2008) to preclude enforcement of a fair share agreement (under which deductions from a non-unionist's weekly pay were provided by the employer to the union); see H Collins, KD Ewing and A McColgan, *Labour Law* 2nd edn (Cambridge, Cambridge University Press 2019) 519–20.

[171] See C Fisk, 'Union Security for the Twenty-First Century', in Bales and Garden (n 135) 336, 338–39; and ch 2.

[172] Ibid, 342–43, discussing the US Supreme Court decision in *Janus v American Federation of State, County, and Municipal Employees, Council 31*, 138 S Ct 2448 (2018).

[173] Block and Sachs (n 82) 86.

[174] See further, ibid, 83–86; C McNicholas, Z Mokhibir and M von Wilpert, *Janus and Fair Share Fees: The Organizations Financing the Attack on Unions' Ability to Represent Workers* (Economic Policy Institute, 21 February 2018).

to mobilise workers (again, especially the young). Many workers are demanding a more combative form of unionism, to put an end to decades of inequality, exploitation, precarious work and state facilitation of employer hostility. Labor/ Labour governments in Australia and the UK have let workers down, by not sufficiently winding back the extreme deregulation of their conservative predecessors. Unions must push their political allies harder, to ensure that when the opportunity arises, state support for unions and workers does more than simply 'encourage' or 'enable' collectivism. Labour law can provide the tools which will assist unions to extend their reach, such as multi-employer bargaining. It will then be up to unions how effectively they use those tools on the ground in workplaces. Although they are unlikely ever to return to the membership levels of the post-war era, the need for unions has never been stronger. This is the opportunity presented by the COVID-19 pandemic, the subject of the book's final chapter.

# 12

# The COVID-19 Pandemic: The Undeniable Case for Unions

## I. Introduction

It was noted in Chapter 1 that the COVID-19 pandemic has presented unions with new challenges, in the wake of decades of state and employer antagonism linked with the rise of neoliberalism, globalisation and deregulation. The global health and economic crisis since early 2020 has had a devastating impact on workers, including job losses, reduced hours of work and income insecurity for those in industries most affected by lockdown measures such as hospitality, aviation and tourism. Workers in essential sectors such as healthcare, transport, food production and retail have had to contend with overwork and exposure to unsafe working conditions. For workers in education, media, professional services and other sectors that have continued, but adjusted operations to comply with government-imposed restrictions, home working and its impact on workers' mental health and care responsibilities have been among the central issues. This chapter outlines how unions in the USA, the UK, Australia and Italy have acted to protect workers' interests during the coronavirus pandemic, particularly in two vital areas: income support and health and safety. It also considers the implications of the crisis for unions, how they have adapted representation and organising using digital tools and the opportunity for unions as the world adjusts to the long-term effects of the pandemic.

## II. Union Involvement in National Responses to the COVID-19 Emergency

ACTU Secretary Sally McManus considers that the pandemic saw the union movement returned to the role 'it should always have [played] – as a widely accepted part of Australia's civil society, and a trusted social partner for governments and businesses'.[1] As lockdowns were implemented almost overnight in March 2020, the Coalition government realised it had to involve workers' representatives in

[1] 'ACTU leader begins push for tripartite job security pact', *Workplace Express* (2 December 2020).

dialogue with business groups to obtain urgent adjustments to employment regulation. This led to a series of joint union-employer applications to the Fair Work Commission (FWC) to vary awards covering hospitality and restaurants (enabling businesses to change operations, eg, shifting to take-away only food service)[2] and clerical work (facilitating working from home for millions of office staff).[3] As the crisis unfolded, the government sought to capitalise on this spirit of cooperation by instigating a wider industrial relations reform process, corralling union and business leaders in months of talks. The objective was to identify changes to workplace legislation that would help the economy recover from the pandemic.[4] However, the process unravelled during the remainder of 2020, as it became clearer to unions that this was simply a ruse for an employer-driven, deregulatory agenda.[5] It ultimately resulted only in changes enabling greater utilisation of casual work,[6] as the remainder of the government's reform legislation was voted down in Parliament in February 2021.

UK unions were closely engaged with the Johnson government, along with the Confederation of British Industry, in the early phase of the crisis, particularly in the development and implementation of the Coronavirus Job Retention Scheme (CJRS).[7] As in Australia, though, this early cooperation dissipated, as British unions became more critical of the government's response to the pandemic.[8] In Italy, which suffered the greatest initial impact of COVID-19 of the four countries, the earliest response measures of Prime Minister Giuseppe Conte's government included a short-time work scheme and a ban on individual and collective dismissals on economic grounds. These measures were implemented unilaterally, followed by consultation with unions and business groups.[9] A national protocol for workplace health and safety was negotiated and revised with the social partners (including the major union confederations) in March and April 2020.[10] Dialogue with unions looked set to increase under the leadership of Mario Draghi, who took over as Prime Minister in February 2021,[11] although cracks appeared as his

[2] *Australian Hotels Association and United Workers Union* [2020] FWCFB 1574; *Application to vary the Restaurant Industry Award 2010* [2020] FWCFB 1741.

[3] *Application to vary the Clerks – Private Sector Award 2010* [2020] FWCFB 1690.

[4] Prime Minister of Australia, *Address, National Press Club* (26 May 2020). Available at: www.pm.gov.au/media/address-national-press-club-260520.

[5] See, eg, P Karp, 'Industrial relations reforms at risk as talks between unions and employer groups break down', *The Guardian* (24 September 2020).

[6] Fair Work Amendment (Supporting Australia's Jobs and Economic Recovery) Act 2021 (Cth).

[7] C Evans, *UK: Working Life in the COVID-19 Pandemic 2020* (European Foundation for the Improvement of Living and Working Conditions, 2021) 7, 12–13.

[8] Ibid, 7; T Hunt, *COVID-19 and the Work of Trade Unions: New Challenges and New Responses* (Unions 21, January 2021) 36.

[9] R Pedersini, *Italy: Working Life in the COVID-19 Pandemic 2020* (European Foundation for the Improvement of Living and Working Conditions, 2021) 7–8.

[10] Ibid, 7; M Franchi, 'Italian PM negotiates coronavirus safety agreement between workers and employers', *Il Manifesto* (15 March 2020).

[11] Pedersini (n 9) 10.

government made clear its plans to end the prohibition of dismissals.[12] In the USA, where lockdowns and other public health responses to the pandemic were implemented on a state-by-state basis, unions have had little formal input into regulatory or policy changes.[13] At the federal level (in relation to income support and other measures) consultation with unions was non-existent under the Trump administration, but they have played a greater role in discussions on the economic policy response to the pandemic since President Biden took office.[14]

## III. Income Protection

The immediate effects of the initial, drastic lockdown measures to control the spread of coronavirus included the rapid closure of businesses and other enterprises and the consequent standing down or dismissal of millions of workers.[15] In Italy, displaced workers were able to access benefits under the pre-existing unemployment insurance scheme.[16] This was supplemented by special government payments of around €600 per month (from March to May 2020) for groups of workers not covered by unemployment protection, including the self-employed and seasonal workers (eg, those in the tourism, entertainment and agricultural sectors).[17] In the US, the Coronavirus Aid, Relief and Economic Security Act 2020 extended the duration of eligibility for unemployment benefits from 26 to 39 weeks, topped up state unemployment benefits with a US$600 per week federal payment and provided additional economic impact payments of US$1,200 to those earning less than US$99,000 per year.[18] Although not involved in the design of this scheme, unions have been active in assisting workers to ensure they receive payments. For example, NYTWA brought a successful lawsuit against New York State to ensure that app-based drivers received the full benefit rate for unemployed employees (rather than the lower self-employed workers' rate).[19]

[12] 'Up to 2mn jobs at risk with end to COVID firing ban – union', *ANSA.it (English edition)* (26 May 2021).

[13] R Bales and C Elko, 'COVID-19 and Labour Law: U.S.' (2020) 13:1S *Italian Labour Law E-Journal* 2, 5.

[14] See, eg, A Shalal and N Bose, 'Biden discusses COVID relief and infrastructure with top labor leaders', *Reuters* (18 February 2021).

[15] See, eg, International Labour Organization (ILO), *ILO Monitor: COVID-19 and the World of Work*, 2nd edn (7 April 2020) 1–4.

[16] F Carta and M De Philippis, *The Impact of the COVID-19 Shock on Labour Income Inequality: Evidence from Italy* (Banca D'Italia, Occasional Papers, Number 606, February 2021) 12.

[17] Ibid, 13; C Gaglione, I Purificato and O Rymkevich, 'COVID-19 and Labour Law: Italy' (2020) 13:1S *Italian Labour Law E-Journal* 3–4.

[18] Bales and Elko (n 13) 2; see further S Padya, 'Unemployment Insurance' in S Padya and J Hirsch (eds), *Work Law Under COVID-19* (open source e-book, 2020) ch 9. Available at: https://worklawcovid19book.netlify.app/ui.html.

[19] NYTWA, 'NYTWA wins big for N.Y. State app drivers' (undated). Available at: www.nytwa.org/home/2020/8/13/b9dgvuvsjk99vse2x5zt3czn3zpt67.

Public pressure from unions in Australia and the UK ensured that their governments introduced more comprehensive income protection programmes. The CJRS, also known as the 'furlough scheme', provided employees who ceased work for at least 21 days because of the pandemic with 80 per cent of their wages (subject to a maximum payment of £2,500 per month, administered via employers).[20] Taxable grants were also made available to eligible self-employed workers under the Self-Employment Income Support Scheme (SEISS),[21] for which unions covering workers in the creative industries had lobbied.[22] UK unions have been instrumental in highlighting the deficiencies of the CJRS and SEISS. For example, IWGB made submissions to a Parliamentary Committee and brought (unsuccessful) legal proceedings on behalf of gig workers who found themselves excluded from *both* income support schemes.[23] IWGB also drew attention to the discretionary nature of the CJRS.[24] That is, employers could choose whether to place employees on furlough or (alternatively) make their positions redundant.[25]

The Australian government only introduced the JobKeeper wage subsidy scheme after the ACTU, VTHC and other union groups agitated strongly for income support measures,[26] with the support of employer organisations. JobKeeper enabled businesses with at least 30 per cent reduced turnover to obtain a wage subsidy of A$1,500 per fortnight, in respect of full-time, part-time and regular casual employees who continued working or were stood down from their employment due to the impact of COVID-19 on the business.[27] However, many workers were excluded from eligibility for JobKeeper, leading unions to take up their cause. The National Tertiary Education Union (NTEU) linked the exclusion of public universities from JobKeeper to the eventual loss of over 17,000 jobs in the sector.[28]

[20] Evans (n 7) 7; KD Ewing and Lord Hendy, 'Covid-19 and the Failure of Labour Law: Part 1' (2020) 49:4 *Industrial Law Journal* 497, 512.

[21] Ewing and Hendy (n 20) 513.

[22] Hunt (n 8) 35.

[23] Ewing and Hendy (n 20) 519–20, referring to *R (Adiatu) v HM Treasury* [2020] EWHC 1554 (Admin).

[24] IWGB, 'Fair Furlough Now! Fight for Furlough: everyone is essential'. Available at: https://iwgb.org.uk/page/fair-furlough-now.

[25] T Novitz, 'COVID-19 and Labour Law: United Kingdom' (2020) 13:1S *Italian Labour Law E-Journal* 6.

[26] See ch 1.

[27] Australian Government, *JobKeeper Payment: Frequently Asked Questions* (9 April 2020). Note that unions (and workers) paid a price for the introduction of JobKeeper, through amendments to the FW Act giving employers wide powers to stand workers down, reduce working hours or change the duties or location of work for recipients of the wage subsidy: see Coronavirus Economic Response Package Omnibus (Measures No 2) Act 2020 (Cth). On these and other aspects of the regulatory response to the pandemic, see the special issue 'COVID-19 and Labour Regulation in Australia' (2021) *Australian Journal of Labour Law*, forthcoming.

[28] N Zhou, 'More than 17,000 jobs lost at Australian universities during Covid pandemic', *The Guardian* (3 February 2021). On the NTEU's ill-fated attempt to forestall redundancies in the higher education sector through the National Jobs Protection Framework (including the union's acceptance of time-limited pay freezes or salary reductions, which a large proportion of the membership rebelled against), see K Broadbent and A Vassiley, 'Universities are cutting hundreds of jobs – they, and the government, can do better', *The Conversation* (16 July 2020).

Hospo Voice and the UWU drew attention to the practical barriers preventing many hospitality workers from accessing JobKeeper, including a range of dubious employer practices.[29] MWC campaigned for the extension of the scheme to the 1.1 million temporary migrant workers who received no support at all, and set up a phonebank to help these workers access the Red Cross's COVID-19 emergency relief payments.[30]

## IV. Protecting Workers' Safety

### A. Sick Leave/Pandemic Leave

In the pandemic: 'Suddenly, just the act of going to work every day became a potential life-or-death question.'[31] Therefore, one of the most crucial roles performed by unions has been safeguarding workers' health and safety. Unions were quick to identify the gaps in sick leave coverage for many workers required to self-isolate while awaiting coronavirus test results, or if they contracted the virus. In Australia, casual employees do not qualify for sick leave. Gig workers are in the same position because they are categorised as independent contractors. The ACTU pushed for paid pandemic leave entitlement for all employees.[32] The FWC inserted provisions, but only for unpaid pandemic leave, in federal awards.[33] Paid pandemic leave was limited to aged care workers, although the ACTU and unions had brought a case seeking its application to front-line health care workers more broadly.[34] The Italian government extended full paid sick leave entitlements to workers required to quarantine, especially if this arose due to disability or immune system diseases and those in non-standard employment.[35] Under the national health and safety

[29] UWU, 'JobKeeper fail: survey finds 7 in 10 hospo workers miss out' (8 May 2020). Available at: www.unitedworkers.org.au/jobkeeper-fail-survey-finds-7-in-10-hospo-workers-miss-out/.

[30] MWC, *2020 Annual Report*, 26; MWC, 'August 2020 Newsletter'. Available at: www.migrantworkers.org.au/august_2020_newsletter. See, further, L Berg and B Farbenblum, *As If We Weren't Humans: The Abandonment of Temporary Migrants in Australia during COVID-19* (Migrant Worker Justice Initiative, 2020).

[31] D DiMaggio and S Sarkar, '2020 in review: workers struggle under the weight of the pandemic', *Labor Notes* (21 December 2020).

[32] ACTU, 'Pandemic leave, WHS reforms needed before workers can return', *Media Release* (5 May 2020); ACTU, 'List of employers who have agreed to two weeks special leave'. Available at: www.australianunions.org.au/cv_good_employers_list.

[33] *Application to vary awards on the initiative of the Commission* [2020] FWCFB 1760 and [2020] FWCFB 1837.

[34] *Health Awards – Pandemic Leave* [2020] FWCFB 3940. Note also the (unsuccessful) efforts of unions covering Qantas employees to contest the airline's refusal to allow them to access their sick leave entitlements while stood down due to coronavirus travel restrictions: see *Communications, Electronical, Electronic, Energy, Information, Postal, Plumbing and Allied Services Union of Australia v Qantas Airways Ltd* (2020) 302 IR 190; 'High Court rebuffs union challenge to Qantas leave ruling', *Workplace Express* (21 May 2021).

[35] ILO, *Measures adopted in Italy to support workers, families and enterprises during the COVID-19 emergency* (Policy Brief, 28 March 2020) 3.

protocol negotiated by the main union confederations, the use of paid leave under collective agreements was strongly encouraged (as part of measures to limit attendance at workplaces continuing their operations to essential staff only).[36]

In the UK, statutory sick pay entitlements were widened to cover employees required to self-isolate in addition to those who were ill, but this still excluded 'limb (b) workers'.[37] IWGB's legal case, referred to earlier,[38] also sought to challenge the discriminatory impacts of this exclusion on those engaged in the gig economy and other low-paid workers (eg, cleaners, care workers). Although unsuccessful, this helped to illustrate 'the inadequacy' of statutory sick pay in the UK, 'undoubtedly caus[ing] many sick workers to continue to work, increasing the risk to those with whom they worked and the public they served'.[39] In the US, prior to the pandemic, there was no right to paid sick leave under federal law (and very few states provided such entitlements).[40] The Families First Coronavirus Response Act 2020 included provision for two weeks' paid sick leave for full-time employees, but various exclusions placed more than half of the workforce (including many essential workers) outside its coverage.[41] United for Respect called on big retailers to provide paid pandemic leave for all workers,[42] while other unions were able to bargain for paid leave with employers like Verizon.[43]

Very early on, Uber and Deliveroo in Australia provided up to 14 days' pay for drivers/riders who either contracted COVID-19 or were otherwise required to quarantine.[44] The TWU's July 2020 agreement with DoorDash saw the platform providing two weeks' earnings to riders in similar circumstances and those at high risk of becoming infected. DoorDash also agreed to implement contactless food delivery and ensure riders were equipped with gloves, hand sanitiser and face masks.[45] Yet, by September 2020, a survey by the TWU/YWC Delivery Riders Alliance found that 51 per cent of food platform riders and drivers were not provided with basic personal protective equipment (PPE) and 78 per cent did not receive any compensation or sick leave when required to self-isolate.[46] In the US, much evidence emerged about the safety risks faced by rideshare drivers, with

[36] L Dorigatti, *Government and social partners protocol to ensure safe working conditions at the workplace* (European Foundation for the Improvement of Living and Working Conditions, 10 April and 17 July 2020).

[37] Ewing and Hendy (n 20) 509–10; the concept of limb (b) workers is explained in ch 10.

[38] See n 23 above.

[39] Ewing and Hendy (n 20) 510; see also Novitz (n 25) 4–5.

[40] E Tippett, 'Paid Leave under the Families First Coronavirus Response Act', in Padya and Hirsch (n 18) ch 7. Available at: https://worklawcovid19book.netlify.app/ffcra.html.

[41] Ibid; P Clark, 'Essential US workers often lack sick leave and health care – benefits taken for granted in most other countries', *The Conversation* (6 May 2020).

[42] United for Respect, 'Five to Survive'. Available at: https://act.united4respect.org/a/five-to-survive.

[43] C Garden, *Workers' collective power in the pandemic*, *The Century Foundation* (10 June 2020). Available at: https://tcf.org/content/commentary/workers-collective-power-pandemic/?session=1.

[44] 'Financial cover for sick, quarantined gig workers', *Workplace Express* (10 March 2020).

[45] *TWU-DoorDash COVID-19 Response* (July 2020); see ch 10.

[46] Delivery Riders Alliance, *Food Delivery Driver/Rider Survey* (September 2020).

a number in New York City dying from COVID-19 infection.[47] While IDG and NYTWA demanded greater protections for drivers, Uber's CEO claimed their independent contractor status prevented the platform from doing this. He called on President Trump to legislate: 'a "third way" that would update our labor laws to remove the forced choice between flexibility and protection for millions of American workers'.[48] The pandemic has thus hammered home the brutal effects of the gig economy's contracting model[49] – on the one hand elevating rideshare and food delivery riders to the status of 'essential workers'[50] while on the other hand, continuing to deprive many of them of basic employment rights.

## B. Strikes, Walkouts and other Actions against Unsafe Working Conditions

Unions in all four countries have supported workers to take a strong stand against insufficient provision of PPE and inadequate employer responses to identified cases of coronavirus. As the pandemic hit Italy hard in the early months of 2020, nationwide strikes protesting about the risks to workers' health[51] led to the negotiation of the safety protocol between the national government, *Confindustria* and the main union confederations. Many more strikes have followed, including in the logistics sector where SI Cobas rejected the premises of the national protocol and urged the time-limited closure of all but essential production.[52] In the gig economy, a self-organised riders' collective (*Rider X i Diritti*) called a strike in June 2020 to protest against the lack of provision of PPE by food delivery platforms,[53] one of

[47] A Correal and A Jacobs, '"A Tragedy is Unfolding": Inside New York's Virus Epicenter', *New York Times* (9 April 2020). The precise number of deaths is not known; Bhairavi Desai of NYTWA stated, almost a year into the pandemic, that '[w]e've lost so many drivers' (referring to the association's membership which includes yellow cab and rideshare drivers): D Naresh, '"We're on the brink of utter collapse": Yellow cab drivers in New York struggle to stay alive as the pandemic rages on', *CNN* (9 January 2021).

[48] J Fan, 'The Uncertain Life of New York City's Immigrant Uber Drivers During the Pandemic', *The New Yorker* (29 April 2020).

[49] See chs 9–10.

[50] M Cherry and A Rutschman, 'Gig Workers as Essential Workers: How to Correct the Gig Economy Beyond the COVID-19 Pandemic' (2020) 35 *ABA Journal of Labor and Employment Law* 11.

[51] P Tamma, 'Coronavirus sparks nationwide strikes in Italy', *Politico* (13 March 2020); Pedersini (n 9) 12. See also (providing CGIL's perspective on the strikes in sectors including metalwork, auto manufacturing, steel production, poultry and meat processing) L Tartaglia, 'Dispatch from Italy: class struggle in the time of coronavirus', *Labor Notes* (20 March 2020).

[52] SI Cobas, 'Italian warehouse workers say: stop all non-essential activity to stop the virus', *Labor Notes* (20 March 2020). See also A Tassinari, R Chesta and L Cini, 'Labour Conflicts over Health and Safety in the Italian Covid19 Crisis' (2020) 12:1 *Interface: A Journal for and about Social Movements* 128, 129–30.

[53] O Razzolini, *Collective Action for Self-Employed Workers: A Necessary Response to Increasing Income Inequality* (Centre for the Study of European Labour Law 'Massimo D'Antona', Working Paper 155/2021) 4.

many stop-works and log-offs initiated by self-organised rider collectives.[54] These actions followed a lawsuit by an elected workers' safety representative against Just Eat, resulting in a Florence Tribunal ordering the platform to provide riders with PPE to properly protect them against COVID-19.[55] Amazon has been the focus of worker protests against unsafe conditions and coronavirus cases among staff in Italy[56] and, as noted in Chapter 1, in the USA.[57] Walkouts to protest safety concerns have taken place across the US, many of them initiated by workers (without union involvement).[58] An analysis from the Brookings Institution linked the high rates of workers' exposure to COVID-19 infection and inadequate safety measures to very low unionisation rates in essential sectors like health care, food and agriculture.[59] Death rates from coronavirus among US aged care staff and front-line health workers have been extremely high, the president of the New York State Nurses Association poignantly observing that: 'Most of us are going to get it and some of us are going to die.'[60]

In the UK, unions covering postal workers, warehouse employees and university staff have taken or threatened industrial action over coronavirus risks.[61] IWGB organised strike action in response to The Doctors Laboratory (TDL)'s failure to address the safety concerns of couriers and its targeting of union activists and whistleblowers for redundancy.[62] This led to findings by the Health and Safety Executive that TDL had not properly implemented cleaning, PPE and social distancing measures to ensure safe working conditions for the couriers.[63] IWGB also brought judicial review proceedings arguing that the UK government had not fully implemented European Union (EU) health and safety directives, leaving gig workers unable to object to unsafe work and insist on the provision of PPE.

[54] Tassinari, Chesta and Cini (n 52) 133–34.

[55] International Lawyers Assisting Workers Network, *Taken for a Ride: Litigating the Digital Platform Model* (Issue Brief, March 2021) 58, referring to the decision in *Parigi v Just Eat Italy* (Ordinary Tribunal of Florence, 21 April 2020). See also R Chiari, 'Intervista a Yiftalem Parigi, primo RLS dei rider di Just Eat', *Il Becco* (7 October 2020), indicating that the riders' representative had obtained support from CGIL in organising the workers to advocate for safety protections.

[56] I Hamilton and R Moynihan, 'Amazon warehouse workers in Italy are striking in outrage at the firm's response to 2 staff contracting coronavirus', *Business Insider* (18 March 2020).

[57] See also S Ghaffary and J Del Rey, 'The real cost of Amazon', *Vox* (29 June 2020).

[58] E Ortiz, 'Target, Walmart workers and others plan "sickout" protests over coronavirus safety', *NBC News* (2 May 2020); M Sainato, 'Strikes erupt as US essential workers demand protection amid pandemic', *The Guardian* (19 May 2020).

[59] J O'Donnell, 'Essential workers during COVID-19: at risk and lacking union representation', *Up Front Blog* (Brookings Institution, 3 September 2020). Available at: www.brookings.edu/blog/up-front/2020/09/03/essential-workers-during-covid-19-at-risk-and-lacking-union-representation/; see also Garden (n 43).

[60] DiMaggio and Sarkar (n 31).

[61] Evans (n 7) 15–16.

[62] IWGB, 'Covid-19 couriers vote to strike following victimisation by NHS courier TDL' (28 May 2020). Available at: https://iwgb.org.uk/post/covid-19-couriers-vote-to-strike-following-victimisation-by-nhs-contractor-tdl.

[63] T Lezard, 'NHS COVID-19 testing contractor in breach of health and safety regulations', *Union News* (2 October 2020). Available at: www.union-news.co.uk/nhs-covid-19-testing-contractor-in-breach-of-health-and-safety-regulations/.

In a judgment handed down on 13 November 2020, the High Court ruled in IWGB's favour, agreeing that the EU safety rights should extend beyond 'employees' and also apply to 'limb (b) workers' under UK law.[64] The government's position in this case reflected its more general shortcomings in protecting essential workers in the UK, including critical PPE shortages and an 'almost reckless' approach to re-opening the economy.[65]

In Australia, the second wave of coronavirus infections which engulfed Melbourne in mid-2020 raised major workplace safety concerns for workers in aged care homes, the Health Workers Union calling for increased inspections by the state safety regulator.[66] UWU led several employee walkouts in other sectors. At a Spotless commercial laundry facility, the company sought orders from the FWC requiring a return to work after employees walked off due to positive tests among the workforce. The company had shut down and cleaned only part of the facility, whereas UWU argued the whole workplace should be closed and workers stood down with full pay to obtain COVID-19 tests.[67] The union's defence of the workers' safety rights led to the laundry being temporarily closed following a Victorian health department inspection, with the workers placed on paid leave.[68] The union adopted the same stance following outbreaks of infection at distribution centres run by Coles, Woolworths and Toll (for Kmart), demanding site closures and comprehensive testing of all workers:[69] a 'collective stand' to ensure workers were not treated as mere 'vectors of transmission'.[70]

## V. Conclusion: Implications of the Pandemic for Trade Unions

Unions in each of the four countries have performed other roles during the COVID-19 crisis. They have advocated for the many millions of workers abruptly

[64] *R (on the application of The Independent Workers Union of Great Britain) v The Secretary of State for Work and Pensions and Others* [2020] EWHC 3050 (Admin). On IWGB's wider campaign, of which the High Court judicial review case formed part, see G Owen, 'Clapped and Scrapped: how exploited couriers in Wales are taking on the world's biggest companies', *voice.wales* (3 March 2021). Available at: www.voice.wales/clapped-and-scrapped-how-exploited-couriers-in-wales-are-taking-on-the-worlds-biggest-companies/.

[65] Ewing and Hendy (n 20) 523–30. See also Institute of Employment Rights, 'UK government downplaying Covid-19 workplace risk, report says' (11 March 2021). Available at: www.ier.org.uk/press-releases/uk-government-downplaying-covid-19-workplace-risk-report-warns/.

[66] 'Victorian workplaces under virus strain', *Workplace Express* (28 July 2020); F Michie, 'Aged care "on the brink" in Victoria, as providers say they may need help from the military', *ABC News* (25 July 2020).

[67] 'Employer seeks anti-strike order after COVID-19 walkout', *Workplace Express* (29 July 2020).

[68] 'Spotless laundry shut down', *Workplace Express* (31 July 2020).

[69] N Bonyhady, 'Staff walk out of Kmart warehouse over contract tracing fears', *The Age* (7 August 2020); S Ananth, 'Workers at Melbourne's Toll warehouse unite against COVID-19', *Jacobin* (6 September 2020).

[70] G Moase, 'A Plague of the Working Classes', *Overland* (11 August 2020).

required to work from home, highlighted the difficulties (especially for women) of juggling work, care and the home-schooling of children[71] and guarded against intrusive employer surveillance.[72] Unions have drawn attention to the pandemic's accentuation of pre-existing inequality, including its harsh health and financial impacts on those in low-paid, insecure work[73] (its 'disproportionate and tragic impact on communities of color' has also been widely observed[74]). Unions have been vocal in arguments supporting the rebuilding of fairer economies and societies as nations emerge from the pandemic.[75] Most recently, they have pushed for workers to have sufficient paid leave to enable them to receive COVID-19 vaccinations,[76] a vital public health measure to get the world back onto the path to recovery.

Of course, the pandemic has also had a massive impact on unions themselves. Like all organisations confronted with the strictures of lockdowns and travel limitations, unions had to adapt, quickly. This meant switching from in-person meetings with workers and delegates in many workplace settings to virtual meetings via Zoom and the provision of information and training through webinars and social media.[77] Union ventures into digital organising and recruitment have been fast-tracked.[78] For example, SDAEA adapted its National Digital Organising Project to mobilise around workers' concerns on pandemic-related issues including ensuring the safety of retail staff as 'essential workers' (utilising text messaging, Zoom meetings and Facebook groups to increase membership).[79] Campaigns to

[71] See, eg, L Dorigatti, *Simplifying the adoption of the smart working regime* (European Foundation for the Improvement of Living and Working Conditions, 31 March and 29 July 2020), referring to CGIL, 'Smart working: Cgil, presentazione indagine con Landini e Camusso' (18 May 2020). Available at: www.cgil.it/smart-working-cgil-lunedi-presentazione-indagine-con-landini-e-camusso/; Novitz (n 25) 9–10.

[72] See, eg, ACTU, *Working from home Charter* (November 2020). See also I Manokha, 'Covid-19: Teleworking, Surveillance and 24/7 Work. Some Reflexions on the Expected Growth of Remote Work After the Pandemic' (2020) 1:2 *Political Anthropological Research on International Social Sciences* 273.

[73] See, eg, TUC, *Insecure work: Why decent work needs to be at the heart of the UK's recovery from coronavirus* (August 2020); L Kelly, 'Insecure work is a virus, and it's making us all sick', *Arena* (28 January 2021).

[74] D Michaels and G Wagner, *Halting workplace COVID-19 transmission: An urgent proposal to protect American workers* (The Century Foundation, 15 October 2020). Available at: https://tcf.org/content/report/halting-workplace-covid-19-transmission-urgent-proposal-protect-american-workers/?agreed=1; see also Novitz (n 25) 8–9.

[75] See, eg, Hospo Voice, *#RebuildHospo: A Post-COVID Roadmap for Secure Jobs in Hospitality* (November 2020); ACTU/Centre for Future Work, *For a Stronger, Balanced and Inclusive Recovery* (April 2021); K Harris and E Shuler, 'Opinion: Unions can help America build back better after COVID-19', *Detroit News* (6 September 2020); TUC (n 73). See also E McGaughey, 'A Social Recovery, Workplace Democracy and Security: COVID-19 and Labour Law' (2021) 32:1 *King's Law Journal* 122.

[76] See, eg, K Makortoff, 'TUC says Covid vaccine efforts hindered by lack of paid time off for jab', *The Guardian* (22 March 2021).

[77] Hunt (n 8) 17–21, 29–30; Australian Trade Union Institute, 'Virtual Organising Conference, 16–20 November 2020'. Available at: https://voc2020.atui.org.au/.

[78] See the US union examples discussed in A Gabriel, 'Virtual labor organising: The ultimate guide for 2021', *Mobilize Blog* (21 April 2021). Available at: https://join.mobilize.us/blog/virtual-labor-organizing-the-ultimate-guide.

[79] ACTU, *Organising with 2020 Vision: Case Studies of New Approaches to Union Growth and Capacity Building* (Australian Trade Union Institute, 19 November 2020) 10–12. On rival union

influence governments and policy-makers have moved mostly online, supplemented by socially distanced rallies and protests as restrictions have eased.[80] As discussed in Chapter 1, digital picket lines have been used both to campaign and to progress industrial demands.

Some unions reported increased resistance from employers to union access to workplaces, often citing spurious safety concerns.[81] This posture spilled over into the collective bargaining sphere: many US unions encountered heightened opposition to organising drives and employers targeting labour activists for layoffs.[82] Generally, all of this reflects the largely *defensive* position which unions were forced into by the pandemic. The core union project of *improving* workers' wages and conditions was temporarily frozen, in part due to the recessionary economic climate. However, as economies recover,[83] unions can look to re-enliven collective bargaining – especially to ensure that the many businesses that have done very well in the pandemic properly reward all those previously 'invisible' workers in essential industries, who kept our societies functioning at great risk to themselves and their families.[84]

From early expectations of membership losses arising from the pandemic-induced slashing of jobs, many unions have experienced increases in membership.[85] As noted in Chapter 2, overall union membership in the US and UK rose in 2020 according to official statistics (although caution was urged on the reliability of those figures).[86] Many unions made joining easier, for example by reducing or temporarily halting membership fees, or offering an initial period of free membership.[87]

RAFFWU's concerns that even in the pandemic, SDAEA was too close to the major retail employers, see D Nicholson, 'Australia's Youngest Union is Organizing Retail and Fast Food Workers', *Jacobin* (11 May 2020); and see ch 6.

[80] Hunt (n 8) 33–34; DiMaggio and Sarkar (n 31); M Franchi, 'The unions are back in the piazzas for the first time since pre-Covid', *Il Manifesto* (20 September 2020).

[81] Hunt, ibid, 26. In Australia, refusal of statutory right of entry based on COVID-19 risks was supported by the FWC in *Construction, Forestry, Maritime, Mining and Energy Union v Cape Preston Port Company Pty Ltd* [2020] FWC 4502; compare *Bervar Pty Ltd (trading as Della Rosa Fresh Food) v United Workers Union* [2020] FWC 4501.

[82] See, eg, J Silver-Greenberg and R Abrams, 'Fired in a pandemic "because we tried to start a union", workers say', *New York Times* (28 April 2020), noting that the NLRB suspended union representation elections for two weeks in the early stage of the pandemic (it later moved to mail-in ballots). See also Hunt (n 8) 38, observing that some UK unions found employers utilising new stalling tactics in bargaining negotiations, facilitated by the online environment. In Italy, negotiations for renewal of national/sectoral collective agreements do not appear to have been impeded by the pandemic: Pedersini (n 9) 12, 15; in other respects, compare A Gianni, 'Giants of Italian business are using Covid to weaken unions', *Il Manifesto* (30 August 2020).

[83] See, eg, J Smyth, 'Australia's economy powers out of Covid-19 recession', *Financial Times* (2 December 2020).

[84] See, eg, G Gall, 'Building picket lines when we can't stand together', *Jacobin* (9 April 2020).

[85] See, eg, A Pattani, 'For healthcare workers, the pandemic is fueling renewed interest in unions', *NPR* (12 January 2021); S O'Connor, 'Trade unions are back after a long absence', *Financial Times* (9 March 2021).

[86] Note, also, that initial reports of pandemic-induced membership gains in Australia were not sustained, as indicated in official statistics measuring union membership levels as at August 2020: see ch 2.

[87] See, eg, Hunt (n 8) 25; NTEU, 'Covid-19: Casual member fee relief' (16 March 2020). Available at: www.nteu.org.au/article/Covid-19%3A-Casual-member-fee-relief-21909.

Some workers joined to obtain immediate assistance from unions as the pandemic threatened their jobs or their health, while others signed up when they saw unions publicly advocating for income protection or workplace safety.[88]

Having demonstrated the power of collective voice and action, unions in the four countries examined in this study can emerge from the COVID-19 crisis with a re-affirmed legitimacy and a renewed sense of purpose. Many workers have been mobilised for the first time, to protect their lives and livelihoods from coronavirus. Unions can build upon this, engaging workers in collective bargaining campaigns to improve the situation in their own workplaces – and the wider project to create more equal societies and economies for all.[89] COVID-19 has made the case for unionising more compelling than ever. Taking advantage of this opportunity will require unions to examine, very closely, what they are doing to innovate, to re-envision organising and representation in the digital world, and to connect with a new generation of workers. It is intended that the suggestions and ideas articulated in Chapter 11 – along with the labour law reform options outlined there – will assist unions in these efforts. More broadly, it is my hope that unions in each of the four countries (and beyond) can learn from the many successful strategies for advancing the interests of workers, and rebuilding collective power, identified throughout this book.

[88] Hunt, ibid, 23.

[89] See, eg, L Wyndham, 'Labour will win by championing everyone', *The American Prospect* (29 April 2020).

# BIBLIOGRAPHY

*Media articles and websites are not included*

## Books

Ashby, S and Bruno, R, *A Fight for the Soul of Public Education: The Story of the Chicago Teachers Strike* (Ithaca, Cornell University Press, 2016).

Auerbach, S, *Legislating for Conflict* (Oxford, Clarendon Press, 1990).

Baccaro, L and Howell, C, *Trajectories of Neoliberal Transformation: European Industrial Relations Since the 1970s* (Cambridge, Cambridge University Press, 2017).

Bloodworth, J, *Hired: Six Months Undercover in Low-wage Britain* (London, Atlantic Books, 2018).

Bogg, A, *The Democratic Aspects of Trade Union Recognition* (Oxford, Hart Publishing, 2009).

Bramble, T, *Trade Unionism in Australia: A History from Flood to Ebb Tide* (Port Melbourne, Cambridge University Press, 2008).

Brook, P, *Freedom at Work: The Case for Reforming Labour Law in New Zealand* (Auckland, Oxford University Press, 1990).

Bukarica, A and Dallas, A, *Good Faith Bargaining under the Fair Work Act 2009: Lessons from the Collective Bargaining Experience in Canada and New Zealand* (Sydney, Federation Press, 2012).

Cant, C, *Riding for Deliveroo: Resistance in the New Economy* (Cambridge, Polity Press, 2019).

Carney, S, *Australia in Accord: Politics and Industrial Relations under the Hawke Government* (South Melbourne, Sun Books, 1998).

Cohen, N and de Peuter, G, *New Media Unions: Organizing Digital Journalists* (Abingdon, Routledge, 2020).

Collins, H, Ewing, KD and McColgan, A, *Labour Law* 2nd edn (Cambridge, Cambridge University Press, 2019).

Creighton, B, Denvir, C, Johnstone, R, McCrystal, S and Orchiston, A, *Strike Ballots, Democracy, and Law* (Oxford, Oxford University Press, 2020).

Crosby, M, *Power at Work: Rebuilding the Australian Union Movement* (Sydney, Federation Press, 2005)

Davies, P and Freedland, M, *Labour Legislation and Public Policy* (Oxford, Clarendon Press, 1993).

Davies, P and Freedland, M, *Towards a Flexible Labour Market: Labour Legislation and Regulation Since the 1990s* (Oxford, Oxford University Press, 2007).

D'Onofrio, G, *Firms, Labour, Migrations and Unions within Tomato Value Chain in Southern Italy* (Milano, Ledizione LediPublishing, 2020).

Ebbinghaus, B and Visser, J, *Trade Unions in Western Europe since 1945* (Basingstoke, Palgrave Macmillan, 2000).

Estlund, C, *Regoverning the Workplace: From Self-Regulation to Co-Regulation* (New Haven, Yale University Press, 2010).

Fairbrother, P and Yates, C (eds), *Trade Unions in Renewal: A Comparative Study* (London, Routledge, 2003).

Fantasia, R and Voss, K, *Hard Work: Remaking the American Labor Movement* (Berkeley, University of California Press, 2004).

Fernie, S and Metcalf, D (eds), *Trade Unions: Resurgence or Demise?* (London, Routledge, 2005).

Feurer, R and Pearson, C (eds), *Against Labor: How U.S. Employers Organized to Defeat Union Activism* (Urbana, University of Illinois Press, 2017).

Frege, C and Kelly, J (eds), *Varieties of Unionism: Revitalization in a Globalizing Economy* (Oxford, Oxford University Press, 2004).

Friedman, M, *Capitalism and Freedom* (Chicago, University of Chicago Press, 1962).

Friedman, M, *Capitalism and Freedom*, 40th Anniversary Edition (Chicago, University of Chicago Press, 2002).

Getman, J, *Restoring the Power of Unions: It Takes a Movement* (New Haven, Yale University Press, 2010).

Gollan, P, Markey, R and Ross, I (eds), *Works Councils in Australia: Future Prospects and Possibilities* (Sydney, Federation Press, 2002).

Gorman, R, Finkin, M and Glynn, T, *Cox and Bok's Labor Law: Cases and Materials*, 16th edn (St Paul MN, Foundation Press, 2016).

Greenhouse, S, *Beaten Down, Worked Up: The Past, Present, and Future of American Labor* (New York, Alfred A Knopf, 2019).

Gumbrell-McCormick, R and Hyman, R, *Trade Unions in Western Europe: Hard Times, Hard Choices* (Oxford, Oxford University Press, 2013).

Hayek, FA, *The Constitution of Liberty* (London, Routledge and Kegan Paul, 1959).

Hayek, FA, *Law, Legislation and Liberty: A New Statement of the Liberal Principles of Justice and Political Economy* (London, Routledge and Kegan Paul, 1979), vol 3.

Hearn, M, *Organising Union: Transport Workers Face the Challenge of Change, 1989–2013* (Carlton, Melbourne University Publishing, 2017).

Howell, C, *Trade Unions and the State: The Construction of Industrial Relations Institutions in Britain, 1890–2000* (Princeton, Princeton University Press, 2000).

HR Nicholls Society, *Arbitration in Contempt* (Melbourne, HR Nicholls Society, 1986).

Humphreys, E, *How Labour Built Neoliberalism: Australia's Accord, The Labour Movement and the Neoliberal Project* (Chicago, Haymarket Books, 2019).

Hyman, R, *Understanding European Trade Unionism: Between Market, Class and Society* (London, Sage Publications, 2001).

Kelly, P, *The End of Certainty: The Story of the 1980s* (St Leonards, Allen and Unwin, 1992).

Kerrissey, J, Weinbaum, E, Hammonds, C, Juravich, T and Clawson, D (eds), *Labor in the Time of Trump* (Ithaca, Cornell University Press, 2020).

Kessler, S, *Gigged: The Gig Economy, the End of the Job and the Future of Work* (London, Random House, 2018).

Kochan, T and Osterman, P, *The Mutual Gains Enterprise: Forging a Winning Partnership among Labor, Management and Government* (Cambridge MA, Harvard Business School Press, 1994).

Larson, E (ed), *Jobs with Justice: 25 Years, 25 Voices* (Oakland, PM Press, 2013).

Lichtenstein, N, *State of the Union: A Century of American Labor* (Princeton, Princeton University Press, revised and expanded edition, 2013).

Locke, R, *Remaking the Italian Economy* (Ithaca, Cornell University Press, 1995).

Loomis, E, *A History of America in Ten Strikes* (New York, The New Press, 2018).

Macdonald, F, *Individualising Risk: Paid Care Work in the New Gig Economy* (Cham, Palgrave Macmillan, 2021).

McAlevey, J, *No Shortcuts: Organizing for Power in the New Gilded Age* (New York, Oxford University Press, 2016).

McAlevey, J, *A Collective Bargain: Unions, Organizing, and the Fight for Democracy* (New York, Harper Collins, 2020).

McCartin, J, *Collision Course: Ronald Reagan, the Air Traffic Controllers, and the Strike that Changed America* (New York, Oxford University Press, 2011).

McCrystal, S, *The Right to Strike in Australia* (Sydney, Federation Press, 2010).

Moody, K, *US Labor in Trouble and Transition: The Failure of Reform from Above, the Promise of Revival from Below* (New York, Verso, 2007).

Moody, K, *In Solidarity: Essays on Working-Class Organization in the United States* (Chicago, Haymarket Books, 2014).

Moody, K, *On New Terrain: How Capital is Shaping the Battleground of Class War* (Chicago, Haymarket Books, 2017).

Muir, K, *Worth Fighting For: Inside the Your Rights at Work Campaign* (Sydney, UNSW Press, 2008).

Mundlak, G, *Organizing Matters: Two Logics of Trade Union Representation* (Cheltenham, Edward Elgar Publishing, 2020).

Munkholm, L, *Re-Inventing Labour Law Enforcement: A Socio-Legal Analysis* (Oxford, Hart Publishing, 2020).

Murray, A, *The Fall and Rise of the British Left* (London, Verso, 2019).

Naughton, R, *The Shaping of Labour Law Legislation: Underlying Elements of Australia's Workplace Relations System* (Chatswood, LexisNexis Butterworths, 2017).

Nolan, D (ed), *The Australasian Labour Law Reforms: Australia and New Zealand at the End of the Twentieth Century* (Sydney, Federation Press, 1998).

Norington, B, *Planet Jackson: Power, Greed and Unions* (Carlton, Melbourne University Press, 2016).

Peetz, D, *Unions in a Contrary World: The Future of the Australian Trade Union Movement* (Cambridge, Cambridge University Press, 1998).

Peetz, D, *Brave New Workplace: How Individual Contracts are Changing Our Jobs* (Crows Nest, Allen and Unwin, 2006).

Peetz, D, *The Realities and Futures of Work* (Acton, Australian National University Press, 2019).

Perlstein, R, *Reaganland: America's Right Turn 1976–1980* (New York, Simon and Schuster, 2020).

Prassl, J, *The Concept of the Employer* (Oxford, Oxford University Press, 2015).

Prassl, J, *Humans as a Service: The Promise and Perils of Work in the Gig Economy* (Oxford, Oxford University Press, 2018).

Reich, A and Pearman, B, *Working for Respect: Community and Conflict at Walmart* (New York, Columbia University Press, 2018).

Reid, A, *United We Stand: A History of Britain's Trade Unions* (London, Penguin Books, 2005).

Rosenblum, J, *Beyond $15: Immigrant Workers, Faith Activists, and the Revival of the Labor Movement* (Boston, Beacon Press, 2018).

Rosenfeld, J, *What Unions No Longer Do* (Cambridge MA, Harvard University Press, 2014).

Rosenblat, A, *Uberland: How Algorithms Are Rewriting the Rules of Work* (Oakland, University of California Press, 2018).

Scholz, T, *Uberworked and Underpaid: How Workers are Disrupting the Digital Economy* (Cambridge, Polity Press, 2017).

Shenker, J, *Now We Have Your Attention: The New Politics of the People* (London, The Bodley Head, 2019).

Simms, M, Holgate, J and Heery, E, *Union Voices: Tactics and Tensions in UK Organizing* (Ithaca, Cornell University Press, 2013).

Srnicek, N, *Platform Capitalism* (Cambridge, Polity Press, 2017).

Stewart, A, Forsyth, A, Irving, M, Johnstone, R and McCrystal, S, *Creighton and Stewart's Labour Law*, 6th edn (Sydney, Federation Press, 2016).

Tattersall, A, *Power in Coalition: Strategies for Strong Unions and Social Change* (Ithaca, ILR Press/Cornell University Press, 2010).

Tiraboschi, M, *Labour Law and Industrial Relations in Recessionary Times* (Newcastle-upon-Tyne, Cambridge Scholars Publishing, 2014).

Treu, T, *Labour Law in Italy*, 3rd edn (Alphen aan den Rijn, Wolters Kluwer, 2011).

Trinca, H and Davies, A, *Waterfront: The Battle that Changed Australia* (Milsons Point, Doubleday, 2000).

Walker, A, *Divided Unions: The Wagner Act, Federalism, and Organized Labour* (Philadelphia, University of Pennsylvania Press, 2020).

Watson, I, Buchanan, J, Campbell, I and Briggs, C, *Fragmented Futures: New Challenges in Working Life* (Sydney, Federation Press, 2003).

Weeks, P, *Trade Union Security Law: A Study of Preference and Compulsory Unionism* (Sydney, Federation Press, 1995).

Weil, D, *The Fissured Workplace: Why Work Became So Bad for So Many and What Can Be Done to Improve It* (Cambridge MA, Harvard University Press, 2014).

# Book chapters

Aloisi, A and Gramano, E, 'A Solution in Search of a Problem? Collective Rights and the Antitrust Labor Exemption in Italy', in S Paul, S McCrystal and E McGaughey (eds), *Labor in Competition Law* (Cambridge, Cambridge University Press, forthcoming, 2022).

Ambrosini, M, De Luca, D and Pozzi, S, 'Immigrants and Trade Unions in Italy: What Prospects for Mobility and Careers? A Reflection Starting from the Role of Union Delegates', in M Espinoza-Herold and M Contini (eds), *Living in Two Homes: Integration, Identity and Education of Transnational Migrants in a Globalised World* (Bingley, Emerald Publishing Limited, 2017) 61.

Arthurs, H, 'Cross-National Legal Learning: The Uses of Comparative Labor Knowledge, Law, and Policy' in K Stone and H Arthurs (eds), *Rethinking Workplace Regulation* (Russell Sage Foundation, 2013) 353.

Bach, S and Gall, G, 'Public Service Voice under Strain in an Era of Restructuring and Austerity', in A Bogg and T Novitz (eds), *Voices at Work: Continuity and Change in the Common Law World* (Oxford, Oxford University Press, 2014) 322.

Bales, R, 'Union Trends' in R Bales and C Garden (eds), *The Cambridge Handbook of U.S. Labor Law for the Twenty-First Century* (Cambridge, Cambridge University Press, 2020) 3.

Benassi, C and Dorigatti, L, 'The Political Economy of Agency Work in Italy and Germany: Explaining Diverging Trajectories in Collective Bargaining Outcomes', in V Doellgast, N Lillie and V Pulignano (eds), *Reconstructing Solidarity: Labour Unions, Precarious Work, and the Politics of Institutional Change in Europe* (Oxford, Oxford University Press, 2018) 124.

Bennett, L, 'Bargaining Away the Rights of the Weak: Non-Union Agreements in the Federal Jurisdiction' in P Ronfeldt and R McCallum (eds), *Enterprise Bargaining, Trade Unions and the Law* (Sydney, Federation Press, 1995) 129.

Benvegnú, C, Haidinger, B and Sacchetto, D, 'Restructuring Labour Responses and Employment in the European Logistics Sector: Unions' Responses to a Segmented Workforce', in V Doellgast, N Lillie and V Pulignano (eds), *Reconstructing Solidarity: Labour Unions, Precarious Work, and the Politics of Institutional Change in Europe* (Oxford, Oxford University Press, 2018) 83.

Blanc, E, 'Rank-and-File Organizing and Digital Mobilizing in the Red State Revolt', in R Givan and A Lang (eds), *Strike for the Common Good: Fighting for the Future of Public Education* (Ann Arbor, University of Michigan Press, 2020) 91.

Blanpain, R, 'Comparativism in Labour Law and Industrial Relations', in R Blanpain (ed), *Comparative Labour Law and Industrial Relations in Industrialized Market Economies* (Alphen aan den Rijn, Kluwer Law International, 2010) 3.

Bogg, A and Novitz, T, 'Recognition in Respect of Bargaining in the United Kingdom: Collective Autonomy and Political Neutrality in Context' in B Creighton and A Forsyth (eds), *Rediscovering Collective Bargaining: Australia's Fair Work Act in International Perspective* (New York, Routledge, 2012) 225.

Brigden, C, 'Power and Space in the Victorian Trades Hall Council' in B Ellem, R Markey and J Shields, *Peak Unions in Australia: Origins, Purpose, Power, Agency* (Sydney, Federation Press, 2004) 219.

Briggs, C, 'The End of a Cycle? The Australian Council of Trade Unions in Historical Perspective' in B Ellem, R Markey and J Shields, *Peak Unions in Australia: Origins, Purpose, Power, Agency* (Sydney, Federation Press, 2004) 236.

Bronfenbrenner, K, Friedman, S, Hurd, R, Oswald, R and Seeber, R, 'Introduction' in K Bronfenbrenner, S Friedman, R Hurd, R Oswald and R Seeber (eds), *Organizing to Win: New Research on Union Strategies* (Ithaca, Cornell University Press, 1998) 1.

Bronfenbrenner, K and Hickey, R 'Changing to Organize: A National Assessment of Union Strategies', in R Milkman and K Voss (eds), *Rebuilding Labor: Organizing and Organizers in the New Union Movement* (Ithaca, Cornell University Press, 2004) 17.

Bronfenbrenner, K and Juravich, T, 'It Takes More Than House Calls: Organizing to Win with a Comprehensive Union-Building Strategy' in K Bronfenbrenner, S Friedman, R Hurd, R Oswald and R Seeber (eds), *Organizing to Win: New Research on Union Strategies* (Ithaca, Cornell University Press, 1998) 19.

Broxmeyer, J and Michaels, E, 'Faith, Community, and Labor: Challenges and Opportunities in the New York City Living Wage Campaign', in R Milkman and E Ott (eds), *New Labor in New York: Precarious Workers and the Future of the Labor Movement* (Ithaca, Cornell University Press, 2014) 70.

Carinci, F, 'Trade Union Freedom, Organization and Activities' in F Carinci and E Menegatti, *Labour Law and Industrial Relations in Italy: Update to the Jobs Act* (Milano, Wolters Kluwer Italia, 2015) 279.

Cattero, B and D'Onofrio, M, 'Organizing and Collective Bargaining in the Digitized "Tertiary Factories" of Amazon: A Comparison Between Germany and Italy', in E Ales, Y Curzi, T Fabbri, O Rymkevich, I Senatori and G Solinas (eds), *Working in Digital and Smart Organizations: Legal, Economic and Organizational Perspectives on the Digitalization of Labour Relations* (Cham, Palgrave Macmillan, 2018) 141.

Cataudella, M, 'Types of Worker and Employment Contract' in F Carinci and E Menegatti, *Labour Law and Industrial Relations in Italy: Update to the Jobs Act* (Milano, Wolters Kluwer Italia, 2015) 1.

Chaudhuri, U and Sarina, T, 'Employer-Controlled Agreement-Making: Thwarting Collective Bargaining Under the Fair Work Act' in S McCrystal, B Creighton and A Forsyth (eds), *Collective Bargaining under the Fair Work Act* (Sydney, Federation Press, 2018) 138.

Cherry, M and Aloisi, A, 'A Critical Examination of a Third Employment Category for On-Demand Work' in N Davidson, M Finck and J Infranca (eds), *Cambridge Handbook on the Law of the Sharing Economy* (Cambridge, Cambridge University Press, 2018) 316.

Coderre-La Palme, G and Greer, I, 'Dependence on a Hostile State: UK Trade Unions Before and After Brexit' in S Lehndorff, H Dribbusch and T Schulten, *Rough Waters: European Trade Unions in a Time of Crisis* (European Trade Union Institute, 2018) 259.

Collins, H, 'Is There a Third Way in Labour Law?', in J Conaghan, R Fischl and K Klare (eds), *Labour Law in an Era of Globalization: Transformative Practices and Possibilities* (Oxford, Oxford University Press, 2002) 449.

Cooper, R and Ellem, B, 'Trade Unions and Collective Bargaining' in M Baird, K Hancock and J Isaac (eds), *Work and Employment Relations: An Era of Change* (Sydney, Federation Press, 2011) 34.

Cooper, R, Ellem, B and Wright, C, 'Policy and the Labour Movement', in B Head and K Crowley (eds), *Policy Analysis in Australia* (Bristol, Policy Press, 2015) 231.

Countouris, N, De Stefano, V and Lianos, I, 'The EU, Competition Law and Workers' Rights' in S Paul, S McCrystal and E McGaughey (eds), *Labor in Competition Law* (Cambridge, Cambridge University Press, forthcoming, 2022).

Curcio, A, 'Italy: The Revolution in Logistics', in D Azzellini and M Kraft (eds), *The Class Strikes Back: Self-Organised Workers' Struggles in the Twenty-First Century* (Chicago, Haymarket Books, 2017) 259.

Daniels, G, 'In the Field: A Decade of Organizing', in G Daniels and J McIlroy (eds), *Trade Unions in a Neoliberal World: British Trade Unions under New Labour* (London, Routledge, 2009) 254.

Dau-Schmidt, K, 'The Problem of "Misclassification" or How to Define Who Is an "Employee" under Protective Legislation in the Information Age', in R Bales and C Garden (eds), *The Cambridge Handbook of U.S. Labor Law for the Twenty-First Century* (Cambridge, Cambridge University Press, 2020) 140.

Dubal, V, 'An Uber Ambivalence: Employee Status, Worker Perspectives, and Regulation in the Gig Economy', in D Acevedo (ed), *Beyond the Algorithm: Qualitative Insights for Gig Work Regulation* (Cambridge, Cambridge University Press, 2020) 33.

Evangelista, M, 'Italy in Crisis: Epper si muove', in M Evangelista (ed), *Italy from Crisis to Crisis: Political Economy, Security, and Society in the 21st Century* (Abingdon, Routledge, 2018) 3.

Fairbrother, P and Stewart, P, 'The Dilemmas of Social Partnership and Union Organization: Questions for British Trade Unions', in P Fairbrother and C Yates (eds), *Trade Unions in Renewal: A Comparative Study* (London, Routledge, 2003) 158.

Fernie, S, 'The Future of British Unions: Introductions and Conclusions', in Fernie, S and Metcalf, D (eds), *Trade Unions: Resurgence or Demise?* (London, Routledge, 2005) 1.

Fisk, C, 'Union Security for the Twenty-First Century', in R Bales and C Garden (eds), *The Cambridge Handbook of U.S. Labor Law for the Twenty-First Century* (Cambridge, Cambridge University Press, 2020) 336.

Fitzpatrick, K, 'Wage Theft and Young Workers' in A Stewart, J Stanford and T Hardy (eds), *The Wages Crisis in Australia: What it is and What to do About it* (Adelaide, University of Adelaide Press, 2018) 174.

Fletcher, B and Hurd, R, 'Beyond the Organizing Model: The Transformation Process in Local Unions' in K Bronfenbrenner, S Friedman, R Hurd, R Oswald and R Seeber (eds), *Organizing to Win: New Research on Union Strategies* (Ithaca, Cornell University Press, 1998) 37.

Ford, M and Novitz, T, 'There is Power in a Union? Revisiting Trade Union Functions in 2019', in A Bogg, J Rowbottom and A Young (eds), *The Constitution of Social Democracy: Essays in Honour of Keith Ewing* (Oxford, Hart Publishing, 2020) 261.

Forsyth, A and Ellem, B, 'Has the Australian Model Resisted US-Style Anti-Union Organising Campaigns? Case Studies of the Cochlear and ResMed Bargaining Disputes', in S McCrystal, B Creighton and A Forsyth (eds), *Collective Bargaining under the Fair Work Act* (Sydney, Federation Press, 2018) 45.

Frege, C, Heery, E and Turner, L, 'The New Solidarity? Trade Union Coalition-Building in Five Countries', in C Frege and J Kelly (eds), *Varieties of Unionism: Revitalization in a Globalizing Economy* (Oxford, Oxford University Press, 2004) 137.

Gahan, P and Pekarek, A, 'Collective Bargaining and Agreement Making in Australia: Evolution of the Legislative Framework and Practice' in B Creighton and A Forsyth (eds), *Rediscovering Collective Bargaining: Australia's Fair Work Act in International Perspective* (New York, Routledge, 2012) 21.

Garelli, R, 'Educators United Online', in R Givan and A Lang (eds), *Strike for the Common Good: Fighting for the Future of Public Education* (Ann Arbor, University of Michigan Press, 2020) 102.

Garden, C, 'Tactical Mismatch in Union Organizing Drives' in R Bales and C Garden (eds), *The Cambridge Handbook of U.S. Labor Law for the Twenty-First Century* (Cambridge, Cambridge University Press, 2020) 199.

Getman, J, 'The Central Role of the Right to Strike', in R Bales and C Garden (eds), *The Cambridge Handbook of U.S. Labor Law for the Twenty-First Century* (Cambridge, Cambridge University Press, 2020) 291.

Givan, R, 'Introduction: On Strike for Our Students and the Common Good' in R Givan and A Lang (eds), *Strike for the Common Good: Fighting for the Future of Public Education* (Ann Arbor, University of Michigan Press, 2020) 1.

Givan, R, 'The Strike Continues …', in R Givan and A Lang (eds), *Strike for the Common Good: Fighting for the Future of Public Education* (Ann Arbor, University of Michigan Press, 2020) 253.

Grandi, G, 'Collective Bargaining' in F Carinci and E Menegatti, *Labour Law and Industrial Relations in Italy: Update to the Jobs Act* (Milano, Wolters Kluwer Italia, 2015) 301.

Hardy, T, 'Reconsidering the Notion of the "Employer" in the Era of the Fissured Workplace: Traversing the Legislative Landscape in Australia' in H Nakakubo and T Araki (eds), *The Notion of the Employer in the Era of the Fissured Workplace: Should Labour Law Responsibilities Exceed the Boundary of the Legal Entity?* (Alphen aan den Rijn, Kluwer Law International, 2017) 53.

Harnett, S, 'Words Matter', in D Acevedo (ed), *Beyond the Algorithm: Qualitative Insights for Gig Work Regulation* (Cambridge, Cambridge University Press, 2020) 169.

Heery, E and Adler, L, 'Organizing the Unorganized', in C Frege and J Kelly (eds), *Varieties of Unionism: Revitalization in a Globalizing Economy* (Oxford, Oxford University Press, 2004) 45.

Heery, E and Simms, M, 'Union Organising under Certification Law in Britain', in G Gall (ed), *Union Recognition: Organising and Bargaining Outcomes* (London, Routledge, 2006) 44.

Holgate, J and Wills, J, 'Organising Labor in London: Lessons from the Living Wage Campaign', in L Turner and D Cornfield (eds), *Labor in the New Urban Battlefields: Local Solidarity in a Global Economy* (Ithaca, ILR Press, 2007) 211.

Howe, J, 'Temporary Migrant Workers and Trade Unions in Australia – A Complex Relationship' in J Tham and C Kelly (eds), *Democracy, Social Justice and the Role of Trade Unions: We the Working People* (London, Anthem Press, 2021) 139.

Kahn-Freund, O, 'Legal Framework', in A Flanders and H Clegg (eds), *The System of Industrial Relations in Great Britain: Its History, Law and Institutions* (Oxford, Blackwell, 1954).

Karp, S and Sanchez, A, 'The 2018 Wave of Teachers Strikes: A Turning Point for Our Schools?', in R Givan and A Lang (eds), *Strike for the Common Good: Fighting for the Future of Public Education* (Ann Arbor, University of Michigan Press, 2020) 191.

Kelly, J, 'Social Partnership Agreements in Britain', in M Stuart and M Martínez Lucio (eds), *Partnership and Modernisation in Employment Relations* (London, Routledge, 2005) 188.

Kelly, J and Frege, C, 'Conclusions: Varieties of Unionism', in C Frege and J Kelly (eds), *Varieties of Unionism: Revitalization in a Globalizing Economy* (Oxford, Oxford University Press, 2004) 181.

Leonardi, S, 'Trade Unions and Collective Bargaining in Italy during the Crisis', in S Lehndorff, H Dribbusch and T Schulten, *Rough Waters: European Trade Unions in a Time of Crisis* (European Trade Union Institute, 2018) 87.

Leonardi, S, Ambra, M and Ciarini, A, 'Italian Collective Bargaining at a Turning Point' in S Leonardi and A Pedersini, *Multi-Employer Bargaining under Pressure: Decentralisation Trends in Five European Countries* (Brussels, European Trade Union Institute, 2018) 185.

Lewis, R, 'Picketing', in R Lewis (ed), *Labour Law in Britain* (Oxford, Basil Blackwell, 1986) 195.

Lichtenstein, N, 'Wal-Mart, John Tate, and Their Anti-Union America' in N Lichtenstein and E Shermer (eds), *The Right and Labor in America: Politics, Ideology and Imagination* (Philadelphia, University of Pennsylvania Press, 2012) 252.

Locke, R and Baccaro, L, 'The Resurgence of Italian Unions?' in A Martin and G Ross, *The Brave New World of European Labour: European Trade Unions at the Millennium* (New York, Berghahn Books, 1999) 217.

Logan, J, 'After EFCA, What Next for Unions? The Future of Labour Law Reform and of Collective Bargaining in the United States', in B Creighton and A Forsyth (eds), *Rediscovering Collective Bargaining: Australia's Fair Work Act in International Perspective* (New York, Routledge, 2012) 270.

Logan, J, '"All Deals Are Off": The Dunlop Commission and Employer Opposition to Labor Law Reform', in N Lichtenstein and E Shermer (eds), *The Right and Labor in America: Politics, Ideology and Imagination* (Philadelphia, University of Pennsylvania Press, 2012) 276.

Lyddon, D, '"Glorious Summer", 1972: The High Tide of Rank-and-File Militancy', in J McIlroy, N Fishman and A Campbell (eds), *The High Tide of British Trade Unionism: Trade Unions and Industrial Politics, 1964–79* (Monmouth, Merlin Press, 2007) 326.

Macdonald, F, Charlesworth, S and Brigden, C, 'Access to Collective Bargaining for Low-Paid Workers' in S McCrystal, B Creighton and A Forsyth (eds), *Collective Bargaining under the Fair Work Act* (Sydney, Federation Press, 2018) 206.

McCallum, R and Ronfeldt, P, 'Our Changing Labour Law' in P Ronfeldt and R McCallum (eds), *Enterprise Bargaining, Trade Unions and the Law* (Sydney, Federation Press, 1995) 1.

McCartin, J and Sneiderman, M, 'Collective Action and the Common Good: Teachers' Struggles and the Revival of the Strike', in R Givan and A Lang (eds), *Strike for the Common Good: Fighting for the Future of Public Education* (Ann Arbor, University of Michigan Press, 2020) 15.

McIlroy, J, 'A Brief History of British Trade Unions and Neoliberalism: From the Earliest Days to the Birth of New Labour' in G Daniels and J McIlroy (eds), *Trade Unions in a Neoliberal World: British Trade Unions under New Labour* (London, Routledge, 2009) 21.

McIlroy, J, 'A Brief History of British Trade Unions and Neoliberalism in the Age of New Labour' in G Daniels and J McIlroy (eds), *Trade Unions in a Neoliberal World: British Trade Unions under New Labour* (London, Routledge, 2009) 63.

McIlroy, J, 'Under Stress but Still Enduring: The Contentious Alliance in the Age of Tony Blair and Gordon Brown', in G Daniels and J McIlroy (eds), *Trade Unions in a Neoliberal World: British Trade Unions under New Labour* (London, Routledge, 2009) 165.
McIlroy, J and Campbell, A, 'The High Tide of Trade Unionism: Mapping Industrial Politics, 1964–79', in J McIlroy, N Fishman and A Campbell (eds), *The High Tide of British Trade Unionism: Trade Unions and Industrial Politics, 1964–79* (Monmouth, Merlin Press, 2007) 93.
McIlroy, J and Daniels, G, 'Introduction: Trade Unions in a Neoliberal World' in G Daniels and J McIlroy (eds), *Trade Unions in a Neoliberal World: British Trade Unions under New Labour* (London, Routledge, 2009) 1.
McIlroy, J and Daniels, G, 'An Anatomy of British Trade Unions since 1997: Strategies for Revitalization', in G Daniels and J McIlroy (eds), *Trade Unions in a Neoliberal World: British Trade Unions under New Labour* (London, Routledge, 2009) 98.
Menegatti, E, 'A Fair Wage for Workers On-demand via App,' in E Ales, Y Curzi, T Fabbri, O Rymkevich, I Senatori and G Solinas (eds), *Working in Digital and Smart Organizations: Legal, Economic and Organizational Perspectives on the Digitalization of Labour Relations* (Cham, Palgrave Macmillan, 2018) 67.
Milkman, R, 'Introduction: Toward a New Labor Movement? Organising New York City's Precariat', in R Milkman and E Ott (eds), *New Labor in New York: Precarious Workers and the Future of the Labor Movement* (Ithaca, Cornell University Press, 2014) 1.
Milkman, R and Voss, K, 'Introduction', in R Milkman and K Voss (eds), *Rebuilding Labor: Organizing and Organizers in the New Union Movement* (Ithaca, Cornell University Press, 2004) 1.
Needleman, R, 'Building Relationships for the Long Haul: Unions and Community-Based Groups Working Together to Organise Low-Wage Workers', in K Bronfenbrenner, S Friedman, R Hurd, R Oswald and R Seeber (eds), *Organizing to Win: New Research on Union Strategies* (Ithaca, Cornell University Press, 1998) 71.
Orr, S, 'Is Democracy in the Cards? A Democratic Defense of the Employee Free Choice Act', in N Lichtenstein and E Shermer (eds), *The Right and Labor in America: Politics, Ideology and Imagination* (Philadelphia, University of Pennsylvania Press, 2012) 296.
Padya, S, 'Unemployment Insurance' in S Padya and J Hirsch (eds), *Work Law Under COVID-19* (open source e-book, 2020).
Page-Tickell, R and Ritchie, J, 'Presence and Pretence: Trade Unions and the Gig Economy', in R Page-Tickell and E Yerby (eds), *Conflict and Shifting Boundaries in the Gig Economy: An Interdisciplinary Analysis* (Bingley, Emerald Publishing Limited, 2020).
Peetz, D, 'Industrial Relations Policy and Penalty' in A Gauja, P Chen, J Curtin and J Pietsch (eds), *Double Disillusion: The 2016 Australian Federal Election* (Canberra, ANU Press, 2016) 519.
Rawling, M and Howe, J, 'The Regulation of Supply Chains: An Australian Contribution to Cross-National Legal Learning', in K Stone and H Arthurs (eds), *Rethinking Workplace Regulation* (Russell Sage Foundation, 2013) 233.
Read, R, 'The Role of Trade Unions and Individual Bargaining Representatives: Who Pays for the Work of Bargaining?' in S McCrystal, B Creighton and A Forsyth (eds), *Collective Bargaining under the Fair Work Act* (Sydney, Federation Press, 2018) 69.
Regini, M, 'Trade Unions' in E Jones and G Pasquino (eds), *The Oxford Handbook of Italian Politics* (Oxford, Oxford University Press, 2015) 528.
Rimmer, M, 'Unions and Arbitration', in J Isaac and S Macintyre (eds), *The New Province for Law and Order: 100 Years of Australian Industrial Conciliation and Arbitration* (Cambridge, Cambridge University Press, 2004) 275.
Rinaldini, M and Marino, S, 'Trade Unions and Migrant Workers in Italy: Between Labour and Social Rights', in S Marino, J Roosblad and R Penninx (eds), *Trade Unions and Migrant Workers: New Contexts and Challenges in Europe* (Cheltenham, Edward Elgar Publishing, 2017) 266.
Ross, I, 'Bargaining in the Federal System' in P Ronfeldt and R McCallum (eds), *Enterprise Bargaining, Trade Unions and the Law* (Sydney, Federation Press, 1995) 30.

Russom, G, 'The Teachers' Strikes of 2018: A Gendered Rebellion', in R Givan and A Lang (eds), *Strike for the Common Good: Fighting for the Future of Public Education* (Ann Arbor, University of Michigan Press, 2020) 173.

Santini, F, 'Strike Action' in F Carinci and E Menegatti, *Labour Law and Industrial Relations in Italy: Update to the Jobs Act* (Milano, Wolters Kluwer Italia, 2015) 319.

Simpson, B, 'Trade Union Immunities', in R Lewis (ed), *Labour Law in Britain* (Oxford, Basil Blackwell, 1986) 162.

Smith, R and Pinto, M, 'Rewriting the Rules: Gig Companies' Drive for Labor Deregulation', in D Acevedo (ed), *Beyond the Algorithm: Qualitative Insights for Gig Work Regulation* (Cambridge, Cambridge University Press, 2020) 189.

Stewart, A, Stanford, J and Hardy, T, 'Conclusion: Wages and Inclusive Growth' in A Stewart, J Stanford and T Hardy (eds), *The Wages Crisis in Australia: What it is and what to do about it* (Adelaide, University of Adelaide Press, 2018) 277.

Stone, K, 'A New Labor Law for a New World of Work: The Case for a Comparative-Transnational Approach', in B Aaron and K Stone (eds), *Rethinking Comparative Labor Law: Bridging the Past and the Future* (Lake Mary, Vandeplas Publishing, 2007) 193.

Stone, K, 'Unions and On-demand Work in the United States' in J López (ed), *Collective Bargaining and Collective Action: Labour Agency and Governance in the 21st Century?* (Oxford, Hart Publishing, 2019) 101.

Stuart, M and Martínez Lucio, M, 'Trade Union Representatives' Attitudes and Experiences of the Principles and Practices of Partnership', in M Stuart and M Martínez Lucio (eds), *Partnership and Modernisation in Employment Relations* (London, Routledge, 2005) 101.

Tippett, E, 'Paid Leave under the Families First Coronavirus Response Act', in S Padya and J Hirsch (eds), *Work Law Under COVID-19* (open source e-book, 2020).

Tranfaglia, MA, 'Agency Work and its Regulatory Challenges: Lessons Learnt Through a Comparative Overview of Australian and Italian Approaches' in J Howe, A Chapman and I Landau (eds), *The Evolving Project of Labour Law: Foundations, Development and Future Research Directions* (Sydney, Federation Press, 2017) 206.

Turner, L, 'Why Revitalize? Labour's Urgent Mission in a Contested Global Economy', in C Frege and J Kelly (eds), *Varieties of Unionism: Revitalization in a Globalizing Economy* (Oxford, Oxford University Press, 2004) 1.

Upchurch, M, 'Partnership: New Labour's Third Way?', in G Daniels and J McIlroy (eds), *Trade Unions in a Neoliberal World: British Trade Unions under New Labour* (London, Routledge, 2009) 230.

Vandaele, K, 'Collective Resistance and Organizational Creativity among Europe's Platform Workers: A New Power in the Labour Movement?', in J Haidar and M Keune (eds), *Work and Labour Relations in Global Platform Capitalism* (Cheltenham, Edward Elgar, 2021), forthcoming.

Vesan, P, 'Labor Market Policy and Politics' in E Jones and G Pasquino (eds), *The Oxford Handbook of Italian Politics* (Oxford, Oxford University Press, 2015) 491.

Waldinger, R, Erickson, C, Milkman, R, Mitchell, D, Valenzuela, A, Wong, K and Zeitlin, M, 'Helots No More: A Case Study of the Justice for Janitors Campaign in Los Angeles', in K Bronfenbrenner, S Friedman, R Hurd, R Oswald and R Seeber (eds), *Organizing to Win: New Research on Union Strategies* (Ithaca, Cornell University Press, 1998) 102.

Zamponi, L and Vogiatzoglou, M, 'Contentious Labour in Italy and Greece: Movements and Trade Unions in Times of Precarity and Austerity' in M Wennerhag, C Fröhlich and G Piotrowski (eds), *Radical Left Movements in Europe* (Farnham, Ashgate, 2017) 82.

## Journal articles

Adams, R and Markey, R, 'How the State Influences Trade Union Growth: A Comparative Analysis of Developments in Europe, North America and Australasia' (1997) 13:4 *International Journal of Comparative Labour Law and Industrial Relations* 285.

Agnoletto, S, 'Trade Unions and the Origins of the Union-Based Welfare State in Italy (1950s–1970s)' (2012) 3:2 *California Italian Studies* 1.

Aleks, R, 'Estimating the Effects of "Change to Win" on Union Organising' (2015) 68:3 *Industrial and Labor Relations Review* 584.

Almond, P and Connolly, H, 'A Manifesto for "Slow" Comparative Research on Work and Employment' (2019) 26:1 *European Journal of Industrial Relations* 59.

Aloisi, A, '"With Great Power Comes Virtual Freedom": A Review of the First Italian Case Holding that (Food-Delivery) Platform Workers are not Employees' (2018) *Comparative Labor Law and Policy Journal* (Dispatch No 13).

Aloisi, A, '"A Worker is a Worker is a Worker": Collective Bargaining and Platform Work, the Case of Deliveroo Couriers' (2019) 5:1 *International Labor Rights Case Law Journal* 36.

Andrias, K, 'The New Labor Law' (2016) 126 *Yale Law Journal* 2.

Armaroli, I, 'Integrating Direct Employee Voice within the Framework of Employee Representation: The Role of an Italian Trade Union in *Organising Disintermediation*' (2020) *Economic and Industrial Democracy* (advance access).

Arup, C, 'Enforcing Labour Standards in the Supermarket Food Supply Chain' (2019) 32:1 *Australian Journal of Labour Law* 103.

Ashby, S, '"Traditional" and "Alt" Labor: Comparisons, Critiques and Perspectives' (2018) 43 *Labor Studies Journal* 101.

Atkinson, J and Dhorajiwala, H, '*IWGB v RooFoods*: Status, Rights and Substitution' (2019) 38:2 *Industrial Law Journal* 278.

Badigannavar, V and Kelly, J, 'Partnership and Organizing: An Empirical Assessment of Two Contrasting Approaches to Union Revitalization in the UK' (2011) 32:1 *Economic and Industrial Democracy* 5.

Bales, R and Elko, C, 'COVID-19 and Labour law: U.S.' (2020) 13:1S *Italian Labour Law E-Journal.*

Barnes, A and Balnave, N, 'Back to Grass Roots: Peak Union Councils and Community Campaigning' (2015) 26:4 *Economic and Labour Relations Review* 577.

Barnes, A and Markey, R, 'Evaluating the Organising Model of Trade Unionism? An Australian Perspective' (2015) 26:4 *Economic and Labour Relations Review* 513.

Battistelli, S and Campanella, P, 'Subcontracting Chain and Working Conditions in Italy: Evidence from the Meat and Food Industry' (2020) 27:2 *Studies on Labour Law and Social Policy* 135.

Benassi, C and Dorigatti, L, 'Out of Sight, Out of Mind: The Challenge of External Work Arrangements for Industrial Manufacturing Unions in Germany and Italy' (2020) 34:6 *Work, Employment and Society* 1027.

Benassi, C, Dorigatti, L and Pannini, E, 'Explaining Divergent Bargaining Outcomes for Agency Workers: The Role of Labour Divides and Labour Market Reforms' (2019) 25:2 *European Journal of Industrial Relations* 163.

Berg, J and Johnston, H, 'Too Good to Be True? A Comment on Hall and Kreuger's Analysis of the Labor Market for Uber's Driver-Partners' (2019) 72:1 *Industrial and Labor Relations Review* 39.

Biasi, M, 'The On-Demand Work (Mis)classification Judgments in Italy. An Overview' (2019) 12:1 *Italian Labour Law E-Journal* 49.

Bogg, A, 'Employment Relations Act 2004: Another False Dawn for Collectivism' (2005) 34:1 *Industrial Law Journal* 72.

Bogg, A, 'The Mouse That Never Roared: Unfair Practices and Union Recognition' (2009) 38:4 *Industrial Law Journal* 390.

Bogg, A, 'Beyond Neo-Liberalism: The Trade Union Act 2016 and the Authoritarian State' (2016) 45:3 *Industrial Law Journal* 299.

Bogg, A, 'Taken for a Ride: Workers in the Gig Economy' (2019) 135 *Law Quarterly Review* 219.

Bogg, A and Ewing, K, 'The Continuing Evolution of European Labour Law and the Changing Context for Trade Union Organising' (2017) 38:2 *Comparative Labor Law and Policy Journal* 211.

Borelli, S, 'Fitting the Panoply in a Binary Perspective: The Italian Platform Workers in the European Context' (2020) 41:2 *Comparative Labor Law and Policy Journal* 365.

Bornstein, J, 'Employees Are Losing: Have Workplace Laws Gone Too Far?' (2019) 61:3 *Journal of Industrial Relations* 438.

Borraccino, G and Gentile, A, 'Trade Unions and Self-Organised Groups of Educational Workers in Italy' (2019) 7:2 *Critical and Radical Social Work* 215.

Bowden, B, 'The Organising Model in Australia: A Reassessment' (2009) 20:2 *Labour and Industry* 138.

Brogan, R, 'The Digital Sweatshop: Why Heightened Labor Protections Must be Implemented Before Crunch Causes the Backbone of the Video Game Industry to Collapse', *Texas Review of Entertainment and Sports Law*, forthcoming.

Brigden, C, 'Creating Labour's Space: The Case of the Melbourne Trades Hall' (2005) 89 *Labour History* 125.

Buchanan, J, Oliver, D and Briggs, C, 'Solidarity Reconstructed: The Impact of the Accord on Relations within the Australian Union Movement' (2014) 56:2 *Journal of Industrial Relations* 288.

Burchielli, R, Delaney, A and Coventry, K, 'Campaign Strategies to Develop Regulatory Mechanisms: Protecting Australian Garment Homeworkers' (2014) 56:1 *Journal of Industrial Relations* 81.

Burroni, L and Pedaci, M, 'Collective Bargaining, Atypical Employment and Welfare Provisions: The Case of Temporary Agency Work in Italy' (2014) 101 *Stato e Mercato* 169.

Cahill, D, 'Change the Rules', *Arena* (June 2019).

Cant, C and Woodcock, J, 'Fast Food Shutdown: From Disorganisation to Action in the Service Sector' (2020) 44:4 *Capital and Class* 513.

Caraway, B, 'OUR Walmart: A Case Study of Connective Action' (2016) 19:7 *Information, Communication and Society* 907.

Carinci, F, 'Fifty Years of the Workers' Statute (1970–2020)' (2020) 13:2 *Italian Labour Law E-Journal* 1.

Carter, B and Cooper, R, 'The Organising Model and the Management of Change: A Comparative Study of Unions in Australia and Britain' (2002) 57:4 *Relations Industrielles/Industrial Relations* 712.

Cha, J, Holgate, J and Yon, K, 'Emergent Cultures of Activism: Young People and the Building of Alliances Between Unions and Other Social Movements' (2018) 45:4 *Work and Occupations* 451.

Cherry, M, 'Beyond Misclassification: The Digital Transformation of Work' (2016) 37 *Comparative Labor Law and Policy Journal* 577.

Cherry, M, 'Proposition 22: A Vote on Gig Worker Status in California' (2021) *Comparative Labor Law and Policy Journal* (Dispatch No 31).

Cherry, M and Aloisi, A, '"Dependent Contractors" in the Gig Economy: A Comparative Approach' (2017) 66 *American University Law Review* 635.

Cherry, M and Rutschman, A, 'Gig Workers as Essential Workers: How to Correct the Gig Economy Beyond the COVID-19 Pandemic' (2020) 35 *ABA Journal of Labor and Employment Law* 11.

Chesta, R, Zamponi, L and Caciagli, C, 'Labour Activism and Social Movement Unionism in the Gig Economy: Food Delivery Workers Struggles in Italy' (2019) 12:3 *Partecipazione e Conflitto* 819.

Chiarini, B, 'The Composition of Union Membership: The Role of Pensioners in Italy' (1999) 37:4 *British Journal of Industrial Relations* 577.

Choi, H and Mattoni, A, 'The Contentious Field of Precarious Work in Italy: Political Strategies, Actors and Coalitions' (2010) 13 *Working USA: The Journal of Labor and Society* 213.

Cillo, R and Pradella, L, 'New Immigrant Struggles in Italy's Logistics Industry' (2018) 16:1 *Comparative European Politics* 67.

Colombo, S and Regalia, I, 'Changing Joint Regulation and Labour Market Policy in Italy during the Crisis: On the Edge of a Paradigm Shift?' (2016) 22:3 *European Journal of Industrial Relations* 295.

Colvin, A, 'Strike Ballot Law and Practice in the United States: Order without Law in Labour Relations?' (2016) 29:2 *Australian Journal of Labour Law* 243.

Comande, D and Giubboni, S, 'The Social Partners in the Welfare System in Italy: From Coordination to Fragmentation' (2020) 26:3 *International Journal of Comparative Labour Law and Industrial Relations* 315.

Compa, L, 'Careful What You Wish For: A Critical Appraisal of Proposals to Rebuild the Labor Movement' (2015) 24:3 *New Labor Forum* 11.

Cooper, R, 'Getting Organised: A White-collar Union Responds to Membership Crisis' (2001) 43:4 *Journal of Industrial Relations* 422.

Cooper, R, 'Peak Council Organising at Work: ACTU Strategy 1994–2000' (2003) 14:1 *Labour and Industry* 1.

Cooper, R and Ellem, B, 'The Neoliberal State, Trade Unions and Collective Bargaining in Australia' (2008) 46:3 *British Journal of Industrial Relations* 532.

Cooper, R, Ellem, B, Briggs, C and van den Broek, D, 'Anti-unionism, Employer Strategy, and the Australian State, 1996–2005' (2009) 34:3 *Labor Studies Journal* 339.

Cox, A, 'The Duty to Bargain in Good Faith' (1958) 71 *Harvard Law Review* 1401.

Crain, M and Matheny, K, 'The "New" Labor Regime' (2017) 126 *Yale Law Journal Forum* 478.

Craver, C, 'The National Labor Relations Act at 75: In Need of a Heart Transplant' (2010) 27:2 *Hofstra Labor and Employment Law Journal* 311.

Creighton, B, 'A Retreat from Individualism? The Fair Work Act 2009 and the Re-collectivisation of Australian Labour Law' (2011) 40 *Industrial Law Journal* 116.

Cunningham-Parmeter, K, 'Gig-Dependence: Finding the Real Independent Contractors of Platform Work' (2019) 39:3 *Northern Illinois University Law Review* 379.

Cuppini, N, Frapporti, M and Pirone, M, 'Logistics Struggles in the Po Valley Region: Territorial Transformations and Processes of Antagonistic Subjectivation' (2015) 114:1 *South Atlantic Quarterly* 119.

Damiani, M, Pompei, F and Ricci, A, 'Opting Out, Collective Contracts and Labour Flexibility: Firm-Level Evidence for the Italian Case' (2020) 58:3 *British Journal of Industrial Relations* 558.

Davies, A, 'Wages and Working Time in the "Gig Economy"' (2020) 31 *King's Law Journal* 250.

Davies, P, 'A Challenge to Single Channel' (1994) 23 *Industrial Law Journal* 272.

Deakin, S, 'Decoding Employment Status' (2020) 31:2 *King's Law Journal* 180.

De Luca, D, Pozzi, S and Ambrosini, M, 'Trade Unions and Immigrants in Italy: How Immigrant Offices Promote Inclusion' (2018) 60:1 *Journal of Industrial Relations* 101.

de Turberville, S, 'Does the "Organizing Model" Represent a Credible Union Renewal Strategy?' (2004) 18:4 *Work, Employment and Society* 775.

Del Conte, M and Gramano, E, 'Looking to the Other Side of the Bench: The New Legal Status of Independent Contractors under the Italian Legal System' (2018) 39:3 *Comparative Labor Law and Policy Journal* 579.

Dias-Abey, M, 'Justice in Our Fields: Can "Alt-Labor" Organizations Improve Migrant Farm Workers' Conditions?' (2018) 53 *Harvard Civil Rights-Civil Liberties Law Review* 167.

Dias-Abey, M, 'Using Law to Support Social Movement-Led Collective Bargaining Structures in Supply Chains' (2019) 32:1 *Australian Journal of Labour Law* 123.

Dukes, R, 'The Statutory Recognition Procedure 1999: No Bias in Favour of Recognition?' (2008) 37 *Industrial Law Journal* 236.

Dukes, R and Kountouris, N, 'Pre-strike Ballots, Picketing and Protest: Banning Industrial Action by the Back Door?' (2016) 45:3 *Industrial Law Journal* 337.

Durazzi, N, 'Inclusive Unions in a Dualized Labour Market? The Challenge of Organizing Labour Market Policy and Social Protection for Labour Market Outsiders' (2017) 51:2 *Social and Policy Administration* 265.

Durazzi, N, Fleckenstein, T and Lee, S, 'Social Solidarity for All? Trade Union Strategies, Labour Market Dualization, and the Welfare State in Italy and South Korea' (2018) 46:2 *Politics and Society* 205.

Eaton, A and Kriesky, J, 'Union Organizing under Neutrality and Card Check Agreements' (2001) 55:1 *Industrial and Labor Relations Review* 42.

Eaton, A and Kriesky, J, 'NLRB Elections versus Card Check Campaigns: Results of a Worker Survey' (2009) 62:2 *Industrial and Labor Relations Review* 157.

Ellem, B, '"We're Solid": Union Renewal at BHP Iron Ore, 1999–2002' (2002) 10:2 *International Journal of Employment Studies* 23.

Ellem, B, 'Peak Union Campaigning: Fighting for Rights at Work in Australia' (2013) 51:2 *British Journal of Industrial Relations* 264.

Ellem, B, Goods, C and Todd, P, 'Rethinking Power, Strategy and Renewal: Members and Unions in Crisis' (2019) 58:2 *British Journal of Industrial Relations* 424.

Engeman, C, 'Social Movement Unionism in Practice: Organizational Dimensions of Union Mobilization in the Los Angeles Immigrant Rights Marches' (2015) 29:3 *Work, Employment and Society* 444.

Epstein, R, 'A Common Law for Labor Relations: A Critique of the New Deal Labor Legislation' (1983) 92 *Yale Law Journal* 1357.

Ewing, K, 'The State and Industrial Relations: "Collective Laissez Faire" Revisited' (1998) 5 *Historical Studies in Industrial Relations* 1.

Ewing, KD, 'The Function of Trade Unions' (2005) 34:1 *Industrial Law Journal* 1.

Ewing, K and Hendy, J, 'New Perspectives on Labour Law – Trade Union Recognition and Collective Bargaining' (2017) 46:1 *Industrial Law Journal* 23.

Ewing, KD and Hendy, Lord, 'Covid-19 and the Failure of Labour Law: Part 1' (2020) 49:4 *Industrial Law Journal* 497.

Fetter, J, 'Work Choices and Australian Workplace Agreements' (2006) 19:2 *Australian Journal of Labour Law* 210.

Fisk, C, 'Sustainable Alt-Labor' (2020) 95:1 *Chicago-Kent Law Review* 7

Fisk, C and Pulver, A, 'First Contract Arbitration and the Employee Free Choice Act' (2009) 70:1 *Louisiana Law Review* 47.

Flanagan, F, 'Theorising the Gig Economy and Home-based Service Work' (2019) 61:1 *Journal of Industrial Relations* 57.

Ford, M and Novitz, T, 'Legislating for Control: The Trade Union Act 2016' (2016) 45:3 *Industrial Law Journal* 277.

Ford, W, 'Being There: Changing Union Rights of Entry Under Federal Industrial Law' (2000) 13 *Australian Journal of Labour Law* 1.

Forsyth, A, 'The "Transplantability" Debate Re-Visited: Can European Social Partnership Be Exported to Australia?' (2006) 27:3 *Comparative Labor Law and Policy Journal* 305.

Forsyth, A, 'Ten Years of the Fair Work Act: (More) Testing Times for Australia's Unions' (2020) 33:1 *Australian Journal of Labour Law* 122.

Forsyth, A, Howe, J, Gahan, P and Landau, I, 'Establishing the Right to Bargain Collectively in Australia and the UK: Are Majority Support Determinations under Australia's Fair Work Act a More Effective Form of Union Recognition?' (2017) 46:3 *Industrial Law Journal* 335.

Forsyth, A and Sutherland, C, 'From "Uncharted Seas" to "Stormy Waters": How Will Trade Unions Fare under the Work Choices Legislation?' (2006) 16:2 *The Economic and Labour Relations Review* 215.

Fosh, P, Morris, H, Martin, R, Smith, P and Undy, R, 'Politics, Pragmatism and Ideology: The "Wellsprings" of Conservative Union Legislation (1979–1992)' (1993) 22:1 *Industrial Law Journal* 14.

Frangi, L and Barisione, M, 'Are You a Union Member? Determinants and Trends of Subjective Union Membership in Italian Society (1972–2013)' (2015) 21:4 *Transfer* 451.

Frangi, L, Zhang, T and Banerjee, R, 'Constructing Inequalities: Tenure Trajectories of Immigrant Workers and Union Strategies in the Milan Construction Sector' (2020) *British Journal of Industrial Relations* (advance access).

Frangi, L, Zhang, T and Hebdon, R, 'Tweeting and Retweeting for Fight for $15: Unions as Dinosaur Opinion Leaders?' (2020) 58:2 *British Journal of Industrial Relations* 301.

Fredman, S, 'The New Rights: Labour Law and Ideology in the Thatcher Years' (1992) 12:1 *Oxford Journal of Legal Studies* 24.

Fredman, S and Du Toit, D, 'One Small Step Towards Decent Work: *Uber v Aslam* in the Court of Appeal' (2019) 48:2 *Industrial Law Journal* 260.

Freeman, R and Rogers, J, 'Open Source Unionism: Beyond Exclusive Collective Bargaining' (2002) 5 *Working USA: The Journal of Labor and Society* 8.

Gaglione, C, Purificato, I and Rymkevich, O, 'COVID-19 and Labour Law: Italy' (2020) 13:1S *Italian Labour Law E-Journal* 1.

Gall, G, 'The Emergence of a Rank-and-File Movement: The Comitati di Base in the Italian Worker's Movement' (1995) 19:1 *Capital and Class* 9.

Gall, G, 'Union Recognition in Britain: The End of Legally Induced Voluntarism?' (2012) 41:4 *Industrial Law Journal* 407.

Gall, G, 'Twenty Years of the Third Statutory Union Recognition Procedure in Britain: Outcomes and Impact' (2020) 49:4 *Industrial Law Journal* 657.

Gall, G and Fiorito, J, 'The Backward March of Labour Halted: Or What is to be Done with "Union Organising"? The Cases of Britain and the USA' (2011) 35:2 *Capital and Class* 233.

Garden, C, 'The Seattle Solution: Collective Bargaining by For-Hire Drivers and Prospects for Pro-Labor Federalism' (2017) 12 *Harvard Law and Policy Review Online* 1.

Garrick, J, 'How Worker Centers Organize Low-Wage Workers: An Exploration of Targets and Strategies' (2021) 46:2 *Labor Studies Journal* 134.

Gasparri, S, Ikeler, P and Fullin, G, 'Trade Union Strategy in Fashion Retail in Italy and the USA: Converging Divergence between Institutions and Mobilisation' (2019) 25:4 *European Journal of Industrial Relations* 345.

Ginsburg, M, 'Nothing New Under the Sun: "The New Labor Law" Must Still Grapple with the Traditional Challenges of Firm-Based Organizing and Building Self-Sustainable Worker Organizations' (2017) 126 *Yale Law Journal Forum* 488.

Goods, C, Veen, A and Barratt, T, '"Is your gig any good?" Analysing Job Quality in the Australian Platform-based Food Delivery Sector' (2019) 61:4 *Journal of Industrial Relations* 502.

Gould, W, 'Politics and the Effect on the National Labor Relations Board's Adjudicative and Rulemaking Processes' (2015) 64 *Emory Law Journal* 1051.

Griffith, K and Gates, L, 'Worker Centers: Labor Policy as a Carrot, not a Stick' (2019) 14 *Harvard Law and Policy Review* 601.

Gross, J, 'Conflicting Statutory Purposes: Another Look at Fifty Years of NLRB Law Making' (1985) 39:1 *Industrial and Labor Relations Review* 7.

Gross, K, 'Separate to Unite: Will *Change to Win* Strengthen Organized Labor in America?' (2005–2006) 25 *Buffalo Public Interest Law Journal* 75.

Guest, D and Piccei, R, 'Partnership at Work: Mutuality and the Balance of Advantage' (2001) 39:2 *British Journal of Industrial Relations* 207.

Gupta, S, Lerner, S and McCartin, J, 'Why the Labor Movement Has Failed – And How to Fix It', *Boston Review* (1 May 2019).

Guzick, W, 'Employer Neutrality Agreements: Union Organizing under a Nonadversarial Model of Labor Relations' (1984) 6 *Industrial Relations Law Journal* 421.

Hall, R, 'The Politics of Industrial Relations in Australia in 2007' (2008) 50 *Journal of Industrial Relations* 371.

Hancock, K, 'The Accord, the Labour Market and the Economy' (2014) 56:2 *Journal of Industrial Relations* 273.

Hardy, T and McCrystal, S, 'Bargaining in a Vacuum? An Examination of The Proposed Class Exemption for Collective Bargaining for Small Businesses' (2020) 42:3 *Sydney Law Review* 311.

Heery, E, 'Unions and the Organising Turn: Reflections after 20 Years of Organising Works' (2015) 26:4 *Economic and Labour Relations Review* 545.

Heery, E, 'Fusion or Replacement: Labour and the "New" Social Movements' (2018) 39:4 *Economic and Industrial Democracy* 661.

Hepple, B, 'Can Collective Labour Law Transplants Work? The South African Example' (1999) 20 *Industrial Law Journal (South Africa)* 1.

Hepple, B, 'Back to the Future: Employment Law under the Coalition Government' (2013) 42:3 *Industrial Law Journal* 203.

Holgate, J, 'An International Study of Trade Union Involvement in Community Organizing: Same Model, Different Outcomes' (2015) 53:3 *British Journal of Industrial Relations* 460.

Holgate, J, 'Community Organising in the UK: A "New" Approach for Trade Unions?' (2015) 36:3 *Economic and Industrial Democracy* 431.

Holgate, J, 'Trade Unions in the Community: Building Broad Spaces of Solidarity' (2021) 42:2 *Economic and Industrial Democracy* 226.

Hose, K and Rimmer, M, 'The Australian Union Merger Wave Revisited' (2002) 44 *Journal of Industrial Relations* 525.

Ianuzzi, F and Sacchetto, D, 'Outsourcing and Workers' Resistance Practices in Venice's Hotel Industry: The Role of Migrants Employed by Cooperatives' (2020) *Economic and Industrial Democracy* (advance access).

Ibsen, C and Tapia, M, 'Trade Union Revitalisation: Where Are We Now? Where To Next?' (2017) 59:2 *Journal of Industrial Relations* 170.

Iglitzin, D and Robbins, J, 'The City of Seattle's Ordinance Providing Collective Bargaining Rights to Independent Contractor For-Hire Drivers; An Analysis of the Major Legal Hurdles' (2017) 38:1 *Berkeley Journal of Employment and Labor Law* 49.

James, P and Karmowsaka, J, 'British Union Renewal: Does Salvation Really Lie beyond the Workplace?' (2016) 47:2 *Industrial Relations Journal* 102.

Jiang, Z and Korczynski, M, 'When the "Unorganisable" Organize: The Collective Mobilization of Migrant Domestic Workers in London' (2016) 69 *Human Relations* 813.

Johnston, H, 'Workplace Gains beyond the Wagner Act: The New York Taxi Workers Alliance and Participation in Administrative Rulemaking' (2018) 43:2 *Labor Studies Journal* 141.

Juravich, T, 'Constituting Challenges in Differing Arenas of Power: Worker Centers, the Fight for $15, and Union Organizing' (2018) 43:2 *Labor Studies Journal* 104.

Kahn-Freund, O, 'On Uses and Misuse of Comparative Law' (1974) 37 *Modern Law Review* 1.

Kaine, S and Josserand, E, 'The Organisation and Experience of Work in the Gig Economy' (2019) 61:4 *Journal of Industrial Relations* 479.

Kaine, S and Rawling, M, '"Comprehensive Campaigning" in the NSW Transport Industry: Bridging the Divide Between Regulation and Union Organizing' (2010) 52:2 *Journal of Industrial Relations* 183.

Kelly, J, 'Trade Union Membership and Power in Comparative Perspective' (2015) 26:4 *Economic and Labour Relations Review* 526.

Kennedy, E, 'Employed by an Algorithm: Labor Rights in the On-Demand Economy' (2017) 40 *Seattle University Law Review* 987.

Kennedy, T, Redford, B, Burns, R and Forsyth, A, 'Rebuilding Worker Power in Australia through Multi-Employer Bargaining' (2021) *Labour and Industry*, forthcoming.

Kimberley, N and McCrystal, S, 'Contested Spaces: Unions and Employer Controlled Access to Space for Organising under the Fair Work Act 2009 (Cth)' (2020) 33:1 *Australian Journal of Labour Law* 139.

Legrand, P, 'The Impossibility of "Legal Transplants"' (1997) 4 *Maastricht Journal of European and Comparative Law* 111.

Leonardi, S, 'Union Organisation of Employees in Atypical and Precarious Work in Italy' (2008) 4:3 *International Journal of Action Research* 203.

Leonardi, S, 'Employee Participation and Involvement: The Italian Case and Trade Union Issues' (2016) 22:1 *Transfer* 81.

Liebman, W, 'Decline and Disenchantment: Reflections on the Aging of the National Labor Relations Board' (2007) 28 *Berkeley Journal of Labor and Employment Law* 569.

Liebman, W, 'Labor Law Inside Out' (2008) 11 *Working USA: The Journal of Labor and Society* 9.

Locke, R, 'The Demise of the National Union in Italy: Lessons for Comparative Industrial Relations Theory' (1992) 45:2 *Industrial and Labour Relations Review* 229.

Locke, R, and Thelen, K, 'Apples and Oranges Revisited: Contextualized Comparisons and the Study of Comparative Labor Politics' (1995) 23:3 *Politics and Society* 337.

Logan, J, 'The Union Avoidance Industry in the United States' (2006) 44:4 *British Journal of Industrial Relations* 651.

Lorber, P, 'National Works Councils: Opening the Door on a Whole New Era in United Kingdom Employment Relations?' (2003) 19:3 *International Journal of Comparative Labour Law and Industrial Relations* 297.

Lyons, T, 'The Labour Movement: My Part in its Downfall', *Meanjin* (Spring 2016) 87.

Magnani, M, 'The Role of Collective Bargaining in Italian Labour Law' (2018) 7:2 *E-Journal of International and Comparative Labour Studies* 1.

Mandelman, M and Manara, K, 'Staying Above the Surface: Surface Bargaining Claims under the National Labor Relations Act' (2007) 24 *Hofstra Labor and Employment Law Journal* 261.

Manokha, I, 'Covid-19: Teleworking, Surveillance and 24/7 Work. Some Reflexions on the Expected Growth of Remote Work After the Pandemic' (2020) 1:2 *Political Anthropological Research on International Social Sciences* 273.

Marginson, P, 'The Changing Nature of Collective Employment Relations' (2015) 37:6 *Employee Relations* 645.

Marino, S, 'Trade Union Inclusion of Migrant and Ethnic Minority Workers: Comparing Italy and the Netherlands' (2012) 18:1 *European Journal of Industrial Relations* 5.

Marino, S, Bernaciak, M, Mrozowicki, A and Pulignano, V, 'Unions for Whom? Union Democracy and Precarious Workers in Poland and Italy' (2019) 40:1 *Economic and Industrial Democracy* 111.

Martínez Lucio, M, 'Beyond Consensus: The State and Industrial Relations in the United Kingdom from 1964 to 2014' (2015) 37:6 *Employee Relations* 692.

Mason, L, 'Locating Unity in the Fragmented Platform Economy: Labor Law and the Platform Economy in the United Kingdom' (2020) 41:2 *Comparative Labor Law and Policy Journal* 32.

McCabe, P, 'Picket Lines and the Principle of Legality' (2020) 33:2 *Australian Journal of Labour Law* 209.

McCallum, R, 'Plunder Downunder: Transplanting the Anglo-American Labour Law Model to Australia' (2005) 26 *Comparative Labor Law and Policy Journal* 381.

McCartin, J, Sneiderman, M and BP-Weeks, M, 'Combustible Convergence: Bargaining for the Common Good and the #RedForEd Uprisings of 2018' (2020) 45:1 *Labor Studies Journal* 97.

McCluskey, L, 'Can Unions Stay Within the Law Any Longer?' (2015) 44:3 *Industrial Law Journal* 439.

McCrystal, S, 'Why Is It So Hard to Take Lawful Strike Action in Australia?' (2019) 61:1 *Journal of Industrial Relations* 129.

McGaughey, E, 'Uber, the Taylor Review, Mutuality and the Duty Not to Misrepresent Employment Status' (2019) 48:2 *Industrial Law Journal* 180.

McGaughey, E, 'A Social Recovery, Workplace Democracy and Security: COVID-19 and Labour Law' (2021) 32:1 *King's Law Journal* 122.

Menegatti, E, 'Mending the Fissured Workplace: The Solutions Provided by Italian Law' (2015) 37 *Comparative Labor Law and Policy Journal* 91.

Milkman, R, 'Back to the Future? US Labour in the New Gilded Age' (2013) 51:4 *British Journal of Industrial Relations* 645.

Minter, K, 'Negotiating Labour Standards in the Gig Economy: Airtasker and Unions New South Wales' (2017) 28 *The Economic and Labour Relations Review* 438.

Mitchell, R, 'Juridification and Labour Law: A Legal Response to the Flexibility Debate in Australia' (1998) 14 *International Journal of Comparative Labour Law and Industrial Relations* 113.

Moase, G, 'A New Species of Shark: Towards Direct Unionism' (2012) 4:2 *Interface: A Journal for and about Social Movements* 280.

Moore, J and Bales, R, 'Elections, Neutrality Agreements, and Card Checks: The Failure of the Political Model of Industrial Democracy' (2012) 87 *Indiana Law Journal* 147.

Muir, K and Peetz, D, 'Not Dead Yet: The Australian Union Movement and the Defeat of a Government' (2010) 9:2 *Social Movement Studies* 215.

Murgia, A and Pulignano, V, 'Neither Precarious nor Entrepreneur: The Subjective Experience of Hybrid Self-Employed Workers' (2019) *Economic and Industrial Democracy* (advance access).

Murgia, A and Selmi, G, '"Inspire and Conspire": Italian Precarious Workers between Selforganization and Self-advocacy' (2012) 4:2 *Interface* 181.

Murray, G, 'Union Renewal: What Can We Learn from Three Decades of Research?' (2017) 23:1 *Transfer* 9.

Murray, J, 'Work Choices and the Radical Revision of the Public Realm of Australian Statutory Labour Law' (2006) 35:4 *Industrial Law Journal* 343.

Negrelli, S and Signoretti, A, 'Between Berlusconi and Monti: Trade Unions and Economic Crisis in Italy' (2014) 59:4 *The Singapore Economic Review* 1.

Nossar, I, Johnstone, R, Macklin, A and Rawling, M, 'Protective Legal Regulation for Home-based Workers in Australian Textile, Clothing and Footwear Supply Chains' (2015) 57:4 *Journal of Industrial Relations* 585.

Novitz, T, 'COVID-19 and Labour Law: United Kingdom' (2020) 13:1S *Italian Labour Law E-Journal* (Special Issue).

Orr, G, 'Conspiracy on the Waterfront' (1998) 11 *Australian Journal of Labour Law* 159.

Orr, G, 'Agency Shops in Australia? Compulsory Bargaining Fees, Union (In)Security and the Rights of Free-Riders' (2001) 14 *Australian Journal of Labour Law* 159.

Oswalt, M, 'Improvisational Unionism' (2016) 104:3 *California Law Review* 597.

Oswalt, M, 'Alt-Bargaining' (2019) 82:3 *Law and Contemporary Problems* 89.

Oswalt, M, 'Short Strikes' (2020) 95:1 *Chicago-Kent Law Review* 67.

Pallini, M, 'Italian Industrial Relations: Toward a Strongly Decentralized Collective Bargaining?' (2016) 38:1 *Comparative Labor Law and Policy Journal* 1.

Paul, S, 'Uber as For-Profit Hiring Hall: A Price-Fixing Paradox and Its Implications' (2017) 38:2 *Berkeley Journal of Employment and Labor Law* 233.

Peetz, D, 'The Impacts and Non-Impacts of Enterprise Bargaining on Unions' (2012) 22:3 *Labour and Industry* 237.

Peetz, D, 'Are Australian trade unions part of the solution, or part of the problem?', *Australian Review of Public Affairs* (February 2015).

Peetz, D and Bailey, J, 'Dancing Alone: The Australian Union Movement Over Three Decades' (2012) 54:4 *Journal of Industrial Relations* 525.

Peetz, D and Pocock, B, 'An Analysis of Workplace Representatives, Union Power and Democracy in Australia' (2009) 47:4 *British Journal of Industrial Relations* 623.

Pencavel, J, 'Company Unions, Wages and Work Hours' (2003) 12 *Advances in Industrial and Labor Relations* 7.

Pennington, A, 'The Fair Work Act and the Decline of Enterprise Bargaining in Australia's Private Sector' (2020) 33:1 *Australian Journal of Labour Law* 68.

Però, D, 'Indie Unions, Organizing and Labour Renewal: Learning from Precarious Migrant Workers' (2020) 34:5 *Work, Employment and Society* 900.

Perrotta, M and Sacchetto, D, 'Migrant Farmworkers in Southern Italy: Ghettoes, *Caporalato* and Collective Action' (2014) 1:5 *Workers of the World* 75.

Picot, G and Tassinari, A, 'Politics in a Transformed Labor Market: Renzi's Labor Market Reform' (2015) 30:1 *Italian Politics* 121.

Pizzoferrato, A, 'Platform Workers in the Italian System' (2019) 12:1 *Italian Labour Law E-Journal* 93.

Prince, S, 'The AB5 Experiment – Should States Adopt California's Worker Classification Law?', *American University Business Law Review*, forthcoming.

Pulignano, V, Carrieri, D and Baccaro, L, 'Industrial Relations in Italy in the Twenty-first Century' (2017) 40:4 *Employee Relations* 654.

Pulignano, V, Gervasi, L and de Franceschi, F, 'Union Responses to Precarious Workers: Italy and Spain Compared' (2016) 22:1 *European Journal of Industrial Relations* 39.

Pulignano, V and Signoretti, A, 'Union Strategies and National Institutions and the Use of Temporary Labour in Italian and US Plants' (2016) 54:3 *British Journal of Industrial Relations* 574.

Rawling, M, Johnstone, R and Nossar, I, 'Compromising Road Transport Supply Chain Regulation: The Abolition of the Road Safety Remuneration Tribunal' (2017) 39:3 *Sydney Law Review* 303.

Recchia, G, 'The Future of Collective Bargaining in Italy between Legislative Reforms and Social Partners' Responses' (2017) 23:4 *Transfer* 457.

Reddy, D, '"There is No Such Thing as an Illegal Strike": Reconceptualizing the Strike in Law and Political Economy' (2021) 130 *Yale Law Journal Forum* 421.

Regalia, I, 'Italian Trade Unions: Still Shifting between Consolidated Organizations and Social Movements?' (2012) 23:4 *Management Revue* 386.

Regalia, I and Regini, M, 'Trade Unions and Employment Relations in Italy during the Economic Crisis' (2018) 23:1 *South European Society and Politics* 63.
Regini, M and Regalia, I, 'Employers, Unions and the State: The Resurgence of Concertation in Italy?' (2007) 20:1 *West European Politics* 210.
Rogers, K, 'Precarious and Migrant Workers in Struggle: Are New Forms of Trade Unionism Necessary in Post-Brexit Britain?' (2017) 41:2 *Capital and Class* 336.
Rosenblum, J, 'Fight for $15: Good Wins, but Where did the Focus on Organizing Go?' (2017) 42:4 *Labor Studies Journal* 387.
Sachs, B, 'Labor Law Renewal' (2007) 1 *Harvard Law and Policy Review* 375.
Sánchez Ocasio, K and Gertner, L, 'Fighting for the Common Good: How Low-Wage Workers' Identities Are Shaping Labor Law' (2017) 126 *Yale Law Journal Forum* 503.
Schiek, D, 'Enforcing (EU) Non-discrimination Law: Mutual Learning between British and Italian Labour Law' (2012) 28:4 *International Journal of Comparative Labour Law and Industrial Relations* 489.
Schoemann, K, 'Digital Technology to Support the Trade Union Movement' (2018) 6 *Open Journal of Social Sciences* 67.
Secunda, P, 'Toward the Viability of State-Based Legislation to Address Workplace Captive Audience Meetings in the United States' (2008) 29 *Comparative Labor Law and Policy Journal* 209.
Simms, M, 'Accounting for Greenfield Union Organizing Outcomes' (2015) 53:3 *British Journal of Industrial Relations* 397.
Simms, M, Eversberg, D, Dupuy, C and Hipp, L, 'Organizing Young Workers Under Precarious Conditions: What Hinders or Facilitates Union Success' (2018) 45:4 *Work and Occupations* 420.
Simms, M, Holgate, J and Roper, C, 'The Trades Union Congress 150 Years On: A Review of the Organising Challenges and Responses to the Changing Nature of Work' (2019) 41:2 *Employee Relations* 331.
Sprague, R, 'Using the ABC Test to Classify Workers: End of the Platform-Based Business Model or Status Quo Ante?' (2020) 11:3 *William and Mary Business Law Review* 733.
Stanford, J, 'The Fair Work Act and Wages' (2020) 33:1 *Australian Journal of Labour Law* 20.
Steinbaum, M, 'Antitrust, the Gig Economy, and Labor Market Power' (2019) 82 *Law and Contemporary Problems* 45.
Stewart, A and McCrystal, S, 'Labour Regulation and the Great Divide: Does the Gig Economy Require a New Category of Worker?' (2019) 32:1 *Australian Journal of Labour Law* 4.
Sutherland, C, 'First Steps Forward (with Fairness): A Preliminary Examination of the Transition Legislation' (2008) 21 *Australian Journal of Labour Law* 137.
Tapia, M and Turner, L, 'Union Campaigns as Counter-Movements: Mobilizing Immigrant Workers in France and the United Kingdom' (2013) 51:3 *British Journal of Industrial Relations* 601.
Tapia, M and Turner, L, 'Renewed Activism for the Labor Movement: The Urgency of Young Worker Engagement' (2018) 45:4 *Work and Occupations* 391.
Tassinari, A, Chesta, R and Cini, L, 'Labour Conflicts over Health and Safety in the Italian Covid19 Crisis' (2020) 12:1 *Interface: A Journal for and about Social Movements* 128.
Tassinari, A and Maccarrone, V, 'The mobilisation of gig economy couriers in Italy: Some lessons for the trade union movement' (2017) 23:3 *Transfer* 353.
Tassinari, A and Maccarrone, V, 'Riders on the Storm: Workplace Solidarity among Gig Economy Couriers in Italy and the UK (2020) 34:1 *Work, Employment and Society* 35.
Tattersall, A, 'How Do We Build Power in Coalition? Rethinking Union-Community Coalition Types 12 Years On' (2018) 28:1 *Labour and Industry* 68.
Terry, M, 'Partnership and the Future of Trade Unions in the UK' (2003) 24:4 *Economic and Industrial Democracy* 485.
Teubner, G, 'Legal Irritants: Good Faith in British Law or How Unifying Law Ends Up in New Divergences' (1998) 61 *Modern Law Review* 11.
Tomassetti, P, 'The Shift towards Single-Employer Bargaining in the Italian Car Sector: Determinants and Prospects at FIAT' (2013) 2:1 *E-Journal of International and Comparative Labour Studies* 93.

Tomassetti, P, 'From Fixed to Flexible? Wage Coordination and the Collective Bargaining System in Italy' (2017) 33:4 *International Journal of Comparative Labour Law and Industrial Relations* 527.

Underhill, E, Groutsis, D, van den Broek, D and Rimmer, M, 'Organising Across Borders: Mobilising Temporary Migrant Labour in Australian Food Production' (2020) 62:2 *Journal of Industrial Relations* 278.

Unidentified student author, '*Chamber of Commerce v City of Seattle*: Ninth Circuit Holds Collective Bargaining Ordinance Not Subject to State Action Immunity' (2019) 132 *Harvard Law Review* 2360.

Unidentified student author, 'California Adopts the ABC Test to Distinguish Between Employees and Independent Contractors' (2020) 133:7 *Harvard Law Review* 2435.

Watson, A, 'Legal Transplants and Law Reform' (1976) 92 *Law Quarterly Review* 79.

Watts, J and Bale, T, 'Populism as an Intra-Party Phenomenon: The British Labour Party under Jeremy Corbyn' (2019) 21:1 *British Journal of Politics and International Relations* 99.

Weststar, J and Legault, M, 'Why Might a Videogame Developer Join a Union?' (2017) 42:4 *Labor Studies Journal* 295.

Wills, J, 'The Geography of Union Organising in Low-Paid Service Industries in the UK: Lessons from the T&G's Campaign to Unionise the Dorchester Hotel, London' (2005) 37:1 *Antipode* 139.

Wood, A, 'Networks of Injustice and Worker Mobilisation at Walmart' (2015) 46:4 *Industrial Relations Journal* 259.

Wood, A, 'Beyond Mobilisation at McDonald's: Towards Networked Organising' (2020) 44:4 *Capital and Class* 493.

Woodcock, J, 'Organizing in the Game Industry: The Story of Game Workers Unite U.K.' (2020) 29:1 *New Labor Forum* 50.

Wright, C, 'The Prices and Incomes Accord: Its Significance, Impact and Legacy' (2014) 56:2 *Journal of Industrial Relations* 264.

Zazzara, G, '"Italians First": Workers on the Right Amidst Old and New Populisms' (2018) 93 *International Labour and Working Class History* 101.

## Policy papers, working papers and reports

ACTU, *unions@work: The Challenge for Unions in Creating a Fair and Just Society* (1999).

ACTU, *Future Strategies: Unions Working for a Fairer Australia* (2003).

ACTU, *Congress 2018 Draft Policies and Resolutions* (ACTU D No 153/2018).

ACTU, *Organising with 2020 Vision: Case Studies of New Approaches to Union Growth and Capacity Building* (Australian Trade Union Institute, 19 November 2020).

ACTU, *Working from home Charter* (November 2020).

ACTU/Centre for Future Work, *For a Stronger, Balanced and Inclusive Recovery* (April 2021).

Ales, A and Senatori, I, 'Collective Bargaining and Workers' (Trade Union) Representation: The Company Level in Italy' (Paper for the Labour Law Research Network Conference, Amsterdam, 2015).

Aloisi, A, *A Fascinating Chapter in the "Gig" Saga: How to Deliver Decent Work to Platform Workers in Italy?* (European Commission Mutual Learning Programme, Peer Review on Platform Work, September 2020).

Andrias, K and Rogers, B, *Rebuilding Worker Voice in Today's Economy* (Roosevelt Institute, 2018).

Australian Government, *Report of the Migrant Workers' Taskforce* (March 2019).

Australian Government, *Australian Government Response: Report of the Migrant Workers Taskforce* (March 2019).

Australian Government, Attorney-General's Department, *Trends in Federal Enterprise Bargaining Report: June quarter 2020.*

Australian Government, *JobKeeper Payment: Frequently Asked Questions* (9 April 2020).

Barenberg, M, *Widening the Scope of Worker Organizing: Legal Reforms to Facilitate Multi-Employer Organizing, Bargaining and Striking* (Roosevelt Institute, 2015).

Berg, L and Farbenblum, B, *As If We Weren't Humans: The Abandonment of Temporary Migrants in Australia during COVID-19* (Migrant Worker Justice Initiative, 2020).

Bernaciak, M, Gumbrell-McCormick, R and Hyman, R, *European Trade Unionism: From Crisis to Renewal?* (Report 133, European Trade Union Institute, 2014).

Block, S and Sachs, B, *Clean Slate for Worker Power: Building a Just Economy and Democracy* (Harvard Law School, 2020).

Bodie, M, *Mandatory Disclosure in the Market for Union Representation* (Saint Louis University Legal Studies Research Paper Series, No 2011-02, 2011).

Borelli, S 'Italy', in I Daugareilh, C Degryse and P Pochet (eds), *The Platform Economy and Social Law: Key Issues in Comparative Perspective* (European Trade Union Institute, Working Paper 2019.10) 63.

Bright, S and Fitzgerald, A, *Snapshot: On-Demand Food Delivery Riders* (TWU/YWC, 2018).

Brindelli, L, 'Contrattazione integrative e retribuzioni nel settoro privato' (Roma, Fondazione Giuseppe Di Vittorio, 2016).

Brock, J, *Getting Organised: Low-Paid Self-Employment and Trade Unions* (The Changing Work Centre, May 2019).

Bronfenbrenner, K, *The Impact of Employer Opposition on Union Certification Win Rates: A Private/Public Sector Comparison* (Working Paper No 113, Economic Policy Institute, 1995).

Bronfenbrenner, K, *No Holds Barred: The Intensification of Employer Opposition to Organizing* (EPI Briefing Paper #235, Economic Policy Institute, 20 May 2009).

Business Council of Australia, *Enterprise-Based Bargaining Units: A Better Way of Working* (Melbourne, BCA, 1989).

Carneiro, B, *Trade Unions and Facebook: The Need to Improve Dialogue and Expand Networks* (ETUI Policy Brief, No 5 2018).

Carta, F and De Philippis, M, *The Impact of the COVID-19 Shock on Labour Income Inequality: Evidence from Italy* (Banca D'Italia, Occasional Papers, Number 606, February 2021).

Chartered Institute of Personnel and Development, *To Gig or Not to Gig? Stories from the Modern Economy* (Survey Report, March 2017).

Clean Clothes Campaign, *Can You Earn a Living Wage in Fashion in Italy?* (Report, 2014).

Clean Slate for Worker Power, *Principles of Sectoral Bargaining: A Reference Guide for Designing Federal, State and Local Laws in the U.S.* (Harvard Labor and Worklife Program, May 2021).

Coatman, C, *The Missing Half Million: How Unions Can Transform Themselves to be a Movement of Young Workers* (TUC, January 2020).

Commonwealth of Australia, *Royal Commission into Trade Union Governance and Corruption* (Final Report, December 2015).

Commonwealth of Australia, Senate Education and Employment References Committee, *A National Disgrace: The Exploitation of Temporary Work Visa Holders* (March 2016).

Congressional Research Service, *State Minimum Wages: An Overview* (CRS Report, R43792, 25 January 2019).

Corti, M, Delfino, M and Spinelli, C, 'The Impact of the Global Economic Crisis on the Evolution of Labour Law in the National Legal Systems: Italian Report' (International Society for Labour and Social Security Law, European Regional Congress, Dublin, 2014).

Darlington, R and Dobson, J, *The Conservative Government's Proposed Strike Ballot Thresholds: The Challenge to Trade Unions* (London, Institute of Employment Rights, 2015).

Delivery Riders Alliance, *It's Even Worse Than You Think. Snapshot: On-Demand Food Delivery Riders* (November 2019).

Delivery Riders Alliance, *Food Delivery Driver/Rider Survey* (September 2020).

Department for Business, Energy and Industrial Strategy, *Trade Union Membership, UK 1995–2019: Statistical Bulletin* (27 May 2020).

Department for Business, Energy and Industrial Strategy, *Trade Union Membership, UK 1995–2020: Statistical Bulletin* (27 May 2021).

De Stefano, V and Aloisi, A, *Digital Age: Employment and Working Conditions of Selected Types of Platform Work – National Context Analysis, Italy* (European Foundation for the Improvement of Living and Working Conditions, 2018).

Donovan, Lord (Chair), *Royal Commission on Trade Unions and Employers' Associations* (Report, Cmnd 3623, 1968).

Dorigatti, L, *Simplifying the adoption of the smart working regime* (European Foundation for the Improvement of Living and Working Conditions, 31 March and 29 July 2020).

Dorigatti, L, *Government and Social Partners Protocol to Ensure Safe Working Conditions at the Workplace* (European Foundation for the Improvement of Living and Working Conditions, 10 April and 17 July 2020).

Economic Policy Institute and National Employment Law Project, *Why the U.S. Needs a $15 Minimum Wage* (Fact Sheet, 26 January 2021).

Evans, C, *UK: Working Life in the COVID-19 Pandemic 2020* (European Foundation for the Improvement of Living and Working Conditions, 2021).

Ewing, KD, Moore, S and Wood, S, *Unfair Labour Practices: Trade Union Recognition and Employer Resistance* (London, Institute of Employment Rights, 2003).

Ewing, KD, Hendy, J and Jones, C (eds), *A Manifesto for Labour Law: Towards a Comprehensive Revision of Workers' Rights* (Liverpool, Institute of Employment Rights, 2016).

Ewing, KD, Hendy, J and Jones, C (eds), *Rolling out the Manifesto for Labour Law* (Liverpool, Institute of Employment Rights, 2018).

*Fairness at Work* (London, Department of Trade and Industry, 1998).

Freedland, M and Prassl, J, *Employees, Workers and the "Sharing Economy": Changing Practices and Concepts in the United Kingdom* (University of Oxford, Legal Research Paper Series No 19/2017, March 2017).

Freeman, R, Barenberg, M and Rogers, J, *The Legal, Economic and Business Case for Neutrality and Majority Verification of Worker Desire for Union Representation* (February 2016).

FWO, *Harvest Trail Inquiry: A Report on Workplace Arrangements along the Harvest Trail* (November 2018).

Gall, G, *'Union Organising' and the Health of the Union Movement in Britain* (London, Institute of Employment Rights, 2010).

Garden, C, *Workers' Collective Power in the Pandemic*, The Century Foundation (10 June 2020).

Haipeter, T, Owczarek, D, Faioli, M and Iudicone, F (eds), *Don't Gig Up: Final Report* (Fondazione Giacomo Brodolini and Partners, 2020).

HM Government, *Good Work Plan* (December 2018).

Holland, P and Hanley, G, *'Organising Works': Is It Meeting the Challenge of Declining Union Membership?* (Monash University, Faculty of Business and Economics, Working Paper 48/02, December 2002).

Hospo Voice, *#RebuildHospo: A Post-COVID Roadmap for Secure Jobs in Hospitality* (November 2020)

Hunt, T, *COVID-19 and the Work of Trade Unions: New Challenges and New Responses* (Unions 21, January 2021).

Industrial Relations Victoria, *Victorian Inquiry into the Labour Hire Industry and Insecure Work: Final Report* (August 2016).

International Lawyers Assisting Workers Network, *Taken for a Ride: Litigating the Digital Platform Model* (Issue Brief, March 2021).

ILO, *Measures adopted in Italy to support workers, families and enterprises during the COVID-19 emergency* (Policy Brief, 28 March 2020).

ILO, *ILO Monitor: COVID-19 and the World of Work*, 2nd edn (7 April 2020).

James, N, *Report of the Inquiry into the Victorian On-Demand Workforce* (Melbourne, Victorian Government, 2020).

Jansson, J and Uba, K, *The Untapped Possibilities of YouTube as a Trade Union Tool* (ETUI Policy Brief, No 7 2018).

Johnston, H and Land-Kazlauskas, C, *Organizing On-Demand: Representation, Voice and Collective Bargaining in the Gig Economy* (Conditions of Work and Employment Series No. 94, Geneva, International Labour Office, 2018).

Joyce, S, Neumann, D, Trappmann, V and Umney, C, *A Global Struggle: Worker Protest in the Platform Economy* (European Trade Union Institute Policy Brief No 2/2020).
Logan, J, *US Anti-Union Consultants: A Threat to the Rights of British Workers* (London, Trades Union Congress, 2008).
Lyons, T, *The Urge to Merge* (Per Capita, March 2016).
Manzo, F and Bruno, R, *On-Demand Workers, Sub-Minimum Wages: Evidence from Transportation Network Provider Trips in the City of Chicago* (Illinois Economic Policy Institute/University of Illinois Project for Middle Class Renewal, 19 January 2021).
Martínez Lucio, M, Koukiadaki, A and Tavora, I, *The Legacy of Thatcherism in European Labour Relations: The Impact of the Politics of Neo-Liberalism and Austerity on Collective Bargaining in a Fragmenting Europe* (London, Institute of Employment Rights, 2017).
McAlpine, K and Roberts, S, *The Future of Trade Unions in Australia* (Paper for the Association of Industrial Relations Academics of Australia and New Zealand Conference, Canberra, 9 February 2017).
McDonald, P, Williams, P, Stewart, A, Mayes, R and Oliver, D, *Digital Platform Work in Australia: Prevalence, Nature and Impact* (University of Adelaide and University of Technology Sydney, 2019).
McNicholas, C, Mokhibir, Z and von Wilpert, M, Janus *and Fair Share Fees: The Organizations Financing the Attack on Unions' Ability to Represent Workers* (Economic Policy Institute, 21 February 2018).
McNicholas, C, Podock, M, Wolfe, J, Zipperer, B, Lafer, G and Loustaunau, L, *Unlawful: U.S. Employers are Charged with Violating Federal Law in 41.5% of All Union Election Campaigns* (Economic Policy Institute, Report, 11 December 2019).
Michaels, D and Wagner, G, *Halting workplace COVID-19 transmission: An urgent proposal to protect American workers* (The Century Foundation, 15 October 2020).
Mishel, L and McNicholas, C, 'Uber drivers are not entrepreneurs', *Economic Policy Institute* (20 September 2019).
Mishel, L, Rhinehart, L and Windham, L, *Explaining the Erosion of Private-Sector Unions* (Economic Policy Institute, Report, 18 November 2020).
Moore, B and Walton, C, *Rise! Empowering Australian Workers through the Collective Spirit and Collaborative Energy of Unions* (ATUI/Strategic Membership Solutions, 7 May 2020).
Moyer-Lee, J and Kountouris, N, 'The "Gig Economy": Litigating the Cause of Labour' in International Lawyers Assisting Workers Network, *Taken for a Ride: Litigating the Digital Platform Model* (Issue Brief, March 2021) 6.
MWC, *Report of the National Conference on Labour Hire Reform* (8 November 2019).
National Employment Law Project, *Rights at Risk: Gig Companies' Campaign to Upend Employment as We Know It* (25 March 2019).
New Zealand Ministry of Business, Innovation and Employment, *The Proposed Fair Pay Agreement System* (undated).
New Zealand Ministry of Business, Innovation and Employment, *Fair Pay Agreements: Approval to Draft* (Cabinet Paper, 7 May 2021).
NUW, *Farm Workers Speak Out!* (July 2019).
Ockenfels-Martinez, M and Farhang, L, *Driving Away Our Health: The Economic Insecurity of Working for Lyft and Uber* (Human Impact Partners and Gig Workers Rising, August 2019).
O'Connor, B, MP, *Wages, Fairness and Inclusive Prosperity* (Speech to the National Press Club, Canberra, 12 December 2018).
OECD, *OECD Employment Outlook 2017* (Paris, OECD Publishing, 2017).
OECD, *Negotiating Our Way Up: Collective Bargaining in a Changing World of Work* (Paris, OECD Publishing, 2019).
O'Farrell, R and Montagnier, P, *Measuring Platform Mediated Workers* (OECD Digital Economy Papers No 282, April 2019).
Oliver, D, Speech to the ACTU Leadership Forum (Melbourne, 4 February 2016).
Open Markets Institute, *Eyes Everywhere: Amazon's Surveillance Infrastructure and Revitalizing Worker Power* (August 2020).

Parliament of Australia, Department of Parliamentary Services, *Trends in Union Membership in Australia* (Research Paper Series, 2018–19, 15 October 2018).

Pasquier, V and Wood, A, *The Power of Social Media as a Labour Campaigning Tool: Lessons from OUR Walmart and the Fight for 15* (Brussels, European Trade Union Institute, Policy Brief No 10/2018) 2.

Pedersini, R, *Italy: Working Life in the COVID-19 Pandemic 2020* (European Foundation for the Improvement of Living and Working Conditions, 2021).

Peetz, D, *Assessing the Impact of 'Work Choices' – One Year On* (Report for the Department of Innovation, Industry and Regional Development, Victoria, 2007).

Peetz, D, 'The ABS Statistics or the Abyss, Statistically?' (Presentation to Queensland Council of Unions Growth Symposium, Brisbane, 14 December 2015).

Prassl, J, *Collective Voice in the Platform Economy: Challenges, Opportunities, Solutions* (Report to the European Trade Union Confederation, 2018).

Prime Minister of Australia, *Address, National Press Club* (26 May 2020).

Productivity Commission, *Workplace Relations Framework: Productivity Commission Inquiry Report* (No 76, 30 November 2015).

Puttick, K, *The Welfare State, Wages and Work: Disintegration or Renewal?* (London, Institute of Employment Rights, 2019).

Rawling, M and Riley Munton, J, *Proposals for Legal Protections for On-Demand Gig Workers in the Road Transport Industry* (A report prepared for the Transport Education Audit Compliance Health Organisation by UTS Faculty of Law, January 2021).

Razzolini, O, *Collective Action for Self-Employed Workers: A Necessary Response to Increasing Income Inequality* (Centre for the Study of European Labour Law 'Massimo D'Antona', Working Paper 155/2021).

Reveille Strategy, *Transformation vs Adaption: Designing New Forms of Union Organising and Membership* (Research Note, June 2016).

Reveille Strategy, 'Digital Organising Immersion Training' (undated).

RSDAA, *Submission on Point-to-Point Transport (Taxis and Hire Vehicles) Regulation 2017 (NSW)* (9 May 2017).

RSDU, *Submission prepared by Max B. – for Ride Share Drivers United, Inquiry into the On-Demand Workforce in Victoria* (undated).

Schnabel, C, *Union Membership and Collective Bargaining: Trends and Determinants* (University of Erlangen-Nuremberg, Labor and Socio-Economic Research Center, LASER Discussion Papers No 121, 2020).

Stanford, J, *Historical Data on the Decline in Australian Industrial Disputes* (Briefing Note, Centre for Future Work, The Australia Institute, 30 January 2018).

Stanford, J, *Subsidising Billionaires: Simulating the Net Incomes of UberX drivers in Australia* (Australia Institute, Centre for Future Work, March 2018).

Stanford, J, *Union Organising and Labour Market Rules: Two Sides of the Same Coin* (Briefing Note, Centre for Future Work, The Australia Institute, 13 June 2019).

Tait, C, *Future Unions: Towards a Membership Renaissance in the Private Sector* (The Changing Work Centre, 2017).

Tait, C and Phibbs, T (eds), *A New Collectivism: How Private Sector Trade Unions Can Innovate and Grow* (Fabian Society, December 2017).

Taylor, M, Marsh, G, Nicol, D and Broadbent, P, *Good Work: The Taylor Review of Modern Working Practices* (2017).

Terzi, A, *An Italian Job: The Need for Collective Wage Bargaining Reform* (Bruegel Policy Contribution, Issue 2016/11, July 2016).

The Senate, Education and Employment References Committee, *Corporate Avoidance of the* Fair Work Act 2009 (September 2017).

The Senate, Education and Employment Legislation Committee, *Fair Work (Registered Organisations) Amendment (Ensuring Integrity) Bill 2019 [Provisions]* (October 2019).

Tranfaglia, MA, *A (Functional-Purposive) Comparative Analysis of the Protection of Workers Involved in Triangular Work Arrangements through Labour Providers in Australia and Italy* (Unpublished PhD Thesis, University of Melbourne, November 2020).

TUC, *Insecure Work: Why Decent Work Needs to be at the Heart of the UK's Recovery from Coronavirus* (August 2020).

TUC, *The TUC's Ten-Point Plan to Protect Jobs, Rights and Public Services After Brexit* (2021).

TUC Digital, *Unions and Digital Disruption* (February 2021).

TWU and Rideshare Driver Co-operative, *Rideshare Driver Survey* (24 October 2018).

Uber, *Submission: Inquiry into the Victorian On-Demand Workforce* (2019).

Unions 21, *Roadmap to Renewal: A Manifesto for Change* (April 2018).

Unions NSW, *Innovation or Exploitation? Busting the Airtasker Myth* (2016).

Urzì Brancati, M, Pesole, A, Férnandéz-Macías, E, *New Evidence on Platform Workers in Europe: Evidence from the Second COLLEEM Survey* (JRC Science for Policy Report, Luxembourg, Publications Office of the European Union, 2020).

UWU, *Submission to the National Agricultural Labour Advisory Committee: National Agricultural Workforce Strategy* (3 August 2020).

Vandaele, K, *Will Trade Unions Survive in the Platform Economy: Emerging Patterns of Platform Workers' Collective Voice and Representation in Europe* (European Trade Union Institute, Working Paper 2018.05).

Vandaele, K, Piasna, A and Drahokoupil, J, *Algorithm Breakers are not a Different 'Species': Attitudes towards Trade Unions of Deliveroo Riders in Belgium* (European Trade Union Institute, Working Paper 2019.06).

Victorian Auditor-General's Office, *Grants to the Migrant Workers Centre: Independent Assurance Report to Parliament* (February 2021).

Visser, J, *Wage Bargaining Institutions – From Crisis to Crisis* (European Commission, Economic Papers 488, April 2013).

Visser, J, *Trade Unions in the Balance* (ILO/ACTRAV Working Paper, International Labour Organization, 2019).

Waheed, S, Herrera, L, Gonzalez-Vasquez, A, Shadduck-Hernández, J, Koonz, T and Leynov, D, *More Than a Gig: A Survey of Ride-hailing Drivers in Los Angeles* (UCLA Labor Center, 30 May 2018).

Walton, C, *Guide to Organising and Campaigning with Digital Tools* (ACTU Union Innovation Hub, April 2021).

Walton, C and Locke, E, *The Overdue Case for Change: A Place for Unions in Modern Australia* (January 2016).

Willman, P, Bryson, A and Forth, J, *New Model Unions: Options for the 21st Century* (Unions 21, August 2019).

YWC, *Young Workers Centre Submission: Inquiry into Corporate Avoidance of the Fair Work Act* (January 2017).

YWC, *Briefing: Criminalising Wage Theft* (May 2018).

# INDEX

Lightning Source UK Ltd.
Milton Keynes UK
UKHW020616051122
411692UK00002B/46

9 781509 924974